THE ROUGH GUIDE TO
BEIJING

This sixth edition
David Leffman

C016366944

KT-177-139

Contents

Introduction to
Beijing

As the capital of one of the world's most dynamic economies, the bold modernity of Beijing (北京, běijīng) should take nobody by surprise. And yet it's hard not to be overawed by the sheer dynamism of this brash, gaudy, elegant, charming, filthy and historic city: whether partying to punk in a club, admiring the bizarre modern architecture spiking the skyline, or pushing your way through the bustling, neon-soaked streets, Beijing is never, ever dull. Yet the city remains firmly rooted in the past: for the last seven hundred years, much of the drama of China's history has been played out here, a place that saw the emperors enthroned at the centre of the Chinese universe inside the Forbidden City, and later witnessed the chaos of the early communist years. Though Beijing has been transformed over the last two decades to such an extent that it is barely recognizable, it still remains – spiritually and geographically – the buzzing heart of the nation.

As the front line of China's constant reinterpretation of the notion of **"modernity"**, the city is on permanent fast forward when it comes to urban development, and is continually being ripped up and rebuilt – a factor responsible for the strange lack of cohesion between Beijing's various districts. The government, meanwhile, seems unable to modernize, remaining as paranoid as ever towards potential dissent – most obvious in all the media restrictions, and the multiple security barriers and bag checks around town – though outside the political arena just about anything goes these days. Students in the latest fashions while away their time in internet cafés, dropouts mosh in grunge clubs, and bohemians dream up boutiques over frappuccinos. Not everyone has benefited from the new prosperity, however: migrant day-labourers wait for work outside the stations, and homeless beggars, not long ago a rare sight, are now as common as in Western cities.

The first impression of Beijing, for both foreigners and visiting Chinese, is often of a bewildering **vastness**, not least in the sprawl of uniform apartment buildings in which

ABOVE THE FORBIDDEN CITY **RIGHT** THE CBD

most of the city's 22 million-strong population are housed, and the eight-lane freeways that slice it up. It's a perception reinforced on closer acquaintance by the concrete desert of **Tian'anmen Square**, and the gargantuan buildings of the modern executive around it. The main tourist sights – the Forbidden City, the Summer Palace and the Great Wall – also impress with their scale, though more manageable grandeur is offered by the city's attractive temples, including the Tibetan-style Yonghe Gong, the Taoist Baiyun Guan, and the astonishing Temple of Heaven, once a centre for imperial rites.

With its sights, history and, importantly, delicious **food** (all of China's diverse cuisines can be enjoyed cheaply at the city's numerous restaurants and street stalls), Beijing is a place that almost everyone enjoys. But it's essentially a private city, one whose surface, though attractive, is difficult to penetrate. The city's history and unique character are in the **details**: to find and experience these, check out the little antiques markets; the local shopping districts; the smaller, quirkier sights; the city's twisted, grey stone alleyway **hutongs**; and the parks, where you'll see old men sitting with their caged songbirds. Take advantage, too, of the city's burgeoning bar scene and nightlife and see just how far the Chinese have gone down the road of what used to be deemed "spiritual pollution". Keep your eyes open, and you'll soon notice that westernization and the rise of a brash consumer society is not the only trend here. Just as marked is the revival of older **Chinese culture**, much of it outlawed during the more austere years of communist rule. Summer evenings see long strings of traditional kites rising up beyond the rooftops; the city's numerous parks are full of martial artists every morning; and there's a renewed interest in traditional music and opera for their own sake, rather than as tourist attractions.

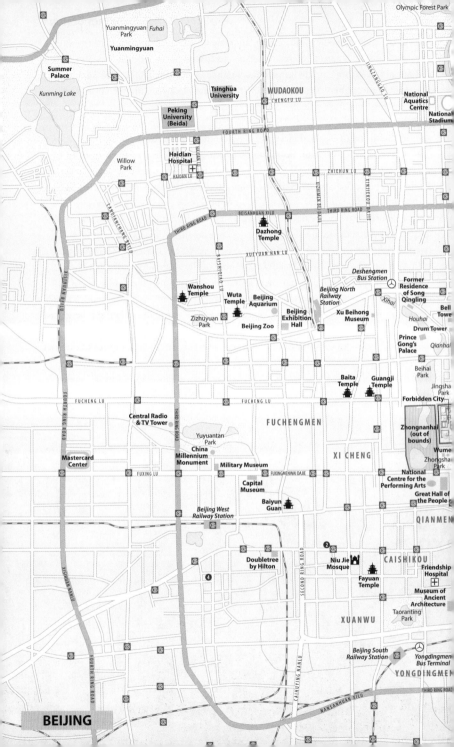

BEIJING

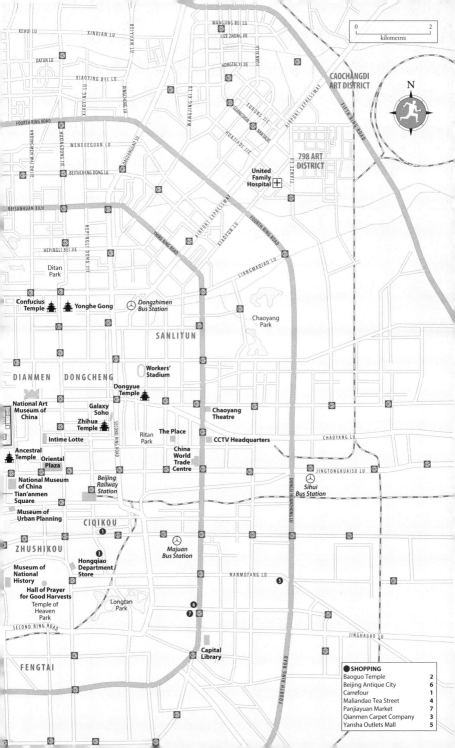

KEHUI LU **XINDIAN LU** **BEIYUAN LU** **WANGJING BEI LU**

LIZE ZHONG JIE

DATUN LU **HONGTAI XI JIE**

XIAOYING BEI LU **HONGTAI XI JIE**

FOURTH RING ROAD

CAOCHANGDI ART DISTRICT

0   2
kilometres

N

WENXUEGUAN LU

BEITUCHENG DONG LU

798 ART DISTRICT

BEISANHUAN XILU

United Family Hospital ✚

HEPINGLI BEI JIE

Ditan Park

AIRPORT EXPRESSWAY

THIRD RING ROAD

FOURTH RING ROAD

XIAOYUN LU

LIANGMAQIAO LU

Confucius Temple   Yonghe Gong   Dongzhimen Bus Station

Chaoyang Park

SANLITUN

DIANMEN   **DONGCHENG**

Workers' Stadium

Dongyue Temple

National Art Museum of China

Galaxy Soho

Zhihua Temple

Chaoyang Theatre

Intime Lotte

SECOND RING ROAD

Ritan Park

The Place

CCTV Headquarters

CHAOYANG LU

Ancestral Temple   Oriental Plaza

China World Trade Centre

JINGTONGKUAISU LU

National Museum of China

Tian'anmen Square

Beijing Railway Station

Sihui Bus Station

Museum of Urban Planning

CIQIKOU   ❶

DONGSI HUANZHONG LU

ZHUSHIKOU

❸

Hongqiao Department Store

Majuan Bus Station

Museum of National History

Hall of Prayer for Good Harvests

NANMOFANG LU

❺

Temple of Heaven Park

Longtan Park

❻

❼

SECOND RING ROAD

JINGHAGAO SU

FENGTAI

Capital Library

FOURTH RING ROAD

● SHOPPING	
Baoguo Temple	2
Beijing Antique City	6
Carrefour	1
Maliandao Tea Street	4
Panjiayuan Market	7
Qianmen Carpet Company	3
Yansha Outlets Mall	5

What to see

The absolute centre of China since the Ming dynasty, the wonderful **Forbidden City** remains Beijing's most popular sight – and rightly so. Immediately to its south is **Tian'anmen Square**, a bald expanse with a hairy history; sights on and around the square include the colossal National Museum and three grand city gates, as well as the corpse of Chairman Mao, lying pickled in his sombre mausoleum.

The wide area spreading north of the Forbidden City is one of the city's most pleasant quarters. First comes **Beihai Park**, the old imperial pleasure grounds, centred on a large lake. North again are two further lakes, **Qianhai** and **Houhai**, and the historic **Drum** and **Bell towers**, set in the heart of one of the city's most appealing *hutong* areas. The *hutongs* are tricky to navigate, but getting lost is part of the fun – nowhere else in Beijing is aimless rambling so amply rewarded. Many sights west of the lakes are remnants of the imperial past, when the area was home to princes, dukes and eunuchs. For a more contemporary side of Beijing, head east instead to the charming street of **Nanluogu Xiang**, one of Beijing's most fashionable areas – youngsters from all over the city come here to stroll and sup coffee, tourists (both foreign and domestic) go trinket mad, while expats tend to make a beeline for the craft breweries.

Further to the east is the **Yonghe Gong**, a spectacular Lamaist temple, which lies across the road from the wonderful **Confucius Temple** – less showy but just as rewarding as a window into traditional Chinese culture. The areas to the east and south are some of the most important pieces of Beijing's modern jigsaw – **Sanlitun**, the city's prime nightlife spot for the last two decades; the **CBD**, boasting high-rises aplenty and with plenty more

ABOVE A BOOK MARKET IN DITAN PARK **RIGHT** THE WATER CUBE

BEIJING ARCHITECTURE

Since the days of dynasty, Beijing has always been image-conscious – anxious to portray a particular face, both to its citizenry and to the world at large. It was during the Ming dynasty that the city took on much of its present shape, including the grid pattern still followed by many of the major streets. Some splendid buildings and complexes from this time remain, including the Forbidden City, Yonghe Gong, the Temple of Heaven and the Drum Tower. One of the world's most vaunted pieces of engineering also took shape at this time – the glorious Great Wall. Rather more humble, though forming an essential part of the city's fabric, were the traditional *hutong* houses that most Beijingers lived in. Though declining in number with each passing year, many of those you'll see today went up in **Qing** times.

Beijing took on an entirely different form during early **communist rule**. When Mao took over, he wanted the feudal city of the emperors transformed into a "forest of chimneys"; he got his wish, and the capital became an ugly industrial powerhouse of socialism. The best (or worst, depending upon your point of view) buildings from the Mao years are the Military Museum, the National Exhibition Hall, or any of the buildings on or around Tian'anmen Square. In the 1980s, when the Party embraced capitalism "with Chinese characteristics", bland international-style office blocks were erected with a pagoda-shaped "silly hat" on the roof as a concession to local taste.

Modern Beijing, eager to express China's new global dominance, has undergone the kind of urban transformation usually only seen after a war. Esteemed architects from across the globe have been roped in for a series of carte blanche projects; the results have been hit and miss, but some have been astounding. The best include the fantastic venues built for the 2008 Olympics (the "Bird's Nest" and "Water Cube"), Paul Andreu's National Centre for the Performing Arts (the "Egg"); and Zaha Hadid's curvy, sci-fi-like Galaxy Soho, completed in 2013. Perhaps most striking of all, however, is the new CCTV state television headquarters (the "Twisted Doughnut") by Dutch architect Rem Koolhaas, which appears to defy gravity with its intersecting Z-shaped towers.

CHINESE SCRIPT

Chinese characters are simplified images of what they represent, and their origins as pictograms can often still be seen, even though they have become highly abstract today. The earliest known examples of Chinese writing are predictions, which were cut into "oracle bones"; these were used for divination during the Shang dynasty, more than three thousand years ago, though the characters must have been in use long before, for these inscriptions already amount to a highly complex writing system. As the characters represent concepts, not sounds, written Chinese cuts through the problem of communication in a country with many different dialects. However, learning the writing system is ponderous, taking children an estimated two years longer than with an alphabet. Foreigners learning Mandarin use the modern **pinyin** transliteration system of accented Roman letters – used in this book – to help memorize the sounds (see p.194).

to come; and **Wangfujing**, with its array of places to shop. The best sight hereabouts is the little oasis of calm that is the **Ancient Observatory**, where Jesuit priests used to chart the movements of the heavens for the imperial court.

South of the Forbidden City you'll find **Qianmen Dajie**, an over-reconstructed shopping street, and the rather more intimate **Dazhalan** district. These feed down towards the magnificent **Temple of Heaven**, a superb specimen of Ming-dynasty design surrounded by pretty parkland. There's less to see west of the Forbidden City, but there are still a few sights worth visiting. These include a couple of charming temples; the **Military Museum**, monument to a fast-disappearing communist ethos; the modern **Capital Museum**; and the city **zoo** and **aquarium**.

In the far north of Beijing proper, you'll find three contrasting groups of sights. Furthest west, providing one of the most pleasant areas to escape from the city bustle, is the **Summer Palace**, centred around peaceful Kunming Lake; Yuanmingyuan, the "old"

Author picks

Our indefatigable author has explored every highway, byway and *hutong* of Beijing to bring you some unique travel experiences. Here are some of his personal favourites.

Hidden treasures Everyone knows about the Wall, the Forbidden City and the Temple of Heaven but to avoid the crowds head a little off the beaten track to the Confucius Temple (p.70), Ancient Observatory (p.74) and Baiyun Guan (p.87).

Get on your bike For all its high-octane development, Beijing remains a great cycling city (p.26). Wend your way through the *hutong* alleys around the Shicha lakes (p.60), cycle south to the Imperial Palace, past Mao's portrait, and pedal back up along the Forbidden City canal.

Contemporary art Beijing's prolific art scene is centred around the famed 798 Art District (p.102) but there are some good galleries closer to the city centre, such as the wonderful Red Gate Gallery (p.76).

Shopping Beijing's mix of earthy markets, boutique districts and super-modern mall complexes make it a fine place to shop (p.161): green tea, fans, seals and antiques are all popular souvenirs, and the city remains a highly affordable place for tailored clothing.

Courtyard living Though many *hutong* dwellings have fallen foul of the wrecking ball, a fair few remain, and it's quite possible to stay in one of many artfully redecorated courtyard houses (p.132).

Park life To de-stress from the city bustle, make for one of Beijing's principal parks – Ditan (p.72), Temple of Heaven (p.79) and Ritan (p.74). They're at their most attractive around sunrise and sunset, when you may see locals practising *tai ji*, dancing in formation, or doing the odd-looking "backwards walk".

Our author recommendations don't end here. We've flagged up our favourite places – a perfectly sited hotel, an atmospheric café, a special restaurant – throughout the guide, highlighted with the ★ symbol.

LEFT GALAXY SOHO **FROM TOP** ANCIENT OBSERVATORY; CÔTE COUR HOTEL; PRACTISING *TAI JI*

summer palace, lies nearby. East of here, past the university district, is the **Olympic Green**, home to some of the remaining venues from the spectacular 2008 Summer Games. East again, en route to the airport, is the fascinating **798 Art District**, centre of Beijing's burgeoning art scene.

Beijing's sprawling outskirts are a messy jumble of farmland, housing and industry, but out in the **Western Hills** you'll find semi-wild parkland, peaceful temples and the disturbing Eunuch Museum. Well outside the city – but an essential stop for many visitors and well within the scope of a day-trip – is the **Great Wall**, which winds over lonely ridges only a few hours' drive north of the capital, while for those with time to spare, the port city of **Tianjin**, and imperial pleasure complex of **Chengde** is easily accessible from the capital by train and bus.

When to go

Beijing's year starts off mean. The long **winter** (November to March) sees temperatures plummet below freezing – sometimes as low as -20°C (-4°F) – and the winds that whip off the Mongolian plains feel like they're freezing your ears off. However, pack the right clothing and this can actually be an enjoyable time to visit, not least since crowds are thin even at the most popular sights. The run-up to **Chinese New Year** (falling in late January or early to mid-February) is a great time to be in the country: everyone is in festive mood and the city is bedecked with decorations. This isn't a good time to travel around, however, as much of the population is on the move, and transport systems become hopelessly overstretched. It's best to avoid Beijing during the first three days of the festival itself, as everyone is at home with family, and a lot of businesses and sights are closed.

The city's short **spring** (April and May) is a lovely season to visit Beijing – it's dry and comfortably warm at this time, though can be windy. Fortunately, the spring dust storms that once plagued the city have lessened of late, though they still occur. **Summer** itself (June to August) is muggy and hot, with temperatures topping 30°C (86°F); in high summer the city is ripe for dining alfresco, and beer consumption goes through the roof. July and August also see plenty of rainfall, though most of it deluges all at once and even then there's still a fair amount of sun.

Ultimately, when all's said and done, the best time to visit Beijing is in the **autumn** (September and October), when the weather is dry and clement. This is also the most likely time for Beijing's semi-mythical "blue-sky days", when air pollution is said to be at its lowest, to occur – the perfect time to climb up Jingshan and see the Forbidden City at its most beautiful.

AVERAGE TEMPERATURES AND RAINFALL IN BEIJING

	Jan	Feb	Mar	Apr	May	Jun	Jul	Aug	Sep	Oct	Nov	Dec
Max/min (°C)	1/-10	4/-8	11/-1	21/7	27/13	31/18	31/21	30/20	26/14	20/6	9/-2	3/-8
Max/min (°F)	34/14	39/18	52/30	70/45	81/55	88/64	88/70	86/68	79/57	68/43	48/28	37/18
Rainfall (mm)	4	5	8	17	35	78	243	141	58	16	11	3

19

things not to miss

It's not possible to see everything Beijing has to offer in one short trip – and we don't suggest you try. What follows is a selective taste of the city's highlights: stunning temples, delicious food, artsy districts and fascinating excursions beyond the city. All entries have a page reference to take you straight into the Guide, where you can find out more.

1 FORBIDDEN CITY
Page 41
For five centuries centre of the Chinese universe and private pleasure ground of the emperor, this sumptuous palace complex ranks as the city's main attraction.

2 BEIJING OPERA
Page 158
Largely incomprehensible to foreigners, and many Chinese, but still a great spectacle.

3 PEKING DUCK
Page 139
You won't be eating the city's most famous dish every day (doing so would probably guarantee heart failure), but try it at least once, as it's supremely tasty.

4 MAO'S MAUSOLEUM
Page 51
Join the queue of awed peasants shuffling past the preserved corpse of the founder of modern China in his giant tomb, fronted by suitably bombastic socialist realist statuary.

5 GREAT WALL AT SIMATAI
Page 109
A dramatic and relatively crowd-free stretch of crumbly, vertiginous fortifications three hours from Beijing.

6 TEMPLE OF HEAVEN
Page 79

Set in the centre of an elegant park, this temple is often regarded as the zenith of Ming architecture.

7 A BEIJING BREAKFAST
See box, p.140

Start your day the local way: seek out some *jianbing* (a kind of savoury pancake), and wash it down with a pot of delicious Beijing yoghurt.

8 798 ART DISTRICT
Page 102

This huge complex of art galleries has become Ground Zero for the city's bohemians and fashionistas.

9 YONGHE GONG
Page 67

A lively, flamboyantly decorated Tibetan temple, where the air is often heady with incense smoke.

10 SUMMER PALACE
Page 96

Once the exclusive retreat of the emperors, this beautiful landscaped park, dotted with imperial buildings, is now open to all.

11 THE CBD
Page 73

The heart of new Beijing, the Central Business District is essentially a playground for some of the world's foremost architects – most dramatically in the seemingly gravity-defying CCTV Headquarters.

12 NANLUOGU XIANG
Page 64

In vogue with local hipsters, this trendy *hutong* of restaurants and boutiques is the perfect spot for a stroll, snack and a coffee.

13

14

15

BEIJING CYCLISTS

Basics

Getting there

Beijing is China's main international transport hub – though nearby Tianjin offers a smaller-scale alternative – with plenty of inbound flights from European, American, Australian and Asian cities. You can also fly or catch trains from cities all over China, or even from faraway Moscow on the vaunted Trans-Siberian railways.

Airfares vary by season, with the highest fares from Easter to October and around Christmas, New Year and just before the Chinese New Year (which falls between late January and mid-February). Note also that flying at weekends is slightly more expensive; prices quoted below assume midweek travel.

Flights from the UK and Ireland

From the UK, there are **direct flights** to Beijing (10–11hr) from London Heathrow with Air China and British Airways, and from Manchester with Hainan Air; figure on a minimum of £460 return. There's also a twice-weekly direct flight from London Gatwick to Tianjin with Tianjin Airlines (17hr; £420).

Airlines offering **indirect flights** to Beijing from the UK, stopping off in the airline's hub city, include Ukraine International Airlines (UIA), KLM, China Southern and Emirates. These are a little cheaper than direct flights, with prices starting from around £350 in low season, rising to £700 in high season. Prices can be substantially higher from the Republic of Ireland; you may want to consider taking a cheap flight to London first.

Flights from the US and Canada

There's no shortage of **direct flights** to Beijing **from North America**; carriers include Air China, Air Canada and United Airlines. It takes around 13hr to reach Beijing **from the west coast**; add 7hr or more to this if you start **from the east coast** (including a stopover on the west coast en route). Some flights cross the North Pole, shaving a couple of hours off the flight time.

In low season, expect to pay US$750–1200 from the west coast (Los Angeles, San Francisco, Vancouver), or US$870–1400 from the east coast (New York, Montreal, Toronto). To get a good fare during high season it's important to buy your ticket as early as possible, in which case you probably won't pay more than US$200 above low-season tariffs.

Flights from Australia, New Zealand and South Africa

You can fly **direct** to Beijing **from Melbourne or Sydney** with Air China and China Eastern Airlines (12hr; Aus$950); otherwise there are a host of indirect options from all state capitals on other Chinese and southeast Asian carriers, which are often substantially cheaper (from Aus$570).

From New Zealand, Air China are the only airline offering direct flights between Auckland and Beijing (12hr; NZ$990); you'll save NZ$100 flying via Guangzhou with China Southern (17hr).

There are **no direct flights** between **South Africa** and Beijing; balancing price and journey time, the best deal is probably with Cathay Pacific (17hr; ZAR7500), travelling via Hong Kong.

Organized tours

Tour operators generally include Beijing as one of a number of destinations in a tour of China. There are very cheap, off-season **flight-and-hotel packages** to Beijing, at prices that sometimes go as low as £600/€700/US$1000. Since six or seven nights in a four-star hotel are included, you're effectively getting accommodation for free, considering the cost of the flight alone. Don't forget, though, that quoted prices in brochures usually refer to the low-season minimum, based on two people sharing – the cost for a single traveller in high season will always work out more expensive.

By train

The classic overland route to Beijing is **through Russia by train**. There are actually two rail lines

---

A BETTER KIND OF TRAVEL

At Rough Guides we are passionately committed to travel. We believe it helps us understand the world we live in and the people we share it with – and of course tourism is vital to many developing economies. But the scale of modern tourism has also damaged some places irreparably, and climate change is accelerated by most forms of transport, especially flying. All Rough Guides' flights are **carbon-offset**, and every year we donate money to a variety of environmental charities.

from Moscow to Beijing: the **Trans-Manchurian** (6 days), which runs almost as far as the Sea of Japan before turning south through Dongbei to Beijing; and the **Trans-Mongolian** (5 days), the more popular option, as it rumbles past Lake Baikal in Siberia, the grasslands of Mongolia, and the desert of northwest China.

You'll need tourist **visas** for Russia, and possibly Mongolia too if you use the Trans-Mongolian train (US citizens don't need these). For detailed, up-to-date **information** on all ways to get tickets, check Ⓦ seat61.com.

Sorting out your travel arrangements on your own from abroad is a complex business and usually more trouble than it's worth; turning up in Russia and buying a ticket from a train station is unlikely to succeed, as tickets sell out quickly. British travellers can cut the complications by using the **online booking system** offered by **Real Russia** (Ⓦ realrussia.co.uk); they mark up prices by about 20 percent but save you a lot of hassle. A second-class Moscow to Beijing ticket booked with them costs around £500–700 depending on the time of year – and of course they will then help you sort out your visas for a small fee (as will all other agencies).

It's also possible to reach Beijing by train from other neighbouring countries. There are direct trains from Hanoi in **Vietnam** (2 weekly; 40hr), and daily services via Nanning. From **Kazakhstan** there are weekly services from both Astana and Almaty; you'll have to change in Urumqi.

Airlines, agents and operators

AIRLINES

Air Canada Ⓦ aircanada.com.
Air China Ⓦ airchina.com.
British Airways Ⓦ britishairways.com.
Cathay Pacific Ⓦ cathaypacific.com.
China Eastern Airlines Ⓦ flychinaeastern.com.
China Southern Ⓦ csair.com/en.
Emirates Ⓦ emirates.com.
Hainan Air Ⓦ hainanairlines.com.
KLM Ⓦ klm.com.
Tianjin Airlines Ⓦ tianjinairlines.co.uk.
UIA Ⓦ flyuia.com.
United Airlines Ⓦ united.com.

AGENTS

Ⓦ **flychina.com** US Good for discount fares from the States.
North South Travel UK ☎ 01245 608291, Ⓦ northsouthtravel .co.uk. Discounted fares worldwide. Profits are used to support projects in the developing world, especially the promotion of sustainable tourism.
STA Travel Ⓦ sta-travel.com. Worldwide specialists in low-cost flights

and tours for students and under-26s, though other customers are welcome too.
Trailfinders Ⓦ trailfinders.com. One of the best-informed and most efficient agents for independent travellers.

SPECIALIST TOUR OPERATORS

Abercrombie & Kent Ⓦ abercrombiekent.com. Luxury tours, including a nine-day "Classic China" trip covering Beijing, Xi'an and Shanghai.
Adventures Abroad US ☎ 1 800 665 3998, Ⓦ adventures-abroad .com. Small-group specialists with two-week tours between Beijing and Shanghai.
Backroads US ☎ 1 800 462 2848, Ⓦ backroads.com. Cycling and hiking between Beijing and Hong Kong.
China Highlights China ☎ 0773 283 1999, Ⓦ chinahighlights .com. China-based company that offers a set of tours of Beijing and the surrounding area.
China Odyssey China ☎ 01569 773 0073, Ⓦ chinaodysseytours .com. Offers four- to seven-day themed Beijing tours, and also visits the former imperial hunting park at Chengde.
CTS Horizons ☎ 020 3750 1655, Ⓦ ctshorizons.com. The China Travel Service's UK branch, offering an extensive range of tours including some cheap off-season hotel-and-flight packages to Beijing, and tailor-made private tours.
Geographic Expeditions US ☎ 1 888 570 7108, Ⓦ geoex.com. Moscow or Central Asia to Beijing overland packages, as well as more conventional trips within China.
Hayes and Jarvis UK ☎ 01293 762404, Ⓦ hayesandjarvis.co.uk. Among the most inexpensive Beijing packages available to British travellers.
Intrepid Adventure Travel Ⓦ intrepidtravel.com. Small-group tours, with an emphasis on cross-cultural contact and low-impact tourism. Covers the staples, including hikes along the Great Wall near Beijing.
Koryo Tours China Ⓦ koryogroup.com. Beijing's most unusual tour agency, arranging visits (heavily controlled, of course) to the paranoid hermit kingdom of North Korea.
Mir Corp US ☎ 206 624 7289, Ⓦ mircorp.com. Specialists in Central Asian and Trans-Siberian rail travel, for small groups as well as individual travellers.
The Russia Experience UK ☎ 0845 521 2910, Ⓦ trans-siberian .co.uk. Besides detailing their Trans-Siberian packages, the website is a veritable mine of information about the railway. More expensive than similar tours offered by Russian agencies, but probably the most hassle-free option.
Sundowners Ⓦ sundownersoverland.com. Tours of the Silk Road, plus Trans-Siberian rail bookings.
Travel China Guide Ⓦ travelchinaguide.com. A Chinese company with a wide range of three- and four-day group tours of Beijing and around.
Wild China Ⓦ wildchina.com. Upmarket adventure travel agency, including a four-day Beijing-specific tour, plus many others, which pass through the city on wider explorations of China.
World Expeditions Ⓦ worldexpeditions.com. Offers a 21-day Great Wall trek, starting in Beijing and heading well off the beaten track, plus cycling tours.

Arrival and departure

Beijing's airport and main train stations are all connected to the city's subway system, though you'll probably still need to use a taxi at some point – accommodation is often an inconvenient distance from the nearest subway station, especially if you're loaded down with luggage. Public buses are a cheaper alternative to cabs, but they'll be very crowded; again, it's best to save the experience for after you've dropped off your bags.

Booking **onward transport** is a simple matter, but for peak seasons – the two-week-long holidays, and just before Chinese New Year (see box, p.28) – you'll need to organize it long in advance. See the box on p.36 for useful **booking site apps**.

By plane

Beijing Capital Airport (北京首都机场, běijīng shǒudū jīchǎng; @en.bcia.com.cn) is 29km northeast of the centre. It serves both international and domestic flights, and has three terminals (T1, T2 and T3) – if you're departing Beijing, be sure to figure out which one you'll be using before heading to the airport. There are banks and ATMs here, and commission rates are the same as everywhere else. Beijing Capital is due to be joined in 2019 by **Beijing Daxing**, which will be the largest airport terminal in the world.

Taxis to the centre

You'll be pestered in the arrivals hall by charlatan taxi drivers; ignore them and use the official **taxi ranks outside**. A trip to the city centre will cost ¥70–150 and takes 50min–1hr 30min, depending on traffic and where you're headed. Drivers are unlikely to speak English, so have the name of your hotel (and address, if possible) printed out in Chinese; staff at the airport information desks can scribble it down for you.

Airport Express to the centre

The **Airport Express** light rail (¥25) runs from T3 and stops at T2 (connected by walkway and free shuttle bus to T1); it then hits Sanyuanqiao subway station (line #10), before terminating at Dongzhimen subway station (lines #2 & #13). The ride from the airport to Dongzhimen takes about 30min from T3, and 20min from T2. The trains run every 15min, 6.30am–10.30pm. Note that cabbies at the Dongzhimen exit rank commonly overcharge new arrivals, so walk a little way and hail a cab from the street.

Buses to the centre

Airport **buses** (¥16) to the city depart from T3, stopping at T2 and T1 on the way; buy tickets from desks inside the terminals. They run regularly along eleven routes; the most useful are line #1 for Guomao, a station near the Central Business District to the east of the centre; and line #3 for Dongzhimen and the main train station. The same routes return to the airport from the city. Journeys take at least 1hr each way.

Tickets

You can **buy domestic airline tickets** online at competitive rates via @elong.net or @english.ctrip .com. You'll need to provide your passport details (make sure you give names exactly as they appear in your passport) and might need to provide a phone number to confirm the booking – your hotel's will do – and to book more than 24 hours in advance if using an overseas credit card. Tickets can also be arranged through accommodation tour

---

ORIENTATION AND THE RING ROADS

Beijing still retains much of its original Ming-dynasty **layout**: that of a large rectangle oriented north and centred on the Forbidden City, all cut up by a grid of main roads. Nowadays these are frenetic, multi-lane highways, and the way they're lined with seemingly identical, endlessly repeating rows of high-rises can make the city feel alienating on a large scale, especially as you whip through in a taxi – though out on the streets, plenty of parks and the surviving *hutong* districts add a good deal of local character.

Beijing's **ring roads** – freeways arranged in nested rectangles rippling out from Tian'anmen Square – are rapid-access corridors around the city. The second and third ring roads, **Erhuan** and **Sanhuan Lu**, are the two most useful, as they cut down on journey times but extend the distance travelled; they are much favoured by taxi drivers. Within the Second Ring Road lie most of the **historical sights**, while many of the most modern buildings (including the smartest hotels, restaurants, shopping centres and office blocks) are along or close to the Third.

desks, at downtown airline offices or airport ticket desks. Travel Stone (☎ 010 56707485, ✆ travel-stone .com) are a recommended independent agent, and about the only place in Beijing where you can buy plane tickets with cash.

By train

Beijing has four useful train stations: Beijing, North, West and South, with the latter two hosting the most high-speed services. Tickets can be bought at the stations or, with a small surcharge, from hotels, travel agents and rail ticket outlets; as always, you'll need your passport to book and board. The stations are all large, busy and have poor signage; arrive with plenty of time to spare, especially if buying tickets or collecting prepaid tickets. All stations have left-luggage offices and are within taxi range of central accommodation.

TRAIN STATIONS

Beijing (北京站, běijīng zhàn) is just southeast of the city centre on subway line #2. It handles relatively slow services to northeastern China and Shanghai – aside from Chengde, there's almost nowhere you can't get to faster from another station – and international routes to Moscow and Ulaan Baatar (see p.21 for details).
Beijing North (北京北站, běijīng běi zhàn) is a minor terminal northwest of the centre, near Xixhimen subway station (lines #2, #4 & #13), with a useful service to Badaling on the Great Wall (see p.105).
Beijing South (北京南站, běijīng nán zhàn) is a modern terminus southwest of the centre on subway lines #4 and #14, handling the majority of high-speed trains to eastern China, including frequent departures to Tianjin and Shanghai.
Beijing West (北京西站, běijīng xī zhàn) is west of the centre on subway lines #7 and #9, and handles normal and high-speed services to southern, central and western destinations – including direct trains to Hong Kong (book at least six days in advance) and Lhasa (for which you'll need a Tibet travel permit).

Tickets

Tickets – always **one-way** – are available sixty days in advance of travel. **Station ticket offices** are brisk and efficient, and while queues can involve an hour or more of jostling, you'll generally get what you're after if you have some flexibility. At the counter, state your destination, the train number if possible, the day you'd like to travel, and the class you want, and have some alternatives handy. If you can't speak Chinese, get someone to write things down for you before setting out, as staff rarely speak English.

Far less crowded are the numerous **advance purchase offices** scattered around Beijing (there

are at least three on Dazhalan Dong Lu, including one outside the cinema – see p.78) where you pay a ¥5 commission per ticket. **Agents**, such as hotel travel services, can also book tickets for a commission of ¥30 or more each.

The best way to **book tickets online**, and have them delivered to your hotel door (or pick up at the departure station), is through ✆ travelchinaguide .com; you'll pay a fee of about US$5 for this. You can also reserve tickets through other websites such as ✆ ctrip.com, but these cannot be picked up by foreigners at in-town railway booking offices, or from the automatic machines at the station (which require a Chinese ID card to use); instead you have to queue at a dedicated window at the station, which has been known to take over an hour – so again, give yourself plenty of time to spare.

By bus

Beijing has many long-distance bus stations, each one serving only a few destinations; trains are almost invariably faster. The most useful options are listed below; if you arrive at any other station, it's generally best to catch a taxi to the nearest subway. Some sights around Beijing are served by buses from stops, rather than stations; details are given in the individual accounts.

BUS STATIONS

Deshengmen (德胜门汽车站, déshèngmén qìchēzhàn) is north of the centre on the Second Ring Road, close to Jishuitan subway station (line #2). Useful for Badaling and Juyong sections of the Great Wall.
Dongzhimen (东直门公共汽车站, dōngzhímén gōnggòng qìchēzhàn) is a large station at the northeast corner of the Second Ring Road on subway lines #2 and #13. It is of most use for buses to Chengde and various sections of the Great Wall.
Sihui (四惠公共汽车站, sìhuì gōnggòng qìchēzhàn), in the southeast on subway line #1, is also good for buses to Chengde (3hr 30min–4hr).

By ferry

International ferries from Incheon in South Korea dock at Tianjin Xingang Passenger Terminal (天津新 港客运站, tiānjīn xīngǎng kèyùn zhàn), around 60km east of Tianjin, itself 120km southeast of Beijing (see p.118). Tickets can be purchased from travel agents in Beijing or Tianjin (ask your hotel for the closest one), or at the port itself. There are frequent minibuses between the port and Tianjin's main train station (¥10), and some shuttle services direct to Beijing (¥70); alternatively, it's ¥100–120 for a taxi from the port to central Tianjin, and you'll easily find others to share the cost if necessary.

Services leave South Korea every Tuesday and Friday (the latter service arrives later in the day, making it harder to get to Beijing), and Tianjin every Thursday and Sunday. The cheapest tickets (around KRW110,000 from Korea, and ¥888 from China) will get you a comfy bed, with curtains to seal yourself off from the communal corridors. Pay a little more, and you'll get a bed in an en-suite private room.

City transport

Beijing is not a city that encourages random exploration on foot: though there are indeed plenty of great districts to walk around, the long spaces between them tend to be filled by busy roads and anonymous blocks of offices and apartments. Fortunately, getting around is pretty straightforward, thanks to the excellent subway system and abundant – and relatively inexpensive – taxis. Still, public transport can sometimes feel overstretched, with buses and subways often packed to bursting and taxis stuck in gridlock – in which case the best solution might be to hire a bike.

Subway

Clean, efficient and very fast, the **subway** system (daily 5.30am–11pm; ⓦbjsubway.com) currently numbers nineteen lines and is by far the most convenient method of public transport – but come prepared for poor signage (it helps to know the next station or terminus in the direction that you're heading), rush-hour overcrowding and lengthy hikes between interchange platforms. Station entrances are marked by a logo of a rectangle inside a "G" shape; you're obliged to pass bags through an airport-style scanner on entry, and might be body-scanned at some stations. **Tickets** cost ¥2 per journey from station ticket machines or when using a transport card. All stops are signed in *pinyin* (the anglicized spelling out of Chinese characters) and announced in English and Chinese over the intercom when the train pulls in.

Buses

Services mostly run daily 5.30am–11pm, though some operate 24hr. Routes are efficiently organized,

---

TRANSPORT CARDS

Anyone staying more than a couple of weeks and intending to use public transport regularly should consider buying a swipe-style **transport card** (一卡通, yīkǎtōng). Available from subway stations, these are valid for bus and subway journeys, getting you a 50 percent discount on the former; they can also be used in taxis, and for payment in some convenience stores. The deposit is ¥20, which you receive back when you return it, and you can put as much money on the card as you like.

---

though none is marked in English at the stops or on the buses – unless you speak Chinese, you'll have to find an English-speaking passer-by (though the **Pandabus app** might help; see box, p.36).

BUS TYPES

City bus and trolleybus Even though the city's 200-plus bus and trolleybus services run regularly, you'll find getting on or off at busy times hard work (rush hours are 7–9am & 4.30–8pm). The fare for ordinary buses is ¥2, or an impressively cheap ¥1 when using a travel card. Buses numbered #201–215 only provide night services.

Tourist bus These look like ordinary buses but have their numbers written in green and operate April–Oct, several times an hour 9am–5pm, between the city centre and certain attractions. Routes #1 and #2 (¥15) circuit via Tian'anmen, the Forbidden City, Beihai Park, Dazhilan and elsewhere around the centre; while Route #3 (¥15) heads out to the Drum Tower, National Stadium, Yuanmingyuan and the Summer Palace.

Taxis

Cabs are fairly inexpensive: with a standing charge of ¥13, then ¥2.3 per kilometre, a ride within the city limits should rarely exceed ¥50 – though traffic at peak hours can see the meter clicking over as you sit in gridlock. Using a taxi after 11pm will incur a surcharge of twenty percent. You can pay either by cash or using a transport card (see box above). Drivers in official licensed cabs are generally honest, but don't let yourself get hustled into one of the freelance taxis that hang around transport links; walk a short distance and hail one, or find a rank (there's one outside each train station). If you feel aggrieved at a driver's behaviour, take their number, displayed on the dashboard, and report it to the taxi **complaint office** (☏010 68351150). Indeed, just the action of writing their number down can produce a remarkable change in demeanour.

STREET NAMES

Beijing street names appear bewildering at first, as a road can have several names along its length, but they are easy to figure out once you know the system. Some names vary by the addition of the word for "inside" or "outside" – **nèi** (内) or **wài** (外) respectively – which indicates the street's position in relation to the former city walls. More common are directional terms – north (**běi**, 北), south (**nán**, 南), west (**xī**, 西), east (**dōng**, 东) and central (**zhōng**, 中). Central streets often also contain the word **mén** (门), which indicates that they once passed through a walled gate along their route. **Jiē** (街) and **lù** (路) mean "street" and "road" respectively; the word **dà** (大), which sometimes precedes them, simply means "big". Thus Jianguomenwai Dajie literally refers to the section of Jianguomen Big Street which once lay outside the city wall gate. Some of these compound street names are just too much of a mouthful, even for locals, and are usually shortened; Gongrentiyuchang Beilu, for example, is usually referred to as Gongti Beilu.

It can be a nightmare to try to find a taxi during wet weather or in certain places, such as Wangfujing, the Forbidden City or (especially) the Sanlitun bar area at kicking-out time – unless, of course, you have a **cab-hailing app** (see box, p.36).

Three Wheelers

Known as "**Three Wheelers**" (三轮车, sānlúnchē), these motorized tricycles come in many shapes and styles, and are widely used by the public for everything from pensioner mobility scooters to low-cost cars. Some are also run as short-range taxis, with some sort of canopied box on the back for passengers, and hang around outside tourist sights and transport stations. Prices are set by haggling and drivers are uniformly out to overcharge customers; if you don't want to find yourself facing a screaming match on arrival, when he claims that the three fingers he held up meant ¥300, not ¥3, get the fare written down before you set off. There are not to be confused with the pedal-powered rickshaws (see p.57) that offer tourists rides through Beijing's more attractive backstreets.

Bicycles

Renting or buying a bike gives you much more independence and flexibility – and, given their ability to skip around traffic jams, they're often faster than taxis. There are **bike lanes** on all main roads and you'll be in the company of plenty of other cyclists. If you feel nervous at busy junctions, just dismount and walk the bike across – plenty of Chinese do.

Renting a bike

Renting a bike costs upwards of ¥20 a day, plus a ¥200–500 deposit – if the nearest hostel can't help out, try the operators listed opposite. Always test the

brakes on a rented bike before riding off, and get the tyres pumped up. Should you have a problem, you can turn to one of the bike repair stalls – there are plenty of these on the pavements next to main roads.

Buying a bike

You can **buy** cheap city bikes from shops around town. Used models cost from around ¥400, though you'll likely pay at least ¥500 for a bottom-of-the-range new one; for something reliable, try Carrefour (see p.168) or the strip of bike shops on the south side of Jiaodaokou, just west of the Ghost Street restaurants (see p.146). You'll need a good lock, as **theft** is very common.

BIKE RENTALS AND TOURS

Alley Coffee 寻常巷陌, xúncháng xiàng mò. 61 Shatan Hou Jie, just east of Jingshan Park ☎ 010 84047228. Backpacker-friendly café with good bikes for rent by the day.

★ **Bike Beijing** 康多自行车店, kāngduō zìxíngchē diàn. 81 Beiheyuan Da Jie, not far from the Forbidden City or Wangfujing ☎ 010 65265857, ⊛ bikebeijing.com. Guided tours in and around the city; mountain biking through the Fragrant Hills and trips to the Great Wall (cycle there, then hike). Helpful, with good English spoken. Rental ¥100 per day.

Natooke 固定齿轮自行车, gùdìng chǐlún zìxíngchē. 19-1 Wudaoying Hutong, near the Lama and Confucius temples ☎ 010 84026925, ⊛ natooke.com. Bike repairs, sales and rental, either by the hour (¥20) or ¥80 per day.

City tours

Standard tours of the city and its outskirts, offered by most accommodation and agents scattered around tourist sights, provide a painless way of seeing the main sights quickly. The price varies considerably depending where you book: a trip to the Summer Palace, Yonghe Gong and a pedicab jaunt around the *hutongs* might cost around ¥460 per person through an upmarket hotel, but only half of this through a hostel. In addition, **hostels** offer good-value evening trips to the acrobatics shows and the opera a few times a week (essentially the same price as the event ticket, with transport thrown in), and trips (occasionally overnighters) to the Great Wall (see p.105). You must book these at least a day in advance.

CITY TOUR COMPANIES

Beijing Cooking School 🕲 beijingcookingschool.com. Ten-day intensive courses in regional Chinese cuisine, with an optional add-on in preparing Peking duck. Course dates are listed on the website.

Beijing Sideways 🕲 beijingsideways.com. Dash around Beijing in a sidecar, its adjoining motorbike driven by a local expat. Plenty of options available, including *hutong* tours, night tours, and trips to the Great Wall.

Catherine Lu 🕲 catherinelutours.com. Locally based mid-range operator, organizing everything from private *hutong* tours to hiking trips along the Great Wall.

China Culture Center 🕲 chinaculturecenter.org. Varied schedule, including cookery courses, guided tours around obvious sights, themed tours and occasional limited-number day-trips to remoter places like Cuandixia.

The China Guide 🕲 thechinaguide.com. Great Wall and tailor-made city excursions lasting one to four days.

CITS 🕲 cits.net; branches include; Parkson Building, 103 Fuxingmen Dajie 🕿 010 66011122 (daily 9am–5pm); the *Beijing Hotel*, 33 Dongchang'an Jie 🕿 010 65120507; and the *New Century Hotel* 🕿 010 68491426, opposite the zoo. This state-run behemoth offers all the regular tours of the city and surroundings.

Granite Studio 🕲 granitestudio.org. Works with The Hutong (see below), but also organizes private guided walks and themed discussions (usually historical) around the city.

★ **The Hutong** 🕲 thehutong.com. This excellent outfit runs some interesting cultural tours, including cookery courses and tea-market trips.

Tours By Locals 🕲 toursbylocals.com. Worldwide network of tours guided by local residents, with over sixty listings for Beijing.

The media

Xinhua is the state-run news agency, supplying most of the national print and TV media. All content is Party-controlled, with limited coverage of social issues and natural disasters, and then with the government portrayed as successfully combating the problem. The heavy hand of Chinese censorship is more obvious in Beijing than anywhere else in the country; ever since President Xi Jinping made highly publicized visits to newspaper offices in 2015 to encourage "patriotism" in the press, any editor who tried to publish stories about serious public discontent at corruption, or were critical of government policies, would doubtless find themselves disgraced, dismissed or even in prison for "revealing state secrets".

Newspapers and magazines

Despite ferocious censorship the official English-language **newspaper**, the *China Daily* (🕲 chinadaily .com.cn), is a decent enough read; surprisingly, the same can be said of the *Global Times* (🕲 www.global times.com.cn), an offshoot of the nationalistic *People's Daily* (🕲 english.peopledaily.com.cn). Imported news publications such as *Time* and *The Economist*, and Hong Kong's *South China Morning Post* (🕲 scmp.com), can be bought at shops in four- and five-star hotels.

There are a number of **free magazines** aimed at the expat community, which contain up-to-date entertainment and restaurant listings and are available at expat bars and restaurants. Look for *The Beijinger* (🕲 thebeijinger.com), *That's Beijing* (🕲 thats mags.com/beijing), *City Weekend* (🕲 cityweekend .com.cn/beijing) and *Time Out* (🕲 timeoutbeijing .com), all of which have reviews and event sections, with addresses written in *pinyin* and Chinese.

For an idea of what Chinese people actually think, check out **Shanghaiist** (🕲 shanghaiist.com). Though focused on Shanghai, it covers trending domestic news stories with a definite cruel and trashy tabloid slant – try searching for the phrase *tuhao* ("nouveau riche") – and offers a rare insight into the underbelly of contemporary Chinese life.

Television

Chinese **television** comprises a dozen or so channels run by the state television company, **CCTV**, plus a host of regional stations; not all channels are available across the country. You'd have to be very bored to resort to it for entertainment: the content comprises news, flirty game shows, travel and wildlife documentaries, soaps and historical dramas, and bizarre song-and-dance extravaganzas featuring performers in fetishistic, tight-fitting military outfits entertaining party officials with rigor-mortis faces. Tune in to **CCTV 1** for general viewing; **CCTV 5** is dedicated to sport; **CCTV 6** shows films (with at least one war feature a day, with the Japanese getting firmly beaten); **CCTV 11** concentrates on Chinese opera; and CCTV 17 is International news in English. The **regional stations** are sometimes more adventurous, with a current trend for frank dating games, which draw criticism from conservative-minded government factions for the rampant materialism displayed by the contestants.

Festivals and events

The festivals and religious observances that dot the Chinese year are enthusiastically celebrated in Beijing, despite the city's modernity. The majority mark the turning of seasons or propitious dates, and are times for gift-giving, family reunions and – especially – feasting.

A festival calendar

Traditional festivals take place according to dates in the **Chinese lunar calendar**, in which the first day of the month is when the moon is blacked out, with the middle of the month marked by the full moon. By the Gregorian calendar, these festivals fall on a different date every year.

JANUARY/FEBRUARY

New Year's Day Jan 1.

Spring Festival Starts on the first new moon of the year, between late Jan and mid-Feb. See box below.

Tiancang (Granary) Festival Chinese peasants celebrate with a feast on the twentieth day of the first lunar month, in the hope of ensuring a good harvest later in the year.

MARCH

Guanyin's Birthday Guanyin, the goddess of compassion and China's most popular deity, is celebrated at Buddhist temples on the nineteenth day of the second lunar month.

APRIL

Qingming April 4 & 5. Also known as Tomb Sweeping Day, this is the time to tidy ancestral graves, leave offerings of food, and burn ghost money – fake paper currency – in honour of the departed.

Beijing International Film Festival Mid- to late April ⓦ www.bjiff.com/en. BJIFF, the city's main cinematic event, is increasingly giving Asia's larger festivals – Hong Kong, Singapore and Busan – a run for their money.

Midi and Strawberry Late April/early May. Quite why the city's two biggest rock festivals have to take place on the same weekend is a mystery, but on the plus side, at least you have a choice. Midi (ⓦ www.midifestival.com) is larger and more commercial, while Strawberry tends to branch out into wider musical genres.

MAY

Labour Day May 1. Labour Day is a national holiday, during which all tourist sites are extremely busy.

Youth Day May 4. Commemorates the student demonstrators in Tian'anmen Square in 1919, which gave rise to the nationalist May Fourth Movement. It's marked in Beijing with flower displays in Tian'anmen Square.

Great Wall Marathon Late May ⓦ great-wall-marathon.com. Thousands of hardened competitors race along a remote and notoriously steep section of the wall.

JUNE

Children's Day June 1. Most school pupils are taken on excursions at this time, so if you're visiting a popular tourist site be prepared for mobs of kids in yellow baseball caps.

Beijing Craft Beer Festival Mid-June. A great time to sample the wares of Beijing's ever-increasing number of microbreweries, plus a few from elsewhere in China. Venue varies.

Dragon Boat Festival The fifth day of the fifth lunar month is a one-day public holiday. People watch dragon-boat racing and eat *zongzi*, sticky rice steamed in bamboo leaves.

JULY

Genghis Khan Extreme Grassland Marathon and Mountain Bike Adventure ⓦgenghiskhanmtbadventure.com. The Genghis Khan team organizes two major events in July: a marathon that, while standard length, runs through the Mongolian grasslands; and a 206km bike ride.

Beijing Dance Festival ⓦ beijingdancefestival.com. A delightful mix of dance – mostly contemporary, with a few traditional and Chinese ethnic minority strands thrown in. Events held at various venues across a couple of weeks.

SPRING FESTIVAL

The **Spring Festival** (late Jan or first half of Feb), is marked by two weeks of celebrations for the beginning of a new year in the lunar calendar (also called **Chinese New Year**). In Chinese astrology, each year is associated with a particular animal from a cycle of twelve, and the passing into a new astrological phase is a momentous occasion. The first day of the festival is marked by a family feast at which *jiaozi* (dumplings) are eaten. To bring luck, people dress in red clothes (red is regarded as a lucky colour) and each family tries to eat a whole fish, since the word for fish (*yu*) sounds like the word for surplus. Firecrackers are let off to scare ghosts away and, on the fifth day, to honour Cai Shen, god of wealth. Another ghost-scaring tradition you may notice is the pasting up of images of door gods at the threshold. Note that it is not an ideal time to travel – everything shuts down, and most of the population is on the move, making public transport impossible or extremely uncomfortable.

FROM TOP SPRING FESTIVAL; FREE THE BIRDS PERFORMING AT MIDI FESTIVAL>

AUGUST

Beijing International Music Festival ⓦ bimfa.org. China's premier classical music event; with as many local as international performers, it's a great opportunity to see how well the scene is developing here.

SEPTEMBER

Moon Festival Also known as the Mid-Autumn Festival, this falls on the fifteenth day of the eighth lunar month. It's celebrated with fireworks, lanterns and displays to Beijing's own Rabbit deity (see p.79). Moon cakes stuffed with preserved eggs and sweet bean paste are eaten, washed down with plenty of raw spirits.

Double Ninth Festival Nine is a number associated with *yang*, or male energy, and on the ninth day of the ninth lunar month qualities such as assertiveness and strength are celebrated. Considered an auspicious time for the distillation (and consumption) of spirits.

China Open Late Sept. Held at the Olympic Green, this premier tennis tournament attracts many of the world's elite.

Beijing International Art Biennale Late Sept in even-numbered years. See p.187.

Confucius Festival Sept 28. The birthday of China's great social philosopher is marked by celebrations at all Confucian temples.

OCTOBER

National Day Oct 1. Everyone has three days off to celebrate the founding of the People's Republic.

Culture and etiquette

When Confucius arrives in a country, he invariably gets to know about its society. Does he seek this information, or is it given him? Confucius gets it through being cordial, good, respectful, temperate and deferential.

Confucius, The Analects

Privacy is a luxury largely unheard of in China – indeed, Chinese doesn't have an exact translation of the word. Public toilets are built with low partitions, restaurants are bright and noisy, all leisure activities are performed in sociable groups, and – even in cosmopolitan Beijing – foreigners can find themselves the subject of frank stares and attention. In addition, behaviour seen as antisocial in the West (notably queue-jumping and spitting) is quite normal in China. After lengthy government campaigns, however, **smoking** – though still widespread elsewhere in the country – is now **banned** in many of Beijing's public spaces, including bars, restaurants and all transport.

Skimpy **clothing** is fine (indeed fashionable), but looking scruffy will only induce disrespect: all

---

WECHAT

While Chinese professionals would once hand out **business cards** at every opportunity, nowadays it's far more common to exchange contact details via the smartphone app **WeChat** (微信, wēixìn; ⓦ wechat.com). And it's not just for business: as foreign social media such as Twitter and Facebook are blocked in China, WeChat is utterly ubiquitous and it's becoming hard to have any sort of a social life without it. Texting is free (it can also handle video messaging and internet calls) and there's a useful **QR scanner** too.

---

foreigners are assumed to be comparatively rich, so why they would want to dress like peasants is quite beyond the Chinese. **Shaking hands** is not a Chinese tradition, though it is now fairly common between men. Businessmen meeting for the first time exchange business cards, with the offered card held in two hands as a gesture of respect – you'll see polite shop assistants doing the same with your change.

Chinese don't usually share restaurant bills; instead, diners contest for the honour of paying it, arguing loudly, grappling at the till or employing devious tactics (like pretending to go to the toilet) in their attempt to get in first. **Tipping** is never expected, though a few upmarket places add a service charge.

If you visit a Chinese house, you'll be expected to present your hosts with a **gift**, which won't be opened in front of you (that would be impolite). Spirits and ornamental trinkets are suitable presents; avoid giving anything too practical, as it might be construed as charity.

Sex, sexuality and gender issues

Women travellers in Beijing usually find the incidence of sexual harassment much less of a problem than in other Asian countries. Being ignored is a much more likely complaint, as the Chinese will generally assume that any man accompanying a woman will be doing all the talking.

Prostitution, though illegal, has made a big comeback – witness all the "hairdressers", saunas and massage parlours, most of which are brothels. Single foreign men may find themselves approached inside certain hotels (not fancy ones, or Western chains), and it's common practice for prostitutes to phone around hotel rooms at all hours of the night – unplug the phone if you don't want to be woken up. Bear in mind that consequences may be unpleasant if you are caught with a prostitute.

Beijing, and China as a whole, has become more tolerant of **homosexuality** in recent years; it's been removed from the list of psychiatric diseases and is no longer illegal. Still, the scene is fairly tame and low-key (see p.156).

Travelling with children

Foreigners with kids can be expected to receive lots of attention from curious locals – and the occasional admonition that the little one should be wrapped up warmer.

Local kids generally don't use **nappies**, just pants with a slit at the back – and when baby wants to go, mummy points him at the gutter. Nappies and baby milk are available from modern supermarkets such as Carrefour (see p.168), though there are few public changing facilities. High-end hotels have **baby-minding** services for around ¥150 an hour. **Breast-feeding** in public is acceptable, though more so outside the train station than in celebrity restaurants.

Sights and activities that youngsters might enjoy are the zoo and aquarium (see p.93), pedal boating on Houhai (see p.61), the acrobat shows (see p.159), the Puppet Theatre (see p.159) and the Natural History Museum (see p.83). If you're tired of worrying about them in the traffic, try taking them to pedestrianized Liulichang Jie (see p.78), the 798 Art District (see p.102), or the parks – Ritan Park (see p.74) has a good playground. Most Beijing attractions are free for children under 1.2m high.

For other child-specific distractions, check out ⓦ beijing-kids.com, which has an excellent "Things to Do" menu, covering places to eat, places to play, and local events.

Travel essentials

Addresses

Unlike in most of China, Beijing **street addresses** are sequential and logically numbered, usually with even numbers one side of the road, and odd numbers the other. In *hutongs*, look for small red metal address plates in Chinese at the corner of doorways; they're useful for locating otherwise hard-to-find bars and businesses. The Chinese call the ground floor the first floor, the first storey is second floor etc; these are given through the Guide as 1F, 2F and so on.

Costs

In terms of **costs**, Beijing is a city of extremes. You can, if you wish to live it up, spend as much here as you would visiting any Western capital; on the other hand, it's also quite possible to live extremely cheaply – most locals survive on less than ¥2000 a month.

Generally, your biggest expense is likely to be **accommodation**. **Food** and **transport**, on the other hand, are relatively cheap. The minimum you can live on comfortably is about £30/€33/US$38/¥250 a day if you stay in a dormitory, get around by bus and eat in simple restaurants. On a budget of £75/€88/US$100/¥650 a day, you'll be able to stay in a modest hotel, travel in taxis and eat in good restaurants. To stay in an upmarket hotel, you'll need to have a budget of around £112/€135/US$150/¥1000 a day.

Discount rates for pensioners and students are available at many sights, though the practice varies from place to place. Students may well be asked for a Chinese student card, though pensioners can often just use their passports to prove they are over 60 (women) or 65 (men). An international youth hostel card gets small discounts at affiliated hostels (and can be bought at the front desk).

Crime and personal safety

Despite the sometimes overbearing obsession with **public security** – the bag scanning and even occasional body searches at Tian'anmen Square, subway stations and many tourist sights – Beijing is in fact a relatively safe place to visit. You're far more likely to get worn down by the crowds, weather or pollution than get mugged, and it's very rare to feel personally threatened around the city centre, even late at night. Even so, you should certainly take the same precautions here that you would at home, and in particular look out for the following scams.

Con artists

Getting **scammed** is by far the biggest threat to foreign visitors, and there are now so many profes-sional con artists targeting tourists that you can expect to be approached many times a day at places such as Wangfujing and on Tian'anmen Square. A sweet-looking young couple, a pair of girls, or perhaps a kindly old man will ask to practise their English or offer to show you round. After befriending you – which may take hours – they will suggest

EMERGENCY NUMBERS

Police ☎110
Fire ☎119
Ambulance ☎120

some refreshment, and lead you to a teahouse or restaurant. After eating you will be presented with a bill for thousands of yuan, your new "friends" will disappear or pretend to be shocked, and some large gentlemen will appear. In another variation, you will be coaxed into buying artwork for a ridiculous sum. It is hard to believe just how convincing these scammers can be: never let a stranger take you to a restaurant or gallery at a first meeting, however innocently friendly they might appear.

Theft

Tourists are an obvious target for petty **thieves**, and you need to be wary on crowded buses and subways, the favoured haunt of pickpockets. Passports and money should be kept in a concealed money belt; a bum bag offers much less protection and is easy for skilled fingers to get into. It's a good idea to keep a few large-value notes separate from the rest of your cash, together with copies of all your important documents.

Hotel rooms are on the whole secure, dormitories much less so – in the latter case it's often fellow travellers who are the problem. Most hotels should have a safe, but it's not unusual for things to go missing from these.

On the **street**, flashy jewellery and watches will attract the wrong kind of attention, and try to be discreet when taking out your cash. Not looking obviously wealthy also helps if you want to avoid being ripped off by street traders and three-wheeler drivers, as does telling them you are a student – the Chinese have a great respect for education, and more sympathy for foreign students than for tourists.

The police

If you do have anything stolen, you'll need to get the police, known as the **Public Security Bureau** or PSB, to write up a loss report in order to claim on your insurance. Their main office is at 2 Andingmen Dong Dajie, 300m east of Yonghegong subway stop (Mon–Fri 8.30am–4.30pm; ☎010 84015292), though police boxes across town are open around the clock.

The **police** are recognizable by their dark blue uniforms and caps, though there are a lot more around than you might at first think, as plenty are undercover. They have much wider powers than most Western police forces, including establishing the guilt of criminals – trials are often used only for deciding the sentence of the accused, though China is beginning to have the makings of an independent judiciary. Laws are harsh, with execution – a bullet in the back of the head – the penalty for a wide range of serious crimes, from corruption to rape, though if the culprit is deemed to show proper remorse, the result can be a more lenient sentence.

While individual police often go out of their way to help foreigners, the institution of the PSB is, on the whole, tiresomely officious.

Electricity

The electrical supply is 220V. **Plugs** come in four types: three-pronged with angled pins, three-pronged with round pins, two flat pins and two narrow round pins. Adaptor plugs are available from hardware and electronic stores.

Entry requirements

All foreign nationals require a **visa** for mainland China, available worldwide from Chinese embassies, specialist tour operators, visa agents, and online. Bear in mind that application requirements are strict but change frequently, and you need to check the latest rules at least three months before you travel; the following information outlines the current situation. Extending your visa in-country (see opposite) can be problematic; go for the longest visa available given your travel plans.

It is best to **apply in your home country**, that is, the same country that issued your passport – so a British national living long-term in Europe on a British passport needs to apply in Britain, not their country of residence. You need to provide a detailed itinerary of your proposed trip, plus proof of having bought a return airfare and having booked accommodation for every night that you're in China. The way around the latter hurdle is to find a hotel via ⓦctrip.com which doesn't require your credit card details to make a reservation, book it for the duration, and then cancel the booking once you have your visa. You'll be asked your occupation – it's not wise to admit to being a journalist, photographer or writer, and in such instances it's best to say "consultant" or similar. Your passport must be valid for at least another six months from your planned date of entry into China, and have at least one blank page for visas.

If you don't apply in your home country, or fall short of expectations in any way, you'll be asked to provide an official introductory letter from an organization inviting you to China, bank statements, and possibly documents proving your annual income and employment record – things that might be impossible to produce if, for instance, you're halfway through a round-the-world trip. The only solution in this case might be to head to Hong Kong and apply through independent agents there, who charge steeply but can usual wrangle a one-month visa.

Visas must be **used** within three months of issue, and the **cost** varies considerably depending on the visa type, the length of stay, the number of entries allowed, and – especially – your nationality. For example, US nationals pay US$140 for a multi-entry tourist visa with up to ten years validity, whereas UK nationals pay £150 for one lasting just two years. **Don't overstay** your visa: the fine is ¥500 a day, along with the possibility that you may be deported and banned from entering China for five years.

Tourist visas (L) are valid for between one month and two years, and can be single- or multiple-entry. **Business** (M) and **Research** visas (F) are valid for between three months and two years and can be either multiple- or single-entry; to apply, you'll need an official invitation from a government-recognized Chinese organization. Twelve-month **work visas** (Z) again require an invitation, plus a health certificate.

Students intending to **study** in China for less than six months need an invitation or letter of acceptance from a college there and will be given an F visa. To study for up to twelve months (X visa), there is an additional form to fill out and you will also need a health certificate.

CHINESE EMBASSIES ABROAD

Australia Ⓦ au.china-embassy.org
Canada Ⓦ ca.chineseembassy.org
Ireland Ⓦ ie.china-embassy.org/eng
New Zealand Ⓦ www.chinaembassy.org.nz
South Africa Ⓦ www.chinese-embassy.org.za
UK Ⓦ www.chinese-embassy.org.uk/eng
US Ⓦ www.china-embassy.org/eng

Visa extensions

Obtaining a **visa extension** in Beijing is possible but involves a good deal of bureaucratic officiousness; authorities here are notoriously unsympathetic. You'll need a passport photo, a receipt from your accommodation as evidence of residence in Beijing, proof that you have international transport out of the country booked, and an itinerary for the rest of your stay (which can be fictitious of course). You may also need to show that you have health insurance, plus train tickets, museum entrance tickets and such like to prove that you are indeed a tourist and haven't been working illegally. Subsequent applications for extensions will be refused unless you have a good reason to stay, such as illness or travel delay.

Apply at least 7 days before your visa expires at the Public Security Bureau, Entry and Exit Division, 2 Andingmen Dong Jie (Mon–Sat 8.30am–4.30pm; ☏ 010 84020101). If successful, a 30-day extension costs ¥160 (US citizens pay ¥1000). The process takes a week, so make sure that you won't need your passport during this time.

Customs allowances

You're allowed to **import** into China up to 400 cigarettes and 1.5l of alcohol and up to ¥20,000 cash. Foreign currency in excess of US$5000 or the equivalent must be declared. It's illegal to import printed or filmed matter critical of the country, but confiscation is rare in practice.

Export restrictions apply on any items over 100 years old that you might buy in China. Taking these items out of the country requires an export form, available from the Friendship Store (see map on pp.68–69); ask at the information counter for a form, take along the item and your receipt, and approval is given on the spot. You needn't be unduly concerned about the process – the "antiques" you commonly see for sale are all fakes anyway.

Embassies

Most **embassies** are either around Sanlitun, in the northeast, or in the Jianguomenwai compound, north of and parallel to Jianguomenwai Dajie. Visa departments usually open for a few hours every weekday morning (check websites for exact times and to see what you'll need to take). During the application process they might take your passport for as long as a week; remember that you can't change money or your accommodation without it.

FOREIGN EMBASSIES IN BEIJING

Australia 21 Dongzhimenwai Dajie ☏ 010 51404111, Ⓦ china.embassy.gov.au.
Canada 19 Dongzhimenwai Dajie ☏ 010 51394000, Ⓦ canadainternational.gc.ca.
Ireland 3 Ritan Donglu ☏ 010 85316200, Ⓦ embassyofireland.cn.
New Zealand Sanlitun Dongsan Jie ☏ 010 85312700, Ⓦ mfat.gov.nz/china.
South Africa 5 Dongzhimenwai Dajie ☏ 010 85320000, Ⓦ www.dirco.gov.za/beijing.
UK 11 Guanghua Lu, Jianguomenwai ☏ 010 51924000, Ⓦ www.gov.uk/government/world/organisations/british-embassy-beijing.
US 55 Anjialou Lu (entrance on Tianze Lu) ☏ 010 85313000, Ⓦ beijing.usembassy-china.org.cn.

Health

Beijing is one of the most polluted capital cities in the world, a problem compounded by heavy industry, heavy traffic, crowded conditions, and occasional dust storms. Unsurprisingly, a host of **cold and flu infections** affect a large proportion of the population, mostly in the winter months. More serious epidemics such as **SARS and bird flu** have hit since the turn of the century; should another major one occur, it's best to refer to the advice of your home government. For the current **Air Quality Index**, check Ⓦ aqicn.org/city/beijing.

Diarrhoea is another common illness to affect travellers, usually in a mild form; it can be caused by stress or simply unfamiliar food. The sudden onset of diarrhoea with stomach cramps and vomiting indicates food poisoning. Get plenty of rest, drink lots of water, and in serious cases replace lost salts with oral rehydration solution (ORS); this is especially important with young children. Take a few sachets with you, or make your own by adding half a teaspoon of salt and three of sugar to a litre of cool, previously boiled water. While down with diarrhoea, avoid milk, greasy or spicy foods, coffee and most fruit, in favour of bland food such as rice, plain noodles and soup. If symptoms persist, or if you notice blood or mucus in your stools, consult a doctor.

> ### EMERGENCY MEDICAL CARE
>
> For emergencies, note that the **Friendship Hospital Foreigners' Service** has English-speaking staff and offers a comprehensive (and expensive) service at 95 Yongan Lu (Ⓣ010 63014411). **Ambulances** can be called on Ⓣ120, but taking a taxi will be cheaper and probably quicker.

To avoid stomach complaints, eat at places that look busy and clean and stick to fresh, thoroughly cooked food. Shellfish is a potential hepatitis A risk, and best avoided. Fresh fruit you've peeled yourself is safe; other uncooked foods – salads and the like – may have been washed in unclean water. **Don't drink tap water**; just about every corner store sells bottled drinking water, in up to five-litre containers (¥1–10).

Hospitals, clinics and pharmacies

Medical facilities in Beijing are adequate: there are some high-standard international clinics, most big hotels have a resident doctor, and for minor complaints there are plenty of pharmacies that can suggest remedies. Most doctors will treat you with Western techniques first, but will also know a little

---

TRADITIONAL CHINESE MEDICINE

Chinese traditional medicine has been used for 2200 years – ever since the semi-mythical Xia king Shennong compiled his classic work on medicinal herbs. Around eight thousand "herbs" derived from roots, leaves, twigs, fruit and animal parts are used, generally taken as a bitter and earthy-tasting tea. **Diagnosis** involves feeling the pulse, examining the tongue and face, and listening to the tone of voice. Infections are believed to be caused by internal imbalances, so the whole body is treated rather than just the symptom. In the treatment of flu, for example, a "cold action" herb would be used to reduce fever, another to induce sweating and so flush out the system, and another as a replenishing tonic.

Just as aspirin is derived from willow bark, many Chinese drugs come from traditional herbal remedies: artemisin, for example, which is an effective anti-malarial treatment. With their presentation boxes of ginseng roots and deer antlers, traditional **Chinese pharmacies** are colourful places; unfortunately, few practitioners or pharmacy staff will be able to speak English, but there are a few good places for international visitors to head to.

Beijing Hospital of Traditional Chinese Medicine 北京中医医院 běijīng, ng zhōngyī yīyuàn. 23 Meishuguan Houjie Ⓣ010 52176667, Ⓦ www.bjzhongyi.com; Nanluoguxiang subway (line #6 or #8). Renowned hospital with a range of services and English-speaking staff; call ahead to book an appointment. Daily 8am–4.30pm.
Meridian Massage Center 明经堂中医诊疗机构, míngjīngtáng zhōngyī zhěnliáo jīgòu. 9–10A Fangyuan Xilu Ⓣ010 84567010, Ⓦ www.mingjingtang.com; Sanyuanqiao subway (line #10). More than a mere massage centre,

this clinic offers various treatments including cupping, moxibustion and acupuncture; courses of the last-named sometimes see electrical charges applied to the needles. Daily 8am–4.30pm.
Tongrentang 同仁堂, tóngréntáng. 24 Dazhalan Jie Ⓣ010 63030221, Ⓦ tongrentang.com; Qianmen subway (line #2). Famed pharmacy with branches all around the country. Their Dazhalan branch is the most beautiful of the lot, and particularly useful since it has English-speaking staff; they're able to advise on appropriate herbal purchases, and offer on-the-spot diagnoses for a range of ailments. Daily 8am–8pm.

traditional Chinese medicine (TCM; see box opposite). If you don't speak Chinese, you'll generally need to have a good phrasebook or be accompanied by a Chinese-speaker.

Pharmacies are marked by a green cross. There are large ones at 136 Wangfujing and 42 Dongdan Bei Dajie (daily 9am–8pm) or you could try the well-known Tongrentang Pharmacy on Dazhalan for traditional remedies (see box opposite).

HOSPITALS AND CLINICS

Beijing International SOS Clinic 国际 SOS, guójì SOS. Suite 105, Kunsha Building, 16 Xinyuanli ☎ 010 64629199, ⓦ internationalsos.com. Foreign-staffed clinic that's correspondingly expensive; it'll be at least ¥1000 for a simple consultation. 24hr.

China–Japan Friendship Hospital 中日友好医院, zhōngrì yǒuhǎo yīyuàn. 2 Yinghua Dong Jie ☎ 010 64282297, ⓦ english.zryhyy.com.cn. In the northeast of the city, this hospital has a dedicated foreigners' clinic. Daily 8–11.30am & 1–4.30pm; 24hr emergency unit.

International Medical and Dental Centre 国际医疗中心, guójì yīliáo zhōngxīn. S-106/S-110 Lufthansa Centre, 50 Liangmaqiao Lu ☎ 010 64651561, ⓦ www.imcclinics.com. Efficiently run clinic with foreign staff and a well-stocked pharmacy. Mon–Fri 9am–5pm.

United Family Hospital 和睦家医院, hémùjiā yīyuàn. 2 Jingtai Lu, appointment ☎ 010 59277000; emergency ☎ 010 59277120, ⓦ ufh.com.cn. The only completely foreign-operated clinic in town; consultations will cost at least ¥1000. Mon–Fri 9am–5pm.

Insurance

You'd do well to take out an **insurance policy** before travelling, to cover against theft, loss and illness or injury. Before paying for a new policy, however, it's worth checking whether you are already covered: some all-risks home insurance policies may cover your possessions when overseas, and many private medical schemes include cover when abroad.

There's little opportunity for dangerous sports in Beijing (unless crossing the road counts) so a standard policy should be sufficient.

Internet

Free wi-fi is ubiquitous, from cafés and tourist areas, to just about every form of accommodation. Almost every Beijinger has a smartphone nowadays, and the best way to keep online is to tote one as well, or failing that, a tablet or laptop. There's only one **social media app** you'll need, and that's WeChat (see box, p.30)

Internet bars (网吧, wǎngbā) are also legion, though never signed in English. They're invariably full of network-gaming teenagers, and **charge** ¥5–10 per hour. You're officially required to show a Chinese ID card before being allowed to use one, though some accept passports. Otherwise backpacker hostels (free or cheap) and hotel business centres (expensive) will have terminals.

Censorship is a major headache for anyone wanting to access foreign websites, thanks to the dryly named "**Great Firewall**" or Net Nanny, which blocks sites deemed undesirable by the state. This currently includes anything connected to Google (so no Google Maps, Gmail or YouTube; those with Gmail accounts might want to set up a new one for their trip with Hotmail, Yahoo or similar), plus all foreign social media, including Twitter and Facebook. To get around it, you need to install a **web proxy** or **VPN** (Virtual Private Network) on your phone or laptop, which needs to be set up before you leave home and will cost a few pounds a month; check online to find the best current option, as unfortunately they get disabled regularly by Chinese censors. Using a VPN in China is illegal, but just about every foreign business runs one.

Laundry

Big hotels, guesthouses and youth hostels offer a **laundry service** for anything upwards of ¥15 per load; alternatively, some hostels have self-service facilities or you can use your room sink – every corner store sells **washing powder** (洗衣粉, xǐyīfěn).

ESSENTIAL APPS

Smooth your way in China with these handy smartphone apps. To make friends, you'll also definitely need **WeChat** (see box, p.30).

Baidu maps (Ⓦmap.baidu.com). Chinese-language take on Google Maps (which is anyway blocked in China unless you're running a VPN). Works in a limited way with *pinyin*, but you'll need to input Chinese characters for best results.

Ctrip & Elong (Ⓦelong.net, Ⓦenglish.ctrip .com). Useful for booking flights and accommodation; use Travel China Guide (see below) for trains. See p.24.

Didi (Ⓦwww.xiaojukeji.com). Uber-like Chinese app for taxis in over 350 cities; you offer a pick-up fee and wait for drivers to respond. Drivers will take cash too, so there's no need for a domestic bank card. Chinese-language only, but not too hard to get to grips with.

ExploreMetro (Ⓦexploremetro.com). Subway maps for Beijing (plus Guangzhou, Hong Kong, Shenzhen and Shanghai, should you be heading there).

Pandabus (Ⓦpandabus.cn). Uses your phone's GPS to show public bus timetables for your location. Also works with English-language searches, though results text will be in Chinese.

Pleco & Dianhua (Ⓦpleco.com, Ⓦdianhuadictionary.com). Comprehensive dictionaries where you can input words in English, *pinyin* or Chinese characters and get a translation. They both come in free and pay-for versions; Pleco scores higher here with optical character recognition.

Travel China Guide (Ⓦtravelchinaguide .com). Best way to book train tickets online and have them delivered to your hotel room (see p.24).

Waygo (Ⓦwaygoapp.com). Use your phone's camera to scan a Chinese-language menu or transport timetable and get a basic translation. Limited but surprisingly useful.

Otherwise, try **Laundry Town** (Ⓦlaundrytown.com /beijing), who charge ¥30/kilo by dry weight, take a couple of days and offer a door-to-door service.

Left luggage

There are left-luggage offices at all three of Beijing's main train stations, and there are also several at the airport; all are well signed. Those at the train stations are open daily 5am–midnight, and cost from ¥15/day; the office at the airport is open 24hr, and costs from ¥20/day.

Living in Beijing

Most resident foreigners in Beijing live in Western-style **expat housing**, often in **Chaoyang** in the east of the city. Rent in these districts is expensive, topping £2250/€2700/US$3000/¥20,000 a month. Living in ordinary neighbourhoods is much cheaper: a furnished two-bedroom apartment can cost around £785/€950/US$1100/¥7000 a month, while a shared room in a flat will be half this.

The easiest way to find an apartment is through a **real estate agent**, who will usually take a month's rent as a fee. There are lots of agents, and many advertise in the expat magazines – an example is *Wo Ai Wo Jia* (Ⓦ5i5j.com). **Homestays** can be cheap, but you won't get much privacy; check

Ⓦchinahomestay.org. As you move in, you and the landlord are supposed to register with the local PSB office – in reality, it's quite possible to let it slide, at least for a while.

Working in Beijing

There are plenty of jobs available for foreigners in mainland China, with a whole section of expat society surviving as actors, cocktail barmen, models and so on. Many foreign workers are employed teaching English at universities, private colleges and schools. There are schemes to place foreign teachers in **Chinese educational institutions** – contact your Chinese embassy (see p.33) for details. Teaching at a university you'll earn ¥6000–16,000 a month, depending on your qualifications; plus there's usually free on-campus accommodation. Contracts are generally for one year.

You'll earn up to ¥250 per hour in a **private school**, though be aware of the risk of being ripped off: the most common complaints are being given more classes to teach than you'd signed up for, and being placed in substandard housing.

Studying in Beijing

Most foreign students come to Beijing to study **Mandarin Chinese**, often at the renowned **Peking University** (usually referred to as Beida, see p.101; Ⓦenglish.pku.edu.cn) or **Tsinghua University**

(Ⓦwww.tsinghua.edu.cn). There are many other subjects available too – from martial arts to traditional opera or classical literature – once you break the language barrier. Courses cost from the equivalent of US$2700 a year, or US$900 a semester. Hotel-style campus accommodation costs around US$20 a day; most people move out as soon as they speak enough Chinese to rent a flat.

The universities also offer short Mandarin **courses** (from one week to two months), or try: **Beijing Foreign Studies University**, 2 Xierhuan Lu (Ⓣ010 68468167, Ⓦwww.bfsu.edu.cn); **Berlitz**, 6 Ritan Lu (Ⓣ010 65930478, Ⓦwww.berlitz.com.cn); the **Bridge School** (Ⓦwww.bridgeschoolchina.com); or the **BDS** at 7 Beixiao Jie, Sanlitun (Ⓣ010 65323005, Ⓦchinese study-lcc.com), where most students are diplomats.

USEFUL RESOURCES

Chinatefl Ⓦ www.chinatefl.com. A good overview of English-teaching opportunities in the Chinese public sector.
CIEE Ⓦ ciee.org. The Council on International Educational Exchange runs programmes for US students of Mandarin or Chinese studies, with placements in Beijing.
Teach Abroad Ⓣ goabroad.com. International teaching website with plenty of Beijing positions.

Mail

The Chinese **postal service** is, on the whole, fast and reliable. Main **post offices** are open Monday to Saturday between 9am and 5pm; smaller offices may close for lunch or at weekends.

The **International Post Office** is on Chaoyangmen Dajie, just north of the intersection with Jianguomen Dajie (Mon–Sat 8am–7pm; Ⓣ010 65128114). Here you can rent a PO box, use their packing service for parcels and buy a wide variety of collectable stamps, though staff are not very helpful.

Postage for a letter (up to 100g) is ¥7, then ¥4.50 for each additional 100g. To send **parcels**, turn up at a post office with the goods you want to send – staff sell boxes to pack them in. Once packed, but before the parcel is sealed, it must be checked at the customs window in the post office. Surface rates for small parcels (up to 2kg) cost ¥5 for the first 50g, then around ¥0.1 per gram thereafter; large packages (up to 30kg) start around ¥100 for the first kilo, then a sliding scale for additional weight. If you are sending valuable goods bought in China, put the receipt or a photocopy of it in with the parcel, as it may be opened for customs inspection farther down the line.

An **Express Mail Service** (**EMS**) operates to most countries and to most destinations within China and is available from all post offices. Besides cutting delivery times, the service ensures that the letter or parcel is sent by registered delivery – though note that the courier service **DHL** (Ⓦcn.dhl.com) is rather faster, and costs about the same; there are also **FedEx** (Ⓦfedex.com) and **UPS** (Ⓦups.com) branches around town.

Maps

In these days of mobile phone apps and good subway connections, printed maps are less vital than before. Be aware, however, that with **Google maps blocked in China**, you'll either need a VPN or to use alternative online mapping services (see box opposite). If all else fails, you can still buy traditional fold-out city maps from hotels, bookshops and street vendors.

Money

Chinese **currency** is formally called the **yuan** (¥), more colloquially known as renminbi (RMB) or kuai; a yuan breaks down into units of ten **jiao** (also called mao). Paper money was invented in China and is still the main form of exchange, available in ¥100, ¥50, ¥20, ¥10, ¥5 and ¥1 notes; though you'll rarely need to use them, there are also notes for jiao, while everything up to and including ¥1 also comes in coin form. At the time of writing the exchange rate was approximately ¥6.6 to US$1, ¥9 to £1, ¥7.5 to €1, ¥5.1 to CAN$1, ¥5 to Aus$1, ¥4.9 to NZ$1 and ¥0.46 to ZAR1. For exact rates, check Ⓦxe.com.

Banks and ATMs

Most **ATMs** accept foreign bankcards, connected to the Cirrus, American Express, Visa, Plus and Master-Card networks. They'll likely charge transaction fees, and your home bank will probably take a slice too. There's usually a maximum of ¥2000 in a single withdrawal, and a maximum 24hr limit of ¥3000–5000, depending on your card.

Banks are usually open from Monday to Friday (9am–5pm), though some branches open on weekends too. All are closed on New Year's Day, National Day, and for the first three days of the Chinese New Year, with reduced hours for the following eleven days. All branches of the Bank of China will give cash advances on Visa cards.

Credit cards and wiring money

Major credit cards, such as Visa, American Express and MasterCard, are accepted only at big tourist hotels and restaurants, and by a few tourist-oriented shops. It's possible to **wire money** to Beijing through

Western Union (⦿westernunion.com); funds can be collected from one of their agents in the city, in post offices and the Agricultural Bank of China.

Opening hours and public holidays

Offices and **government agencies** are open from Monday to Friday, usually from 8am to noon and then from 1pm to 5pm; some open on Saturday and Sunday mornings, too. **Shops** are generally open from 10am to 7pm or 8pm Monday to Saturday, with shorter hours on Sunday; large shopping centres are open daily and don't close till around 9pm.

Public holidays have little effect on business, with only government departments and certain banks closing. However, on New Year's Day, during the first three days of the Chinese New Year, and on National Day, most businesses, shops and sights will be shut, though some restaurants stay open.

Crowds are heaviest at attractions at the weekends, during public holidays, and through June–August, when visitor numbers at popular sights reach critical mass. Note that most government-run attractions – including museums, temples and even the Forbidden City – are **closed on Mondays**. Specific opening hours are listed throughout the Guide.

PUBLIC HOLIDAYS

Jan 1 New Year's Day (one day)
Feb/March Chinese New Year/Spring Festival (one week)
Early April Qingming Festival (one day)
May 1 Labour Day (one day)
June Dragon Boat Festival (two days)
September Mid-Autumn Festival (one day)
Oct National Day (one week)

Phones

Everywhere in China has an **area code** that must be used when phoning from outside that locality; Beijing's is 010. Local calls are free from landlines, and long-distance China-wide calls are ¥0.3 a minute. International calls cost from ¥3.5 a minute (much cheaper if you use an IP internet phone card – see below).

The most prevalent **public phones** are located on the outside of small stores – you won't have to look long to find one. Simply pick up, dial and pay the amount on the meter afterwards. Most of these however, will not handle international calls. The cheapest way to call overseas with any phone is to use an **IP card**, which comes in ¥100 units. You dial a local number, then a PIN, then the number you're

calling. Rates are as low as ¥2.4 per minute to the US and Canada, ¥3.2 to Europe. IP cards are sold from corner stores, mobile-phone emporiums, and from street hawkers (usually outside the mobile-phone emporiums).

Note that calling from **tourist hotels**, whether from your room or from their business centres, will attract a surcharge that may well be extortionate.

Mobile phones

Mobile coverage in Beijing is excellent and comprehensive; they use the GSM system. Assuming your phone is unlocked and compatible, the cheapest deal is to buy a Chinese **SIM card** (SIM卡, SIM kǎ or 手机卡, shǒujīkǎ) for your phone from street kiosks or any China Mobile, China Unicom or China Telecom shop. The regulations state that you have to show a Chinese ID Card or foreign passport to buy a SIM card; depending on where you are, however, you might be sold one without anyone checking, or find that sales staff will only accept Chinese ID.

The basic SIM card **costs** ¥100, which gets you 300MB download and 100min of phone time; you extend this with prepaid **top-up cards** (充值卡, chōngzhí kǎ) from the same outlets. Making and receiving domestic calls this way costs ¥0.2 per minute, and texts ¥0.1; you can usually only send texts overseas, not call.

If your phone is locked or uses another system, it could well be cheaper to **buy a new handset** rather than pay your provider's roaming charges; the cheapest (non-smart) phones cost around ¥200. Make sure the staff change the operating language into English for you. You can also **rent mobile phones** from China Mobile, which is most conveniently arranged online at ⦿china-mobile -phones.com. The phone can be picked up from your hotel and left there when you leave. Phones

---

USEFUL DIALLING CODES

To **call mainland China from abroad**, dial the international access code, then 86, then the number (omitting the initial zero). To **call abroad from mainland China**, dial ☎00, then the country code (see below), then the number (omitting the initial zero, if any):

Australia 61
New Zealand 64
Republic of Ireland 353
South Africa 27
UK 44
US and Canada 1

cost US$10 for the first two days, then US$1 per additional day, and all calls are at the local rate.

Time

Beijing, like the rest of China, is 8hr ahead of GMT, 13hr ahead of US Eastern Standard Time, 16hr ahead of US Pacific Time and 2hr behind Australian Eastern Standard Time. It does not observe daylight saving time.

Toilets

Chinese toilets can be pretty disgusting, and though Beijing is one of the best places in the country in such regards, it's still common to find loos that are filthy or provide no privacy whatsoever. Things are certainly improving, though, even in the city's famed *hutong* alleys – many of the communal toilets (which all locals have to use, since they've none of their own) have been spruced up and are kept clean, with some now even allowing wheelchair access. Although public toilets are quite common and almost always free, the best advice when around town is to head for the nearest shopping mall or five-star hotel; many of Beijing's sights now also feature decent toilets. Lastly, some facilities only have Chinese markings to designate male and female sections: it's helpful to remember that the ladies' one (女) looks a bit like a (crouching) woman, and the chaps' one (男) somewhat like a man with a window for a head.

Tourist information

Hostels are generally the best source of information about Beijing, even putting many top hotels to shame in this respect. For details of English-language listings magazines, see p.142.

ONLINE RESOURCES

The Beijing Page Ⓦ beijingpage.com. A comprehensive and well-organized page of links, with sections on tourism, entertainment and industry.

CCTV Ⓦ english.cctv.com. Featuring a live video stream plus other programmes available to watch on demand, this is the website of the Chinese state television's English-language service.

China Bloglist Ⓦ chinabloglist.org. Directory with links to over 500 blogs about China, most of whose writers claim unique insights into the country, its people and culture.

China Business World Ⓦ cbw.com. A corporate directory site with a useful travel section, detailing tours and allowing you to book flights and hotels.

China Vista Ⓦ chinavista.com. China-based website with snippets about Chinese culture, history, attractions and food.

eBeijing Ⓦ www.ebeijing.gov.cn. Government-run but surprisingly useful website on Beijing, with plenty of general information on tourism, culture, study programmes and even visas.

I am Xiao Li Ⓦ youtube.com. If David Lynch had designed a Mandarin Chinese course, it would have looked like this. Very disturbing.

Middle Kingdom Life Ⓦ middlekingdomlife.com. Online manual for foreigners planning to live and work in China, providing a sane sketch of the personal and professional difficulties they're likely to face.

Popup Chinese Ⓦ popupchinese.com. Great resource for learning Mandarin Chinese, from beginner to advanced; you need to open an account for full access, but even the free material includes podcasts, videos, useful tools and tests.

Travel China Ⓦ travelchinaguide.com. Unusual in covering obscure places and small-group tours, as well as the normal run of popular sites and booking links.

Visit Beijing Ⓦ english.visitbeijing.com.cn. Useful what's-on style listings site and webzine, run by the otherwise lacklustre Beijing Tourism.

Yesasia Ⓦ yesasia.com. Online shopping for Chinese movies, CDs, books, pop collectables, etc.

Youku Ⓦ youku.com. With YouTube blocked, this popular site fills the gap, with millions of clips and home videos. In Chinese, but easy enough to navigate.

Zhongwen.com Ⓦ zhongwen.com. Especially interesting if you're a student of Chinese, this site includes background on the Chinese script, several classic texts (with links to some English translations) and even a bunch of suggested renderings into Chinese of common first names.

Travellers with disabilities

Beijing makes few provisions for disabled people. Subject to continual, arbitrary redevelopment along whatever is the current government whim, parts of the city can be guaranteed to resemble a building site with uneven, obstacle-strewn paving; elsewhere you can expect intense crowds and vehicle traffic, and few access ramps. **Public transport** is generally inaccessible to wheelchair users, though a few of the upmarket **hotels** are equipped to assist disabled visitors; in particular, Beijing's several *Holiday Inns* (Ⓦ ihg.com/holidayinn) and *Hiltons* (Ⓦ hilton.com) have rooms designed for wheelchair users.

The disabled in Chinese are usually kept hidden away; attitudes are not, on the whole, very enlightened, and disabled visitors should be prepared for a great deal of staring. Given the situation, it may be worth considering an **organized tour**. Make sure you take spares of any specialist clothing or equipment, extra supplies of drugs (carried with you if you fly), and a prescription including the generic name – in English and Chinese characters – in case of emergency. If there's an association representing people with your disability, contact them early on in the planning process.

MAO PORTRAIT, TIANAN'MEN

The Forbidden City and Tian'anmen Square

A sealed-off stomping ground for century upon century of emperors, Beijing's lauded Imperial Palace – better known in the West by its unofficial title, the Forbidden City – is the most famous tourist draw in all China. For its five centuries in action, throughout the reigns of 24 emperors of the Ming and Qing dynasties, civilian Chinese were forbidden from even approaching its massive, ochre red walls. With its emperor sitting in state among a maze of eight hundred yellow-tiled buildings and nine thousand chambers, the Forbidden City was the core of the capital, the empire and the Chinese universe. It remains an extraordinary place today, unsurpassed in China for its monumental scale, harmonious design and elegant grandeur.

This central pivot of dynastic splendour sits just off **Tian'anmen Square**, which, at over 400,000 square metres, is the greatest public space on earth. A monument to China's post-imperial era, the square is an infamous place, which in its austerity provides a complete contrast to the Forbidden City's luxury and ornamentation. Laid out in 1949, it's a modern creation in a city that, traditionally and very deliberately, had no places where crowds could gather. As one of the square's architects put it: "Beijing was a reflection of a feudal society… We had to transform it; we had to make Beijing into the capital of socialist China." They created a vast concrete plain bounded by stern, monumental buildings – not least the **Great Hall of the People** to the west and the **National Museum of China** to the east – and where, fittingly, the very founder of modern China, Chairman Mao, has been laid to rest.

Note that, because of this area's hugely symbolic importance, and its role through the last century as a focus for **public dissent** – most recently in 2013, when Muslim separatists drove a car into the gates of the Forbidden City, killing five – this is the most security-conscious (or perhaps paranoid) place in the whole country: expect bag searches, body scans and random pat-downs at **checkpoints** surrounding the area.

The Forbidden City

故宫, gùgōng • Tues–Sun: April–Oct 8.30am–5pm & Nov–March 8.30am–4.30pm; plus Mon June 1–Aug 31 • April–Oct ¥60; Nov–March ¥40; audio guide ¥40 • ⓦ www.dpm.org.cn • Subway line #1 to Tian'anmen East (Exit A) or Tian'anmen West (Exit B)

In every respect, the **Imperial Palace** – or, most evocatively, the **Forbidden City** – lies at the very heart of Beijing. To do it justice, plan to spend at least a whole day here, though you could wander the complex for a week and keep discovering new aspects, especially now that many of the smaller buildings are doubling as museums of dynastic artefacts. The central main halls, with their wealth of imperial pomp, may be the most magnificent structures, but for many visitors it's the side rooms, with their displays of the more intimate accoutrements of court life, that bring home the realities of existence for the inhabitants in this, the most gilded of cages. It is somewhat ironic that the "Forbidden" City now admits up to an incredible 80,000 visitors each day – though as the largest palace complex in the world, it's only at peak times along the central strip of buildings that you'll ever feel crowded out by a critical mass of sightseers.

The Forbidden City is encased by **a moat and turreted walls** – best viewed from their northeast corner, at the intersection of Beichizi Dajie and Jingshanqian Jie – and laid out according to the geomantic laws of **feng shui** (see box below). The City's spine is composed of eleven colossal, south-facing halls or gates, interspersed by enormous

---

FENG SHUI IN THE FORBIDDEN CITY

Literally "wind and water", **feng shui** (风水, fēng shuǐ) is a form of geomancy, which assesses how objects must be positioned so as not to disturb the spiritual balance between the negative (*yin*) and positive (*yang*) elements of the surrounding landscape. Homes, temples, tombs and even entire cities should face south, a "lucky" direction that benefits from the invigorating advantages of *yang* energy. Other buildings and hills offer protection from unlucky *yin* directions (mainly the north), both real and imagined – cold winds, evil spirits or steppe barbarians. Water is thought to carry along good luck and wealth, and is a further barrier to evil spirits; as are mirrors and "spirit walls" inside doorways – or even Great Walls to the north of a country – which bounce bad fortune back the way it has come.

All the halls of the Forbidden City were laid out according to these geomantic theories. The buildings face south, ramparts of compacted earth and a 50m-wide moat isolate the complex from the commoners outside, with the only access being through four monumental gateways in the four cardinal directions. The layout is the same as that of any grand Chinese house of the period: reception rooms and official buildings at the front (south), screening and protecting the private chambers buried deeper within the northern heart of the complex.

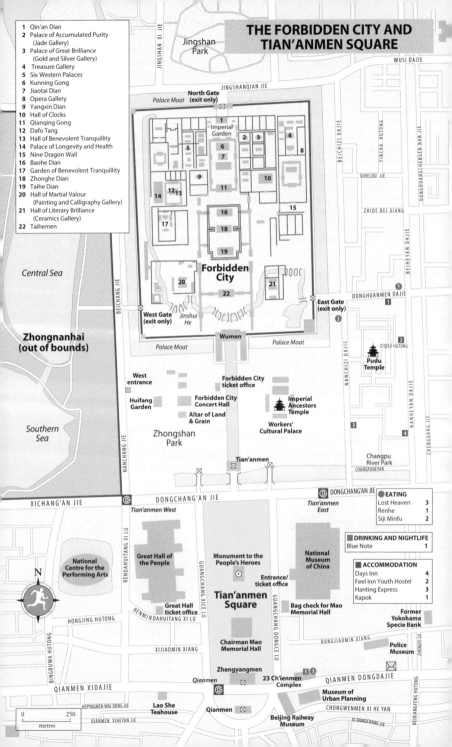

THE FORBIDDEN CITY AND TIAN'ANMEN SQUARE

1 Qin'an Dian
2 Palace of Accumulated Purity (Jade Gallery)
3 Palace of Great Brilliance (Gold and Silver Gallery)
4 Treasure Gallery
5 Six Western Palaces
6 Kunning Gong
7 Jiaotai Dian
8 Opera Gallery
9 Yangxin Dian
10 Hall of Clocks
11 Qianqing Gong
12 Dafo Tang
13 Hall of Benevolent Tranquillity
14 Palace of Longevity and Health
15 Nine Dragon Wall
16 Baohe Dian
17 Garden of Benevolent Tranquillity
18 Zhonghe Dian
19 Taihe Dian
20 Hall of Martial Valour (Painting and Calligraphy Gallery)
21 Hall of Literary Brilliance (Ceramics Gallery)
22 Taihemen

Jingshan Park

WUSI DAJIE

JINGSHAN XI JIE

JINGSHANQIAN JIE

Palace Moat

North Gate (exit only)

BEICHIZI DAJIE

YINCHA HUTONG

DONGHUANGCHENG GEN NAN JIE

Imperial Garden

QIHELOU JIE

ZHIDE BEI XIANG

BEIHEYAN DAJIE

Central Sea

BEICHANG JIE

Forbidden City

West Gate (exit only)

Jinshui He

East Gate (exit only)

DONGHUANMEN DAJIE

Zhongnanhai (out of bounds)

Palace Moat

Wumen

Palace Moat

NANCHIZI DAJIE

CIQIKU HUTONG

Pudu Temple

NANHEYAN DAJIE

ZHENGLIANG JIE

West entrance

Forbidden City ticket office

Huifang Garden

Forbidden City Concert Hall

Imperial Ancestors Temple

Southern Sea

Altar of Land & Grain

Workers' Cultural Palace

Changpu River Park

CHANGPUHEYAN

NANCHANG JIE

Zhongshan Park

Tian'anmen

DONGCHANG'AN JIE

Tian'anmen East

XICHANG'AN JIE

DONGCHANG'AN JIE

Tian'anmen West

RENDAHUITANG XI LU

National Centre for the Performing Arts

Great Hall of the People

GUANGCHANG XICE LU

Monument to the People's Heroes

National Museum of China

Entrance/ ticket office

N

Great Hall ticket office

RENMINDAHUITANG XI LU

Tian'anmen Square

GUANGCHANG DONGCE LU

Bag check for Mao Memorial Hall

Former Yokohama Specie Bank

HONGJING HUTONG

XIJIAOMIN XIANG

DONGJIAOMIN XIANG

Police Museum

ZHENGYI LU

BINGBUWA HUTONG

Chairman Mao Memorial Hall

Zhengyangmen

Qianmen

23 Ch'ienmen Complex

QIANMEN DONGDAJIE

BEIXIANGFENG HUTONG

QIANMEN XIDAJIE

HEPINGMEN WAI DONG JIE

Lao She Teahouse

Qianmen

Museum of Urban Planning

CHONGWENMEN XI HE YAN

0 — 250 metres

QIANMEN XIHEYAN JIE

Beijing Railway Museum

XI DAMOCHANG JIE

EATING
Lost Heaven 3
Renhe 1
Siji Minfu 2

DRINKING AND NIGHTLIFE
Blue Note 1

ACCOMMODATION
Days Inn 4
Feel Inn Youth Hostel 2
Hanting Express 3
Kapok 1

1

flagstoned courtyards and flanked by more than eight hundred smaller buildings decked in imperial red and yellow. There are also a number of recurring **motifs** to follow as you progress deeper into the belly of the Imperial Palace: sundials feature in many squares as symbols of the emperor's authority over time-keeping; huge bronze cauldrons – once used to store water in case of fire – punctuate the open spaces; while auspicious statues and carvings of dragons, cranes, turtles and lions are abundant (see box, p.44).

Brief history

Construction of the Forbidden City began in 1407 during the reign of **Emperor Yongle**, the monarch responsible for switching the capital from Nanjing back to Beijing in 1403 (see p.176). His programme to construct a complex worthy enough to house the Son of Heaven involved up to ten thousand artisans, and perhaps a million labourers, and was completed in 1420. From then until 1644, the Forbidden City served as the **seat** of successive emperors of the Ming dynasty, as well as the political and ceremonial heart of government. In 1912, upon the abdication of Puyi – the last emperor of China – parts of the City were opened to the public, though Puyi actually lived in its inner sanctums until 1924 with the blessings of the Republican government. The City suffered some damage during the Cultural Revolution, though this was limited by an army battalion that was sent to guard the palace during the uprisings.

ARRIVAL AND INFORMATION   **THE FORBIDDEN CITY**

Access The Forbidden City can only be entered from the south, either off Tian'anmen Square via the triple-arched Tian'anmen gate (the middle arch is hung with Chairman Mao's portrait), or from either Zhongshan Park or the Workers' Cultural Palace (see p.50). Either way you end up in a large square outside the Wumen gate, with ticket

---

FORBIDDEN CITY EXHIBITIONS

The buildings spreading out either side of the Forbidden City's central axis house a variety of exhibitions of Chinese and international historical artefacts and treasures (check what's on at ⓦ www.dpm.org.cn); you'll find a map showing their location on the back of your entrance ticket. While exploring this maze of smaller halls and courtyards is an excellent way of experiencing a more intimate side of the Forbidden City, it has to be said that many of the older displays are badly captioned and unimaginative, and that some of the finest imperial treasures were looted by foreign forces and the Chinese Nationalists during the twentieth century. The exception is the recently opened area in the northwestern side of the complex, whose halls display some impressive imperial artworks.

The Treasure Gallery (¥10). In buildings east of the Hall of Supremacy. Gold, silver, pearl and jade items demonstrating the wealth, majesty and luxury of imperial life.

Hall of Clocks (¥10). This hall, always a favourite, displays the result of one Qing emperor's passion for liberally ornamented Baroque timepieces, most of which are English and French, though the rhino-sized water clock by the entrance is Chinese. There's even one with a mechanical scribe who can write eight characters. Some clocks are wound to demonstrate their workings at 11am and 2pm.

Ceramics Gallery Hall of Literary Brilliance (free). A wonderful, air-cooled selection of fine pots, statues and porcelain treasures; keep an eye out for the Ming and Qing vases.

Dafo Tang (free). Buddhist artwork, but not what you'd expect: a room full of exquisite miniatures in coloured hardstone, some set with tiny jewels; look for the slightly comical set of eighteen *luohans*, Buddha's disciples.

Painting and Calligraphy Gallery Hall of Martial Valour (free). Pieces demonstrating the art, skill and beauty of artists and literary aesthetics.

Jade Gallery Palace of Accumulated Purity (free). An assortment of intricate jade objects from the imperial court.

Gold and Silver Gallery Palace of Great Brilliance (free). Precious religious, decorative, dress and sacrificial items.

Opera Gallery Hall for Viewing Opera (free). Fascinating display of all the finery of the Chinese opera.

Hall of Benevolent Tranquillity (free). Excellent sculpture gallery featuring Tang-dynasty camels, Song-dynasty wooden Bodhisattvas showing a heavy Indian influence, and life-sized ceramic *arhats* from the Ming dynasty.

1

offices to the west, and a booth hiring out audio tours closer to the actual entrance under Wumen. There's a maximum of 80,000 visitors allowed in daily; this sounds enormous but during public holidays and pretty much any time through July and August you'd be lucky to get in after 1pm. Once inside, visitors have freedom to wander most of the site, though not all buildings are open.

Tickets Note that passport ID is required to buy a ticket.

Tours If you want detailed explanations of everything you see, you can tag along with one of the numerous tour groups, pick up a specialist book (on sale at Wumen), or take the audio tour, also available at Wumen; it's GPS-enabled, so automatically provides a short, digestible and informative narrative commentary as you progress through the complex. If you take this option, it's worth retracing your steps afterwards for an untutored view and exploring the side halls that aren't included on the tour.

Services There are plenty of clean toilets inside the complex and a few places to get a snack or a drink, but bring a packed lunch if you're planning to spend most of the day here. Also come prepared for the weather: there's little shelter between halls, and the Forbidden City's vast, open squares are baking hot in summer and seriously cold in winter.

Wumen

午门, wǔmén

A huge building whose central archway was reserved for the emperor's sole use, **Wumen** (Meridian Gate) is the largest and grandest of the Forbidden City gates. From a vantage point at the top, each new lunar year the Sons of Heaven would announce to their court the details of the forthcoming calendar, including the dates of festivals and rites, and, in times of war, inspect the army. It was customary for victorious generals returning from battle to present their prisoners here for the emperor to decide their fate. He would be flanked, as on all such imperial occasions, by a guard of elephants, the gift of Burmese subjects. In the Ming dynasty, this was also where disgraced officials were flogged or executed.

In the wings on either side of Wumen are two drums and two bells; the drums were beaten whenever the emperor went to the Temple of the Imperial Ancestors, the bells rung when he visited the temples of Heaven (see p.79) and Earth.

Jinshui He and Taihemen

金水河, jīnshuǐ hé; 太和门, tàihé mén

On the far side of Wumen you find yourself in a vast paved court, cut east–west by the curving **Jinshui He**, or Golden Water Stream, which protects the complex from evil spirits (they are unable to cross water). The five marble bridges each represent a

---

IMPERIAL SYMBOLISM

Almost every colour and image in the Imperial Palace is richly symbolic. **Yellow** was the imperial **colour**; yellow robes were restricted to the royal family (or, in exceptional circumstances, handed out to officials as a sign of favour), and only imperial buildings could use yellow roof tiles. **Purple** was just as important, though used more sparingly; it symbolized joy and represented the pole star, centre of the universe according to Chinese cosmology (the implication of its use – usually on wall panels – was that the emperor resided in the earthly equivalent of the celestial zenith).

The **sign** for the emperor was the **dragon** and for the empress, the **phoenix**; you'll see these two creatures represented on almost every building and stairway. The **crane** and **turtle**, depicted in paintings, carved into furniture or represented as freestanding sculptures, represent longevity of reign. You'll see plenty of **lion** statues too, guarding gateways and important buildings in pairs: the male holds down a ball representing the earth, while the female holds down a cub (representing, some say, the male). The few **deer** sculptures scattered around are associated with immortality and high rank; there's also at least one **qilin** (with a lion's head, goat's body, dragon horns and cloven hooves), a generally auspicious creature.

The **numbers** nine and five crop up all over the complex, manifested in how often design elements are repeated; nine is lucky and associated with *yang*, or male energy, while five, the middle single-digit number, is associated with harmony and balance. Nine and five together – power and balance – symbolize "the heavenly son", the emperor. The heavy wooden doors on imperial gateways are always dotted with rows of nine golden studs (which, incidentally, gave their name to fried "door-stud" buns, a popular Beijing snack); lesser officials had to use fewer studs.

Confucian virtue (see box, p.71), and are carved with torches, a symbol of masculinity. Beyond is the second ceremonial gate, **Taihemen**, the Gate of Supreme Harmony, its entrance guarded by a pair of enormous bronze lions, their flanks stained in a ghostly green patina. The large courtyard beyond is where the principal imperial audiences were held, a space reputedly able to accommodate the entire court of up to 10,000 people. They made their way in through the lesser side gates – military men from the west, civilian officials from the east – and waited in total silence as the emperor ascended his throne. Then, with only the Imperial Guard remaining standing, they prostrated themselves nine times.

The galleries running round the courtyard served as the imperial storerooms. The buildings either side are the **Hall of Martial Valour** to the west and **Hall of Literary Brilliance** to the east; the latter under the Ming emperors housed all 11,099 volumes of the encyclopedia Yongle commissioned in 1403. They now serve as the Painting Gallery and Ceramics Gallery respectively (see box, p.43).

The central halls

The three main **central halls** stand directly north of Taihemen, dominating the court. The main halls, made of wood, are built in traditional style all on the same level, on a raised stone platform. Their elegant roofs, curved like the wings of a bird, are supported entirely by pillars and beams; the weight is cleverly distributed by ceiling consoles, while the walls beneath are just lightweight partitions. Doors, steps and access ramps are always odd in number, with the middle passageway reserved for the emperor's palanquin. Grand though they are, visit in winter or the height of summer and you'll wonder how anyone could face lengthy spells seated in these essentially open, stone halls.

Taihe Dian
太和殿, tàihé diàn

Raised on a three-tiered marble terrace is the tallest and most spectacular of the three main ceremonial halls, the **Taihe Dian**, Hall of Supreme Harmony. This vast structure, nearly 38m high, was the tallest in China during the Ming and Qing dynasties – no civilian building was permitted to be taller. Taihe Dian was used for the most important state occasions: the emperor's coronation, birthday or marriage; ceremonies marking the new lunar year and winter solstice; proclamations of the results of the imperial examinations; and the nomination of generals at the outset of a military campaign. During the Republic, it was proposed that parliament should sit here, though the idea wasn't put into practice.

Decorated entirely in red and gold, Taihe Dian is the most sumptuous building in the entire complex. In the central coffer, a sunken panel in the ceiling, two gold-plated dragons play with a huge pearl. The gilded rosewood chair beneath, the dragon throne, was the exact centre of the Chinese universe. A marble pavement ramp, intricately carved with dragons and flanked by bronze incense burners, marks the path along which the emperor's sedan chair was carried whenever he wanted to be taken somewhere, while the grain measure and sundial just outside are symbols of imperial justice.

Zhonghe Dian
中和殿, zhōnghé diàn

Beyond the Taihe Dian, you enter the **Zhonghe Dian**, Hall of Central Harmony, another throne room, where the emperor performed ceremonies of greeting to foreign dignitaries and addressed the imperial offspring (the progeny of his several wives and numerous concubines). It owes its name to a quote from the *I-Ching*, a Chinese tome dating back to 200 BC: "avoiding extremes and self-control brings harmony", the idea being that the middle course would be a harmonious one. The emperor also examined the seed for each year's crop in the hall, and it was used, too, as a dressing room for major events held in the Taihe Dian.

1

Baohe Dian

保和殿, bǎohé diàn

The **Baohe Dian**, or Preserving Harmony Hall, was the venue for state banquets and imperial examinations; graduates from the latter were appointed to positions of power in what was the world's first recognizably bureaucratic civil service. Huge ceremonies took place here to celebrate Chinese New Year; in 1903, this involved the sacrifice of 10,000 sheep. The hall's galleries, originally treasure houses, display various finds from the site, though the most spectacular, a vast marble block carved with dragons and clouds, stands at the rear of the hall. A Ming creation, reworked in the eighteenth century, it's among the finest carvings in the palace and certainly the largest – the 250-tonne chunk of marble was slid here from far outside the city, by flooding the roads in winter to form sheets of ice.

The imperial living quarters

Lined up along the central axis, immediately north of the central halls and repeating their hierarchy, are the three principal palaces of the **imperial living quarters**: the Qianqing Gong, the Jiaotai Dian and the Kunning Gong. Slightly more weatherproof than the main halls, they are also more compact, though still grandly scaled.

Qianqing Gong

乾清宮, qiánqīng gōng

Its terrace surmounted by incense burners in the form of cranes and tortoises (see box, p.44) the extravagant **Qianqing Gong**, or Palace of Heavenly Purity, was originally the imperial bedroom. It was here in 1785 that Qianlong presided over the famous "banquet of old men" that brought together three thousand men of over sixty years of age from all corners of the empire. Used for the lying-in-state of the emperor, the hall also played a role in the tradition that finally solved the problem of **succession** (hitherto fraught with intrigue and uncertainty, as the principle of primogeniture was not used), a practice begun by Qing Emperor Yongzheng. Keeping an identical document on his person, Yongzheng and his successors deposited the name of his chosen successor in a sealed box hidden in the hall. When the emperor died, it was sufficient to compare the two documents to proclaim the new Son of Heaven.

Jiaotai Dian

交泰殿, jiāotài diàn

Beyond the Qianqing Gong is the **Jiaotai Dian** (Hall of Union), the empress's throne room where the 25 imperial document seals were kept. The ceiling here is possibly the finest in the complex, a gilt confection with a dragon surrounded by phoenixes at the centre; also here is a fine, and very hefty, water clock. The two characters *wu wei* at the back of the hall mean "non-action" – a reference to the Taoist ideal of not disturbing the natural order of things.

DINING, IMPERIAL STYLE

The **emperor** ate twice a day, at 6.30am and around noon. Often **meals** consisted of scores of dishes, with the emperor eating no more than a mouthful of each – to eat more would be to express a preference, and that information might reach a potential poisoner. According to tradition, no one else was allowed to eat at his table, and when banquets were held he sat at a platform well above his guests. Such occasions – which lasted up to three days and involved between 108 and 320 dishes – were extremely formal and not to everyone's liking. A Jesuit priest invited to such a feast in 1727 complained, "A European dies of hunger here; the way in which he is forced to sit on the ground on a mat with crossed legs is most awkward; neither the wine nor the dishes are to his taste… Every time the emperor says a word which lets it be known he wishes to please, one must kneel down and hit one's head on the ground. This has to be done every time someone serves him something to drink."

CONCUBINES

Numbering in their thousands, the imperial **concubines** trod a line between consort and whore. At night, the emperor chose a girl from his harem by picking out a tablet bearing her name from a pile on a silver tray – though the court astrologer had to approve the decision. She would be delivered to the emperor's bedchamber naked but for a yellow cloth wrapped around her, and carried on the back of one of the court's many eunuchs (see box, p.115), since she could barely walk with her bound feet. Eunuchs would be on hand for the event, standing behind a screen and shouting out cautions for the emperor not to get too carried away and risk harming the imperial body. Favoured wives and concubines were the only women in dynastic China with power and influence (though there has been at least one acknowledged female ruler in Chinese history, the Tang-dynasty empress Wu Zetian); Dowager Empress Cixi (see box, p.99) was a telling example of just how powerful an ambitious concubine could become.

Kunning Gong

坤宁宫, kūnníng gōng

The **Kunning Gong**, or Palace of Earthly Tranquillity, was where the emperor and empress traditionally spent their wedding night. By law the emperor had to spend the first three nights of his marriage, and the first day of the Chinese New Year, with his wife. On the left as you enter is a large sacrificial room, its vats ready to receive offerings (1300 pigs a year during the Ming dynasty). The wedding chamber is a small room off to one side, painted entirely in red and covered with decorative emblems symbolizing fertility and joy. It was last pressed into operation in 1922 for the wedding of 12-year-old Pu Yi, the last emperor, who, finding it "like a melted red wax candle", decided that he preferred the westerly Yangxin Dian (Mind Nurture Palace: 养心殿, yǎngxīn diàn) and relocated there.

Six Western Palaces

西六宫, xīliù gōng

To the west of the living quarters is an interlinked set of halls and courtyards known as the **Six Western Palaces** after its main buildings, which once housed the imperial women. Smaller and more intimate than the central halls, they still mark their status with yellow tiles and green-glazed brickwork. The most famous of the group is the Palace of Gathered Elegance (储秀宫, chǔxiù gōng), which originally accommodated concubines under the Ming but rose in status thanks to Cixi, who lived here before she became Empress Dowager in 1861. It was lavishly redecorated to mark her fiftieth birthday in 1884 (as was the Palace of Supreme Principle for her fortieth birthday; the ageing emperor Qianlong had abdicated in favour of his son here in 1799). Later the palace became the private residence of the wife of Puyi, the last emperor, and he was visiting her here when Nationalist forces broke into the Forbidden City and evicted them both in 1924; it now houses an exhibition on Puyi's life. You should also visit the adjacent Palace of Eternal Spring (长春宫, chángchūn gōng), another of Cixi's former residences; a set of paintings here illustrates the classic Ming novel of manners, *The Dream of Red Mansions*.

Palace of Longevity and Health

寿康宫, shòukāng gōng

This auspiciously named complex was built for Qianlong's mother in 1736; the centrepiece is a red sandalwood throne from 1771, made by Suzhou craftsmen to celebrate her eightieth birthday. The pleasantly small-scale adjoining apartments, with their carpets, tasteful hangings and screens, are a relief from the rest of the Forbidden City; there's a feeling that you could actually live a normal life here, not just as a pawn in some vast gilded cage. A few select treasures are on display in a side wing, including a scroll painting and copy of the Heart Sutra in gold ink by Qianlong – from which it seems that he was a much finer calligrapher than artist.

1

Garden of Benevolent Tranquillity

慈宁宫花园, cínínggōng huāyuán

Fronting the Hall of Benevolent Tranquillity, which houses an excellent sculpture exhibition (see box, p.43), the garden dates to 1583, a place where Empress Dowagers and consorts could rest. At the moment this seems at first to be little more than an uninspiring strip of bare earth, where neat rectangles of archeological excavations have exposed paving and bricks; but behind a wall there's a pleasant garden with shady pine trees and a neat grouping of small, brightly painted pavilions, one of them covered in Tibetan murals.

Nine Dragon Wall

九龙壁, jiǔlóng bì

Over on the east side of the Forbidden City, the **Nine Dragon Wall** is a relatively recent addition (1772). This 30m-long screen of dragons, each toying with a pearl, is composed of 270 pieces of coloured glaze. Note that the third white dragon has a mysterious wooden replacement piece to its jigsaw pattern: just before presentation of the screen to the emperor, the ceramic tile was damaged and, to save the lives of the designers, the inconspicuous replacement was quickly carved from wood.

The Imperial Garden

御花园, yù huāyuán

Up towards the Forbidden City's northernmost reaches, the Kunningmen (Gate of Terrestrial Tranquillity) opens into the **Imperial Garden**, by this stage something of a respite from the Forbidden City's cumulatively overwhelming scale and architecture. There are a couple of **cafés** here amid a pleasing network of ponds, artistically shaped rocks, walkways and pavilions, designed to be reminiscent of southern Chinese landscapes. In the middle of the garden is the **Qin'an Dian** (Hall of Imperial Tranquillity), where the emperor came to worship a Taoist water deity, Xuan Wu, who was responsible for keeping the palace safe from fire. You can exit here into Jingshan Park (see p.57), which provides an overview of the complex.

Tian'anmen

天安门, tiān'ānmén • Daily 8.30am–4.30pm • Entrance at junction of Xichang'an Jie and Dongchang'an Jie • ¥15; tickets available from the Forbidden City ticket offices (see p.43) • Subway line #1 to Tian'anmen East (Exit A) or Tian'anmen West (Exit B)

Tian'anmen, the Gate of Heavenly Peace, is the main entrance to the Forbidden City. An image familiar across the world, it occupies an exalted place in Chinese iconography, appearing on policemen's caps, banknotes, coins, stamps and most pieces of official paper. As such it's a prime object of pilgrimage, with many visitors milling

---

THE EMPEROR SPEAKS TO HIS PEOPLE

During the Ming and Qing dynasties, Tian'anmen was where the **ceremony** called "the golden phoenix issues an edict" took place. The minister of rites would receive an imperial edict inside the palace and take it to Tian'anmen on a silver "cloud tray", he and his charge under a yellow umbrella. Here, the edict was read aloud to the officials of the court who knelt below, lined up according to rank. Next, the edict was placed in the mouth of a gilded wooden phoenix, which was lowered by rope to another cloud tray below. The tray was then put in a carved, wooden dragon and taken to the Ministry of Rites to be copied out and sent around the country.

Mao too liked to address his subjects from here. On October 1, 1949, he delivered the **liberation speech** to jubilant crowds below, declaring that "the Chinese people have now stood up"; in the 1960s, he spoke from this spot to massed ranks of Red Guards and declared that it was time for a "cultural revolution" (see p.180).

1

around and taking pictures of the large **portrait of Mao** (the only one still on public display), which hangs over the central passageway. Once reserved for the sole use of the emperor, but now standing wide open, the entrance is flanked by the twin slogans "Long Live the People's Republic of China" and "Long Live the Great Union between the Peoples of the World".

The entry ticket allows you to climb up onto the **viewing platform** above the gate. Security is tight: all visitors have to leave their bags and go through a metal detector before they can ascend. Inside, the fact that most people cluster around the souvenir stall – which sells official certificates to anyone who wants their visit here documented – reflects the fact that there's not much to look at.

The parks

Tian'anmen gate is flanked by two parks, **Zhongshan** to the west, and the grounds of the **Workers' Cultural Palace** to the east. These are great places to escape the rigorous formality of Tian'anmen Square, not to mention the crowds of the Forbidden City; they also double as an alternate means of access to the latter.

Zhongshan Park

中山公园, zhōngshān gōngyuán • Entrances on Xichang'an and Nanchang Jie • **Park** Daily 6am–9pm • ¥3 • **Flower exhibition and Huifang Garden** Daily 9am–4.30pm • ¥5 • ⓦ www.zhongshan-park.cn • Subway line #1 to Tian'anmen West (Exit B)

Delightful **Zhongshan Park** boasts the ruins of the **Altar of Land and Grain**, a site of biennial sacrifice during the Qing and Ming dynasties. It was built during Yongle's reign in 1420, and hosts harvest-time events closely related to those of the Temple of Heaven (see p.79). Elsewhere in the park you'll find pavilions, attractively gnarled trees, covered walkways, ornamental rocks and a concert hall (see p.160). There's also a **flower exhibition** and the **Huifang Garden**; the former is a so-so collection of hothouse blooms, while the latter is a beautiful, bamboo-strewn section of the park.

Workers' Cultural Palace

劳动人民文化宫, láodòng rénmín wénhuàgōng • Entrances on Dongchang'an Jie and Nanchizi Dajie • Daily 6.30am–7.30pm • ¥2, or ¥15 including Front Hall • ⓦ www.bjwhg.com.cn • Subway line #1 to Tian'anmen East (Exit A)

Don't be put off by the unfortunate name: the **Workers' Cultural Palace** originally served as the **Temple of Imperial Ancestors** (太庙, tài miào), and though the halls were co-opted as an entertainment complex after the communist takeover in 1949, they've retained their imposing appearance. Something of a minor Forbidden City in layout, it's also far more manageable, infinitely less crowded (aside from couples being photographed for their weddings), and equally beautiful in parts. Only the main hall, the first of three, is open to the public; it's unusual for being built on a three-tiered terrace, but otherwise follows the standard red-walls-yellow-roof pattern. The side wings are worth checking out for temporary art exhibitions.

Pudu Temple

普渡寺, pǔdù sì

The small block east of the Workers' Cultural Palace is filled by a network of smart new *hutongs* (see box, p.61), the upmarket houses hidden away behind heavy wooden gates and high grey-brick walls. Through the middle runs little Ciqiku Hutong, once lined with porcelain warehouses and now home to **Pudu Temple**. This was once part of the Ming Imperial Palace, appropriated at the start of the Qing dynasty by the powerful regent **Dorgon**; long after his death, it was converted in his honour into a Manchu-style temple – the only one in the capital. Deconsecrated during the early twentieth century and successively used as a school, a sports grounds and a taxation museum, there are now plans to renovate the semi-derelict building; at the time of writing it was only possible to walk around the outside and admire the green- and yellow-glazed hexagonal wall tiles.

Tian'anmen Square

1

天安门广场, tiān'ānmén guǎngchǎng • Daily sunrise to sunset • Free • Subway line #1 to Tian'anmen East (Exit D), or line #2 to Qianmen (Exit A)

For many Chinese tourists, gigantic **Tian'anmen Square** is a place of pilgrimage. Crowds flock to gaze at Chairman Mao's portrait on Tian'anmen, the huge gate to the north (see opposite), then head south to **Mao's mausoleum**, quietly bowing their heads by the **Monument to the People's Heroes** en route. Despite its scale the square is rather dull considering its recent history as a focus for public dissent, and it's sometimes better to look upwards, where you'll often see incredibly long chains of kites disappearing into Beijing's soup-like sky. Crowds gather at **sunrise** and **sunset** to see the national flag at the northern end of the square raised in a military ceremony.

Monument to the People's Heroes

Towards the northern end of the square is the **Monument to the People's Heroes**, a 38m-high obelisk commemorating the victims of the revolutionary struggle. Its foundations were laid on October 1, 1949, the day that the establishment of the People's Republic was announced. Bas-reliefs illustrate key scenes from China's revolutionary history; one of these, on the east side, shows the Chinese destroying British opium (see p.177) in the nineteenth century. The calligraphy on the front is a copy of Mao Zedong's handwriting and reads "Eternal glory to the Heroes of the People". The platform on which the obelisk stands is guarded, and a prominent sign declares that commemorative gestures, such as the **laying of wreaths**, are banned – for why, see the box below.

The Chairman Mao Memorial Hall

毛主席纪念堂, máozhǔxí jìniàntáng • Sept–June Tues–Sun 8am–noon; July & Aug daily 7–11am (expect a 30min queue to get in at peak times) • Free (bring ID) • Bags & camera deposit on the east side of the square (¥2–15 each depending on size) • No photography

Mao's mausoleum, constructed in 1977 by an estimated one million volunteers, is an ugly building that looks like a drab municipal facility. It contravenes the principles of *feng shui* (see box, p.41) – presumably deliberately – by interrupting the line from the palace to Qianmen and by facing north. Mao himself wanted to be cremated, and the

---

DISSENT IN TIAN'ANMEN SQUARE

Designed way back in the seventeenth century and enlarged during the post-imperial era as a space for mass declarations of loyalty, Tian'anmen Square has as often been a venue for expressions of popular **dissent**. The first protests here occurred on May 4, 1919, when thousands of students demonstrated against the Treaty of Versailles, under which the victorious Allies granted several former German concessions in China to the Japanese. In 1925, the inhabitants of Beijing again occupied the square, following the massacre of Chinese demonstrators by British troops at Shanghai. Angered by the weak government's constant capitulations to the Japanese, protesters marched the following year as well, and were fired on by soldiers.

Tian'anmen Square hosted its first communist-era demonstrations in 1976, when thousands assembled to voice dissatisfaction at their leaders by laying wreaths for the recently deceased moderate, Zhou Enlai; in 1978 and 1979, large numbers came to discuss new ideas of democracy, triggered by writings posted along "Democracy Wall" on the edge of the Forbidden City. People gathered again in 1986 and 1987, frustrated by the Party's refusal to allow limited municipal elections to be held. But it was in **1989** that Tian'anmen Square gained international attention; from April to June of that year, nearly a million protesters assembled to demonstrate against the slow pace of reform, lack of civil liberties and widespread corruption. The government, infuriated at being humiliated by their own people, declared martial law on May 20, and on June 4 the military moved into the square. The ensuing **killing** was indiscriminate; tanks ran over tents and machine guns strafed the avenues. No one knows exactly how many died in the massacre – probably thousands. Hundreds were arrested afterwards and some remain in jail, though others have since joined the administration.

1

erection of the mausoleum was apparently no more than a power assertion by his would-be successor, Hua Guofeng. In 1980 Deng Xiaoping, then leader, said it should never have been built, although he wouldn't go so far as to pull it down.

Much of the interest of a visit here lies in witnessing the sense of awe of the Chinese confronted with their former leader, the architect of modern China who achieved an almost god-like status during his life. The atmosphere is one of reverence; turn off your phone's ringtone and keep quiet.

Viewing the Chairman

Once inside the mausoleum, the queue – almost exclusively working-class out-of-towners – advances surprisingly quickly, and takes just a couple of minutes to file through the chambers. Mao's **corpse**, draped with a red flag within a crystal coffin, looks unreal, which it may well be; a wax copy was made in case the preservation went wrong. Mechanically raised from a freezer every morning, it is said to have been embalmed with the aid of Vietnamese technicians who had previously worked on the body of Ho Chi Minh. Apparently, 22 litres of formaldehyde went into preserving his body; rumour has it that not only did the corpse swell grotesquely when too much fluid was used, but that Mao's left ear fell off during the embalming process, and had to be stitched back on.

Zhengyangmen

正阳门, zhèngyángmén • Daily 8.30am–4pm • ¥20 • Subway line #2 to Qianmen (Exit A)

For a great view over the square head to its south gate, **Zhengyangmen**. A squat, 40m-high structure with an arched gateway through the middle, it's similar in design to its northern counterpart, Tian'anmen. From the top you'll get an idea of how much more impressive the square must have looked before Mao's mausoleum was stuck in the middle of it. There's also a small **museum** here, featuring a random smattering of historical exhibits.

CHAIRMAN MAO

A revolution is not a dinner party.

Mao Zedong

Mao Zedong (毛泽东, Máo Zédōng), the son of a well-off Hunnanese farmer, believed that social reform lay in the hands of the peasants. Having helped found the Chinese Communist Party, in Shanghai in 1921, he quickly organized a peasant workers' militia – the Red Army – to take on the Nationalist government. A cunning guerrilla leader, Mao was an admirer of China's despotic first emperor, Qin Shihuang, and learned military tactics by studying Sun Tzu's *Art of War* and the strategic board game, *weiqi*. In 1934 Mao's army was pushed from its rural base by government forces and began the epic **Long March** – with 80,000 men walking 10,000km over a year – during which time Mao took firm control of the Party from its Russian-backed advisers.

In 1949, now at the head of a huge communist army, Mao finally drove the Nationalists out of China and became the new nation's "Great Helmsman" – and here the trouble started. The chain-smoking poet rebel indulged what appeared to be a personal need for permanent revolution in catastrophes such as the **Great Leap Forward** of the 1950s and the **Cultural Revolution** of the 1960s. His policies caused enormous suffering; some estimate that Mao was responsible for the deaths of over 38 million people – mostly from famine. Towards the end of his life Mao became increasingly paranoid and out of touch, surrounded by sycophants and nubile dancers – at least, this was the situation described by his physician, Li Zhisui, in his book *The Private Life of Chairman Mao*.

Today the official Chinese position on Mao is that he was "70 percent right, 30 percent wrong". Although public images of him have largely been expunged, the personality cult he fostered lives on, particularly in taxis where his image is hung like a lucky charm from the rear-view mirror, and he's often included among the deities in peasant shrines. Today his **Little Red Book** – source of many memorable one-liners, such as "Political power grows from the barrel of a gun" – is no longer required reading, but English translations are widely available from souvenir vendors.

Around Tian'anmen Square

Several important buildings lie at Tian'anmen Square's periphery, notably the **Great Hall of the People** and splendid **National Museum of China** – not to be missed if you have the slightest interest in Chinese history. Less vaunted are the **Railway Museum** and **Museum of Urban Planning**, not to mention the **23 Ch'ienmen Complex**, at the edge of the former foreign legation quarter further east (see p.55).

Great Hall of the People

人民大会堂, rénmín dàhuìtáng • Entrance off Tian'anmen Square • Daily when not in session: April–June 8.15am–3pm; July & Aug 7.30am–4pm; Sept–Nov 8.30am–3pm; Dec–March 9am–2pm • ¥30 (bring ID) • Subway line #1 to Tian'anmen West (Exit C) or line #2 to Qianmen (Exit C)

Taking up almost half the west side of Tian'anmen Square is the monolithic **Great Hall of the People**, one of ten Stalinist-style buildings constructed in 1959 to celebrate "ten years of liberation". This is the venue of the **National People's Congress**, the Chinese legislature, and the building is closed to the public when in session – you'll know whether it's accessible by the hundreds of black limos with darkened windows parked outside. It's not really a sight as such, but you can take a turn through the building; you get shown a selection of the 29 cavernous, dim reception rooms, each named after a province of China (including Taiwan) and decorated in the same manner as the lobby of any mid-range Chinese hotel – shabby red carpets, lifeless murals and armchairs lined up against the walls.

This venue has long been a place for high-level meet-and-greets. Nixon dropped by in 1972, and when Margaret Thatcher came here in 1982 she tripped on the steps – regarded in Hong Kong as a terrible omen for the negotiations she was having over the territory's future. In 1989, the visiting Mikhail Gorbachev had to be smuggled in through a side entrance in order to avoid the crowds of protesters outside.

The National Museum of China

中国历史博物馆, zhōngguó lìshǐ bówùguǎn • Entrance off Tian'anmen Square • Tues–Sun 9am–5pm, last ticket 3.30pm • Free (bring ID) • ☎ 010 65116400, ⓦ en.chnmuseum.cn • Subway line #1 to Tian'anmen East (Exit D)

Tian'anmen Square's eastern flank is dominated by the colossal **National Museum of China**, one of the world's largest museums. Modern and well laid-out, it's also exhaustingly comprehensive; you're best off beginning with the main exhibition on Floor 1 (actually down in the basement) and only then, if you've still enough energy, heading upstairs to the special collections.

Floor 1

Floor 1 provides a mighty trawl through Chinese history, with archeological and artistic treasures from every period and every part of the country. It kicks off with hominid fossils and far more recent Neolithic skulls and tools from the Zhoukoudian caves, just outside Beijing. The 4000 year-old **Yangshao Culture**, based along the lower Yellow River, is represented by a grave flanked by tiger and dragon mosaics made from shells, and typical earthenware pottery with swirled black patterns. There are early **jade** objects too, testifying to China's long fascination with this translucent, hard stone – stylized dragons, long tubular *cong*, pierced *bi* discs – plus a diorama of a contemporary thatched settlement. Technologically sophisticated **bronze** vessels appeared around 1600 BC, their intricate, finely chased patterns bursting fully formed from nowhere; don't miss the extraordinary bronze mask with eyes popping out on stalks from Sichuan's enigmatic Sanxingdui culture.

China's early dynasties are represented by a **burial suit** made of hundreds of jade tiles; a stone tablet from 219 BC extolling the virtues of Qin Shihuangdi, the despotic first emperor whose famous Terracotta Army guards his tomb near Xi'an; and **Han pottery models** of domestic architecture. A disturbing **bronze drum** from distant Yunnan province, showing a diorama of a crowded village marketplace with tame leopards

1

being led around on chains and a man tied to a sacrificial pillar, hints at what was happening along the empire's fringes. And so it continues: tricolour pottery of foreign-looking, bearded soldiers from the cosmopolitan Tang; a model of China's oldest surviving wooden structure, the eleventh-century Fogong Temple pagoda; Ming marble tablets covered with carvings of *qilin* and phoenix unearthed from the foundations of Beijing's original city wall; a stone rubbing of a star chart from 1247; a dragon-spouted water clock from 1316; a plain-looking ink slab once owned by the famed Song dynasty poet-official, Su Dongpo; and enough porcelain, paintings and carvings to make the most ardent art historian punch-drunk.

The upper floors

If you're not utterly worn out after Floor 1, vist the upper three levels which focus on specific themes. Floor 4's main attraction is the cases of **currency** used through the ages, from prehistoric cowrie shells and spade-shaped bronze tokens, to silver ingots, the earliest-known paper notes (issued by the Mongol Yuan dynasty in 1260), and stone moulds used for making common "copper cash" – of which just about every known type is represented. Floor 3 features a **Hall of Buddhist Sculptures**, the pick of which is a Song-dynasty Guanyin, whose languid posture and draped robes are Indian-inspired, and a pair of Ming polychrome representations of Wenshu, the Buddhist incarnation of Wisdom, seated on lions. The best feature of Floor 2, which focuses on often bombastic **Socialist Art**, are the temporary exhibitions in the wings.

Qianmen

前门, qiánmén • Subway line #2 to Qianmen (Exit C)

Before Beijing's walls were demolished, **Qianmen** – literally "Front Gate", and also, confusingly, known as Zhengyangmen Front Tower – controlled the entrance to the inner city from the outer, suburban sector. A mighty block of a gateway, with a double-tiered roof and zig-zag stairway at the rear, it dates back to the fifteenth century, and in imperial days the shops and places of entertainment banned from the interior city were concentrated around here. Nowadays, the gate has given its name to the pedestrianized area immediately south (see p.78).

Beijing Railway Museum

北京铁路博物馆, běijīng tiělù bówùguǎn • Off Qianmen Dongdajie • Tues–Sun 9am–5pm • ¥20, high-speed cabin an extra ¥20 • ☏ 010 67051638 • Subway line #2 to Qianmen (Exit B)

Appropriately located in the old Qianmen Railway Station, itself an important historic structure dating to 1906 (see box opposite), the **Beijing Railway Museum** – officially the Zhengyangmen branch of the China Railway Museum, which is based at Chaoyang in the northeast of the city – explores the history of China's national rail system, and the vehicles using it. Train buffs should love it, though others may find the various

---

CASH AND TAELS

From the fifth century onwards, China's only officially minted currency was the so-called "**copper cash**", a round bronze coin with square central hole. Strung together in their hundreds, these were fine to buy everyday household goods with at the local market, but were worth so little that it wasn't physically possible for merchants to carry enough to conduct any real trade – during the nineteenth century, half a kilo of them only just equalled the value of a British shilling. For any serious dealings you needed shoe-shaped **silver ingots** measured in Chinese ounces, or **taels**. As these were issued locally and the quality of silver varied so much from place to place, the problem here was that travellers needed to have their ingots assessed at almost every big city they passed through by local money changers – who naturally claimed that "foreign" ingots were underweight and of inferior purity. Incredibly, the first standardized silver coins were introduced as late as 1889, but even then they failed to catch on until well into the twentieth century.

1

RAILS AND REVOLUTION

Given that it was a dispute over railways that finally brought the tottering Qing dynasty down in 1912, the Beijing Railway Museum's location – inside China's first ever proper train station, and within sight of the Forbidden City – is poignant. China's late nineteenth-century politics were played out through its railways: foreign powers (and some Chinese) desperately wanted to improve China's infrastructure – and their access to markets in the remote interior – by building railways; conservative Chinese politicians, alarmed at the thought of foreigners using trains to extend their already outrageous hold on the country, worked equally hard against their construction.

The **first commercial line** was laid between Shanghai and the nearby port of Wusong in 1876, but was almost immediately shut down and torn up by the government. In 1881, a 10km-long industrial line was built at **Tangshan** to transport coal; this was later extended west to Tianjin and east to the coast at Shanhaiguan – 300km in all – at the orders of the powerful statesman Li Hongzhang. By the time the first long-distance passenger service, the **Jing-Han line** between Beijing and the Yangzi River port of Hankou, opened in 1906, many more were planned or under construction. But when the imperial government announced that they were going to **nationalize** all these railways – taking profits out of the hands of local provincial authorities, who had part-funded the lines – widespread anti-Qing riots erupted all over China. With civil war looming, in 1912 the warlord Yuan Shikai forced the abdication of the last emperor, four-year-old Puyi, and ushered in the short-lived Chinese Republic.

artefacts, models and grainy old photos of heroic construction crews building bridges, laying lines and excavating tunnels during the 1950s only mildly interesting – not helped by the lack of English captioning. For most, the highlight is upstairs on the top floor: a full-size replica of the driver's cabin on a high-speed train, which you can get inside and pretend you are driving.

The Museum of Urban Planning

规划博物馆, guīhuà bówùguǎn • Qianmen Dongdajie • Tues–Sun 9am–5pm • ¥30 • Ⓦ www.bjghzl.com.cn • Subway line #2 to Qianmen (Exit B)

The quirky **Museum of Urban Planning** is little visited: perhaps the frankly unbelievable displays portraying Beijing as a "low-carbon eco-city" stretch most visitors' credulity. Head up the escalators and you'll find the **interactive area**; here you can sit in a boat in a mirrored room, where a giant TV screen will attempt to convince you that you're navigating Beijing's waterways and (weirdly, given the nature of boats, and of Beijing's air) flying through azure-blue skies.

The non-ironic highlights of the museum are all map-based. First, and visible on a wall from the escalator, is a fascinating **bronze model** showing the city as it used to look in imperial times, back when every significant building was part of an awesome, grand design. Then comes another TV screen, which slowly spools through a digitized version of an ancient scroll, heading through **Old Beijing** from south wall to north wall, via the Forbidden City. The star attraction, though, is an enormous and fantastically detailed underlit **model of the city** that takes up the entire top floor. At a scale of 1m:1km it covers more than three hundred square metres, and illustrates what the place will look like once it's finished being ripped up and redesigned in 2020.

23 Ch'ienmen

前门东大街二十三号, qiánmén dōngdàjiē èrshísān hào • 23 Qianmen Dongdajie • Daily 24hr • Free • Subway line #2 to Qianmen (Exit A)

23 Chi'enmen is a reconstructed compound at the edge of the former legation compound that once housed the US embassy between 1861 and 1949. Once you get in past the guard, you'll find the nineteenth-century-style buildings mostly occupied by upmarket foreign businesses, though there's also some fine dining available at the Yunnanese restaurant *Lost Heaven* (see p.142).

BEIHAI PARK

North of the centre

The area north of the Forbidden City has a good collection of sights you could happily spend days exploring. Just beyond the palace are two of Beijing's finest parks: centred on a small hill, Jingshan offers superlative city views from its peak; while Beihai is set around a magnificent lake. North of here, another lake system – Shicha Hai – sits among a charmingly old-fashioned *hutong* district, which was once the home of aristocrats and literati; buried deep within the labyrinthine alleys is impressive Prince Gong's Palace, once the residence of an imperial power broker.

East of Shicha the most obvious landmarks are the enormous **Bell and Drum towers**, which once used to toll out the hours of the day and still rise grandly over the surrounding few blocks of *hutongs*. Sights as such are thin on the ground here – though the eccentric **Wine Museum** is worth a look – and again it's the warren of old lanes that really appeal. Rather too many people gravitate towards attractive but overcrowded **Nanluogu Xiang**, a leafy, renovated street packed with snack stalls and artsy souvenir shops; you might get more out of an unstructured amble through the less-visited lanes instead, hunting out bars or aiming south through a low-key residential quarter towards the Forbidden City.

2

TOURS	NORTH OF THE CENTRE

Tours The idea of being pedalled around Beijing's backstreet alleyways in an old-style rickshaw sounds great, though few drivers speak much English and in reality it's hard not to feel a bit of a plum. Private operators cruise the entire area and are tricky to avoid; barter hard and you should pay around ¥60 for a half-hour, ¥200 for anything extensive, and expect to be taken to a few shops where the driver gets commission. You'd be better off, however, booking a tour from the office on the west side of the Drum Tower (¥100/hr). Best of all – if pricier – are bike or walking tours run by agencies such as The Hutong or Bike Beijing (see p.26).

Jingshan Park

景山公园, jǐngshān gōngyuán • Daily: April–Oct 6am–9pm; Nov–March 6.30am–8pm • ¥2 • Subway line #6 or #8 to Nanluoguxiang (Exit A)

A visit to **Jingshan Park** is a natural way to round off a trip to the Forbidden City, whose exit is just across the road from the park. The small **hill** here, crowned with pavilions, was a by-product of the digging of the palace moat, and served as both a windbreak and a barrier to keep malevolent northern spirits from entering the imperial quarter of the city. It's notorious for the suicide in 1644 of the last Ming emperor, **Chongzhen**, after the armies of the peasant rebel Li Zicheng had stormed into Beijing. Chongzhen killed two of his consorts and then hanged himself from a locust tree at the bottom of the hill, having penned a moving plea for the rebels to spare his subjects. The site is well-marked on the eastern side of the park, though the tree that stands here is not the original.

"Jingshan" means "View Hill", and panoramas from the summit – though barely 46m high – are the best in Beijing, taking in the whole extent of the Forbidden City and (if the weather cooperates) a fair swathe of the city outside. To the west is Beihai Park and its lake; to the north the Bell and Drum towers; and to the northeast the Yonghe Gong (see p.67).

Red Building

北京大学红楼, běijīng dàxué hónglóu • Wusi Dajie • Tues–Sun 9am–4pm • Free • Subway line #6 or #8 to Nanluoguxiang (Exit B)

Built in 1918, this famous wing of Peking University nurtured several early twentieth-century revolutionaries, including Mao. Inside, temporary exhibitions focusing on vintage art – such as advertising posters from the 1930s – set the period for permanent displays about literary luminaries associated with the **May Fourth Movement.** This movement began after WWI, when the victorious Allies carved up Germany's former overseas territories at the Treaty of Versailles; the Chinese had expected that German-held concessions in China would be returned to her sovereignty, and were outraged when they were instead gifted to Japan. Pick of the lives profiled here are of the renowned author **Lu Xun**; and magazine editor **Chen Duxiu**, who agitated for citizens' rights, freedom of speech and an end to Japanese aggression – demands that saw him imprisoned. If none of this grabs you, at least check out the fascinating noticeboards outside, with photos of recent **archeological discoveries** from around China.

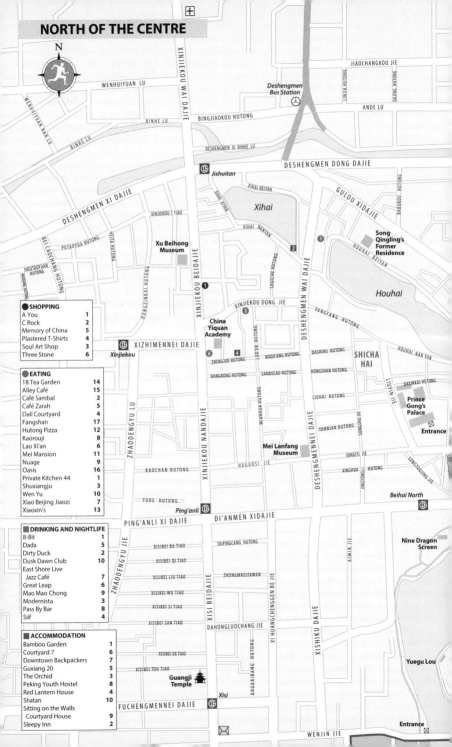

NORTH OF THE CENTRE

N

WENHUIYUAN LU

WENHUIYUAN NAN LU

XINJIEKOU WAI DAJIE

JIAOCHANGKOU JIE

BINHE LU

BINGJIAOKOU HUTONG

Deshengmen
Bus Station

ANDE LU

LINJIA HUTONG

DESHENGMEN XI BINHE LU

DESHENGMEN DONG DAJIE

BINHE LU

Jishuitan

XIHAI BEIYAN

GULOU XIDAJIE

DESHENGMEN XI DAJIE

BEI CAOCHANG HUTONG

XINJIEKOU 7 TIAO

XIHAI NANYAN

Xihai

Song
Qingling's
Former
Residence

PUTAOYUA HUTONG

HEITA HUTONG

XIHAI MANYAN

HOUHAI BEIYAN

HOUTAOYUAN
HUTONG

Xu Beihong
Museum

DONGZIKAI HUTONG

XINJIEKOU BEIDAJIE

XINJIEKOU DONG JIE

SHICHE HUTONG

DESHENGMEN WAI DAJIE

Houhai

YANGFANG HUTONG

HOUHAI NAN YAN

XIZHIMENNEI DAJIE

Xinjiekou

China
Yiquan
Academy

DOU JIE HUTONG

DASHIHU HUTONG

SHICHA
HAI

DAXINKAI HUTONG

ZHENGJUE HUTONG

BOQICANG HUTONG

HONGSHAN HUTONG

LUYIN JIE

ZHAODENGYU LU

HANGKONG HUTONG

SANBULAO HUTONG

CIUHAI HUTONG

Prince
Gong's
Palace

Entrance

MANFANG HUTONG

YANNIAN HUTONG

SONGSHU JIE

XINJIEKOU NANDAJIE

HUGUOSI JIE

Mei Lanfang
Museum

DESHENGMENNEI DAJIE

DINGFU JIE

XINGHUA HUTONG

LONGTOUJING JIE

BAOCHAN HUTONG

Beihai North

YUDE HUTONG

JINGYANG HUTONG

Ping'anli

DI'ANMEN XIDAJIE

PING'ANLI XI DAJIE

Nine Dragon
Screen

ZHAODENGYU JIE

XISIBEI BA TIAO

TAIPINGCANG HUTONG

AIMIN JIE

XISIBEI QI TIAO

ZHONGMAOJIAWAN

XI HUANGCHENGGEN BEI JIE

XISHIKU DAJIE

XISIBEI LIU TIAO

XISI BEIDAJIE

XISIBEI WU TIAO

XISIBEI SI TIAO

XISIBEI SAN TIAO

DAHONGLUOCHANG JIE

Yuegu Lou

XISIBEI ER TIAO

DAGUBANG HUTONG

XISIBEI TOU TIAO

Guangji
Temple

Xisi

Entrance

FUCHENGMENNEI DAJIE

WENJIN JIE

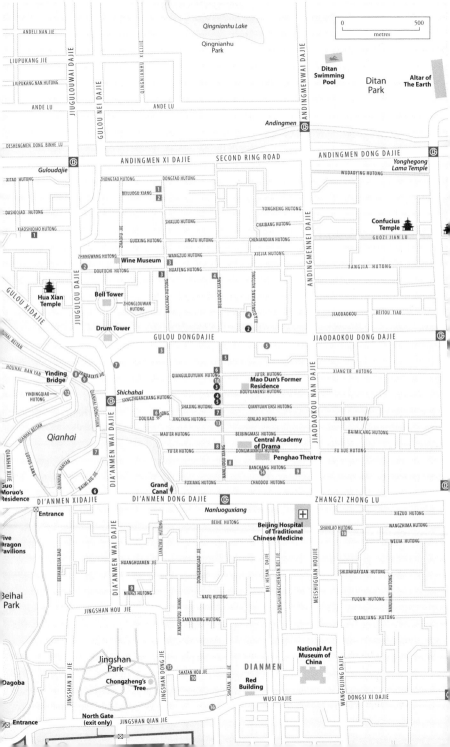

Beihai Park

北海公园, běihǎi gōngyuán · South gate accessed by Wenjin Jie; north gate via Di'anmen Xidajie · Daily: April–Oct 6.30am–9pm; Nov–March 6.30am–8pm; sights close 5pm · ¥10; ¥20 including entry to all buildings · Ten-person cruise boats ¥580/hr, or ¥60pp/hr; pedaloes ¥40/hr · Subway line #6 to Beihai North (Exit D)

Just a few hundred metres west of Jingshan Park, **Beihai Park**, most of which is taken up by a lake, is a favourite spot for many locals. Supposedly created by Kublai Khan, long before any of the Forbidden City structures were conceived, the park is of an ambitious scale: the lake was man-made, the island in its midst created with the excavated earth. Qing Emperor Qianlong oversaw its landscaping into a classical Chinese garden in the eighteenth century, and it is rated as one of the best places in all China to see summertime **lotus flowers** in bloom. Featuring willows and red-columned galleries, it's a lovely spot to retreat from the city and recharge.

The Round and the island

Just inside the main gate, which lies on the park's southern side, is the **Round**, an enclosure of buildings behind a circular wall, which has at its centre a courtyard where there's a large jade bowl said to have belonged to Kublai Khan. The white-jade Buddha in the hall behind was a present from Burmese Buddhists.

From here, a walkway provides access to the island, which is dotted with buildings, including the **Yuegu Lou**, a hall full of steles (stone slabs carved with Chinese characters), and the bulbous white **dagoba** sitting on the crown of the hill, built in the mid-seventeenth century to celebrate a visit by the Dalai Lama. It's a suitable emblem for a park that contains a curious mixture of religious constructions, storehouses for cultural relics and imperial garden furniture. Inside the dagoba is a shrine to the demon-headed, multi-armed Lamaist deity, Yamantaka.

North of the lake

On the north side of the lake stands the impressive **Nine Dragon Screen**, built in 1756 to ward off evil spirits. An ornate wall of brightly coloured glazed tiles, depicting nine stylized, sinuous dragons on each side, it's one of China's largest at 27m in length. Nearby are the **Five Dragon Pavilions**, supposedly in the shape of a dragon's spine. Even when the park is crowded at the weekend, the surrounding gardens and rockeries remain tranquil and soothing, a popular area with courting couples, some of whom like to dress up for photos in period costume (there's a stall outside the Nine Dragon Screen) or take boats out on the lake.

Shicha Hai

什刹海, shíchàhǎi · Nearby stations include Shichahai (line #8, any exit) on the eastern shore of Qianhai; Beihai North (line #6, Exit B), near Prince Gong's Mansion and Qianhai; and Jishuitan (line #2, Exit B) at the tip of Xihai

Three artificial lakes, collectively known as **Shicha Hai**, form a diagonal ribbon north of Beihai Park: first comes **Qianhai**, joined to elongated **Houhai** by a narrow waist, and then, over busy Deshengmen Wai Dajie, is the isolated blob of little **Xihai**. Created during the Yuan dynasty, they were once the terminus for a canal network that served the capital, and the surrounding tangle of **hutong alleyways** (see box opposite) were long favoured as a place to live by the aristocracy, many of whose former mansions survive – most notably **Prince Gong's Palace**. There are plenty of other, less elaborate historic homes to tour around, including that of **Song Qingling**, the wife of China's first Republican head of state, Sun Yatsen. However, as they all follow a similar pattern – featuring early twentieth-century Chinese-Western buildings with pleasant courtyards – there's no need to see all of them; the palace plus one should suffice.

HUTONGS AND HOUSES

In Qing times, the blocks between Beijing's broad main roads were filled by a labyrinthine maze of stone alleyways known as **hutongs**. Once "as fine and numerous as the hairs of a cow" (as one Chinese guidebook put it), today plenty of these residential warrens survive, though in nothing like their original extent: the best examples surround Shichahai, spreading eastwards for a few blocks towards Dongzhimen Nanxiaojie. Some formed low-rent areas for commoners, while others were favoured by aristocratic Manchu families; many have plaques at their entrances explaining their names and histories.

As Beijing was slowly modernized through the twentieth century, so the *hutong* districts were nibbled away; they might be historic and look romantic, but homes were often cramped and poorly maintained, with little heating and no plumbing or sewerage (residents used public toilets). The biggest clearances came in the years running up to the Beijing Olympics in 2008, when China was keen to showcase the capital's modernity to the world; but since then – and in response to increasingly vocal complaints about the destruction of Beijing's architectural heritage – there has been a move towards modernizing, rather than demolishing, the remaining *hutongs*. The results can be seen around Nanluogu Xiang (see p.64) and Wudaoying (see p.70), where residents and the government each paid half the cost for having streets smartened up, roof tiles replaced, walls mended, and public toilets improved. The financial burden was offset, in many cases, by tenants leasing out their front rooms: these are the shops, cafés, galleries and bars you see along these streets today.

The typical *hutong* dwelling is a **siheyuan** (四合院, sìhéyuàn), a single-storey **courtyard house**. These follow a plan that has hardly changed since the Han dynasty, and is in essence identical to that of the Forbidden City. A typical courtyard house has its entrance in the south wall, where you should also find a **Taishan stone**, a small tablet carved with the characters for a protective phrase said to ward off bad fortune. Just outside the front door stand two flat stone blocks – sometimes carved into lions – for mounting horses and to demonstrate the family's wealth and status. Step over the threshold and you are confronted with a freestanding wall; this is to keep out evil spirits, which can only travel in straight lines. Behind it is the outer courtyard, with the servants' quarters to the right and left. The entrance to the inner courtyard, where the family lived, would be in the north wall. The most important rooms, used by the elders, are those at the back, facing south.

Qianhai and Houhai

前海, qiánhǎi and 后海, hòuhǎi • Daily 24hr • Free • Pedaloes ¥120/hr; battery-powered boat ¥200/hr • Beihai North, Nanluoguxiang (both line #6) or Jishuitan subway (line #2)

Just north of Beihai Park are **Qianhai** and **Houhai** lakes, spanned at their narrowest point by the little humpbacked **Yinding Bridge** (银锭桥, yíndìng qiáo). A path lined with willows circuits the shore; you can rent a boat in summer, ice-skate in winter or simply pull up for a meal or a drink at one of the many waterside restaurants – though you probably won't be tempted to join the hardy locals who actually swim in the lakes daily. Note that, despite the area's popularity as an entertainment area, prices are high; you're better off enjoying the scenery here and then heading east towards venues around Nanluogu Xiang. On the way, it's easy to miss an unappreciated historic marker: a stone post on Di'anmen Dong Dajie, which marks where the mighty **Grand Canal** – an 1800km-long waterway reaching all the way south to Hangzhou – once entered Beijing.

Guo Moruo's Residence

郭末若故居, guōmòruò gùjū • Qianhai Xijie • Tues–Sun 8am–6pm • ¥20 • Subway line #6 to Beihai North (Exit B then second left)

Just west of Qianhai, though a little tricky to find, you'll find **Guo Moruo's Residence**. Guo (1892–1978) was a controversial figure: a poet, archeologist, historian and early member of the Communist Party who spent a decade in exile in Japan, he was also accused of being a sycophant to Mao – despite which he and his family were persecuted during the Cultural Revolution. While in exile, Guo married a Japanese woman, but after his return to China in 1937 the war made it impossible for her to join him and he later remarried, this time to a Shanghai actress. His elegantly furnished house is worth a peek, less for the exhibits of dusty books and bric-a-brac than for an insight into how snug courtyard houses could be.

Prince Gong's Mansion

恭王府, gōngwáng fǔ • Qianhai Xijie • Daily: April–Oct 8am–5pm; Nov–March 9am–4pm • ¥40 • Subway line #6 to Beihai North (Exit B); turn left up Sanzuoqiao Hutong, then left at the crossroads

Prince Gong's Mansion was once the residence of the influential Prince Gong Yixin, brother of Emperor Xianfeng, unwilling signatory to the humiliating Peking Convention of 1860 which ended the Second Opium War, and instigator of a palace coup the following year that brought Empress Dowager Cixi to power. A reformer who wanted to modernize China, he later fell out with his conservative patron, but remained head of the court's Department of Foreign Affairs, which he had founded.

The palace's many courtyards, joined by covered walkways, have been restored to something like their former elegance. In the very centre is the **Yin'an Dian**, a hall where the most important ceremonies and rites were held; keep a look out for the sumptuously painted ceiling of **Xi Jin Zhai**, used as a studio by Prince Gong. The northern boundary of the courtyard area is marked by a 151m-long wall; sneak around this and you'll be on the southern cusp of a gorgeous **garden** area, set around an attractive lake.

Mei Lanfang Museum

梅兰芳博物馆, méilánfāng bówùguǎn • 9 Huguosi Jie, off Deshengmennei Dajie • Tues–Sun 9am–4pm • ¥10 • ☎ 010 66183598 • subway line #4 or #6 to Ping'anli (Exit C) or #6 to Beihai North (Exit A)

Some 600m west of Prince Gong's Palace, the small **Mei Lanfang Museum** was once the home of the greatest Beijing opera singer of the twentieth century, Mei Lanfang (1894–1961). Mei's eventful life – famed for his female roles, he was a serial womanizer with two wives, and ended his career as director of the Beijing opera – was the basis for the 2008 movie *Forever Enthralled* by Chen Kaige (who also made the other Beijing opera epic, *Farewell My Concubine*). It's a pretty place, featuring pictures of Mei Lanfang in character as a woman, playing a role from *Legend of the White Snake*.

Song Qingling's Former Residence

宋庆龄故居, sòngqìnglíng gùjū • 46 Houhai Beiyan • Daily 9am–4.30pm • ¥20 • Subway line #2 to Jishuitan (Exit B)

On the northern shore of Houhai, **Song Qingling's** former residence is a Qing mansion with an agreeable, spacious garden. The wife of Sun Yatsen, leader of the short-lived republic that followed the collapse of imperial China (see p.179), Song commands great respect in China, and the exhibition inside details her busy life. It's all fairly dry, but check out the revolver Sun Yatsen – obviously not a great romantic – gave his wife as a wedding gift. More interesting, perhaps, is the chance to take a rare glimpse at a typical Chinese mansion from the beginning of the twentieth century – all the furnishings are pretty much as they were when she died, and her personal effects, including letters and cutlery, are on display.

Xu Beihong Museum

徐悲鸿纪念馆, xúbēihóng jìniànguǎn • 53 Xinjiekou Beidajie • Tues–Sun 9am–noon & 1–5pm • ¥5 • ⓦ www.xubeihong.org /English/museum.htm • Subway line #2 to Jishuitan (Exit C)

West of Xihai, the **Xu Beihong Museum** commemorates the life and works of Xu Beihong (1895–1953), who did for Chinese art what his contemporary Lu Xun (see p.92) did for literature – modernize an atrophied tradition. Xu had to look after his entire family from the age of 17 after his father died, and spent much of his early life labouring in semi-destitution and obscurity before receiving the acclaim he deserved. His extraordinary talent is well in evidence here in seven halls, which display a huge collection of his works. These include many spirited ink paintings of frolicking **horses**, for which he was most famous, and Western-style oil paintings, which he produced while studying in France (and which are now regarded as his weakest works); the large-scale allegorical images also on display allude to tumultuous events in modern Chinese history. However, the pictures it's easiest to respond to are his delightful sketches and studies, in ink and pencil, often of his infant son.

The Drum and Bell towers

Rising high above the surrounding buildings to the east of Shichahai, it's no surprise that the **Drum and Bell towers**, two utterly monstrous relics of ancient Beijing, have survived intact through the ages. They originally marked out the city's day, which was divided up into twelve two-hour blocks called *geng*, each named after a zodiac animal; today their upper storeys provide great views of the surrounding area.

The Drum Tower

鼓楼, gǔlóu • Junction of Gulou Xidajie, Gulou Dongdajie and Di'anmen Wai Dajie • Daily 9am–5pm; drumming hourly 9.30–11.30am & 1.30–4.45pm • ¥20, or ¥30 combined ticket with the Bell Tower (see below) • Subway line #8 to Shichahai (Exit A2), or line #2 or #8 to Guloudajie (Exit G)

The formidable two-storey **Drum Tower**, a squat, wooden, fifteenth-century Ming creation set on a red-painted stone base, is the southern member of the pair of towers. In every city in China, drums were beaten at dawn and dusk; dusk saw the closing of the city gates and a traffic curfew within the walls, known as *jingjie*, "Cleaning the Streets". It's a steep slog up to the top, where there's a small display of ancient time-keeping devices – decoratively shaped sticks of incense that took a known time to burn, and a *kelou*, or water clock – not to mention a **troupe of drummers** in traditional costume who whack away at the giant drums inside. Views to the junction of Xichang'an Jie and Dongchang'an Jie are fantastic, but unfortunately only the southern end – the one facing the Bell Tower – is open.

The Bell Tower

钟楼, zhōnglóu • Junction of Gulou Xidajie, Gulou Dongdajie and Di'anmen Wai Dajie • Daily 9am–5pm • ¥20, or ¥30 combined ticket with the Drum Tower (above) • Subway line #8 to Shichahai (Exit A2), or line #2 or #8 to Guloudajie (Exit G)

At the other end of the small plaza from the Drum Tower, the **Bell Tower** is somewhat different in appearance, being made of stone and a bit chunkier. The original structure was of Ming vintage, though the tower was destroyed by fire and rebuilt in the eighteenth century. It still, however, boasts the original **bronze bell** – at 7m high and weighing 63 tons, by far the largest in China – which until 1924 was traditionally rung every two hours to mark out the time of day. Again, it's a steep climb to the top but, unlike at the Drum Tower, you're able to see in all directions.

According to one well-known legend, **casting** such a huge bell proved nearly impossible. Firstly, the mould was made using the lost wax process, where a full-sized model of the bell made of butter and beeswax – only feasible in winter, when the ingredients would solidify – was covered in clay. Once the clay had set, molten bronze was poured in through holes, vaporizing and replacing the butter-wax model; but here the craftsmen failed time after time. With the deadline looming, and facing the wrath of an impatient emperor, things were looking bleak for the workmen until the foundry master's daughter jumped into the molten mix; with added girl, the casting succeeded. The little **Hua Xian Temple** (花仙娘娘庙, huāxiān niángniáng miào), nearby at 24 Xiao Heihu Hutong, dedicated to the girl, was apparently built over the site of the original foundry.

Wine Museum

北京乾鼎老酒博物馆, běijīng gāndìng lǎojiǔ bówùguǎn • 69 Zhaofu Jie, Zhangwang Hutong • Daily 9am–4.30pm • ¥29 • Ⓜ www.dwwine.cn • Subway line #8 to Shichahai (Exit A2)

Despite being tucked away down a side street, you can't miss the eccentric **Wine Museum**, given that its side wall is studded in metre-high wine jars. Inside, the whole single-floor display is crammed with glass cabinets of **Chinese grain spirits**, *baijiu*, all arranged by province. Foreigners find *baijiu* something of an acquired taste – aside from its sheer strength (often 50º proof or above), it has a distinctly raw aroma – but famous labels like Moutai or Wuliangye are essential for toasts at any Chinese banquet. Most bottles here date from the 1980s, but one is eighteenth century and a couple – they're the earthenware bottles in the Guizhou cabinet – are from the Ming dynasty (before 1644).

Nanluogu Xiang and around

南锣鼓巷, nánluógǔ xiàng • Subway line #6 to Nanluoguxiang (Exit E)

There aren't, to be frank, too many streets in Beijing that could be called attractive, but the pedestrianized north–south *hutong* of **Nanluogu Xiang** is an exception: lined with trees, dotted with cafés, boutiques and restaurants, it has become a prime strolling street for the city's teenagers and bright young things. Unfortunately, Nanluogu Xiang's crushing popularity might be its downfall: in the evenings it's hard to walk from one end of the street to the other in less than half an hour, tour groups have already been banned, and there's talk of putting in **gates** in order to limit the numbers of visitors.

If it all proves too much, you might want to explore the alleys shooting off to the east and west of Nanluogu Xiang, where there are a handful of **bars** and enough open-air mahjong games, rickety mom-and-pop stores, and old men sitting out with their caged birds to maintain that ramshackle, backstreet Beijing charm. South across **Di'anmen Dong Dajie**, more unreconstructed *hutongs* spread down to Jingshan Park and the Forbidden City – another great slice of ordinary street life.

Mao Dun's Former Residence

茅盾故居, máodùn gùjū • 13 Houyuanensi Hutong • Tues–Sun 9am–4pm • ¥5

The only actual sight in the Nanluogu Xiang area is **Mao Dun's Former Residence**, a charming little courtyard house. Mao Dun was the pen name of Shen Dehong, writer, communist and ex-minister of culture, whose best work is *Midnight*, a tale of cosmopolitan Shanghai. His house today has been preserved since he died in 1981, and is full of manuscripts and knick-knacks, with some elegant period furniture.

CCTV BUILDING

East of the centre

Central Beijing's eastern districts make up the city's most cosmopolitan and fashionable area. Just east of Tian'anmen Square, the surprisingly quiet former legation quarter opens into the madcap area of Wangfujing, Beijing's shrine to shopping, which buzzes by day and evening. North of Wangfujing, and surrounded by an increasingly trendy *hutong* area, sit Yonghe Gong and the Confucius Temple, two of Beijing's most beguiling temple complexes. Some way to the east is Sanlitun; most famous as a bar district, it is raucous and gaudy by night but engagingly civilized during the daytime, with its many small cafés and restaurants perfect for people-watching. It is also a great place to shop, with several architecturally adventurous malls.

South of Sanlitun lies Beijing's **Central Business District (CBD)**. Despite a core centred around leafy **Ritan Park**, first impressions are overwhelmingly modern: multi-lane highways, multistorey office blocks, and a whole crop of fantasy-inspired showcase architecture – the most famous example being the **CCTV Tower**. All in all, the CBD is about as far away from traditional China as you can get, but there are a few interesting historical sights on its periphery: the **Ancient Observatory**, full of oversized bronze astronomical instruments; a section of once-mighty Ming-dynasty **city wall**; and the unusual Dongyue and Zhihua **temples**, which all offer some respite from rampant modernity.

The former legations quarter

Subway line #2 to Qianmen (Exit A), or line #2 or #5 to Chongwenmen (Exit A1, A2 or D)

Filling a full three blocks between Tian'anmen Square and Chongwenmennei Dajie to the east, the **former legations quarter** was created at the behest of foreign officials in 1861, and run as an autonomous district with its own postal system, taxes and defences. Rebuilt after being virtually destroyed during the xenophobic Boxer Rebellion, by the 1920s more than twenty nations had legations here – including the Americans, at 23 Ch'ienmen (now accessed off Qianmen Dong Dajie; see p.55) – most built in the style of their home countries, with imported fittings but using local materials. Today it's part film-set facade, with modern offices hiding behind Republican-era Neoclassical frontages, though some genuinely old pieces survive.

Dongjiaomin Xiang

东交民巷, dōngjiāomín xiàng

Cutting eastwards through the district for 1.5km, **Dongjiaomin Xiang** – formerly Legation Street – is the longest alley in all Beijing. Enclosed by old buildings and shady trees, and with minimal vehicle traffic, it feels utterly removed from Tian'anmen Square, immediately to the west. Most of the old buildings now house police departments, though there are a few exceptions that you can visit. For example, the turreted, red-brick former Yokohama Specie Bank at the corner of Zhengyi Lu has now become the **China Court Museum** (中国法院博物馆, zhōngguó fǎyuàn bówùguǎn; Tues–Sun 9am–5pm; free but bring ID). Despite explanatory text asserting greater judicial transparency, and cases full of antique block-printed books covering legal procedure, don't be surprised to find that there's very little content here; the most compelling reason to come is the excellent diorama of the old legation district, with buildings labelled in English, inside the former bank vault.

Further along the road, past the unrestored shell of the French Post Office at number 19, is the Gothic Revival St Michael's Church (圣弥额尔天主堂, shèngmí é'ěr tiānzhǔtáng). Yielding to local taste, the pillars are painted red as in Chinese temples, and the statues of the saints are labelled in Chinese characters.

Police Museum

警察博物馆, jǐngchá bówùguǎn • 36 Dongjiaomin Xiang • Tues–Sun 9am–4pm • ¥5 • ☎ 010 85225018 • Subway line #2 to Qianmen (Exit A)

Appropriately located opposite China's Supreme Court, the **Police Museum** exhibits anything vaguely related to crime or public order on its four floors, including plenty of uniforms and weapons, forensics tools and an ingenious Qing-dynasty fire engine. It's not for the squeamish: there's a skull that's been caved in by an axe, as well as some horrific crime-scene photos and ancient execution tools – and you can cap off a visit with a blast on the firing range on the fourth floor, though all you get to shoot is, alas, a laser gun. Check out the gift shop tat – all sorts of authority figure key-ring dolls are on offer, including one of the internet censor.

Wangfujing

王府井大街, wángfǔjǐng dàjiē • Subway line #1 to Wangfujing (Exit B, C1 or C2)

Wangfujing Dajie – or just Wangfujing – is where the capital gets down to the business of shopping in earnest. The haunt of quality stores for over a century, today it's flush with giant, upscale shopping malls: the **Oriental Plaza** stretches east for nearly a kilometre, and is packed with international fashion labels (plus some local hopefuls, such as the brilliantly named "Marc O'Polo"); it's where to go if you need a new Audi car, Bose sound system or a battery for your sports watch. Less ambitious alternatives include the older-style Beijing Mall, and APM, a bright, cheerful place packed with young families.

Besides the shopping (and the opportunity to eat scorpions and the like at the Xiaochi Jie **night market** – see p.140), a few minor sights might lure you away from Wangfujing's southern core. Be warned that the whole district is packed with **scam artists** (see p.31).

St Joseph's Church

大圣若瑟堂, dàshèng ruòsè táng • 74 Wangfujing Dajie • Daily in morning; Mass Mon–Sat 6.30am & 7am, Sun 6.15am, 7am & 8am • Free • Subway line #1 to Wangfujing (Exit B, C1 or C2)

An island of faith in a sea of consumerism, **St Joseph's** was founded by Jesuits in 1655, and though this technically makes it one of the oldest surviving churches in Beijing, it has in fact been destroyed and rebuilt several times – most recently in 1904, following the Boxer Rebellion. The stocky, grey Romanesque facade hides a bright, airy interior, lightened by elegant columns; look for paintings by the Jesuit priest **Giuseppe Castiglione** (known in Chinese as Lang Shining), an influential artist who blended Western and Chinese techniques and is perhaps best known for his portraits of the emperor Qianlong.

Lao She's Former Residence

老舍故居, lǎoshě gùjū • 19 Fengfu Hutong, just north of Dengshikou Xi Jie • Tues–Sun 9am–4.30pm • ¥10 • Subway line #5 to Dengshikou (Exit A)

Growing up amid the chaos of the early twentieth century – his father was killed by Allied forces during the Boxer Rebellion – it's perhaps not surprising that the often satirical writings of author **Lao She** (1899–1966) are shot through with Dickensian social commentary. His best-known works are the play *Teahouse* and novels *Dragon's Beard Ditch* and *Rickshaw Boy* (see p.192), all of which portray the often tragic lives of ordinary people in Republican China.

Sadly, Lao She's literary talents, and his refusal to align himself with the communist cause, saw him hounded to **suicide** during the Cultural Revolution. He was posthumously rehabilitated, and this pleasantly unpretentious courtyard house has become something of a shrine, though there's little of specific interest besides a persimmon tree planted by Lao.

National Art Museum of China (NAMOC)

中国美术馆, zhōngguó měishùguǎn • 1 Wusi Dajie • Daily 9am–5pm • Free (bring ID); charges for special exhibitions • ☎ 010 84033500, ⊛ namoc.org • Dongsi subway (lines #5 & #6)

Once regarded as a stuffy academy, the grand **National Art Museum of China** now embraces modern trends such as installation and video art. There's no permanent display and it usually holds a couple of shows at once; past subjects have included ethnic embroidery from southwestern China, seal carving, and Socialist Realist propaganda posters – put up not to inspire renewed zeal but as a way to reconsider past follies.

Yonghe Gong

雍和宫, yōnghé gōng • Yonghegong Beidajie • Daily: April–Oct 9am–4.30pm; Nov–March 9am–4pm • ¥25 • ☎ 010 64044499 • Subway line #2 or #5 to Yonghegong (Exit C)

You won't see many bolder or brasher temples than the **Yonghe Gong**, built towards the end of the seventeenth century as an imperial residence of Prince Yin Zhen. In 1723,

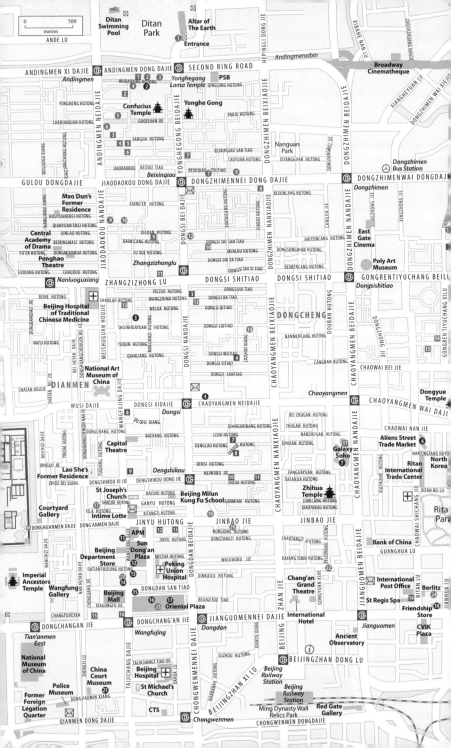

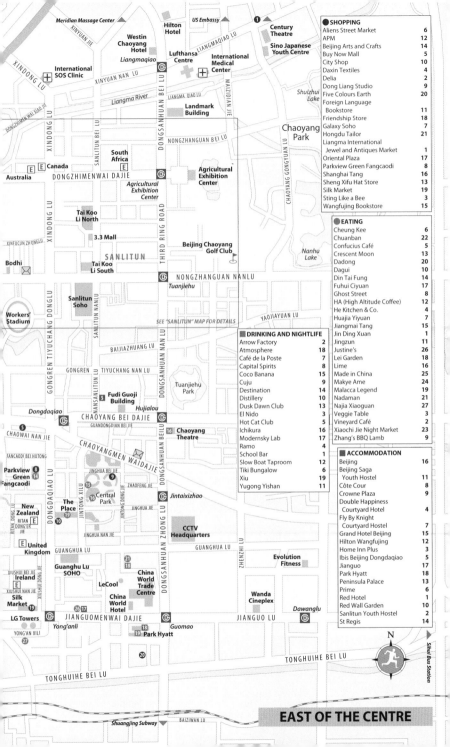

after the prince became Emperor Yong Zheng and moved into the Forbidden City, the temple was retiled in imperial yellow and restricted to religious use. It became a **lamasery** in 1744, housing monks from Tibet and Inner Mongolia. Remarkably, it escaped the ravages of the Cultural Revolution, but has since become associated with the tragedy surrounding the election of the state-approved **Panchen Lama** – a Tibetan spiritual leader – who was sworn in here in 1995. Just prior to this, the Dalai Lama's own choice for the post, 6-year-old Gedhum Choekyi Nyima, had "disappeared" – becoming the youngest political prisoner in the world. Neither he nor his family have been heard of since.

Today, surrounded by shops selling Tibetan medicines, *thankas* (nit-pickingly detailed religious painting) and all manner of temple accessories – prayer flags, giant bronze deity statues, incense and paper foil "gold" ingots for burning as offerings – Yonghe Gong still functions as an active Tibetan Buddhist centre, its five halls full of imposing statuary and the courtyards thick with incense, monks, pilgrims and tourists. Visitors are free to wander throughout the complex, though the experience is perhaps largely an aesthetic, rather than a spiritual one.

The Yonghe Hall

雍和殿, yōnghédiàn

The **Yonghe Hall**, the second one along as you move north through the complex, is the temple's main building, though this may not be immediately apparent. Here you'll find three large statues – gilded representations of the past, present and future Buddhas, respectively standing to the left, centre and right.

The Pavilion of Eternal Blessings

永佑殿, yǒngyòudiàn

Buddhas of longevity and medicine stand in the third hall, the **Pavilion of Eternal Happiness**, though they're far less interesting than the *nandikesvras*, representations of Buddha having sex, in a side room. Once used to educate emperors' sons, the statues are now covered by drapes. The chamber behind, the **Hall of the Wheel of Law**, has a gilded bronze statue of Gelugpa, the founder of the Yellow Hats (the largest sect within Tibetan Buddhism), and paintings that depict his life, while the thrones at its side are for the Dalai Lama (each holder of the post used to come here to teach).

The Hall of Boundless Happiness

万福殿, wànfúdiàn

In the last, grandest hall, the **Wanfu Pavilion** (or Hall of Boundless Happiness), stands an 18m-high statue of the Maitreya Buddha, the world's largest carving made from a single piece of wood – in this case, the trunk of a Tibetan sandalwood tree. Gazing serenely out, the giant reddish-orange figure looms over you; details, such as his jewellery and the foliage fringing his shoulders, are beautifully carved. It took three years for the statue, a gift to Emperor Qianlong from the seventh Dalai Lama, to complete its passage to Beijing.

Confucius Temple

孔庙, kǒngmiào • Guozijian Jie • Tues–Sun 8.30am–5pm • Performances April–Oct 10am, 11am, 2pm, 3pm & 4pm • ¥30 • Subway line #2 or #5 to Yonghegong Lama Temple (Exit D)

West across the road from Yonghe Gong sits a block of attractive, leafy residential lanes, the highest-profile of which is **Wudaoying Hutong** – a lower-key, and far less busy, version of Nanluogu Xiang (see p.64) – with many others in the area worth exploring for their emerging bar scene.

Pretty much in the middle of all this is Beijing's **Confucius Temple**, a calm oasis divided into two areas: the **temple complex** to the east, and the equally large old

CONFUCIUS

Confucius was born in 552 BC into a declining aristocratic family in an age of petty kingdoms, where life was blighted by constant war and feuding. An itinerant scholar, he observed that life would be much improved if people behaved decently, and he wandered from court to court, teaching adherence to a set of moral and social values designed to bring the citizens and the government together in harmony. Ritual and propriety were the system's central values, and great emphasis was placed on the five "**Confucian virtues**": benevolence, righteousness, propriety, wisdom and trustworthiness. An arch-traditionalist, he believed that society required strict hierarchies and total obedience: a son should obey his father, a wife her husband, and a subject his ruler.

Nobody paid Confucius much attention during his lifetime, and he died in obscurity. But during the Han dynasty, six hundred years later, **Confucianism** became institutionalized, underscoring a hierarchical system of administration that prevailed for the next two thousand years. Seeing that its precepts sat well with a feudal society, rulers turned Confucianism into the state philosophy, and from the Tang dynasty onwards, officials were appointed on the basis of their knowledge of the Confucian texts (see p.191).

The great sage fell from official favour in the twentieth century with the rise of the egalitarian communists, and today there are no functioning Confucian temples left in China. Ironically, however, those temples that have become museums or libraries have returned to a vision of the importance of learning, which is perhaps closer to the heart of the Confucian system than ritual and worship.

imperial college, **Guozi Guan**, to the west. In between the two sits a corridor known as the **Hall of Steles**, where the entire Confucian cannon – comprising some 630,000 characters – was carved onto huge stone tablets between 1726 and 1738.

The temple complex

Founded at the start of the fourteenth century, the temple is a charming place filled with carved steles, red-lacquered wood and gnarled cypresses, some of which are over 700 years old; one, to the southwest of the complex, is now a mulberry tree too, the ambitious mulberry seed apparently dropped into the trunk by a bird. Most of the buildings here are relatively modern, though parts of the colossal **Dacheng Hall** date back to 1411. The halls to its east and west were once sacrificial venues, but are now employed as half-hearted art galleries. Small performances, featuring dancing girls in costume, take place to the rear of the complex – the Confucius connection is rather weak, but they're enjoyable to watch nonetheless.

Guozi Jian

国子监, guózǐ jiàn

To the west of the temple complex is **Guozi Jian**, the old imperial college – the temple's junior by only two years. Just inside the gigantic main gate, you'll be confronted by the **Memorial Arch**, glazed in with orange and green tiles and featuring the (slightly tatty) calligraphy of Emperor Qianlong. Behind this is the **Biyong Hall**, set in a circular lake filled with carp; Qianlong used to give speeches here, backed by an elaborate folding screen, and replicas of both are now in place.

The side halls feature an exhibition on China's **examination system**, based on the Confucian Classics, whereby government officials were chosen at the local, provincial and national level. Scholars would spend years studying, often bankrupting themselves and their families while attempting to pass the exams and so "climb the ladder to the clouds" – to gain official position. Not surprisingly, many resorted to **cheating**: one of the exhibits here is of a metre-long "crib sheet" covered in microscopic script, found concealed in a candidate's belt. There are few English captions, but check out the official robes emblazoned with finely embroidered square badges, whose designs indicated the wearer's official rank.

Ditan Park

地坛公园, dìtán gōngyuán • Main entrance at Guanghua Lu • Daily 6am–9.30pm • ¥2, ¥5 extra for altar and museum • Subway line #2 or #5 to Yonghegong (Exit A)

North of Yonghe Gong, across a multi-lane traffic system, **Ditan Park** was one of the imperial city's quartet of sacrificial grounds (along with Tiantan, Ritan and Yuetan parks). As befits this park's name – *dì* means "earth" – this was where the emperor once performed rituals to honour the earth god, using the huge, tiered stone platform just up from the south entrance as an **altar**. A small **museum** next to it holds the emperor's sedan chair – covered, of course, so that no commoner could glimpse the divine presence on his journey here. Wandering among the trees is probably the most diverting way to spend time in the park; at weekends the place is busy with old folk playing croquet, kids playing fishing games and martial artists practicing routines. The place is at its liveliest during Chinese New Year, when it hosts a temple fair (see box, p.183).

Sanlitun

三里屯, sānlǐtún • Subway line #10 to Tuanjiehu, exits A or D

The most famous **nightlife district** in Beijing, if not all China, **Sanlitun** has come a long way since the first watering holes opened up on "Bar Street"– still a popular name for

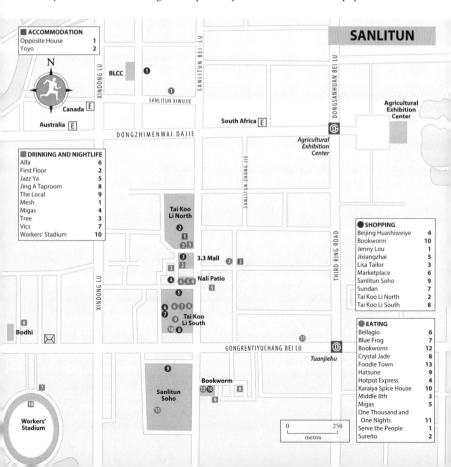

ACCOMMODATION
Opposite House	1
Yoyo	2

DRINKING AND NIGHTLIFE
Alfa	6
First Floor	2
Jazz Ya	5
Jing A Taproom	8
The Local	9
Mesh	1
Migas	4
Tree	3
Vics	7
Workers' Stadium	10

SHOPPING
Beijing Huashiweiye	4
Bookworm	10
Jenny Lou	1
Jixiangzhai	5
Lisa Tailor	3
Marketplace	6
Sanlitun Soho	9
Sundan	7
Tai Koo Li North	2
Tai Koo Li South	8

EATING
Bellagio	6
Blue Frog	7
Bookworm	12
Crystal Jade	8
Foodie Town	13
Hatsune	9
Hotpot Express	4
Karaiya Spice House	10
Middle 8th	3
Migas	5
One Thousand and One Nights	11
Serve the People	1
Sureño	2

Sanlitun Lu, the north–south road that bisects the area. Many of these older bars, amazingly, still survive, though look decidedly seedy compared with the rest of the district's fancy boutiques and shopping malls, and cosmopolitan array of cafés and restaurants. For all this, there are virtually no tourist sights in the area – the bronze treasures in the **Poly Art Museum** are the only real exception.

Sanlitun is centred on **Tai Koo Li** (太古里, tàigǔlǐ), a perpetually crowded, upper-end shopping and dining complex whose frontage is boldly patterned in orange and red squares emblazoned with the UNIQLO logo. Tai Koo Li's north and south buildings form a confusing, multilevel open-air maze of courtyards, walkways and escalators; the pattern is repeated directly south over the main road at the towering **Sanlitun Soho** building. Southwest of all this is the **Workers' Stadium** (工人体育场, gōngrén tǐyùchǎng), colloquially known to Beijingers by the abbreviated term "Gongti" and itself surrounded by industrial-sized nightclubs.

Poly Art Museum

保利大厦, bǎolì dàshà • Poly Plaza, Dongzhimen Nandajie • Mon–Sat 9.30am–4.30pm • ¥20 • ☎ 010 65008117, ⓦ en.polypm .com.cn/english/bwge.php • Subway line #2 to Dongsishitiao (Exit D)

Within the **Poly Plaza**, a boring-looking office block, lies a small **museum** that has one of the most select collections of antiquities in the capital. In the hall of ancient bronzes you'll find four of the twelve bronze animals that were looted from the old Summer Palace (see p.100); the pig, tiger, ox and monkey were bought in the West by patriotic businessmen, and their return was much heralded. Another two were returned in 2013, and now take pride of place in the National Museum of China (see p.53); the four here may follow in due course. The second hall displays ancient Buddha statues.

Dongyue Temple

东岳庙, dōngyuè miào • Chaoyangmen Wai Dajie • Tues–Sun 8am–5pm • ¥10 • Subway line #6 to Dongdaqiao (Exit A)

Stuck in the no-man's land between Sanlitun and Beijing's CBD, the decidedly surreal **Dongyue Temple** dates back to the Ming dynasty. Pass under the Zhandaimen archway – originally constructed in 1322 – and you enter a courtyard with around thirty dusty annexes, where stern Taoist deities hold court over brightly painted figures, many with monstrous animal heads, excess limbs and the like. Each hall represents a bureaucratic department of the afterlife: there's the "Department of Suppressing Schemes", "Department of Wandering Ghosts", even a "Department for Fifteen Kinds of Violent Death". Halls at the rear of the complex delve into the significance of **Chinese zodiac animals** in art, and are illustrated with antique roof tiles, jewellery and clay models – keep an eye open for Beijing's own Rabbit deity (see box, p.79). Look, too, for the truly **ancient trees** swamped in auspicious red ribbons in the temple courtyards, dedicated to the patron deity of literature, Wenchang; there's also a sculpture of Wenchang's trusty steed, the "**Bronze Wonder Donkey**". Scholars used to visit the temple to pray to Wenchang for success in the exams.

The Central Business District

Bristling with glassy skyscrapers, Beijing's **CBD** is a ritzy area with an international flavour in its embassies and expat-heavy apartment complexes – two typical examples being **Central Park** and **The Place**, which face each other over Jintong Xilu. Traditional tourist sights are scarce; this area is all about entertainment and modern architecture – not least the zany CCTV building – though you might also feel tempted to visit the famed **Silk Market**, a giant six-storey mall of fake goods (see p.165).

CCTV Headquarters

央视大楼, yāngshì dàlóu • Guanghua Lu • Closed to visitors • Subway line #10 to Jintaixizhao (Exit C)

By far the most distinctive of the CBD's many weird and wonderful structures is the headquarters of **CCTV**, the national state broadcaster. Designed by Dutch architect Rem Koolhaas and completed in 2012, the 230m-high building's extraordinary Escheresque shape – its two leaning towers are joined at top and bottom with horizontal letter Vs, the point of the uppermost "V" seeming to defy gravity – has quickly made it a world-famous symbol of the city. However, it seems as if China's decade-long flirtation with foreign-designed, cutting-edge architecture may be over: in 2016 the Chinese government **banned** any further "oversized, xenocentric and weird" construction projects, perhaps reflecting President Xi Jingping's own conservative beliefs.

Ritan Park

日坛公园, rìtán gōngyuán • 24hr • Free • Subway line #1 to Yong'anli (Exit A1) or line #6 to Dongdaqiao (Exit D)

Central to the CBD is **Ritan Park**, once the setting for an annual ritual sacrifice to the sun deity Risheng, and paired with westerly Yuetan Park's association with the moon (see box, p.79). Today, Ritan Park is popular with embassy staff and courting couples, who make use of its numerous secluded nooks; it's an attractive place, nicely proportioned and laid out with paths winding between groves of cherry trees, rockeries and ponds.

Jianguomenwai diplomatic compound

The area surrounding Ritan Park has a casual, affluent, cosmopolitan atmosphere thanks to its large contingent of foreigners, many of them staff from the **Jianguomenwai diplomatic compound**, an odd place with neat buildings in ordered courtyards, and frozen sentries on plinths. Though their embassy lies elsewhere, you'll see plenty of Russians (and Cyrillic script) here; many have set up shop in this area, most notably in the strange **Ritan International Trade Center**, most of whose shops have closed doors and, oddly, no customers.

Zhihua Temple

智化寺, zhìhuà sì • 5 Lumicang Hutong • Tues–Sun 8.30am–4.30pm • ¥20, first 200 people free on Wed • Music performances 10am & 3pm • Subway line #2 or #6 to Chaoyangmen (Exit G or H)

Though a bit dusty and desolate, and hidden away down an obscure back lane, **Zhihua Temple** constitutes the largest collection of wooden Ming-dynasty structures in Beijing. It was founded in 1444 as the family temple of eunuch **Wang Zheng**, a domineering imperial favourite; the original complex was vast, though only four halls now survive along what would have been the central axis. Pick of the sights here are the main hall's antique wooden beams and a mural of "Dizang and the Ten Kings of Hell", plus a large Buddha statue in the rear hall surrounded by 9000 Buddha miniatures. Make sure you also catch the haunting 15min-long performances of **religious music**, with an orchestra of monks playing gongs, cymbals, drums and woodwind – a tradition handed down from the Ming dynasty.

Ancient Observatory

古观象台, gǔguānxiàngtái • 2 Dongbiaobei Hutong • Tues–Sun 9am–5pm • ¥20 • ☎ 010 65269468 • Subway line #1 or #2 to Jianguomen (Exit C)

An unexpected survivor marooned amid high-rises and a complex expressway intersection, the **Ancient Observatory** comes as a delightful surprise. The first observatory on the site was founded in the thirteenth century to reform the inaccurate Chinese calendar, and was later staffed by Muslim scientists, as medieval Islamic science

3

THE JESUITS IN CHINA

Jesuit missionaries began to arrive in China in the sixteenth century. Though they weren't allowed to preach freely at first, they were tolerated for their scientific and astronomical skills, and were invited to stay at court: precise astronomical calculations were invaluable to the emperor who, as master of the calendar, was charged with determining the cycle of the seasons in order to ensure good harvests, and observing the movement of celestial bodies to harmonize the divine and human order. Some Jesuits rose to high positions in the imperial court, and in 1692 they finally won the right to preach in China.

Matteo Ricci (1552–1610) was the most illustrious of these early Jesuit missionaries, arriving at Beijing in 1603 and winning the respect of the local literati with his extensive knowledge of cartography, astronomy, mathematics and the physical sciences. A keen Chinese scholar, he translated the Confucian Analects (see p.191) into Portuguese and created the first system for romanizing Chinese characters. Other influential Jesuits included **Johann Adam Schall von Bell** (1592–1666), who advised China to adopt Western measurements; the polymath **Ferdinand Verbiest** (1623–1688), who besides commissioning a huge woodblock map of the world for the emperor, designed six new instruments to add to the armillary sphere already at the Observatory; and **Kilian Stumpf** (1655–1720), who designed a new azimuth theodolite.

---

enjoyed pre-eminence. In the early seventeenth century it was placed in the hands of Jesuit missionaries under Matteo Ricci (see box above), who proceeded to impress the emperor by making a series of precise astronomical forecasts.

The current squat stone tower dates to 1442, and remained in continuous use until 1929. At its base is an exhibition hall, with a small display about the Observatory's history, and a courtyard dotted with busts of famous **Chinese astronomers**: Xu Guangji (1562–1633) who worked with Matteo Ricci to translate Western scientific texts; Zhang Heng (78–139), inventor of the armillary sphere and seismometer; Zu Chongzhi (429–500), observer of the equinox; and Yi Xing (683–727), Buddhist monk who reorganized the calendar. High up on top of the tower itself are eight bronze **astronomical instruments**, designed by the Jesuits during the eighteenth century – stunningly sculptural armillary spheres, theodolites and the like, all beautifully ornamented with entwined dragons, lions and clouds. The observatory was looted in 1900 by French and Germans, but all the instruments were returned after WWI.

Ming Dynasty Wall Relics Park

明城墙遗址公园, míngchéngqiáng yízhǐ gōngyuán • Off Chongwenmen Dongdajie • Daily 8am–5pm • ¥10 • Subway line #2 or #5 to Chongwenmen (Exit B)

Rising up above Beijing's main train station is the last remaining section of the city's massive old stone wall, which now forms part of the **Ming Dynasty Wall Relics Park**. The skinny stretch of parkland is a grand place to be in the spring, when blossom bursts from its many plum and cherry trees, but the wall itself makes for a fine diversion at any time of year. From its uppermost vantage points, you can peer down to see trains coursing in and out of the railway station; also make time to ascend the main tower, whose innards are a temple-like feast of vermillion-painted columns.

Red Gate Gallery

红门画廊, hóngmén huàláng • Levels 1 & 4, Dongbianmen watchtower • Daily 9am–5pm • Free • ☎ 010 65251005, ⓦ redgategallery.com • Subway line #1 or #2 to Jianguomen (Exit C)

Housed within an eastern fragment of the old city wall, the **Red Gate Gallery** opened up in 1991, in the process becoming Beijing's first private contemporary gallery. However, the curators have steadfastly refused to rest on their laurels, and their venue remains a little more adventurous than its city-centre competition; a continuous procession of cutting-edge Chinese work has cultivated a good reputation overseas.

DAZHALAN LU

South of the centre

Visitors usually head south of Tian'anmen Square for one main reason – to see the ravishing Temple of Heaven Park, which contains a visually arresting complex of blue-tiled halls surrounded by acres of quiet lawn and woodland. The nearby Qianmen, Dazhalan and Liulichang shopping areas are another big pull, the main streets packed with tourists but also featuring some surprisingly quiet backstreets where you might even get a glimpse of old Beijing. Close to the Temple of Heaven lies another site of imperial ritual, the Temple of Agriculture, now the engrossing Museum of Ancient Architecture, while west of here are Niu Jie – at the heart of the city's Muslim quarter – and the tranquil Fayuan Temple, both well worth a look.

> ## BEIJING'S UNDERGROUND CITY
>
> On Dongdamochang Jie, a narrow alley just southeast of Qianmen, lies an interesting window
> into Beijing's not-so-distant days of communist paranoia. A faded English sign is all there is to
> show that this was one entrance to the **Underground City**, a warren of bunkers constructed
> under Beijing during the 1960s. Built by "volunteers" at the behest of Chairman Mao in
> response to the perceived nuclear threat from the Soviet Union, it once had entrances all over
> the city, a control centre in the Western Hills, and supply arteries big enough for trucks to drive
> down. Fortunately, it was never put to use, and wouldn't have been much use even if it were
> – it was too close to the surface to offer protection against any but the smallest conventional
> bombs. Opened briefly as a tourist attraction in 2000, today the tunnels have all fallen into
> disrepair, and their entrances are sealed off.

Qianmen Dajie

前门大街, qiánmén dàjiē · Subway line #2 to Qianmen (Exit C or B) · Trams 9am–6pm during holidays only; ¥25

Stretching immediately south of Qianmen (see p.54), 800m-long **Qianmen Dajie** was
once the Imperial Way. Broad and pedestrianized – though rather too shadeless for
comfortable strolling in summer – the street was gentrified to within an inch of its
life in preparation for the 2008 Olympics, and now comprises a corridor of
upmarket stores and restaurants (including *Quanjude*, see p.148) behind a frankly
over-restored, unconvincing pastiche of dynastic facades. During holidays, you can
ride a restored **tram** along Qianmen Dajie's length, a relic from the days when the
city had a full network.

Dazhalan

大栅栏路, dàshílan · Subway line #2 to Qianmen (Exit C)

One of the most traditional shopping districts left in Beijing, **Dazhalan** –
pronounced "Dashilar" by any good Beijinger – is split by Meishi Jie into two
separate pedestrianized sections. Narrow and flanked in grand 1920s facades housing
venerable clothing and tea stores, easterly **Dazhalan Dong Jie** runs for around 250m
between Meishi Jie and Qianmen Dajie, and is perpetually packed with sightseers.
Historic places to eat include branches of the Tianjin dumpling store *Goubuli* (see
p.148) and Muslim hotpot chain, *Dong Lai Shun* (see p.148) – where you should
look for the doorway sculpture of Beijing's Rabbit deity (see box opposite). There's
also the aromatic headquarters of the famous Chinese pharmacy, **Tongrentang** (see
box, p.34), guarded by a pair of stone *qilin*; the **Ruifuxiang Silk Store** (see p.165),
with its elaborate ironwork frontage; and the still-functioning **Daguanlou Cinema**
(大观楼电影院, dàguān lóu diànyǐngyuàn; seats ¥45) at number #36, which was
established in 1903 by entrepreneur Ren Qingtai, and screened the first ever
Chinese-made feature here, *Dingjun Mountain*. The cinema's period lobby hosts a
small display on early Chinese cinema.

Dazhilan's west section, **Dazhalan Xi Jie**, passes a couple of busy backpacker hostels
(see p.136) and tourist restaurants before the crowds tail off and you enter into an
interesting warren of tidied-up residential *hutongs* spreading west for a block to
Nanxinhua Jie. It's a great place for a purposeless amble, though there's always
Liulichang Jie or the Huguang Guildhall (see opposite) if you need a specific target.

Liulichang Jie

琉璃厂街, liúlíchǎng jiē

Literally meaning "coloured glaze factory street", after the erstwhile businesses here that
once made glazed tiles for the roofs of the Forbidden City, **Liulichang Jie** lies to the
west of the Dazhalan area. Its eastern arm, Liulichang Dong Jie, is full of **curio stores**

BEIJING'S RABBIT GOD

In a doorway halfway along the north side of Dazhalan Dong Jie is a brightly painted sculpture of Tu'er Ye (兔儿爷, tù ér yé), Beijing's own **Rabbit god**. First invoked during a plague during the Qing dynasty, the cult caught on, vanished, and then was revived during the 1980s. Nowadays he's something of a symbol of Beijing, and you see rabbit images – long ears pointing skywards, often dressed as a general and riding a tiger – all over the place, from shops on Nanluogu Xiang selling souvenir figurines to subway advertising. He's also informally worshipped during the Mid-Autumn Festival at Dongyue Temple and unpretentious **Yuetan Park** in western Beijing; yuetan means "moon altar" and rabbits are associated with the moon goddess in Chinese mythology.

selling everything from reproduction antique porcelain to folk art (see p.162; remember to bargain hard); while the western arm, Liulichang Xi Jie, is known for its **bookshops and art supply stores**, especially the venerable *Rongbaozhai* (see p.162).

Huguang Guildhall

湖广会馆, húguǎng huìguǎn • 3 Hufang Lu • Daily 10am–9pm • Free; performances from ¥160 (see p.158) • ☎ 010 63045396, ⓦ huguangguildhall.com • Subway line #7 to Hufangqiao (Exit D)

Every large town in China once featured multiple provincial guildhalls, where visiting merchants and dignitaries from specific provinces could stay, eat, discuss business and be entertained. Founded in 1807, Beijing's **Huguang Guildhall** – one of the last surviving in the city – catered to Hunan and Hubei provinces; its stage once hosted operatic greats such as Mei Lanfang (see p.62), and Sun Yatsen oversaw the foundation of the Nationalist Guomindang party here in 1912. Today it's primarily a venue for Beijing opera, but even if you don't catch a performance it's worth dropping in to see the spectacular **teahouse theatre**, still with its original wooden fittings.

Temple of Heaven Park

天坛公园, tiāntán gōngyuán • Daily 6am–9pm • Park only ¥15, or combination ticket including Hall of Prayer for Good Harvests, Circular Mound Altar and Echo Wall ¥35 • ⓦ en.tiantanpark.com • Subway line #5 to Tiantandongmen (for the east gate; Exit A1), line #5 or #7 to Ciqikou (for the north gate; Exit D), or line #7 to Zhushikou (for the west gate; Exit B)

Large and tranquil, the **Temple of Heaven Park** is possibly the best in Beijing. Regarded as the pinnacle of Ming architectural design, for five centuries its buildings occupied the very heart of imperial ceremony and symbolism, and for many modern visitors its unity and beauty remain more appealing – and on a far more accessible scale – than the Forbidden City. It's also easy to find peaceful seclusion away from the temple buildings, where old men gather with their pet birds and crickets, while from dawn onwards, martial artists can be seen practising among the groves of 500-year-old thuja trees.

Brief history

Construction of the Temple of Heaven was begun during the reign of Emperor Yongle, and completed in 1420. The temple complex was conceived as the prime meeting point of earth and heaven, and symbols of the two are integral to its design. Heaven was considered round, and the earth square; thus the round temples and altars stand on square bases, while the park has the shape of a semicircle beside a square. The intermediary between earth and heaven was, of course, the Son of Heaven – the emperor, in other words.

The temple was the site of the most important ceremony of the imperial court calendar, when the emperor prayed for the year's harvests at the **winter solstice**. Purified by three days of fasting, he made his way to the park on the day before the

CHINESE MARTIAL ARTS

Visit any of Beijing's parks early on in the day – especially at the weekends – and you'll almost certainly see **martial artists** running through their routines. Beijing became a hotbed for Chinese martial arts in the late nineteenth century, when the aristocracy often hired famous masters as teachers, though China's northeastern provinces – especially Hebei, Henan and Shandong – had long been famous for their varied martial styles. These included **xingyi**, a powerful linear system said to have derived from spear routines; **bagua**, which features circle-walking and smooth but very rapid changes of direction and tempo; and **ta ji**, whose slow and circular movements occasionally erupt into explosive outbursts. You can see all these styles being performed today – sometimes with weapons too – but while elsewhere in China many people practise martial arts primarily for health, in Beijing they tend to be far more serious, and it's not unusual to see full-contact sparring.

solstice, accompanied by his court in all its magnificence. On arrival at The Temple of Heaven, the emperor would meditate in the Imperial Vault, ritually conversing with the gods on the details of government, before spending the night in the Hall of Prayer for Good Harvests. The following day he sacrificed animals before the Circular Mound Altar. It was forbidden for commoners to catch a glimpse of the great annual procession to the temple, and they were obliged to bolt their windows and remain in silence indoors. Indeed, the Temple of Heaven remained sacrosanct until it was thrown open to the people on the first Chinese National Day of the Republic, in October 1912. The last person to perform the rites was General Yuan Shikai, the first president of the Republic, on December 23, 1914. He planned to declare himself emperor but his plans were thwarted by his opponents, and he died a broken man in 1916.

Hall of Prayer for Good Harvests

¥20, or included in combination ticket

At the north end of the park, the stunning **Hall of Prayer for Good Harvests** is made entirely of wood, without the aid of a single nail; the circular, tent-like structure rises from a tiered marble terrace to no fewer than three blue-tiled roofs. Four compass-point pillars, representing the seasons, support the vault, enclosed in turn by twelve outer pillars (one for each month of the year and hour of the day). The dazzling colours surrounding the central dragon motif on the coffered ceiling give the interior an ultramodern look; it was in fact rebuilt, faithful to the Ming design, after the original was destroyed by lightning in 1889. The official explanation for this appalling omen was that it was divine punishment meted out on a sacrilegious caterpillar, which was on the point of crawling to the golden ball on the hall's conical apex when the lightning struck. Thirty-two court dignitaries were executed for allowing this to happen, and fifty huge camphorwood trunks used in the reconstruction had to be imported from distant Guizhou province.

Imperial Vault of Heaven and the Echo Wall

¥20, or included in combination ticket

Directly south of the Hall of Prayer for Good Harvests, the **Imperial Vault of Heaven** is an octagonal tower made entirely of wood, with a dramatic roof of dark blue, glazed tiles, supported by eight pillars. This is where the emperor would change his robes and meditate. The shrine and stone platforms inside held stone tablets representing the emperor and his ancestors, and the two chambers either side carried tablets representing the elements. The tower is encircled by the **Echo Wall**, said to be a perfect whispering gallery, although the unceasing cacophony of tourists trying it out makes it impossible to tell.

Circular Mound Altar

¥20, or included in combination ticket

Heading south from the Imperial Vault of Heaven, you'll soon be upon the **Circular Mound Altar**, which consists of three marble tiers representing (from the top down) heaven, earth and man. The tiers are comprised of blocks arranged in various multiples of nine, cosmologically the most powerful number, symbolizing both heaven and emperor. The centre of the altar's bare, roofless top tier, where the Throne of Heaven was placed during ceremonies, was considered to be the middle of the Middle Kingdom – the very centre of the earth. Various acoustic properties are claimed for the altar; from this point, it is said, all sounds are channelled straight upwards to heaven. To the east of the nearby fountain, which was reconstructed after fire damage in 1740, are the ruins of a group of buildings used for the preparation of sacrifices.

Hall of Ceremonial Music and Palace of Abstinence

¥10

Established in 1420 as a training centre for the court's Taoist musicians – over two thousand of them – the **Hall of Ceremonial Music** was later disbanded after it became a focus for dubious commercial enterprises during temple fairs; today there's a small museum of musical instruments and statues of famous musicians. The recently reconstructed **Palace of Abstinence** is a huge Ming-style complex surrounded by a moat, complete with regal red walls and gold-studded gates; it was where the emperor purified himself before making the annual sacrifices, abstaining from meat, drink, music and women.

4

Museum of Natural History

自然博物馆, zìrán bówùguǎn • Tianqiao Nandajie • Tues–Sun 9am–5pm • Free, but call ahead to reserve ticket • ☎ 010 67020733, ⓦ bmnh.org.cn • Subway line #7 to Zhushikou (Exit C)

Just north of Temple of Heaven Park's west gate, the **Museum of Natural History** is highly popular with local and foreign kids alike – they never fail to be impressed by the dinosaur skeletons (China has some of the richest fossil beds in the world, with hardly a year passing without some dramatic discovery). On the upper levels of the building, China's prodigious wealth of animal and – less engrossingly displayed – plant life is laid out in cases of specimens.

Museum of Ancient Architecture

古代建筑博物馆, gǔdài jiànzhù bówùguǎn • Dongjing Lu, south off Nanwei Lu (look for the red arch) • Tues–Sun 9am–4pm • ¥15, first 200 visitors free on Wed • ☎ 010 63172150, ⓦ bjgjg.com • Subway line #7 to Zhushikou (Exit D)

One of Beijing's most underrated attractions, the **Museum of Ancient Architecture** is housed in the splendid Xiannong Temple, founded in 1420. Complementing the nearby Temple of Heaven, it was dedicated to the god of earth – *xiannong* translating as "Ancestral Farmer" – and every year the emperor ritually ploughed a furrow to ensure a good harvest. The **Hall of Worship** holds oddments such as the gold-plated plough used by the emperor, as well as a display explaining the building's history; another wing is devoted to Beijing's own *siheyuan* (see box, p.61), with models, photos and floor plans.

The bulk of the exhibition is housed in the main **Taisui Hall**, which sports a beautifully ornate ceiling and a collection of exhibits showing how China's traditional buildings were put together. There are more wooden models, many with cutaways, of famous and distinctive buildings, including a "wind and rain bridge" from Guangxi province's Dong people; elegant Huizhou houses, with their fire-baffle eaves, from Anhui; a diorama of a traditional formal Chinese garden from Suzhou; Naxi homes from Lijiang in Yunnan; and the apartment-like roundhouses of Fujian's Hakka people. Also on hand are samples of *dougongs*, interlocking, stacked brackets, as complex as puzzle boxes. The giant floor model of how Beijing looked in 1949 – before the communists demolished most of it – is informative, revealing how all the surviving imperial remnants are fragments of a grand design, with a precise north–south imperial axis and sites of symbolic significance at each of the cardinal points. For those who prefer spectacle, there's a great sinuous wooden dragon on show, once part of a temple ceiling.

The Muslim quarter

Subway line #7 to Guang'anmennei (Exit B)

Beijing's **Muslim quarter** is focused on congested **Niu Jie** (牛街, niújiē; Ox Street). It's a chaotic thoroughfare lined with offal stalls, steamy restaurants and hawkers selling fried dough rings, rice cakes and *shaobing*, Chinese-style muffins with a meat filling. The white caps and the beards sported by the men distinguish these people of the Muslim **Hui minority** – of which there are nearly 200,000 in the capital – from the Han Chinese. There have been Muslims in China at least since the tenth century, when Arabic traders visited southern ports, but the Hui are descendants of Central Asian soldiers and merchants who followed the Mongol Yuan army into China during their twelfth-century conquests.

Note that Guang'anmennei subway station is right next to the **Baoguo Temple antiques market** – see p.162.

Niu Jie mosque

牛街清真寺, niújiē qīngzhēnsì • Niu Jie • Daily from first to last prayers • ¥10, free for Muslims • ☎ 010 63532564 • Subway line #7 to Guang'anmennei, Exit D, or bus #6 from the north gate of Temple of Heaven Park

Niu Jie's focus is the **mosque** on its eastern side, an attractive, colourful marriage of Chinese and Islamic design, with abstract and flowery decorations and text in Chinese and Arabic over the doorways. Unlike Chinese temples, which inevitably face south (see p.183), the mosque's entrance is on the west side, oriented towards Mecca. You won't get to see the handwritten copy of the Koran, dating back to the Yuan dynasty, without special permission, or be allowed into the main prayer hall if you're not a Muslim, but you can inspect the courtyard, where a copper cauldron, used to cook food for the devotees, sits near the graves of two Persian imams who came here to preach in the thirteenth century. Also in the courtyard is the "tower for viewing the moon", which allows imams to ascertain the beginning and end of Ramadan, the Muslim period of fasting and prayer.

Fayuan Temple

法源寺, fǎyuán sì • Fayuansi Qianjie • Daily 8.30am–5pm • ¥5 • ☎ 010 63534171 • Subway line #4 to Caishikou (Exit D) or Taoranting (Exit A), or a short walk from Niu Jie mosque

One of Beijing's oldest temples, though the present structures are in fact Qing and thus relatively recent, **Fayuan Temple** is a striking Buddhist place of worship. A long way from tourist Beijing, it's appealingly ramshackle and quiet, with the well-worn prayer mats and shabby fittings of a working temple. Monks sit outside on broken armchairs counting prayer beads, or bend over books in halls that stink of butter – burned in lamps – and incense. The courtyards hold a treasury of steles carved with imperial edicts mounted on the backs of stone tortoises, alongside architectural fragments from earlier incarnations of the temple; also look for large white-barked pines, a tree native to northeastern China. The rear halls are home to a miscellany of sculpture, the finest of which is a 5m-long wooden reclining Buddha.

NATIONAL CENTRE FOR THE PERFORMING ARTS

West of the centre

Tourism drops off sharply west of the Forbidden City, partly because the attractions are widely scattered, but mostly because this is Beijing's financial district, and first impressions are of oversized main roads, glistening office blocks and alienating acres of concrete paving. However, there's enough tucked away here to entertain the curious for a few days: a number of wonderful temples, a fine museum and a pair of appealing parks, as well as the city's principal zoo and aquarium. The quirky blend of architecture might appeal too, with postmodern whimsy and Stalinist brutalism sitting side by side. The area's principal sights come in three main bands, each of which can, if you get your skates on, be eaten up in a single day; the northernmost can also be combined with a boat trip to the Summer Palace (see box, p.97).

5

The first band of sights lies on the main road west from Tian'anmen; before long you'll be outside the superb **Capital Museum**, a visit to which can be combined with a trip south to **Baiyun Guan**, a pleasant Taoist temple that seems worlds away from its earthy surroundings. West of the Capital Museum is the **Military Museum**; head north here and you'll find the **World Art Museum** and **Yuyuantan Park**.

The second main batch of sights lies one block to the north, between Xisi and Fuchengmen subway stations. Here, among the area's last clutch of *hutongs*, lie the **Guangji and Baita temples**, as well as a museum dedicated to **Lu Xun**, China's most famous modern writer. The third band of sights lies north again, stretching west of Xizhimen station. The architecturally fascinating **Beijing Exhibition Hall** marks the eastern perimeter of the city **zoo**, which itself borders the absorbing **Wuta Temple**. West again is another temple, **Wanshou**, which sits next to charming **Zizhuyuan Park**.

West along Xichang'an Jie

From Tian'anmen, traffic fires along **Xichang'an Jie**, a gigantic thoroughfare which mutely morphs through several different name changes on its way out west. Close to Tian'anmen is the hectic **Xidan shopping district** (西单, xīdān); though it has few sights, it does boast a few points of interest to travellers among the mammoth malls. The area's main sights lie a fair way further west, clustered around the Muxidi and Military Museum subway stations (both on line #1). Of greatest interest are the **Capital Museum** and **Baiyun Guan** Taoist temple, which are within walking distance of each other; in between the two runs a small stream, whose banks are a favourite with local fishermen. It's quite possible to walk northwest along (and, in some places, above) this waterway to lovely **Yuyuantan Park**, on the periphery of which are the **Military Museum** and **World Art Museum**.

Zhongnanhai
中南海, zhōngnánhǎi · Subway line #1 to Tian'anmen West (Exit A)

Immediately west of the Forbidden City is the large **Zhongnanhai** complex, much of it parkland, which functions as the Communist Party headquarters – armed sentries ensure that only invited guests get inside. Once home to the Empress Dowager Cixi (see box, p.99), since 1949 it's been the base of the party's Central Committee and the Central People's Government; Mao Zedong and Zhou Enlai both worked here. In 1989, pro-democracy protesters camped outside hoping to petition their leaders, and a decade later a similarly large protest was held by Falun Gong practitioners, whose quasi-religious sect remains proscribed by a government fearful of its still sizeable following and resultant potential threat to the Party.

Further west, the present-day Aviation Office stands on the site of the **Democracy Wall**, which received its name during the so-called "Beijing Spring" in 1978 when posters questioning Mao and his political legacy were pasted here.

National Centre for the Performing Arts
中国国家大剧院, zhōngguó guójiā dàjùyuàn · 2 Xichang'an Jie · ☎ 010 66550000, ⓦ en.chncpa.org · Subway line #1 to Tian'anmen West (Exit C)

Designed by French architect Paul Andreu and nicknamed – for obvious reasons – the "Egg", the **National Centre for the Performing Arts**, off Zhongnanhai's southeastern corner, opened up in 2007. This glass-and-titanium dome houses a concert hall, two theatres and a 2500-seat opera house (see p.160). Visitors enter through a tunnel under the surrounding moat, the park-like banks of which are the best vantage point for this wonderful specimen of modern architecture – look east to the po-faced monumentalism of the Great Hall of the People to see how far China's architecture has come in a few short decades.

Bank of China

中国银行, zhōngguó yínháng • Fuxingmen Neidajie • Subway line #1 or #4 to Xidan (Exit F1 or F2)

Overlooking Xidan station is the huge headquarters of the **Bank of China**, built in 2002. It was designed by superstar Chinese architect I.M. Pei, who was also responsible for designing the bank's towering, knife-like offices in Hong Kong – of which, frankly, this looks like a cut-down, recycled version set inside an sandstone block.

Capital Museum

首都博物馆, shǒudū bówùguǎn • Fuxingmenwai Dajie • Tues–Sun 9am–5pm • Free (bring ID) • ☎ 010 63370491, Ⓦ capitalmuseum.org.cn/en • Subway line #1 to Muxidi (Exit C1)

The gigantic **Capital Museum** is a modern beauty, and its exhibitions are in two sections: the **cube** features displays on Beijing, and cultural relics are inside the arresting **cylinder**, a giant bronze construction which shoots diagonally down through the roof as if from heaven. The museum is a vast place which needs a tiring half-day to cover in full; if you're short on time or energy skip the cube and head for the rarer pieces in the cylinder instead. Note that the ground-floor café serves a good Chinese lunch buffet for ¥48.

The cylinder

The cylinder's ground-floor gallery holds **Ming and Qing paintings**, mostly landscapes – well presented, but not as comprehensive as the display in the Forbidden City (see box, p.43). The calligraphy upstairs can be safely missed unless you have a special interest, but the **bronzes** on level three are pretty interesting: a sinister third-century BC owl-headed dagger, for example, or the strangely modern-looking (though actually more than 3000 years old) three-legged *ding* cooking vessels decorated with geometric patterns. The display of **jade** on the fourth and fifth floors is definitely worth lingering over, especially the lovely white quail-shaped vessels. The qualities that combine to create the best jade is an esoteric subject – it's all about colour, lustre and clarity – but anyone can appreciate the workmanship that has gone into the buckles, boxes and statuettes here.

The cube

The quality of the cube's exhibition halls are mixed. The second level hosts a confusing show on the **history of Beijing**: exhibits are jumbled together – a modern lathe is displayed next to a stele, for example – without enough English captions to make any sense of it all for the visitor. The next level up displays models of historical buildings, which can be skipped in favour of the show-stealing **Buddhist figurines** on the fourth floor. As well as depictions of serene long-eared gentlemen, there are some very esoteric Lamaist figures from Tibet; the goddess Marici, for example, comes with her own pig-drawn chariot and other fierce deities have lion heads or many arms. The cube's fifth floor focuses on old **Beijing folk traditions** and artistry, with full-sized mock-ups of streets, houses and rooms decorated with period furniture and pictures. There are also some lively dioramas of street life, featuring festivals, wedding processions and trades, plus recordings of the calls used by the different hawkers who once pedalled their wares in Beijing's *hutongs*.

Baiyun Guan

白云观, báiyún guàn • Off Baiyun Lu • Daily 8.30am–4.30pm • ¥10 • ☎ 010 63463531 • Subway line #1 to Muxidi (Exit C1)

The Taoist **Baiyun Guan** (White Cloud Temple) was founded in 741 and later rose to prominence after Genghis Khan became impressed by the teachings of the Quanzhen (Complete Reality) school, and gifted the temple grounds to the patriarch **Qiu Changchun**. The original monastery was destroyed during the Ming dynasty, but was soon rebuilt and today remains an influential centre for Quanzhen Taoism (see box, p.91), with the Chinese Taoist Association based here. A popular place for pilgrims, with a busy, thriving feel, it's at its most colourful during the Chinese New Year temple fair.

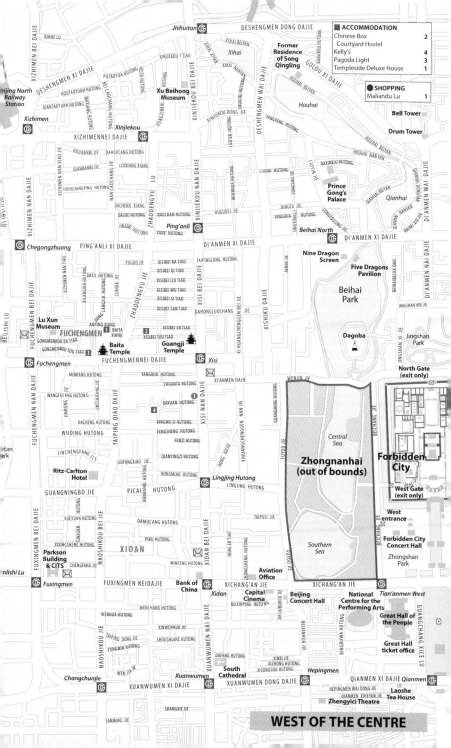

5

The temple complex

At the entrance, Baiyun Guan's **three gateways** symbolize the three states of Taoism – desire, substance and emptiness. Once through them, you'll find that each hall is dedicated to a different deity, whose respective domains of influence are explained in English outside; the thickest plumes of incense emerge from the hall to the gods of wealth. The eastern and western halls hold a great collection of Taoist relics, including some horrific **paintings of hell** showing people being sawn in half. In the western courtyard a shrine houses twelve deities, each linked with a different animal in the Chinese version of the zodiac; here, visitors light incense and kowtow to the deity that corresponds to their birth year. Also in the courtyard is a **shrine to Wenchang**, the patron deity of scholars (see p.73), with a 3m-high bronze statue of him outside. Rubbing his belly is supposed to bring success in academic examinations.

Worship in China can be a lively affair, and there are a number of on-site amusements. Three **monkeys** depicted in relief sculptures around the temple are believed to bring you good luck if you can find, and stroke, them all. One is on the gate, easy to spot as it's been rubbed black, while the other two are in the first courtyard. Another playful diversion is trying to ding the bell under the courtyard bridge by throwing a coin at it. In the back courtyard, devotees close their eyes and try to walk from a wall to an incense burner.

Military Museum

军事博物馆, jūnshì bówùguǎn • Fuxing Lu • Tues–Sun 8.30am–5pm • ¥8 • ☎ 010 66866244, ⓦ eng.jb.mil.cn • Subway line #1 or #9 to Military Museum (Exit A)

This brutally old-fashioned museum – full of big, bad communist art and politically laboured captions such as "Hall of Agrarian Revolutionary War" – was closed for a thorough, desperately needed modernization at the time of writing. Until it all reopens around 2018, hangars have been set up in the courtyard where you can get up close to tanks, fighter jets and even a couple of small gunboats, mostly of Cold War vintage.

China Millennium Monument and World Art Museum

Off Fuxing Lu • Tues–Sun 8.30am–5.30pm • ¥30 • ☎ 010 59802222, ⓦ worldartmuseum.cn • Subway line #1 or #9 to Military Museum (Exit A or E2)

Immediately northwest of the Military Museum, a fenced-off avenue leads up to the grandiose **China Millennium Monument** (中华世纪坛, zhōnghuá shìjì tán), which looks something like a cross between an Aztec temple and a giant sundial and offers a good view north from the top over Yuyuantan Park (see below). Inside is a circular atrium, where a bizarre frieze depicting China "past, present and future" surrounds eight columns; upstairs, the **World Art Museum** (世界艺术馆, shìjiè yìshùguǎn) hopes to foster cultural understanding by displaying temporary (and often excellent) exhibitions from abroad.

Yuyuantan Park

玉渊潭公园, yùyuāntán gōngyuán • Daily: April–May & Sept–Nov 6am–8.30pm; June–Aug 6am–9.30pm; Dec–March 6.30am–7pm • ¥2, or ¥10 during the March–April cherry blossom season • ⓦ www.yytpark.com • Line #1 or #9 to Military Museum (Exit E2)

Giant **Yuyuantan Park**, set around a canal and lake system draining into the Summer Palace lakes some 10km to the northwest (see p.96), offers a respite from the area's honking traffic. In springtime, crowds come to admire its famed **cherry blossoms** – some three thousand cherry trees have been planted in their own garden, on the northwestern side of the park – but it's a pleasant place all through the year, with plenty of pathways, pavilions and other ornamental shrubs to admire.

Central Radio and TV Tower

中央广播电视塔, zhōngyāng guǎngbō diànshì tǎ • Off the Third Ring Road • Daily 8.30am–10pm • ¥90 • ⓦ www.beijingtower.com.cn • Subway line #10 to Xidiaoyutai (Exit C)

Accessible by footbridge from the northwest corner of Yuyuantan Park, Beijing's giant, needle-like **Central Radio and TV Tower** is the city's tallest structure at 405m

5

TAOISM

Humans model themselves on earth
earth on heaven
heaven on the way
and the way on that which is naturally so

Lao Zi, Daodejing

Taoism is a religion deriving from the *Daodejing* or "Classic of the Way of Virtue", an obscure, mystical text (see p.191) comprising the teachings of the semi-mythical **Lao Zi**, who lived around 500 BC. The Tao (道, dào), which literally means "**Way**", is defined as being indefinable; accordingly the book begins: "The Tao that can be told/is not the eternal Tao/The name that can be named/is not the eternal name." Taoism's central tenet is that of *wu wei*, literally non-action, perhaps better understood as "no action which goes against the natural order of things". Taoists believe that the art of living lies in understanding and conforming with this principle, and they emphasize contemplation, meditation and eschewal of dogma.

Taoism developed, at least partially, in reaction to the rigour and formality of Confucianism (see box, p.71); and it similarly became organized as a religion only after Buddhism arrived in China during the first century. Taoism's holy men tend to be artisans and workmen rather than upright advisers, and in focusing on the relationship of the individual with the natural universe, Taoism represents a retreat from the political and social. The communists, accordingly, regard Taoism as fatalistic and passive.

high. You need to pick the right day (check the AQI reading before heading out here – see p.34), but in clear weather views from telescopes dotted around the 238m-high outdoor viewing platform reach to the Forbidden City, the Water Cube and Birds Nest at Olympic Park, and even the CCTV tower – though not, unfortunately, into Zhongnanhai (see p.86), which is screened by some judiciously placed buildings. Come at lunchtime or dinner and take advantage of the **revolving restaurant** too – see p.148.

Fuchengmennei Dajie

阜城门内大街, fùchéngménnèi dàjiē

A few interesting sights – two **temples** and the **Lu Xun Museum** – lie north of **Fuchengmennei Dajie**, a road zipping between Fuchengmen and Xisi subway stations. You can arrive at one station and depart from the other, walking to all three sights in between; most of this area is rather earthy, but appealing in an old-Beijing kind of way. It also features a few back-lane places to stay (see p.135).

Guangji Temple

广济寺, guǎngjì sì • Fuchengmennei Dajie • Daily 6am–4.30pm • Free • Subway line #4 to Xisi (Exit A)

A quiet complement to the Baita Temple further west, the **Guangji Temple** is the administrative headquarters of China's Buddhist Association. Though there's little here for the casual visitor – indeed, the halls are often closed to the public – the temple boasts important collections of painting, sculpture and scriptures (including Tripitakas written in blood from the Song and Ming dynasties), and the big trees and air of established calm make it a pleasant place to drop in to for a few minutes.

Baita Temple

白塔寺, báitǎ sì • Fuchengmennei Dajie • Tues–Sun 9am–5pm • ¥20 • Subway line #2 to Fuchengmen (Exit B), or line #4 to Xisi (Exit A)

The massive white **dagoba** of the famous **Baita Temple** is visible from afar, rising over the rooftops of the *hutongs* that surround it (though only possible to access from the

5

south along busy Fuchengmennei Dajie). The bulbous, 35m-high tower was completed in 1279 by Nepali architects as an attempt by Kublai Khan to gain the goodwill of an increasingly fractious Tibet; today you'll see Tibetan pilgrims in dark red robes circling it clockwise. The temple is famous for its translations of Tibetan scriptures and a collection of thousands of small statues of Buddha (one covered in rubies), very impressive en masse. Another hall holds bronze *luohans* – Buddha's original group of disciples – including one with a beak, small bronze Buddhas and other, outlandish Lamaist figures. The silk and velvet priestly garments on display here were unearthed from under the dagoba in 1978. A shop beside it sells religious curios, such as Buddha images printed on dried leaves.

Lu Xun Museum

鲁迅博物馆, lǔxùn bówùguǎn • 19 Gongmenkou Er Tiao, off Fuchengmennei Dajie • Tues–Sun 9am–4pm • Free (bring ID) • Ⓦ www.luxunmuseum.com.cn • Subway line #2 to Fuchengmen (Exit B)

A large and extensively renovated courtyard house, the **Lu Xun Museum** was once home to Lu Xun (1881–1936), widely accepted as the greatest Chinese writer of the modern era. Lu Xun gave up medicine to pursue a literary career, with the aim of highlighting social ills through writing pithy, satirical stories in an accessible vernacular. He bought this house in 1924, but as someone who abhorred pomp, he might feel a little uneasy here nowadays: his possessions have been preserved like treasured relics, giving a good idea of what Chinese interiors looked like at the beginning of the twentieth century, and there's a photo exhibition lauding his achievements. Unfortunately there are no English captions, though a bookshop on the west side of the compound sells English translations of his work.

Xizhimen

西直门, xīzhímén

Xizhimen – the area west of Shichahai (see p.60) – seems initially to be little more than a functional transport hub, but move out beyond the north train station and there are a handful of sights to take in, perhaps en route to the Yuanmingyuan or Summer Palace (which you can get to from here **by boat**; see box, p.97). Pick of the places to aim for are the very unusual **Wuta Temple** and – perhaps surprisingly – the city **zoo and aquarium**.

Beijing Exhibition Centre

北京展览馆, běijīng zhǎnlǎn guǎn • Xizhimenwai Dajie • Ⓦ bjexpo.com • Subway line #4 to Beijing Zoo (Exit C2)

Built by the Russians in 1954, and easily distinguishable by its slim, star-topped spire, the giant **Beijing Exhibition Centre** is by far the city's best overtly communist construction – a work of grandiose Socialist Realism with fine details, including heroic workers atop columns carved with acorns. It's certainly worth inspection; though its cavernous halls are usually closed, the architecture can be appreciated from side roads to the east and west.

THE TRUE STORY OF AH Q

Lu Xun's most famous work is **The True Story of Ah Q**, a novella written in 1921 but set a decade earlier during the fall of the Qing dynasty. It tells the tale of the worthless peasant Ah Q, who stumbles from disaster to disaster, rationalizing each physical defeat into a moral victory, until he is eventually executed as a revolutionary, having understood nothing about the circumstances that led to his doom. In this, Lu Xun satirized contemporary China, a country which had refused to learn any lessons from its repeated defeats at the hands of bullying foreign powers, and was once again allowing itself to plunge headlong into the chaos of civil war.

The road on the east side leads to the **Huangdichuan wharf** for boats to the Summer Palace (see box, p.97). Head up the alley on the west side and you'll come to the city's oldest Western restaurant, the *Moscow* – the food is mediocre, but check out the grand decor if you're passing.

The zoo and aquarium

动物园, dòngwùyuán • Xizhimenwai Dajie • Daily: April–Oct 7.30am–6pm; Nov–March 7.30am–5pm • ¥15, or ¥18 including panda house • ☎ 010 68390274, ⓦ www.bjzoo.com • Beijing Zoo subway (line #4)

Beijing's park-like city **zoo** is most worth visiting for its panda house. Here you can join the queues to have your photo taken sitting astride a plastic replica of the creature, then push your way through to glimpse the living variety – kept in relatively palatial quarters and familiar through the much-publicized export of the animals to overseas zoos for mating purposes.

While many of the zoo's other residents live in comparatively drab conditions, they all seem fairly well cared for and this certainly isn't the worst-kept collection in the country. There are Chinese rarities such as yangtze alligators, bar-headed geese and golden monkeys, plus tigers, otters and a children's zoo, with plenty of farmyard animals and ponies to pet.

Aquarium

Daily: April–Oct 9am–5.30pm; Nov–March 10am–5pm • ¥160

Accessed through the zoo, the **Beijing Aquarium** is surprisingly good. As well as thousands of varieties of fish, including sharks – which you view while walking through a giant glass tunnel under the tank – it has various daily performances featuring elephant seals and dolphins in its Sea Theatre. Lower-key sections include a handling pool, where sea cucumbers, starfish and even green turtles can be patted in passing; and there's even a performance by Asian archerfish, which shoot jets of water at bait held above their tank.

Wuta Temple (aka Zhenjue Temple)

五塔寺, wǔtǎ sì, 真觉寺, zhēnjué sì • Wutasi Lu, off Zhongguancun Nandajie • Daily 9am–4.30pm • ¥20, free to first 300 visitors on Wed • Subway line #4 or #9 to National Library (Exit C)

The canalside **Wuta Temple** boasts a central hall radically different from any other sacred building you'll see in the capital. Known as the "Diamond Throne Pagoda" and completed in 1473, it's a stone cube decorated on the outside with reliefs of animals, Sanskrit characters and Buddha images – each has a different hand gesture – and topped with five layered, triangular spires. It's visibly Indian in influence, and is said to be based on a temple in Bodhgaya, where the Buddha gained enlightenment. There are 87 steps to the top, where you can inspect the spire carvings at close quarters – including elephants, images of Four Kings of Deva, *arhats* and auspicious Buddhist symbols – and, at the centre of the central spire, a pair of feet.

Besides the temple's multiple names, the large open courtyard in front is also known as the **Beijing Stone Carving Museum**, and is packed with stone sculptures relocated from other, now defunct, temples and tombs. Most obvious are the spirit way guardian figures: camels, rams, lions and civil and military officials, some of these last named with generous beards. Look too for an impressive seventeenth-century sarcophagus, carved to look like a temple hall. On the east side of the courtyard is a line of seventeenth-century **tombstones of Jesuit priests** made in traditional Chinese style, with turtle-like dragons at the base and text in Chinese and Latin.

Zizhuyuan Park

紫竹院公园, zǐzhúyuàn gōngyuán • Best accessed via east gate on Zhongguancun Nandajie • Daily 6am–8pm • Free • Subway lines #4 or #9 to National Library (Exit D)

Centred on a three interconnected lakes, pretty **Zizhuyuan Park** possesses something of the compartmentalized feel of a traditional Chinese garden. Despite its considerable

5

size, strategically placed willows and thick groves of bamboo (*zizhuyuan* means "purple bamboo courtyard") provide the screens necessary to break up what would otherwise be long, empty views. The gardens were first laid out as far back as 1577, and now feature ornamental bridges, rambling paths and small pavilions at strategic intervals; it's somewhere to visit on the walk between Wuta and Wanshou temples.

Wanshou Temple

万寿寺, wànshòu sì • Guangyuanzha Lu • Daily 9am–4pm • ¥20, free to first 300 visitors on Wed • Subway line #4 or #9 to National Library (Exit A)

Dating from the Ming era and a favourite of the Dowager Empress Cixi (see box, p.99), who used to rest up here during her processions to the Summer Palace, **Wanshou Temple** is the last survivor of the several dozen that once lined the local canalsides. Besides the usual buildings (though the eighteen wooden *luohan* statues are pretty good, and one of the halls sports a huge bronze pagoda inside), it also houses a small **museum of ancient art** packed with fine Ming and Qing relics, mostly paintings, calligraphy, jadeware and ceramics. There's nothing spectacular on view, but it's definitely worth a look if you are in the area.

SEVENTEEN-ARCH BRIDGE, KUNMING LAKE

The far north

In the far northwest corner of Beijing is the wonderful Summer Palace; an imperial retreat that has retained the charm of centuries gone by, it's an excellent place to get away from the smog of the city, and deservedly one of Beijing's most-visited sights. Though eclipsed by its newer neighbour, the "old" Summer Palace of Yuanmingyuan – destroyed by European forces in 1860 – also merits a visit, if only for the contrast provided by its ruins. From here, it's not too far to Dazhong Temple, or by bus to the Botanical Gardens, Xiangshan Park and other excursions to the west of Beijing (see p.113). Continuing east will bring you to the area redeveloped for the 2008 Olympics, though it's somewhat neglected since that heady summer. East again, and on the way to the airport, is the quirky 798 Art District – somewhere to explore China's contemporary art movement.

The Summer Palace

颐和园, yíhé yuán • Daily 8am–7pm, buildings close at 5pm • Park entry ¥30, including access to Paiyun Dian, Foxiang Ge and Dehe Yuan ¥60 • ☎ 010 62881144 • Subway line #4 to Xiyuan (for the East Gate; Exit C2) or Beigongmen (for the North Gate; Exit D); also accessible by boat (see box opposite)

Now an immensely attractive public park, the **Summer Palace** still retains the air of the lavish imperial playground it once was, when the Qing court would abandon their Forbidden City and decamp to this perfect location during Beijing's sweltering summers. Spread around the shores of **Kunming Lake**, overlooked by the wooded, pagoda-studded heights of **Wanshou Hill** and with views stretching off into the countryside, it's huge enough to absorb the bustling crowds that nowadays flock here throughout the year. Many of the palace edifices are intimately linked with the **Empress Dowager Cixi** (see box, p.99) – anecdotes about whom are the stock output of the numerous tour guides – but to enjoy the site, you need know very little of its history: the whole complex forms a startling visual array, akin to a traditional Chinese landscape painting brought to life.

Brief history

There have been imperial summer pavilions at the Summer Palace since the eleventh century, although the present park layout is essentially eighteenth-century, created by the Manchu Emperor Qianlong. However, the key character associated with the palace is the **Dowager Empress Cixi**. The Summer Palace was very much her pleasure ground; it was she who restored the buildings here in 1888 after the originals were desecrated by Anglo-French forces during the Opium Wars – a fact echoed by almost every sign here – and later used them to imprison her nephew, the luckless emperor Guangxu.

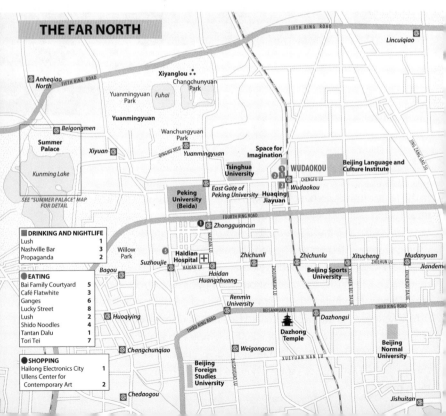

THE FAR NORTH

DRINKING AND NIGHTLIFE

Lush	1
Nashville Bar	3
Propaganda	2

EATING

Bai Family Courtyard	5
Café Flatwhite	3
Ganges	6
Lucky Street	8
Lush	2
Shido Noodles	4
Tantan Dalu	1
Tori Tei	7

SHOPPING

Hailong Electronics City	1
Ullens Center for Contemporary Art	2

BY BOAT TO THE SUMMER PALACE

The fastest route to the Summer Palace is by subway, but there's also a **boat service** from Huangdichuan wharf (皇帝船码头, huángdìchuán mǎtóu; departures hourly 10am–4pm; ¥40), tucked away behind the Beijing Exhibition Centre just east of Beijing Zoo, that takes the old imperial approach along the now dredged and prettified Long River. Your vessel is either one of the large, dragon-shaped cruisers or a smaller speedboat holding four people, passing the Wuta Temple, Zizhuyuan Park, and a number of attractive bridges and willow groves en route.

6

The palace compound

City buses, most tours and those coming via Xiyuan subway station will enter via the **East Gate**, which brings you straight to the main palace compound. Those arriving at Beigongmen subway station will enter through the **North Gate**, on the other side of Wanshou Hill; from here, it's a walk of around 1km – either through the woods or over the hill via Zhihuihai – to the palace compound.

Renshou Dian

The strange bronze animal in the first courtyard is a *kylin* (with the head of a dragon, deer antlers, a lion's tail and ox hooves), said to be able to detect disloyal subjects. The building behind is the **Renshou Dian** (Hall of Benevolence and Longevity), a majestic, multi-eaved hall where the empress and her predecessors gave audience; it retains much of its original nineteenth-century furniture, including an imposing red sandalwood throne carved with nine dragons and flanked

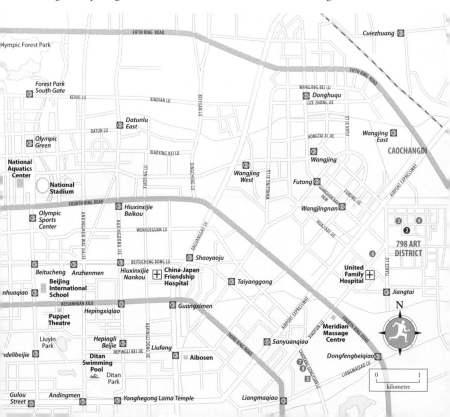

by peacock feather fans. The inscription on the tablet above reads "Benevolence in rule leads to long life". Look out, too, for the superbly well-made basket of flowers studded with precious stones.

Dehe Yuan

¥5, or included in full-priced entry ticket

The **Dehe Yuan** (Palace of Virtue and Harmony) is dominated by a three-storey theatre, complete with trap doors in the stage for surprise appearances and disappearances by the actors. Theatre was one of Cixi's main passions – she even took part in performances, playing the role of Guanyin, the goddess of compassion. Today some of the halls function as a **theatre museum**, with displays of costumes, props and waxworks of Cixi and attendants. The most unusual exhibit is a vintage Mercedes-Benz car, a gift to the warlord Yuan Shikai (see p.179) in the early twentieth century and the first car to appear in China.

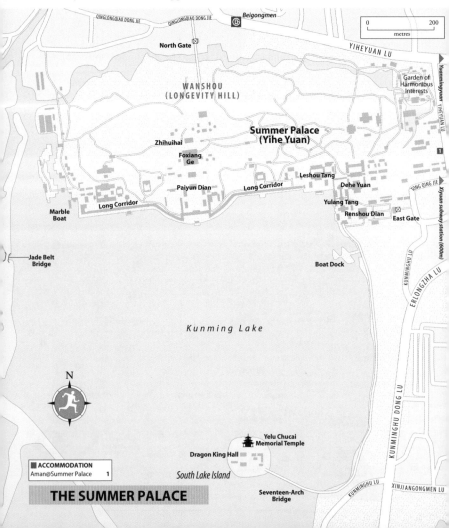

THE SUMMER PALACE

EMPRESS DOWAGER CIXI

Born in 1835 to a minor Manchu official, **Cixi** entered the imperial palace aged fifteen as Emperor Xianfeng's concubine, quickly becoming his favourite and bearing him a son, Tongzhi. A palace coup in 1860 saw her rise to power, and when Xianfeng died the following year she became regent to Tongzhi, ruling in his place through a ruthless mastery of intrigue and court politics. When, after a life of dissipation and debauchery, Tongzhi himself died of smallpox in 1874, she installed her nephew Guangxu as a puppet ruler and continued on as regent, concentrating all real imperial power in her hands as Empress Dowager. In 1898, Guangxu made an attempt to depose his aunt by supporting the **Hundred Days Reform movement** – which, among other things, sought to introduce a constitutional monarchy – but Cixi enlisted the help of the duplicitous warlord Yuan Shikai, had the movement's ringleaders executed, and imprisoned Guangxu in the Summer Palace for much of the rest of his life.

With foreign powers taking great chunks out of China's borders through the latter part of the nineteenth century, Cixi was moved to respond by supporting the xenophobic **Boxer Rebellion** (see p.178), which laid siege to Beijing's foreign legation quarter. But the Boxers were defeated, Beijing was looted by foreign armies and Cixi and Guangxu disguised themselves as peasants and fled to Xi'an. On her return two years later Cixi clung to power, despite an almost total loss of prestige outside the palace, attempting to delay the inevitable fall of the Qing dynasty. One of her last acts before she died in 1908 was to arrange for Guangxu's murder.

Cixi's reign and personality have received mixed press over the years, from the British authorities of the time, who likened her to a rather sinister version of Queen Victoria, to author Jung Chang's worshipful recent reappraisal, *Empress Dowager Cixi*. Overall, there's little doubt that Cixi's fondness of extravagance drained the state's coffers, and her deeply conservative policies were inappropriate for a time when the nation was calling out for reform.

Yulang Tang

The large, lakeside **Yulang Tang** (Jade Waves Palace) is where the Emperor Guangxu was kept in captivity (see box above); the pair of "mother and son" rocks in the front courtyard were put there by Cixi to chastise Guangxu for being unfilial. The main hall contains a tablet of Cixi's calligraphy, reading "The magnificent palace inspires everlasting moral integrity". One character has a stroke missing; apparently no one dared tell her.

Leshou Tang

North of Yulang Tang, behind Renshou Dian, are Cixi's private quarters, three large courtyards connected by a winding gallery. The largest, the **Leshou Tang** (Hall of Joy and Longevity), houses Cixi's hardwood throne and was where she took her infamous meals of 128 courses. The chandeliers were **China's first electric lights**, installed in 1903 and powered by the palace's own generator.

The north shore of Kunming Lake

From Leshou Tang, the **Long Corridor** leads to the northwest corner of Kunming Lake. Flanked by various temples and pavilions, the corridor is actually a 700m covered way, its inside walls painted with more than eight thousand restored images of birds, flowers, landscapes and scenes from history and mythology. Near its western end is Cixi's ultimate flight of fancy, a magnificent lakeside pavilion in the form of a 36m-long **marble boat**, boasting two decks. Completed using funds intended for China's Northern Navy, it was regarded by Cixi's acolytes as an ironic snub to her detractors, though probably contributed to the fleet's heavy defeat during the 1895 war with Japan. Close to the marble boat is a jetty – the tourist focus of this part of the site – with **rowing boats** for hire (see box, p.100).

Wanshou Hill

About halfway down the Long Corridor you'll see an archway and a path that leads away from the lake to climb **Wanshou Hill**, whose slopes are covered in mature pine woodland. Passing through two gates you enter **Paiyun Dian** (Cloud Dispelling Hall;

6

¥20, or included in full-priced entry ticket), which was used by Cixi as a venue for her extravagant birthday parties. The elegant objects on display here are twentieth-birthday presents to her from high officials (the rather flattering oil painting of her was a gift from the American artist Hubert Vos). Near the top of the hill, **Foxiang Ge** (Tower of Buddhist Incense; ¥10, or included in full-priced entry ticket) is a charming three-storey octagonal pagoda built in 1750, which commands a panoramic view of the whole park; the area around it is a popular picnic spot.

The impressive **Zhihuihai** (Sea of Wisdom), a hall at the top of the hill, is an unusual stone cube tiled in a rich green and yellow and dotted with niches holding ceramic Buddha statuettes (many beheaded, most likely during the 1960s). Inside, the gloomy, narrow interior contains a large, beatific statue of Guanyin flanked by the Bodhisattvas Wenshu (representing wisdom) and Puxian (philanthropy).

Garden of Harmonious Interests

At the foot of the hill on the far (north) side lies the little-visited back lake. Walk east along the side of this lake for 500m and you arrive at the **Garden of Harmonious Interests**, a pretty collection of lotus-filled ponds and pavilions connected by bridges. Cixi used to fish from the large central pavilion; to keep her sweet, eunuchs dived in and attached fish to her hook. One bridge is called "Know the Fish Bridge" after an argument between the famous Chinese philosopher Zhuangzi and his friend Huizi: Zhuangzi declared that the fish he could see were happy; Huizi snorted, "How could you know? You're not a fish", whereupon Zhuangzi countered, "You're not me, so how do you know I don't know?"

The south of the park

The scenery is wilder and the crowds thinner at the southern part of Kunming Lake. The obvious attraction is the white **Seventeen-Arch Bridge**, 150m long and topped with 544 cute, vaguely canine lions, each with a slightly different posture. The bridge leads to **South Lake Island**, where Qianlong used to review his navy, and which holds a brace of fine halls, most striking of which is the **Yelu Chucai Memorial Temple**. Yelu, an adviser to Genghis Khan during the Yuan dynasty, is entombed nearby, in the company of his wives and concubines, slaughtered for the occasion. The small, colourful **Dragon King Hall** nearby was used to pray for rain.

Yuanmingyuan

圆明园, yuánmíng yuán • Qinghua Xilu • Daily 8am–6pm, buildings close at 5pm • Park entry ¥10, all-inclusive ticket ¥25 • Boat tours ¥20 • ☎ 010 62628501 • Subway line #4 to Yuanmingyuan (Exit B)

...after pillaging it, [we] burned the whole place, destroying in a vandal-like manner most valuable property, which could not be replaced for millions... you can scarcely imagine the beauty and magnificence of the palaces we burned... it was a scene of utter destruction which passes my description.

Captain Charles Gordon

Beijing's original summer palace, the elegant, European-style **Yuanmingyuan** was designed by Jesuit architects during the early eighteenth century for the Emperor Kangxi. Once nicknamed China's Versailles, it boasted the largest royal gardens in the world, containing some two hundred pavilions and temples set around a series of lakes and natural springs.

BOATING AND SKATING ON KUNMING LAKE

Boating on Kunming Lake is a great way to appreciate the site from a distance (boats or pedaloes can be hired at various jetties for ¥60/hr, plus ¥300 deposit). In winter, the Chinese **skate** on the lake here – a spectacular sight, as some of the participants are really proficient. Skates are available for rent by the lakeside (¥10/hr).

Today the extensive landscaped gardens remain, but every building on the site – including the main palace complex – was **destroyed** by Anglo-French forces in 1860, in retaliation for mistreatment of British prisoners during the Opium Wars (see p.177). As witnessed by Charles "China" Gordon, the foreign troops had previously looted the imperial treasures, an unedifying history described on signs all over the park.

There are **three separate sections** to Yuanmingyuan, together forming a gigantic area of lotus ponds, islands, willow-fringed walkways and decorative arched bridges. For the most impressive ruins – those of the main palace buildings, Xiyanglou – head up to the park's northeast.

6

Xiyanglou

西洋楼, xīyáng lóu · ¥20, or part of all-inclusive ticket

Xiyanglou lies straight up through the centre of the park, about 1.5km from the entrance. Here, richly carved stone columns, architraves and fountains, all embellished in a fusion of European Rococo style and Chinese motifs, lie smashed to pieces and tumbled about in piles – or, in a few cases, have been painstakingly reassembled. Most complete (extensive reconstruction was underway at the time of writing) are the maze and its central pavilion, and the former decorative entranceway. On-site photos and drawings show the palace's original layout, before its destruction.

Peking University (Beida)

北京大学, běijīng dàxué · Haidian · Free, though you may be asked for ID · ⓦ english.pku.edu.cn · Subway line #4 to East Gate of Peking University (Exit D or A)

On the way to or from the Summer Palace, you may care to stop by China's most prestigious university, known by all and sundry by the contraction "**Beida**". Besides its academic acumen, its well-maintained campus, full of old buildings and gardens, make it nicer than most of the city's parks. The **lake** is a popular place to skate in the winter – you can rent skates for ¥10 an hour.

Originally established by Americans during the early twentieth century, the university stood in Jingshan Park before moving to its present site in 1953. Half-deserted during the Cultural Revolution (see p.180), it became a power base for the radical left in their campaign against the reformer Deng Xiaoping in 1975. The university's intake again suffered during the post-1989 clampdowns, but now Beida is once again home to China's brightest academics – and a sizeable population of foreign students, primarily here to learn Mandarin.

Dazhong Temple

大钟寺, dàzhōng sì · Beisanhuan Xilu · Tues–Sun 9am–4.30pm · ¥20 · Subway line #13 to Dazhongsi (Exit A)

Dazhong Temple houses an odd collection of several hundred **bronze bells**, collected from temples all over the country and works of art in their own right, their surfaces embossed with texts in Chinese and Tibetan, abstract patterns and images of auspicious beasts. The scaly, dragon-like creature shown perching on top of each bell is a *pulao*, a legendary animal supposed to shriek when attacked by a whale (the wooden hammers used to strike the bells are carved to look like whales). The history of Chinese bell-making, with English captions, is covered in the side halls; the shape of Chinese bells dampens vibrations, so they only sound for a short time and can be used as instruments (the shop sells CDs).

Make sure you head to the back hall, where you'll find a Ming creation called the **King of Bells**, after which the temple is named (*dazhong* means "big bell"). As tall as a two-storey house and weighing 46 tonnes, it can reputedly be heard up to 15km away. Climb a platform above it to get a closer look at some of the 250,000 Chinese characters on its surface, and join visitors in trying to throw a coin into the small hole in the top for good luck.

Olympic Park

奥林匹克公园, àolínpǐkè gōngyuán • Subway line #8 or #15 to Olympic Park (Exit A2), or line #8 to Forest Park South Gate (exits A or B)

China used the 2008 Olympics to make an impact on the world stage, and facilities built for the occasion were accordingly lavish. The **Olympic Park** – a 1.5km-long strip of concrete paving with the outstanding **National Stadium** and **Aquatics Centre** at one end, and the entrance to the **Forest Park** at the other – was placed on the city's north–south axis, to be bang in line with the Forbidden City. In addition, subway line #8 (eight being a highly auspicious number in China) was built for the occasion.

6

National Stadium

奥林匹克体育馆, àolínpǐkè tǐyùguǎn • Daily: April–Oct 8.30am–7pm; Nov–March 9am–5.30pm • General entry ¥50, full ticket ¥110

Centrepiece of the Olympic Park is the 90,000-seat **National Stadium**, nicknamed the "**Bird's Nest**" on account of its exterior steel lattice. It was built at a cost of over US$400m by Herzog & de Meuron, with design input from artistic dissident Ai Weiwei. The stadium made a grand stage for many memorable events, including the spectacular opening display, but since the Olympics it hasn't seen much use beyond hosting concerts and football games; it's eventually expected to become part of a larger shopping and event complex. The general entry ticket covers a museum with displays about the building's construction and closing ceremonies; the full ticket allows access to the steel "Bird's Nest" structure, from where you can look down into the stadium.

National Aquatics Center

国家游泳中心, guójiā yóuyǒng zhōngxīn • Daily: April–Oct 9am–8pm; Nov–March 9am–5.30pm • ¥30 • Swimming pool Mon–Fri 12.30–5.30pm, Sat & Sun 9am–5.30pm; 2hr maximum stay • ¥60

Next door to the National Stadium, the **National Aquatics Center** quickly became known as the **Water Cube**, thanks to its bubble-like exterior membrane. Part of it is now occupied by the **Beijing Watercube Waterpark**, which – though expensive – is a lot of fun. There are several recreational pools with wave machines, water slides and diving boards; and also an Olympic-sized competition pool.

Forest Park

奥林匹克森林公园, àolínpǐkè sēnlín gōngyuán • Daily: March 15 to Nov 15 6am–9pm; Nov 16 to March 14 6am–8pm • Free • Subway line #8 to Forest Park South Gate (Exits A or B)

Some 1.5km north from the sports facilities along a sterile, blazing concrete corridor (catch the subway) lies a real oasis of picturesque calm, the **Forest Park**: 680 hectares of recently landscaped woodland, lotus lakes and bright, colourful flowerbeds, divided into north and south sections by the Fifth Ring Road. You could spend a pleasant few hours wandering around the footpaths here – there are marked walking circuits of 3–10km in length – and, as very few people get past the entrance area, it's easy to have a quiet time.

798 Art District

798艺术区, qījiǔbā yìshùqū • Daily 24hr, though many galleries close on Mon • Free • ⓦ 798district.com • Bilingual maps available from a stall at the entrance • Subway line #14 to Jiangtai (Exit B), then walk north for 15min

Though it's way out en route to the airport, the **798 Art District** – a collection of more than a hundred galleries and studios – is a magnet for Beijing's arty crowd. Originally this suburb-sized complex was an electronics factory, built by East Germans; when that closed down in the 1990s, artists moved in and converted the airy, light and, above all, cheap spaces into studios. Though the government initially wanted to shut this bohemian area down, it survived to become an established focus for China's modern art movement, even if much of what is here today is unashamedly commercial and populist rather than avant-garde. Still, browsing here is a lot of fun, even more so when you uncover original-minded work or exhibitions, and the actual quality on show is high – as are prices.

798 has the feel of a campus, with a grid of pedestrianized, tree-lined streets dotted with wacky sculptures – a caged dinosaur, a forlorn gorilla – and the gnarliness of the industrial buildings (those in "Power Square" are particularly brutal) softened by artsy graffiti. Exhibitions open every week and all art forms are represented, from installations by international artists such as Antony Gormley, to modern Chinese ceramics and traditional calligraphy. Note that unlike most Beijing attractions, it's actually better at the weekend, when there's a real buzz about the place; on weekdays it can feel a little dead – especially on **Mondays** when most galleries are closed. If you're here in spring, don't miss the **798 Art Festival**, usually scheduled for April – check the website for details.

Caochangdi

曹场地, cǎochǎngdì • Off the Airport Expressway, near the Fifth Ring Rd • Free • Subway line #14 to Jiangtai (Exit B), then catch a cab (¥10)

If the 798 Art District is just too commercial for you, head to **Caochangdi**, a couple of kilometres further towards the airport. This overspill gallery area, away from the tourists and boutiques, is where the hard-core avant-gardists escaped to when 798 became too mainstream for them – though it's increasingly becoming the place for parties and hype. Many of the spaces here were designed by artsy provocateur Ai Weiwei.

BEST GALLERIES AT 798 AND CAOCHANGDI

798

Beijing Commune 北京公社 běijīng gōngshè ☏010 84562862, ⊛beijingcommune.com. Small place renowned for its imaginatively curated shows. Tues–Sun 10am–6pm.

Galleria Continua 常青画廊 chángqīng huàláng ☏010 59789505, ⊛galleriacontinua.com. Beijing branch of Italian gallery, hosting international and home-grown art stars across three floors' worth of space. They tend to choose artists "with something to say", and rotate exhibitions 3–5 times per year. Tues–Sun 11am–6pm.

Long March Space 长征空间 chángzhēng kōngjiān ☏010 59789768, ⊛longmarchspace .com. This space is popular for its attempts to reach out to the masses with education programmes (as its name hints). Tues–Sun 11am–7pm.

Tokyo Gallery+ 东京艺术工程 dōngjīng yìshùgōngchéng ☏010 59784838, ⊛tokyo -gallery.com. The first gallery to set up shop here, and still one of the best, with a large, elegant space for challenging shows. Tues–Sun 10.30am–5pm.

Platform China 站台中国, zhàntái zhōngguó ☏010 57626068, ⊛platformchina.org. This gallery encourages international exchanges but is keen on promoting new Chinese talent; one recent exhibition featured Wang Xingwei's Goya-like canvases of very Chinese subjects. Tues–Sun 10am–6pm.

Ullens Centre for Contemporary Art 尤伦斯当代艺术中心 yóulúnsī dāngdài yìshùzhōngxīn ☏010 59780200, ⊛ucca.org.cn. This huge non-profit space is more of a museum than a gallery; nothing is for sale and it is the only place that charges an entrance fee. There are three exhibition halls and a programme of regular events (all detailed on the website). Daily 10am–7pm; ¥60 (online tickets ¥50).

White Space 空白空间 kòngbái kōngjiān ☏010 84562054, ⊛whitespace-beijing.com. This well-run space has a reputation for putting on challenging shows by up-and-coming Chinese artists. Tues–Sun 10am–6pm.

CAOCHANGDI

Beijing Art Now Gallery (BANG) 北京现在画廊, běijīng xiànzài huàláng ☏010 51273292, ⊛beijingartnow.com. Located on a lakeshore, this gallery has long been a driving force behind China's contemporary art scene, supporting the likes of Zhang Fazhi, Yang Shaobin and Fang Lijun. Tues–Sun noon–6pm.

Pékin Fine Arts 北京艺门, běijīng yìmén ☏010 51273220, ⊛pekinfinearts.com/en. High-profile gallery showcasing upmarket commercial work by a range of artists from across Asia, though naturally with a keen China focus. Tues–Sun 10am–6pm.

Three Shadows Photography 三影堂, sānyǐng táng ☏010 64322663, ⊛threeshadows.cn. This Ai Weiwei-created space is the only dedicated photographic gallery in Beijing, featuring an exhibition area, library and darkrooms. Tues–Sun 10am–6pm.

6

Around Beijing

Some inviting destinations, offering both countryside and culture, lie within a few hours of the capital. Most compelling is the Great Wall, whose remains, either unrestored and crumbling or spruced up for tour groups, can be seen in a number of places in the hills north of the city. Most people heading out this way also take in the renowned Ming Tombs, and though these have more in the way of associations than real sights, it's a good spot for a picnic. West of the capital, and easily accessible from the centre, lies the undulating, wooded landscape known as the Western Hills; dotted with temples, it is a refreshing retreat from Beijing's summertime climate. The striking Fahai, Tanzhe and Jietai temples are out this way too, as is the unusual Tianyi Tomb, with its disturbing Eunuch Museum.

Equally confrontational, perhaps, is the modern **Sino-Japanese War Museum** in Beijing's southwestern suburbs, though the far older **Marco Polo Bridge** nearby is a more obvious target. Much further afield, there's a choice between trips to the antique village of **Cuandixia**, the city of **Tianjin** – totally different in character from the capital, though only a brief high-speed train ride away – and semi-rural **Chengde**, with its vast spread of imperial hunting grounds and collection of Qing architecture.

The Great Wall

长城, chángchéng

This is a Great Wall, and only a great people with a great past could have a great wall, and such a great people with such a great wall will surely have a great future.

Richard M. Nixon

Stretching from Shanhaiguan, by the Yellow Sea, to Jiayuguan Pass in the Gobi Desert – a distance of around three thousand kilometres (or, according to a recent survey taking in all the disconnected sections, over 20,000km) – the **Great Wall** is an astonishing feat of engineering. The practice of walling off the country's northern frontier began in the fifth century BC and continued until the sixteenth century, creating a broken ribbon of fortifications which came to be known as **Wan Li Changcheng** (roughly, "Long Wall of Ten Thousand Miles") – "the Great Wall" to English-speakers. Today, it's a source of great national pride, and also big business: restored sections are besieged daily by rampaging hordes of tourists, while its image adorns all manner of products, from wine to cigarettes.

For all this, even the most blatantly commercial and overrun section at **Badaling** is still easily one of China's most spectacular sights. The section at **Mutianyu** is somewhat less crowded; distant **Simatai** much less so, and more beautiful. To see the wall in its crumbling glory, head out to **Jingshanling**, **Jiankou** or **Huanghua**, as yet largely untouched by development. For trips to other unreconstructed sections, check out ⓦwildwall.com.

Badaling

八达岭, bādálǐng • Daily 7am–6pm • ¥45 • Cable car ¥80

The best-known section of the wall is at **Badaling**, 70km northwest of Beijing. It follows the highest contours of a steep range of hills, forming a formidable defence, so much so that this section was never attacked directly but instead taken by sweeping around from the side after a breach was made in the weaker, low-lying sections.

THE WALL'S LONG HISTORY

The Chinese have walled their cities throughout recorded history, and during the Warring States period (around the fifth century BC) simply extended the practice to separate rival territories. The Great Wall's origins lie in these fractured lines of fortifications and in the vision of the first Emperor **Qin Shi Huang** who, having unified the empire in the third century BC, joined and extended the disparate sections to form one continuous defence against barbarians. It restricted the movement of the nomadic peoples of the distant, non-Han minority regions, preventing plundering raids.

Under subsequent dynasties, whenever insularity rather than engagement drove foreign policy, the wall continued to be maintained. It's the fifteenth-century **Ming wall** that you see today, the 7m-high, 7m-thick barrier crowned in 25,000 battlements: signals made by gunpowder blasts, flags and smoke swiftly sent news of enemy movements to the capital. But a wall is only as strong as its guards, and it was one of these – Wu Sangui – who allowed the Manchu armies through at the end of the Ming dynasty. Disdained by the Qing, the wall slowly crumbled away, and it wasn't until the 1950s that the first stretches were restored and opened up to tourists.

As the most accessible section, Badaling is also the most packaged, and you're greeted on arrival by a giant tourist circus of restaurants and souvenir stalls selling "I climbed the Great Wall" T-shirts. One thing worth a browse here is the **Great Wall Museum** (included in the main ticket), with plenty of aerial photos, models and construction tools. Otherwise it's hard to feel that there's much genuine about the experience; indeed, the wall itself is hardly original here, as the "restorers" basically rebuilt it wholesale on the ancient foundations.

ARRIVAL AND DEPARTURE

BADALING

Many tours arrive in the early afternoon (when the place is at its busiest), spend an hour or two on site and then return, which only allows the most cursory of jaunts. It's just as easy, and cheaper, to travel under your own steam; note that you can also get to/from the Ming Tombs (and Beijing's subway network) from here.

By bus From Deshengmen station in Beijing, near the Jishuitan subway stop, catch bus #877 (1hr; ¥12). From (and to) the Ming tombs, catch bus #879 (50min; ¥8).

By train From Beijing North station (13 daily; 1hr 15min); the wall entrance is a 2km walk from Badaling station. Services depart Beijing 6am–9.30pm, and from Badaling 8.20am–9.30pm.

BEIJING AND AROUND

7

GREAT WALL TOURS

While you can get to the wall on your own, most Beijing accommodation can organize a day-trip to Badaling, Mutianyu or Simatai sections, often including the Ming Tombs, for ¥250–450 per person. The cost depends on the section involved, whether lunch is part of the package, and whether you spend half the trip at souvenir markets along the way (many low-paid guides top up their wages with commissions). Trips are either in a taxi or small minivan (probably with a minimum of two passengers), or you'll be packed off with an agency tour. Some hostels also offer **hiking** and overnight camping trips to less-visited sections from about ¥340; or contact Beijing Hikers (ⓦbeijinghikers.com), who are expensive individually but might be able to tack you on to an existing tour.

If you're just here for the day, you can avoid high on-site prices by bringing your own food and drink. At all the less-visited places, expect to be followed along the wall by a villager selling drinks, for at least an hour; if you don't want to be pestered, make it very clear from the outset that you are not interested in anything they are selling – though after a few kilometres you might find that ¥5 can of Coke very welcome.

ACCOMMODATION

Cao's Courtyard 曹家四合院客栈, cáojiā sìhéyuàn kèzhàn. 18 Chadao Village, Yanqing ☎1851 4663311. Pleasant, low-key compound-style hotel with simple but comfortable en-suite rooms – and, of course, a courtyard terrace. It's only a short walk from the train station, and about 10min from the wall. **¥280**

Commune by the Great Wall 长城脚下的公社, chángchéng jiǎoxiàde gōngshè. By the Shuiguan Great Wall, 4km east of Badaling ☎010 81181888, ⓦwww.communebythegreatwall.com. Each of the eleven striking buildings was designed by a different architect (the complex won an architectural award at the 2002 Venice Biennale) and is run as a small boutique hotel. It's an incredible setting, though for this price the food is average and the complex itself is looking a little tired throughout. **¥2600**

Juyong Pass

居庸关, jūyōng guān • Daily 8am–5pm • ¥45

The closest section to Beijing, the wall at **Juyong Pass**, only fifteen minutes' bus ride south of the Badaling section, has been rather over-restored by enthusiastic builders. That said, it's not too popular, and thus not too crowded. Strategically, this was an important stretch, guarding the way to the capital, just 50km away. From the two-storey gate, the wall climbs steeply in both directions, passing through modern copies of the mostly Ming fortifications. The most interesting structure, and one of the few genuinely old ones, is the intricately carved stone base of a long-vanished stupa just beyond here. Access to unreconstructed sections is blocked, but you can walk for about an hour in either direction.

ARRIVAL AND DEPARTURE   JUYONG PASS

By bus From Deshengmen bus station in Beijing (near Jishuitan subway stop), catch bus #345, #670 or others to Shahe, then catch a Chang #68 bus to Juyong (total journey 2hr; ¥12).

By train Take a Badaling train from Beijing North station (see p.24), then a Juyong shuttle bus from Badaling station.

Huanghua

黄花长城, huánghuā chángchéng • Daily 8am–4.30pm • ¥45

The section of the wall at **Huanghua**, 60km north of Beijing, dates to 1404 and is a good example of Ming defences, with wide ramparts, intact parapets and beacon towers. It climbs both sides of a steep, V-shaped valley, with its central section submerged by a small reservoir; on arrival, you'll be dropped off on a road that cuts through the wall. The section to the left is too hard to climb, but the section on the right, past the reservoir, shouldn't present too many difficulties for the agile; indeed, the climb gets easier as you go, with the wall levelling off along a ridge.

The wall here is attractively ruined – so watch your step – and its course makes for a pleasant walk through some lovely countryside. Keep going for about 2km, to the seventh tower, and you'll reach some steps that lead south down the wall and onto a stony path. Follow this path down past an ancient barracks to a pumping station, and you'll come to a track that takes you south back to the main road, through a graveyard and orchards. When you hit the road you're about 500m from where you started; head north and after 150m you'll come to a bridge where taxis and buses to Huairou congregate.

ARRIVAL AND DEPARTURE   HUANGHUA

By bus Take bus #916 from Dongzhimen bus station to Huairou (怀柔, huáiróu; ¥12), and then bus #H21 to the reservoir (小西湖, xiǎo xīhú; ¥10). The last bus from Huairou to Beijing is at 7pm.

ACCOMMODATION

Guesthouses Locals rent out spare rooms in their houses, with the usual spartan facilities: hard beds, bare furnishings and only cold water on tap, which they might be able to heat up for you. Most also offer meals. Bargain hard over the rates. **¥50–100**

Mutianyu

慕田峪, mùtiányù • Daily 7am–6pm • ¥45 • Bus from service centre to cable-car station ¥10 • Cable car up ¥80; Slideway down ¥40; combined ¥100

Mutianyu Great Wall, 90km northeast of the city, is the second most popular section, with a huge service centre some 3km from the base of the wall where all transport terminates. However, Mutianyu is geared towards families rather than tour buses and is relatively quiet, with superb ridgetop views of lush, undulating hills crowned by the wall; well-endowed with guard towers, it was built in 1368.

From the entrance, steep steps lead up to the wall; you can get a cable car up (and the toboggan-like Slideway down), though it's not far to walk. The stretch of wall you can walk here is about 3km long, with barriers in both directions to stop you continuing any further.

ARRIVAL AND DEPARTURE   MUTIANYU

However you reach Mutianyu, returning by other means shouldn't be a hassle, provided you do so before 6pm; plenty of minibuses wait in the car park to take people back to the city. If you can't find a minibus back to Beijing, get one to the town of Huairou (怀柔, huáiróu) from where you can get regular bus #916 back to the capital – the last bus leaves at 6.30pm.

By bus Take bus #916 from Dongzhimen to Huairou (1hr; ¥12); get off at Mingzhu Square, where you can catch a shuttle bus (¥5) or minibus (¥50 per person) to the wall.

ACCOMMODATION AND EATING

★**Brickyard Retreat** 瓦厂, wǎ chǎng. The Schoolhouse, 12 Mutianyu village ☎010 61626506, ⓦ brickyardmutianyu.com. Former schoolhouse and tile factory now converted into a charming restaurant and boutique guesthouse; the comfortable rooms feature industrial chic brick and tile decor, plus big windows with views of mountains and the (distant) Great Wall. No TV or phones in rooms. The restaurant serves hearty Chinese and Western dishes, made largely with home-grown ingredients. **¥1600**

Shambhala@the Great Wall 新红资避暑山庄, xīnhóngzī bìshǔ shānzhuāng. Xiaguandi village, near Huairou, about 2hr north of Beijing ☎010 84018886, ⓦ shambhalaserai.com. This former hunting lodge is now an idyllic boutique hotel, set in attractive countryside. Each of the ten traditional courtyard buildings was constructed from local materials, with a mix of Chinese, Tibetan and Manchu themes; the rooms, all protected by a stone animal, feature Qing-style carved beds. There's also an on-site spa for some serious pampering, and the place is a short walk from the Great Wall. **¥850**

Jiankou

箭扣, jiànkòu • Daily 7am–5pm • No official entry fee; villagers charge ¥20 to enter the drop-off hub at Xizhai village (see opposite)

A fairly intrepid destination is **Jiankou**, about 30km northwest of Huairou town (怀柔, huáiróu), itself north of Beijing. The wall here is white, as it's made of **dolomite**, and there is a **hikeable** and very picturesque section that winds through thickly forested mountain. Don't make the trip without a local guide; much of the stonework is loose on the wall, which is a little tricky to find in the first place. You really need to watch your step, and some nerve-racking sections are so steep that they have to be climbed on all fours.

Hiking Jiankou

You need to be in good shape to **hike** the full 20km track at Jiankou; also be aware that the path has been **blocked off** at one of the watchtowers and that edging around this, with a long drop below, is extremely dangerous. The far western end of the hike starts at **Nine Eye Tower**, one of the biggest watchtowers on the wall, and named after its nine peepholes. It's a tough 12km from here to the **Beijing Knot** – a watchtower where three walls come together (and, incidentally, the flattest area to set up a tent). Around here the views are spectacular, and for the next kilometre or so the hiking is easier, at least until you reach a steep section called "Eagle Flies Vertically". Though theoretically you can scale this, then carry on for another 10km to Mutianyu, it is not recommended; the hike gets increasingly dangerous and includes some almost vertical climbs, such as the notorious "sky stairs".

7

ARRIVAL AND DEPARTURE   JIANKOU

While Jiankou is just about feasible as a day-trip from Beijing, realistically you'll need to either camp up on the wall, or stay to the north at the transit point of Xizhai village (西栅子, xīzhàzi), where you can pick up guides.

By bus Catch bus #867 or #936 from Dongzhimen to Yujiayuan (于家园, yújiā yuán; ¥13), from where there are 2 buses daily to Xizhai (¥8), at 11.30am & 4.30pm.

ACCOMMODATION

Jiankou Zhao's Hostel 箭扣赵家, jiànkòu zhào jiā. Near the car park in Xizhai village ☎ 010 89696677. Plenty of local farmers rent out rooms, but it's recommended that you call in at this spartan but clean hostel. Mr Zhao is full of information on the hike, and will either guide you himself or sort out someone else to do it. The home-cooked food, incidentally, is excellent – ask if he has any trout. Dorms **¥15**, rooms **¥70**

Simatai

司马台, sīmǎtái • Daily 8am–4pm & 6–9pm • ¥40 • Cable car ¥20 • Gubei old town ¥180

Some 110km northeast of Beijing, **Simatai** fulfils most visitors' expectations of the Great Wall: a pale ribbon snaking across purple hills, with crumpled blue mountains in the distance. It sports a few late innovations such as spaces for cannon, with the inner walls at right angles to the outer wall to thwart invaders who breached the first defence. A rather more modern intrusion is the construction of waterside **Gubei** (古北水镇, gǔběi shuǐ zhèn), also known as Water Town, a generic – though surprisingly convincing – "old town" which serves as the gateway to Simatai.

From Gubei, a winding path takes you up to the wall, where most visitors turn right. Regularly spaced watchtowers allow you to measure your progress uphill along the ridge. The walk over the ruins isn't an easy one, and gets increasingly precipitous – but with better views – after about the tenth watchtower. After the fourteenth tower (2hr on), the wall peters out and the climb becomes quite dangerous – don't go any further.

Note that because of the new lake and the blocking-off of one of the towers en route, you can **no longer hike** to Jinshanling.

ARRIVAL AND DEPARTURE   SIMATAI

The journey out from the capital to Simatai takes about 3hr by private transport. It's easiest to arrange a tour all the way from Beijing; you can travel here independently, but this is only worth doing if you want to stay for a night or two.

By bus Take bus #980 from Dongzhimen to Miyun (密云, mìyún; ¥15), and then bus Mi37, Mi50 or Mi51 to Simatai village; alternatively, you can take a taxi from Miyun, which costs over ¥100 return.
By taxi A rented taxi will cost about ¥850 return, including a wait.

7

ACCOMMODATION AND EATING

For **food**, head to one of the nameless places at the side of the car park, where the owners can whip up some very creditable dishes; if you're lucky, they'll have some locally caught wild game in stock.

Dongpo 东坡农家乐园, dōngpō nóngjiā lèyuán. 250m north of the wall ☎1361 3143252 (no English spoken and erratic mobile signal). One of many similar "farmhouse"-style options run by locals, with simple facilities; one room has a traditional *kang* (heated brick bed), and there's a shared bathroom with solar hot water. Ask about the short hike from the guesthouse to Wangjing tower. They also offer free pick-up from the Jinshanling service centre (see below). Book in advance. **¥300**

Jinshanling

金山岭长城, jīnshānlǐng chángchéng • Daily 8am–5pm • ¥65 • Cable car ¥40

Jinshanling, about 135km from Beijing and not far west of Simatai, is one of the least visited and best preserved parts of the wall, with jutting obstacle walls and oval watchtowers, some with octagonal or sloping roofs.

Turn left along the wall and you soon encounter a largely unreconstructed section, allowing you to experience something of the wall's magnitude; a long and lonely road that unfailingly picks the toughest line between peaks. Take the hike seriously, as you are scrambling up and down steep, crumbly inclines, and you need to be sure of foot. Eventually you reach a **blocked watchtower**, where you'll have to turn back; note that in any case the new lake makes it impossible to reach Simatai – a once-popular hike.

Alternatively, if you head right when you get onto the wall at Jinshanling, you quickly reach an utterly abandoned and overgrown section. After about four hours' walk along here, you'll reach a road that cuts through the wall, and from here you can flag down a passing bus back to Beijing. This route is only recommended for the intrepid.

ARRIVAL AND DEPARTURE

JINSHALING

By bus From outside Wangjing West subway station in Beijing (line #13 or #15), catch a bus to Luanping (滦平, luánpíng; every 40min 7am–4.30pm; ¥32) and get out at the Jinshanling service centre. There are a handful of free shuttle buses daily from the service centre to the wall, or simply hike 2km.

The Ming Tombs

十三陵, shísān líng • Subway line #8 to Zhuxinzhuang and then catch the Changping line to the Ming Tombs station, from where there's a shuttle bus for the final 4km • To reach Badaling from the tombs, catch bus #879 (50min; ¥8)

After their deaths, all but three of the sixteen Ming-dynasty emperors were entombed in giant underground vaults in a valley 50km northwest of Beijing. The site – known in English as the **Ming Tombs** – was chosen by the third Ming emperor, Yongle, for its beautiful scenery of gentle hills and woods, still one of the loveliest landscapes around the capital. Two of the tombs, Chang Ling and Ding Ling, were restored in the 1950s, and the site is marked above ground by grand halls, platforms and a spirit way.

That said, there's little to actually see here, and unless you've a strong historical bent a trip probably isn't worth making for its own sake – although the area is a nice place to picnic, and easy to reach from the city or Great Wall at Badaling. To get the most out of a visit, consider spending a full day here, hiking around the smaller tombs further into the hills (you should be able to buy a map of them at the site).

The Spirit Way

神道, shéndào • Daily 7am–7pm • ¥35

The approach to the Ming Tombs, the 7km **Spirit Way**, is the site's most exciting feature, and it's well worth backtracking along from the ticket office. The road

FROM TOP CHANG LING, MING TOMBS (P.112); BISHU MOUNTAIN RESORT, CHENGDE (P.125) >

commences with the **Dahongmen** (Great Red Gate), a triple-entranced triumphal arch, through the central opening of which only the emperor's dead body was allowed to be carried. Beyond, the road is lined with colossal stone statues of animals and men. Alarmingly larger than life, they all date from the fifteenth century and are among the best surviving examples of Ming sculpture. Their precise significance is unclear, although it is assumed they were intended to serve the emperors in their next lives. The animals depicted include the mythological *qilin* (a reptilian beast with deer's horns and a cow's tail) and the horned, feline *xiezhi*, a symbol of righteousness; the human figures are stern military mandarins. Animal statuary reappears at the entrances to several of the tombs, though the structures themselves are something of an anticlimax.

Chang Ling

长陵, cháng líng · Daily 8.30am–5pm · ¥50

At the end of the spirit way stands the tomb of Yongle himself: **Chang Ling**, the earliest at the site. There are plans to excavate the underground chamber – an exciting prospect since the tomb is contemporary with some of the finest buildings of the Forbidden City in the capital. At present, the enduring impression above ground is mainly one of scale – vast courtyards and halls, approached by terraced white marble. Its main feature is the **Hall of Eminent Flowers**, supported by huge columns consisting of individual tree trunks which, it is said, were imported all the way from Yunnan province in China's southwest.

Ding Ling

定陵, dìng líng · Daily 8.30am–5pm · ¥65

The main focus of the Ming Tombs area is **Ding Ling**, the underground tomb-palace of the Emperor Wanli, who ascended the throne in 1573 at the age of 10. Reigning for almost half a century, he began building his tomb when he was 22, in line with common Ming practice, and hosted a grand party within on its completion. The mausoleum, a short distance east of Chang Ling, was opened up in 1956 and found to be substantially intact, revealing the emperor's coffin, flanked by those of two of his empresses, and floors covered with scores of trunks containing imperial robes, gold and silver, and even the imperial cookbooks. Some of the treasures are displayed in the tomb, a huge musty stone vault, undecorated but impressive for its scale; others – having deteriorated after their excavation in 1956, thanks to the poor preservation techniques available at the time – have been replaced by replicas.

Aviation Museum

航空博物馆, hángkōng bówùguǎn · Tues–Sun 8am–5.30pm · Free; two inside halls ¥20 each · ☎ 010 66916919 · Subway line #5 to Tiantongbeiyuan, then bus #643 to the museum; taxi from Ming Tombs ¥45

Some 60km north of Beijing in Xiaotangshan township (小汤山镇, xiǎotāngshān zhèn), the enormous **Aviation Museum** is a fascinating place containing over three hundred aircraft, displayed in a giant hangar inside a hollow mountain and off a runway-like concourse; it's like being in a small airport. The aircraft on show range from the copy of the Wright brothers' plane flown in 1909 by Feng Ru, a pioneering Chinese aviator, to Gulf War helicopter gunships. As well as plenty of fighter planes – many of which saw action in the Korean War – the bomber that flew in China's first atom bomb test is here, as is **Mao's personal jet** (with his teacup and frilly cushions still inside) and the plane that scattered the ashes of the deceased Zhou Enlai, which is covered with wreaths and tributes. But unless you have a special interest in aircraft, it's mainly the sight of these archaic downed machines en masse – like the setting for a J.G. Ballard story – that makes the place memorable.

Longqing Gorge

龙庆峡, lóngqìng xiá • ¥40; ¥140 including escalator, cruise and Flower Cave • Bungee jump ¥150 • Train S2 from Beijing North to Yanqing (延庆镇, yánqìng zhèn), then bus #875

North from Beijing there are vast swathes of new tree growth: the **Great Green Wall**, a long-term re-vegetation project begun in the 1970s to check soil erosion. In the arid landscape beyond this barrier is **Longqing Gorge**, a local recreation spot at the edge of a reservoir some 90km northwest of the capital. This is somewhere to arrange a boat cruise through the fairly impressive gorge, explore gaudily lit caves and go **bungee jumping** – and to ride the **escalator**, which is contained inside the plastic body of a golden dragon up the dam. The main attraction, though, is the **Ice Lantern Festival** held here (late Jan & Feb, sometimes into March), at which groups of artists sculpt ice carvings of cartoon characters, dragons, storks and figures from Chinese popular culture; with coloured lights inside for a gloriously tacky psychedelic effect, they look great at night.

The Western Hills

西山, xīshān

Thanks to their coolness at the height of summer, Beijing's rugged **Western Hills** are somewhere to escape urban life for a while. They were long favoured as a restful retreat by religious men, intellectuals, and even politicians – Mao lived here briefly, and the Politburo assembles here in times of crisis.

The hills are divided into three parks, the nearest to the centre being the **Botanical Gardens**, 6.5km northwest of the Summer Palace. Two kilometres further west, **Xiangshan** is the largest and most impressive of the parks, but just as pretty is **Badachu**, its eight temples strung out along a hillside 2.5km to the south of Xiangshan. The hills take roughly an hour to reach on public transport, and each section really deserves a day to itself.

The Botanical Gardens

植物园, zhíwù yuán • Daily 7.30am–6pm • ¥10; including conservatory and temple ¥50 • ⓦ www.beijingbg.com

The **Botanical Gardens**, just over 5km west of the Summer Palace as the crow flies, feature over two thousand varieties of trees and plants arranged in formal gardens (and usually labelled in English). They're at their prettiest in summer, though the terrain is flat and the landscaping is not as original as in the older parks. The impressive **conservatory** has desert and tropical environments and a lot of fleshy foliage from Yunnan. Behind the **Wofo Temple** is a bamboo garden, from which paths wind off into the hills; one heads northwest to a pretty cherry valley, just under 1km away, where Cao Xueqin is supposed to have written *Dream of Red Mansions* (see p.192).

Wofo Temple

卧佛寺, wòfó sì • Daily 8.30am–4pm • ¥5, or free with Botanical Gardens through ticket (see above)

The gardens' main path leads after 1km to the **Wofo Temple**, whose main hall houses a huge **reclining Buddha**, more than 5m in length and cast in copper. With two giant feet protruding from the end of his painted robe and a pudgy baby-face, calm in repose, he looks rather cute, although he is not actually sleeping but dying – about to enter nirvana. Suitably huge shoes, presented as offerings, are on display around the hall.

ARRIVAL AND DEPARTURE

THE BOTANICAL GARDENS

By bus Bus #331 from outside the Yuanmingyuan (see p.100) travels via the north gate of the Summer Palace to the Western Hills. Bus #360 also heads this way from the zoo.

By subway Take line #4 to Beigongmen; outside Exit A, catch bus #563 or #331 to the gardens.

Xiangshan Park

香山公园, xiāngshān gōngyuán • Daily 6am–6pm • ¥10 • Cable car ¥60 • ⓦ xiangshanpark.com

Two kilometres west of the Botanical Gardens lies **Xiangshan Park**, a range of hills dominated by Incense Burner Peak in its western corner. It's at its best in the autumn (before the sharp November frosts), when the leaves turn red in a massive profusion of colour. Though busy at weekends, the park is too large to appear swamped and is always a good place for a hike and a picnic. Take the path up to the peak (1hr) from where, on clear days, there are magnificent views down towards the Summer Palace and as far as distant Beijing.

Zhao Miao

昭庙, zhāo miào • Daily 7am–4pm • Free with park entry

Right next to the north gate of the park is the **Zhao Miao** (Temple of Brilliance), one of the few temples in the area that escaped vandalism by Western troops in 1860 and 1900. It was built by Qianlong in 1780 in a Tibetan style, designed to make visiting Lamas feel at home.

Biyun Temple

碧云寺, bìyún sì • Daily 8am–5pm • ¥10

Some 400m west of the park's north gate is the superb **Biyun** ("Azure Clouds") **Temple**, a striking building dominated by extraordinary conical stupas. Inside, rather bizarrely, a tomb houses the hat and clothes of **Sun Yatsen** – his body was held here for a while before being moved in 1924. The giant main hall is now a maze of corridors lined with five hundred *arhat* statues, and it's a magical place. The benignly smiling golden figures are all different – some have two heads or sit on animals, one is even pulling his face off.

ARRIVAL AND DEPARTURE   XIANGSHAN PARK

By bus Bus #331 heads here from outside the Yuanmingyuan (see p.100) via the north gate of the Summer Palace, both of which are also on subway line #4.

Bus #360 also travels this way from the zoo.

By subway Take line #4 to Beigongmen; outside Exit A, catch bus #696 or #331 to the park.

ACCOMMODATION

Fragrant Hills Hotel 香山饭店, xiāngshān fàndiàn. Close to the main entrance of Xiangshan Park ☎ 010 62591166, ⓦ www.xsfd.com. This hotel makes a good base for a weekend escape and some in-depth exploration of the Western Hills. A startlingly incongruous sight, the light, airy hotel looks like something between a Tibetan temple and an airport lounge. It was designed by I.M. Pei, also responsible for Beijing's Bank of China building (see p.87). **¥988**

Badachu

八大处, bādàchù • Daily 6am–6.30pm • ¥10; cable car up ¥50; sled down ¥60 • Subway line #1 to Pingguoyuan (Exit C), then bus #972; or bus #347 from the zoo

A forested hill 10km south of Xiangshan Park, **Badachu** ("Eight Great Sites") derives its name from the presence of eight temples here. Fairly small affairs, lying along the path that curls around the hill, the temples and their surroundings are nonetheless quite attractive, at least on weekdays; don't visit at weekends when the place is swamped.

At the base of the path, right outside Lingguang Temple, is an elegant thirteen-storey pagoda holding what is said to be one of **Buddha's teeth**, relocated here from the fourth temple (Dabei), about halfway up the hill. The third temple, little Sanshan Nunnery, is the most pleasant at Badachu, with well-proportioned halls, a goldfish pond, and a relaxing teahouse in the courtyard. Look for the statue of the rarely depicted, boggle-eyed thunder deity Lei Gong inside the main hall here. The other temples make good breaks in the rest of your climb to the summit ridge.

Fahai Temple and Tianyi Tomb

Subway line #1 to Pingguoyuan, then a taxi (¥15–20); or bus #336, #396, #746, #929 or #959 3km to Shougang Xiao stop on Jinding Bei Jie, and then walk uphill along Moshikou Da Jie to either site

Roughly 20km west of the capital, and barely a kilometre apart are **Fahai Temple**, which sports some impressive frescoes, and the **Tianyi Tomb**, dedicated to a Ming-dynasty palace eunuch, which hosts a disturbing **museum**. Though it's straightforward enough to reach the area, both sites sit among a crowded network of narrow market streets, and it's unlikely that a taxi will be able to get all the way there. Expect to walk for at least 1km, asking directions as you go.

Fahai Temple

法海寺, fǎhǎi sì • North off Moshikou Da Jie • Daily 9am–5pm • Free entry; ¥100 to see the real frescoes, ¥20 to see copies

Though its exterior is unremarkable, **Fahai Temple** is worth a visit for its beautifully vibrant, richly detailed **Buddhist frescoes**. The halls where the frescoes are painted are rather dark, so you're issued with a small torch at the entrance, but if you've got a decent one of your own then take it along. The lively, expressive images, painted in the 1440s, depict the pantheon of Buddhist deities travelling for a meeting. Look out for the elegant god of music, Sarasvati, whose swaying form seems appropriately melodic, and the maternal-looking god of children, Haritidem, with her attendant babies. There are plenty of animals, too; as well as the rather dog-like lions, look out for the six-tusked elephant (a symbol of the Bodhisattva Puxian) – each tusk represents a quality required for the attainment of enlightenment.

7

Tianyi Tomb

田义墓, tiányì mù • 80 Moshikou Da Jie • Daily 9am–4pm • ¥8

The **Tianyi Tomb** is that of an influential Ming-dynasty palace **eunuch** and power-broker who became a favourite of the emperor Wanli. He was buried here, at the foot of auspiciously south-facing hills, after 63 years of faithful service to the

---

EUNUCHS

In a practice dating back at least to the Han dynasty, China's ruling houses employed **eunuchs** as staff, not least as a means of ensuring the authenticity of the emperor's offspring – and, as the eunuchs would never have any family, an extreme solution to the problem of nepotism. In daily contact with the royals, they often rose to considerable power, but this was bought at the expense of their dreadfully low standing in the public imagination; as palace bureaucrats, they were also despised (often with good reason) for being utterly corrupt and scheming. Their numbers varied greatly from one dynasty to the next – the Ming court is supposed to have employed 20,000, but this is probably an overestimate; the relatively frugal Qing Emperor Kangxi reduced the number to nine thousand.

Most of the eunuchs (or "bob-tailed dogs" as they were nicknamed) came from poor families, and volunteered for their emasculation as a way of acquiring wealth and influence. The operation, which removed both the testicles and penis, cost six silver pieces and was performed in a hut just outside the palace walls. Hot pepper-water was used to numb the parts, then after the blade had flashed the wound, it was sealed with a solder plug. The plug was removed three days later – if urine gushed out, the operation was a success. If it didn't, the man would die soon, in agony. Confucianism held that disfiguration of the body impaired the soul, so in the hope that he would still be buried "whole", the eunuch carried his severed genitalia in a bag hung on his belt. One problem eunuchs were often plagued with was bed-wetting, hence the old Chinese expression, "as stinky as a eunuch".

Eunuchry was finally **banned** in 1924, and the remaining 1500 eunuchs were expelled from the palace. An observer described them "carrying their belongings in sacks and crying piteously in high-pitched voices". The last imperial eunuch, Sun Yaoting, died in 1996 at the age of 93, and inspired a fascinating book chronicling the mysteries and horrors of his life at the imperial court, Jia Yinghua's The Last Eunuch of China: The Life of Sun Yaoting.

imperial household; there's a small spirit way flanked by civil and military guardian statues, plus a host of impressive steles outlining Tianyi's life story and achievements. The tomb itself, marked by a concreted-over mound at the back of the complex, is unimpressive, but you can descend into the vault beneath where a heavy stone door and vacant platform are all that remain after the site was looted in 1911. Back near the entrance, a courtyard holds further steles and stone guardian animals, plus surrounding halls form a small **Eunuch Museum** (宦官博物馆, huànguān bówùguǎn), featuring gruesome photos and models, a castration knife, and the mummified body of another Qing-dynasty eunuch who was buried at the site.

The Sino-Japanese War Museum and Marco Polo Bridge

Subway line #14 to Dawayao, then a taxi or three-wheeler (¥10–15) for the final 2km; or it's an unpleasant 30min walk around a complex traffic flow

Some 15km southwest of Beijing, a remnant of the old Imperial Highway crosses the Yongding River over the twelfth-century arches of the **Marco Polo Bridge**, a site infamous in China as where the Japanese launched their attack on the capital in 1937 – an event seen by some as the opening battle of World War II, and commemorated here at the **Sino-Japanese War Museum**. The bridge is intriguing, and the museum – enclosed inside the 8m-high reconstructed walls of the Ming-dynasty **Wanping Fortress** (宛平城, wǎnpíng chéng) – is perhaps less bombastic than you'd expect, though horrifically graphic at times.

Sino-Japanese War Museum

中国人民抗日战争纪念馆, zhōngguó rénmín kàngrìzhànzhēng jìniànguǎn • Daily 9am–4.30pm • Free

The **Sino-Japanese War Museum** is usually packed with school groups being given an education in national outrage. Eight themed halls detail the conflict's history, which reach back to Japan's occupation of northeastern China after the original Sino-Japanese War of 1894–95. Japan went on to annex Manchuria and finally sparked all-out war by attacking the Wanping Fortress here, outside Beijing, on September 18, 1937. Cases of spears, sabres and chain whips illustrate how ill-equipped Chinese guerrilla forces were to tackle a modern army – and also, perhaps, how brave. One surprising aspect is how inclusive the museum is: British, US, Russian and even Guomindang campaigns against Japan are all given space, painting a picture of an international effort to save China from the invaders. One hall is devoted to Japanese atrocities, such as the notorious Nanjing Massacre, yet the exhibition's captions are relatively muted: this is an exhaustive documentation of China's case against Japan, rather than an attempt to browbeat visitors with dogma.

Marco Polo Bridge

卢沟桥, lúgōu qiáo • April–Oct 7am–8pm; Nov–March 7am–6pm • ¥20

Head out through the western gate of the Wanping Fortress, and it's a short walk to where the eleven granite arches of the 266m-long **Marco Polo Bridge** span a vestigial stretch of river, now dammed upstream. Built in 1192, the bridge was seen by Marco Polo some seventy years later, who wrote that "there is not a bridge in the world to compare to it" – though the version here today, its parapets lined with a parade of stone lions, mostly dates to 1698. A plaza at the eastern end sports life-sized bronze statues of camel trains, a memento of the trade artery that once was the Imperial Highway, which stretched west from here through Xi'an and Lanzhou to distant Xinjiang, Tibet and Mongolia. A section of impressively rutted flagstones run down the centre of the bridge, deeply grooved by baggage carts. For the best photographs, get here around sundown.

Jietai and Tanzhe temples

Due west of Beijing, the splendid **Jietai and Tanzhe temples** sit in the wooded country outside the industrial zone that rings the city. Though relatively little visited by tourists, the temples rate among the best places to escape the city smoke, a haven of clean air, peace and solitude. Getting there and back can be time-consuming, so take a picnic and make a day of it.

Jietai Temple

戒台寺, jiètái sì • Daily 8am–5pm • ¥45

Sitting on a hillside 35km west of Beijing, **Jietai Temple** looks more like a fortress than a temple, surrounded as it is by forbiddingly tall, red walls. First constructed during the Sui dynasty (581–600), it's an extremely atmospheric, quiet place, made slightly spooky by its dramatically shaped pines – eccentric-looking venerable trees growing in odd directions. Indeed one, leaning out at an angle of about thirty degrees, is pushing over a pagoda on the terrace beneath it. In the **main hall** is an enormous tenth-century platform of white marble at which novice monks were ordained. At 3m high, it's intricately carved with figures – monks, monsters (beaked and winged) and saints. The chairs on top are for the three masters and seven witnesses who oversaw ordinations. Another, smaller, side hall holds a beautiful wooden altar that swarms with dragon reliefs.

Tanzhe Temple

潭柘寺, tanzhè sì • Daily 8am–5pm • ¥55 (¥85 combined ticket with Jietai Temple)

Twelve kilometres beyond Jietai, **Tanzhe Temple** has the most beautiful and serene location of any temple near the city. It's also one of the oldest, having been constructed during the Jin dynasty (265–420 AD), and one of the largest too, though there are no longer any monks living or working here. The temple is formed from a number of different shrines, all of them accessed by following the labyrinth of alleyways and steps leading up the hillside.

The temple complex

Wandering through the complex, past a terrace of stupas (each one raised to the memory of former monks), you reach an enormous central courtyard, with an ancient, towering gingko tree at its heart that's over a thousand years old (christened the "King of Trees" by Emperor Qianlong). Across the courtyard, a second, smaller gingko, known as "The Emperor's Wife", was once supposed to produce a new branch every time a new emperor was born. From here you can take in the other buildings, arrayed on different levels up the hillside, or look around the lush gardens, whose bamboo is supposed to cure all manner of ailments. Back at the entrance, the spiky *zhe* trees nearby (*Cudrania tricuspidata*, or **Chinese mulberry**), after which the temple is named, "reinforce the essence of the kidney and control spontaneous seminal emission", according to Chinese medicine.

ARRIVAL AND DEPARTURE   JIETAI AND TANZHE TEMPLES

By public transport For either temple, first take subway line #1 to its western terminus at Pingguoyuan. From here, bus #948 goes to Jietai; while bus #931 also travels via Jietai to terminate at Tanzhe Temple (this bus has two routes, so make sure the driver knows where you're going). A taxi between the two temples will cost around ¥35.
By taxi A taxi to visit both temples should cost around ¥400 from the city centre.

Cuandixia

爨底下, cuàndǐxià, also known as 川底下, chuāndǐxià • ¥35

Around 90km west of Beijing, **Cuandixia village** has some of this part of the country's finest surviving Ming- and Qing-dynasty village architecture. It's a splendid setting: fanning downhill from a ridge, against a backdrop of the rugged Jingxi mountains, the village forms a tight cluster of eighty-odd traditional, grey-tiled courtyard houses built on stone terraces. Cuandixia sits close to one of the old imperial post roads – now Highway #109 – which explains the village's one-time, now faded, prosperity; many of the houses are decorated with auspicious murals, and feature carvings in stone and wood. A local oddity is that almost everyone in the village is surnamed **Han**, after the original clan which migrated here from Shanxi province some five centuries ago. A few small temples and viewpoints above the village make for some easy hikes, and if you're enjoying the experience you might want to check out similar villages nearby: Huanglingxi (黄岭西村, huánglǐngxī cūn), Shaungshitou (双石头村, shuāngshítou cūn) and the old garrison town of Baiyu (柏峪村, bǎiyù cūn).

ARRIVAL AND DEPARTURE   CUANDIXIA

By public transport Take subway line #1 to Pingguoyuan, walk 150m west to the bus station; there are 2 buses daily direct to Cuandixia at 7.30am & 12.40pm. Return buses depart Cuandixia at 10.30am & 3.30pm. The journey takes 2–3hr in total from downtown Beijing.

By tour Several Beijing tour operators offer private excursions to Cuandixia, but these are expensive for solo travellers: try ⓦ thechinaguide.com or ⓦ chinaculturecenter.org, who might be able to tack you on to an existing tour.

ACCOMMODATION

Unless on a tour, you'll have to spend the night at Cuandixia, and though there's little to see or do as such, it's a refreshing break from the capital.

Homestays Many places have signs up offering basic homestay accommodation and meals, though be aware

that nobody in the village speaks English. **¥150**

Tianjin

天津, tiānjīn

Just 130km southeast of Beijing (a mere 30min by high-speed train), **TIANJIN** is predictably overshadowed by the national capital, despite being a major city in its own right. While it's true that specific attractions here are fairly low-key – a couple of **antiques markets**, the excellent **Yangliuqing Woodblock Printing Museum** and a fun **river cruise** – Tianjin's core of **colonial-era architecture** is completely different from anything you'll see in Beijing, making it an interesting place to spend a day.

Brief history

Sited 60km upstream from the mouth of the **Hai River** (海河, hǎi hé), and astride the **Grand Canal** – a vast transport network which ran for 1500km down through eastern China – Tianjin first gained importance as a **port** for Beijing, the dock for vast quantities of tribute rice paid annually to the emperor. Following the nineteenth century Opium Wars, foreign powers established Tianjin as one of their **treaty ports**, specially designated Chinese cities where they could live and conduct trade inside self-administered **concession districts**. Tianjin's concession was especially lavish, flanking the banks of the Hai River in Neoclassical buildings whose styling picked out separate French, British, German, Russian and even Italian quarters. Tensions between the indigenous population and foreigners exploded in the **Tianjin Massacre** of 1870, when a Chinese mob attacked a French-run orphanage, killing nuns, priests and the French consul in the belief that the Chinese orphans had been kidnapped and were merely awaiting the pot. Tianjin had its peace shattered again during the **Boxer Rebellion** in 1900 (see p.178), after which the foreigners levelled the walls around the old Chinese city and installed their own military here, to ensure easy access to Beijing.

The foreign concessions survived until WWII, after which Tianjin went into a decline. Today though, the port has once again become a major international shipping hub. As evidence of new wealth, the skyline is pierced by **skyscrapers**, the tallest of which is currently the 337m-high *Tianjin World Financial Center*. *Goldin Finance 117* and *Rose Rock IFC*, two near-600m-tall beasts – though plagued by construction hiccups – are scheduled to bring Tianjin into the world's select 100-storey-plus club around 2018.

South of the river

The bulk of Tianjin's surviving **colonial architecture** lies south of the river, an area exuding an oddly continental feel by the pastel colours and wrought-iron scrollwork balconies of the French Concession. From the main train station, cross via the **Jiefang Bridge**, a steel girder drawbridge completed in the 1920s, to **Jiefang Bei Lu**; there's an old French Concession boundary marker stone set into the wall at the intersection with **Binjiang Dao**, beyond which ordinary Chinese were once barred. The most appealing clutch of old lanes and facades lie either side of Binjiang Dao and **Heping Lu**, two pedestrianized, over-restored shopping streets lined with upmarket international

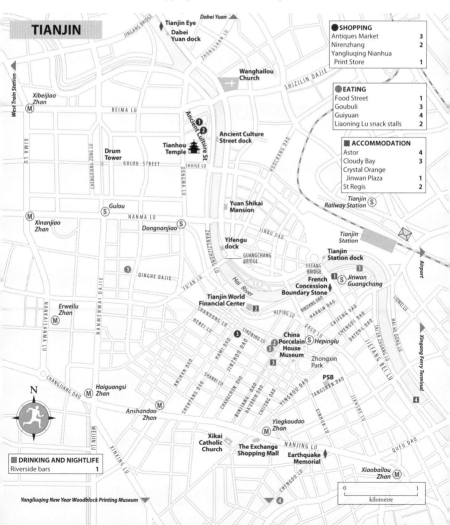

TIANJIN

● SHOPPING	
Antiques Market	3
Nirenzhang	2
Yangliuqing Nianhua Print Store	1

● EATING	
Food Street	1
Goubuli	3
Guiyuan	4
Liaoning Lu snack stalls	2

■ ACCOMMODATION	
Astor	4
Cloudy Bay	3
Crystal Orange Jinwan Plaza	1
St Regis	2

■ DRINKING AND NIGHTLIFE	
Riverside bars	1

Yangliuqing New Year Woodblock Printing Museum

boutiques. It's a good area just to wander around and maybe sample some of Tianjin's street snacks, but as a specific target the **antiques market** on Shengyang Dao (see p.122) is of most interest to visitors.

Below busy Nanjing Lu, **Chengdu Dao** runs southwest through a quiet district of rectangular, low-rise, 1930s Art Deco residences, which once made up the heart of the British Concession and still echo parts of north London (indeed, Chengdu Dao was formerly "London Road"). Push on in this direction and you'll eventually reach the **woodblock printing museum.**

China Porcelain House Museum

中国瓷房子博物馆, zhōngguó cífángzi bówùguǎn • Chifeng Dao • Daily 9am–6pm • ¥35 • Metro line #3 to Hepinglu

While most people won't feel the need to go inside, the **China House Museum** is a must-see for its insane premises – a colonial mansion clad entirely in broken glazed pottery, replete with extensive additional curlicues. This is the work of Zhang Lianzhi, a Tianjin native who purchased the house in 2002; he has since gone on to fill it with thousands of ceramic pieces, mainly from the Qing dynasty, though some go back to the Tang (618–907). A couple of rooms at the front of the property function as small shops, though prices verge on the extortionate.

Yangliuqing New Year Woodblock Printing Museum

杨柳青木版年画博物馆, yángliǔqīng mùbǎn niánhuà bówùguǎn • 111 Donghou Sanhe Li/Binguan Lu • Tues–Sun 9am–4.30pm • Free • Metro line #3 to Wujiayao

Hidden down an obscure lane 2km southwest of the city centre, the under-visited **Yangliuqing New Year Woodblock Printing Museum** houses an outstanding collection of colourful folk art pictures, traditionally pasted up outside homes to usher in luck over the coming year. Though there were many centres for the craft across China, Yangliuqing village (in Tianjin's western suburbs) became famous during the Qing dynasty, when a host of family-run studios competed to produce prints of folk tales, deities, fat babies, and scenes from daily life. Naturalistic and technically complex, they were often unusually large (some measure over a metre across) and typically used colours hand-painted over a block-printed outline.

A century of civil war devastated the industry, however, and by the 1950s many of the old designs had been lost. The museum's archive has gathered together over 1300 survivals, with a broad range on display over two floors; look for the cheery Mao-era illustrations, promising happiness and prosperity for all; and the four large "Tale of White Snake" prints, each showing successive stages in the printing process.

North of the river

There's a clutch of sights to the north and west of central Tianjin; you can use the Hai's riverbanks as a pleasant means of access from the train station, or **cruise** the area by boat (see opposite). The most compelling attractions in this direction are the Buddhist **Dabei Yuan** and **Ancient Culture Street**, though the latter has been over-renovated in faux-dynastic style.

Dabei Yuan

大悲院, dàbēi yuàn • Tianwei Lu, off Wuma Lu • Daily 9am–4pm • ¥5 • Dabei Yuan ferry dock or metro line #3 to Jinshiqiao

Tianjin's major Buddhist temple, **Dabei Yuan**, is located on a narrow lane off Zhongshan Lu in the northern part of the city. Large bronze vessels full of water stand outside the buildings, a fire precaution that has been in use for centuries. Outside the first hall, which was built in the 1940s, the devout wrap their arms around a large bronze incense burner before lighting incense sticks and kowtowing. In the smaller, rear buildings – seventeenth-century structures extensively restored after the Tangshan earthquake – you'll see the temple's resident monks, while small antique wood and bronze Buddhist figurines are displayed in a hall in the west of the complex.

Tianjin Eye

天津之眼, tiānjīn zhīyǎn • Jingang Bridge • Daily 9.30am–9.30pm • ¥70 • Dabei Yuan ferry dock or metro line #3 to Jinshiqiao

The 120m-tall **Tianjin Eye** is perched west of the Dabei Yuan, right over the Hai River on Jingang Bridge. Eight-seater pods carry passengers up to the skyline on a 30min cycle, providing superlative views of the river and an ever-more modern cityscape.

Ancient Culture Street

古文化街, gǔwénhuà jiē • Between Beima Lu and Shuige Lu • Ancient Culture Street ferry dock or metro line #2 to Dongnanjiao

Every city in China worth its salt has an antique-style district, often no more than a few years old. Tianjin's incarnation, **Ancient Culture Street**, runs west of the river, its entrance marked by colourful arches. There are a few genuinely old structures here (including a section of Ming-dynasty cobbled road) but – despite all the curling roofs, carved balconies and wooden shopfronts – not much in the way of venerable atmosphere or culture. Part of the problem is the overload of souvenir stalls, and one has to wonder how on earth *Doraemon* key rings and butt-wiggling dog dolls can be representative of "old Tianjin".

One actual piece of culture on Ancient Culture Street is the heavily restored **Tianhou Temple** (天后宫, tiānhòu gōng; daily 9am–5pm; ¥10), founded in 1326. It's dedicated to the southern Chinese deity Tian Hou (also known as Matsu), protector of sailors and fishermen, and the imported cult is evidence of Tianjin's port status as far back as the Yuan dynasty. An exhibition of local crafts fills the side halls.

7

ARRIVAL AND DEPARTURE **TIANJIN**

By plane Binhai International airport (天津滨海国际机场, tiānjīn bīnhǎi guójì jīchǎng) lies 15km east of Tianjin; it has connections to every major city in China, as well as multiple international destinations. Airport shuttle buses serve various parts of the city, including the main train station (every 30min 6am–7.30pm; 20min; ¥15).

By train High-speed trains from Beijing's South station (every few minutes from dawn to around 10pm; 30min; ¥52) generally arrive at Tianjin's main train station (天津站, tiānjīn zhàn), located on the north bank of the river at the nexus of metro lines #2, #3 and #9. A few services terminate at Tianjin's West station (火车西站,

huǒchē xīzhàn; metro line #1).

By ferry Tianjin Xingang Passenger Terminal (天津新港客运站 tiānjīn xīngǎng kèyùn zhàn), around 60km east of Tianjin, has international services to Incheon in South Korea. Tickets can be purchased from travel agents all over Tianjin (ask your hotel for the closest one; many even sell tickets themselves), or at the port itself. There are frequent minibuses between the port and Tianjin's main train station (¥10), and some shuttle services direct to Beijing (¥70); alternatively, it's ¥100–120 for a taxi from the port to central Tianjin, and you'll easily find others to share the cost if necessary.

TIANJIN BY BOAT

A fun way to view Tianjin's old city is aboard the **ferries and cruises** along a short section of the Hai River, between the train station and Tianjin Eye; you pass many (reconstructed) colonial-era facades finished in the French, British and Italian style, interspersed with blocks of contemporary riverside architecture. Keep an eye open too for the former riverside **mansion of Yuan Shikai**, the warlord who brought down the Chinese empire (see p.179), and the **Wanghailou Church** on the north bank, site of the 1870 massacre (see p.118). There are also many notable **bridges**, not least the plank-and-steel-girder Jiefang Bridge opposite the station, and the impressively heavy-looking stone Guangcheng Bridge, complete with gilded Neoclassical statues, which could have been transplanted from London.

PRACTICALITIES
Haihe Cruises ☎022 58306789, ⓦwww .haihetour.com. Runs 50min cruises from Tianjin station dock daily, on the hour 9am–5pm (¥80) and 7.30pm & 8.30pm (¥100). The journey takes you non-stop upstream to Dabei Yuan dock at the Tianjin

Eye before returning.
By ferry Regular ferries travel from the station via docks at Ancient Culture Street, Yifengu and Dabei Yuan; they depart every 30min, 9am–4.30pm. A 1-day pass costs ¥100.

GETTING AROUND

By metro Tianjin's useful metro system (from ¥2 per journey) currently comprises subway lines #1, #2, #3, and the Jinbing light rail #9 (though this isn't of any use for visitors). More lines are under construction.

By bus Buses run 5am–midnight, with fares a standard ¥1.5 throughout the city centre. The most useful route is #600, which starts behind the main train station, then heads out on a circular route past (or close to) all the main city sights.

By taxi Cabs are plentiful – flag fall is ¥9, and ¥15 is sufficient for most journeys around town.

ACCOMMODATION

Given the ease of access from Beijing, there's no need to stay overnight in Tianjin, but there are some good hotels in town, and – hostel aside – prices here are a good deal cheaper than those in the capital for what you get.

Astor 利顺德大饭店, lìshùndé dà fàndiàn. 33 Tai'er Zhuang Lu ☎022 58526888, ⓦstarwoodhotels.com. A charming hotel located in a former British mansion dating back to 1863. Modern but still featuring elegant colonial panelling, antique-style light fittings, polished wooden floors and woollen carpets, this is one of the most stylish places to stay in Tianjin. **¥900**

Cloudy Bay 云雾之湾国际青年旅舍, yúnwùzhīwān guójì qīngnián lǚshě. 120 Ha'erbin Lu ☎022 27230606, ⓦyhachina.com. Welcoming youth hostel featuring slightly fuddled staff, clean rooms with bright paint jobs and a great roof terrace-bar. Look for a blue-and-white building just south of the Xinhua Dao intersection. Dorms **¥70**, doubles **¥300**

Crystal Orange Jinwan Plaza 桔子水晶酒店(津湾广场店), júzi shuǐjīng jiǔdiàn (jīnwān guǎngchǎng diàn). Jinwan Plaza, Jiefang Dao ☎022 60973088. Smart budget chain hotel inside a mock-colonial block, conveniently located close to the station and the old town. The cheapest rooms are windowless, but it's all modern and well appointed. **¥500**

St Regis 瑞吉金融街酒店, ruìjí jīnróngjiē jiǔdiàn. 158 Zhangzizhong Lu ☎022 58309999, ⓦstarwoodhotels.com. Hard to fault either the location of this upmarket business venue – a waterfront site bang in the city centre – or the modern, square-with-hole building design. All rooms are spacious, and come with butler service too. **¥850**

EATING

For local snacks – such as deep-fried squid, *erduoyuan* (rice cakes fried in sesame oil; the name means "ear hole") or *mahua* (fried dough twists) – try Liaoning Lu, west off pedestrianized Binjiang Dao. **Food Street** (食品街, shípǐn jiē) on Qinghe Dajie, east of Nanmenwai Dajie, comprises an indoor eating area crammed with restaurants to suit all budgets.

Goubuli 狗不理包子铺, gǒubùlǐ bāozi pù. 77 Shandong Lu ☎022 27302540. Famed as much for its name (meaning "Dogs Wouldn't Touch It") as for its food, this Tianjin stalwart serves succulent – if very expensive – *baozi* dumplings, as well as a host of standard restaurant dishes. Always crowded despite poor service. Expect to pay ¥60 for a plate of *baozi* in the downstairs canteen, or around ¥80 per main dish in the upstairs restaurant. Daily 10am–9pm.

★Guiyuan 桂园餐厅, guìyuán cāntīng. 103 Chengdu Dao, across from the intersection with Guangxi Lu ☎022 23397530. Slightly shabby, very busy place on three floors, serving Tianjin specialities; expect to share a table with strangers unless you want a long wait. Everyone orders "eight-treasure tofu" (八珍豆腐, bāzhēn dòufu; mostly braised seafood) and "black garlic beef" (黑蒜子牛肉粒, hēi suànzǐ niúròulì), a delicious Chinese take on French pepper steak. No English signage or menu. Daily 11am–2pm & 5–9pm.

DRINKING

When it comes to drinking, it's hard to beat the small curl of bars on the **river bank** opposite the train station; many sell draught beer from just ¥12, and their outdoor terraces are glorious places to sit on a sunny day.

SHOPPING

Antiques Market Underneath the Taiwanese restaurant (台湾菜馆, táiwān càiguǎn), west of the Drum Tower on Chengxiang Zhong Lu. Though tourists flock to the Shenyang Dao market (see p.120), more serious collectors target this subterranean, rather more upmarket den, where you're likely to find far more gaudy (and possibly genuine) items. Market open daily 10am–5pm, though individual dealers keep their own hours; Thursday is the busiest day.

Nirenzhang 泥人张, nírénzhāng. Ancient Culture St. Brightly painted clay figurines are a traditional Tianjin folk art, and among fairly crude models of simpering deities are some really fine pieces of famous figures and ordinary people engaged in their daily activities – though prices are steep. Daily 10am–7pm.

Yangliuqing Nianhua Print Store 杨柳青年画店, yángliǔqīng niánhuà diàn. Ancient Culture St. The

best available range of these bold, eye-catching posters, though sadly that's not saying much: nowadays the industry seems keen on churning out lurid images of fat babies. The museum (see p.120) has a similar selection, but also books (some in English). Daily 10am–7pm.

Chengde

承德, chéngdé

Around 250km northeast of Beijing towards the Manchurian borderlands, unassuming **CHENGDE** boasts a highly colourful history. It was founded as a summer retreat for the Manchu emperors, and its fringes remain dotted with regal **temples** – not to mention an enormous, sprawling palace-and-park hill complex, the **Bishu Mountain Resort**. Otherwise, despite a million-strong population, the city itself is fairly small-scale, with new high-rises along its traffic-clogged main artery, **Nanyingzi Dajie**, yet to obscure the view of outlying mountains and cabbage fields.

7

Brief history

Originally called "Rehe", the site was discovered by the Qing-dynasty emperor **Kangxi** at the end of the seventeenth century. Attracted by the cool summer climate and rugged landscape, he built lodges here and indulged in a fantasy Manchu lifestyle, hunting and hiking like his northern ancestors. By 1711 there were 36 palaces, temples, monasteries and pagodas set in a great walled park, its ornamental pools and islands dotted with beautiful pavilions and linked by bridges.

The building programme expanded under Kangxi's grandson, **Qianlong** (1736–96), when it became diplomatically useful to spend time north of Beijing, forging closer links with troublesome **Mongol tribes**. Chengde was thus a thoroughly pragmatic creation, devised as a means of defending the empire by overawing Mongol princes with splendid audiences, hunting parties and impressive military manoeuvres.

The British

The first **British Embassy** to China, under Lord Macartney, visited Qianlong at Chengde court in 1793. They were well received by the emperor, though the visit was hardly a success. Macartney caused an initial stir by refusing to **kowtow**, while Qianlong was disappointed with the gifts the British had brought and, with Manchu power at its height, rebuffed all British trade demands, remarking: "We possess all things. I set no value on objects strange or ingenious, and have no use for your country's manufactures." His letter to the British monarch concluded, magnificently, "O king, Tremblingly Obey and Show No Negligence!"

THE PANCHEN LAMA IN CHENGDE

In 1786, the **Panchen Lama** was summoned from Tibet by Emperor Qianlong for his birthday celebrations, an adroit political move designed to impress the followers of Lamaist Buddhism. The Buddhists included a number of minority groups who were prominent thorns in the emperor's side, such as Tibetans, Mongols, Torguts, Eleuths, Djungars and Kalmucks. Some accounts (not Chinese) tell how Qianlong invited the Panchen Lama to sit with him on the Dragon Throne, which was taken to Chengde for the summer season. He was certainly feted with honours and bestowed with costly gifts and titles, but the greatest impression on him and his followers must have been made by the replicas of the Potala and of his own palace, constructed at Chengde to make him feel at home (see p.127) – a munificent gesture, and one that would not have been lost on the Lamaists. However, the Panchen Lama's visit ended questionably when he died, possibly poisoned, in Beijing; his coffin was returned to Tibet with a stupendous funeral cortege.

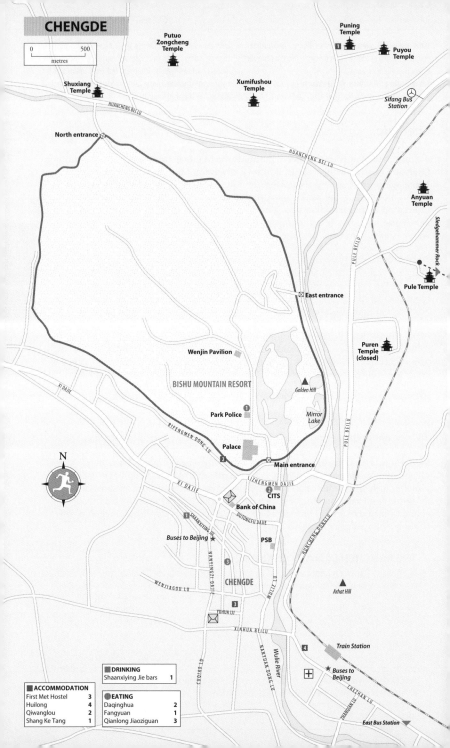

Bishu Mountain Resort

避暑山庄, bìshǔ shānzhuāng • Daily 8am–5.30pm • April 16 to Oct 15 ¥145; Oct 16 to April 15 ¥90 • Bus #1, #5, #15 or #30 from Chengde

Surrounded by a 10km-long wall and larger than the Summer Palace in Beijing, **Bishu Mountain Resort** sits immediately north of the city centre, with its **main gate**, Lizhengmen, in the south wall, off Lizhengmen Dajie. The **palace quarter**, just inside the complex to the west of the main gate, is built on a slope facing south, and consists of four groups of dark wooden buildings spread over an area of 100,000 square metres. This is where the Qing emperors lived, feasted, hunted, and occasionally dealt with affairs of state. The palace buildings just inside the main entrance are unusual for imperial China as they are low, wooden and unpainted, in marked contrast to the grandeur of Beijing's palaces. It's said that Emperor Kangxi wanted the complex to mimic a simple Manchurian village, though with 120 rooms and several thousand servants he wasn't exactly roughing it.

The **park** itself, with its artfully contrived paths and streams, rockeries and hills, is a fantasy re-creation of the Chinese landscapes that the emperors would have seen on their tours – an attempt to harmonize nature. Lord Macartney noted its similarity to the "soft beauties" of an English manor park of the Romantic style.

Covering the park and its buildings takes at least a day, and an early start is recommended. It's at its nicest in the early morning anyway, though the park is simply too big to get overcrowded – if you head north beyond the lakes, you're likely to find yourself alone.

The Front Palace

The southernmost **Front Palace** is the most interesting, as many of the rooms have been restored to their full Qing elegance, decked out with graceful furniture and ornaments. Even the everyday objects are impressive: brushes and ink stones on desks, ornate fly whisks on the arms of chairs, little jade trees on shelves. Other rooms house displays of ceramics, books and exotic martial-art weaponry. The Qing emperors were fine calligraphers, and examples of their work appear throughout the palace.

There are 26 buildings in this group, arranged south to north in nine successive compounds, which correspond to the nine levels of heaven. The main gate leads into the **Outer Wumen**, where high-ranking officials waited for a single peal of a large bell, indicating that the emperor was ready to receive them. Next is the **Inner Wumen**, where the emperor would watch his officers practise their archery. Directly behind, the **Hall of Frugality and Sincerity** is a dark, well-appointed room made of cedarwood, imported at great expense from south of the Yangzi River by Qianlong, who had none of his grandfather Kangxi's scruples about conspicuous consumption. Topped with a curved roof, the hall has nine bays, and patterns on the walls include symbols of longevity and good luck. The **Four Knowledge Study Room** behind was where the emperor worked, changed his clothes and rested. A vertical scroll on the wall outlines the knowledge required of a gentleman: he must be aware of what is small, obvious, soft and strong.

Rear Palace

The main building in the **Rear Palace** is the **Hall of Refreshing Mists and Waves**, the living quarters of the imperial family, and beautifully turned out in period style. It was in the west room here that Emperor Xianfeng signed the humiliating Beijing Treaty in the 1850s, giving away more of China's sovereignty and territory after their defeat in the Second Opium War. The **Western Apartments** are where the Empress Dowager Cixi (see box, p.99) lived when she was one of Xianfeng's concubines. A door connects the apartments to the hall, and it was through here that she eavesdropped on the dying emperor's last words of advice to his ministers, intelligence she used in her rise to power.

7

Outer complexes

The outer two complexes are much smaller than the inner. The **Pine and Crane Residence**, a group of buildings parallel to the front gate, is a more subdued version of the Front Palace, and was home to the emperor's mother and his concubines. In the **Myriad Valleys of Rustling Pine Trees**, to the north of here, Emperor Kangxi read books and granted audiences, and Qianlong studied as a child. The group of structures southwest of the main palace is the **Ahgesuo**, where male descendants of the royal family studied during Manchurian rule; lessons began at 5am and finished at noon. A boy was expected to speak Manchu at six, Chinese at twelve, be competent with a bow by the age of fourteen and marry at sixteen.

The lake

Boat rental ¥60/hr, from behind the palace, on the lakeshore

Renting a **rowing boat** is the best way to get around the **lake area** of the park – a network of pavilions, bridges, lakes and waterways – though you can easily walk. Much of the architecture here is a direct copy of southern Chinese buildings. In the east, the **Golden Hill**, a cluster of buildings grouped on a small island, is notable for a hall and tower modelled after the Golden Hill Monastery in Zhenjiang, Jiangsu Province. The **Island of Midnight and Murmuring Streams**, roughly in the centre of the lake, holds a three-courtyard compound which was used by Kangxi and Qianlong as a retreat, while the compound of halls, towers and pavilions on **Ruyi Island**, the largest, was where Kangxi dealt with affairs of state before the palace was completed.

Wenjin Pavilion

文津阁, wénjīn gé

Just beyond the lake area, on the western side of the park, is the grey-tiled **Wenjin Pavilion**, surrounded by rockeries and pools for fire protection. Originally this served as an imperial library housing a complete edition of the *siku quanshu*, an eighteenth-century encyclopedia of all Chinese knowledge, comprising an enormous 36,381 volumes. From the outside, the structure appears to have two storeys; in fact there are three – a central section is windowless to protect the books from the sun. Sadly, the building is closed to the public.

North of the lake

A vast expanse of grassland extends from north of the lake area to the foothills of the mountains, comprising **Wanshun Wan** ("Garden of Ten Thousand Trees") and **Shima Da** ("Horse Testing Ground"). The hilly area in the northwest of the park has a number of rocky valleys, gorges and gullies with a few tastefully placed lodges and pagodas. The deer, which graze on tourist handouts, were reintroduced after being wiped out by imperial hunting expeditions.

The temples

The **temples** in the foothills of the mountains around Chengde were built in the architectural styles of different ethnic nationalities, constructed less to express religious sentiment than as a way of showing off imperial magnificence, and also to make envoys from anywhere in the empire feel more at home. Though varying in design, all the temples share **Lamaist features** – Qianlong found it politically expedient to promote Tibetan and Mongolian Lamaism as a way of keeping these troublesome minorities in line.

Puning Temple

普宁寺, pǔníng sì • Daily 8am–5.30pm • April–Oct ¥80; Nov–March ¥60 (joint ticket with adjacent Puyou Temple) • Bus #6 from Lizhengmen Dajie

Puning Temple was built in 1755 to commemorate the Qing victory over Mongolian rebels at Junggar in northwest China, and is based on the oldest Tibetan monastery, the

VISITING THE TEMPLES

The temples are now in varying states of repair, having been left untended for decades. Of the original twelve, two have been destroyed and another three are dilapidated; the remaining seven stand in two groups: a string of five just beyond the northern border of Bishu Mountain Resort; and two more to the east of the park. If you're short on time the **Puning Temple** is a must, if only for the awe-inspiring statue of Guanyin, the largest wooden statue in the world.

A good itinerary is to see the northern cluster in the morning, return to town for lunch, and in the afternoon head for the Pule Temple and Sledgehammer Rock, a bizarre protuberance that dominates the eastern horizon of the town (see p.128).

Samye. Like traditional Tibetan buildings, it lies on the slope of a mountain facing south, though the layout of the front is typically Han, with a gate hall, stele pavilions, a bell and a drum tower, a Hall of Heavenly Kings, and the Mahayana Hall. This is the only working temple in Chengde, and though the atmosphere is not especially spiritual – it's usually clamorous with day-trippers – the temple and its grounds exude undeniable charm.

The East Hall

The **East Hall**'s central statue, flanked by *arhats*, depicts **Ji Gong**, a freethinking Song dynasty monk who drank quite a bit and caused chaos wherever he went, but had a talent for turning the tables on petty bureaucrats who were bullying ordinary people. Unusually – he's often portrayed emaciated and in rags – here he's dressed in rich robes and wearing a crown, but can still be identified by his fan-leaf palm.

Mahayana Hall

The rear section of the temple, separated from the front by a wall, comprises 27 Tibetan-style rooms laid out symmetrically, with the **Mahayana Hall** in the centre. The hall is dominated by a 23m-high **wooden statue of Guanyin**, the Goddess of Mercy. She has 42 arms with an eye in the centre of each palm, and three eyes on her face, which symbolize her ability to see into the past, present and future. The hall has two raised entrances, and it's worth looking at the statue from these upper viewpoints as they reveal new details, such as the eye sunk in her belly button, and the little Buddha sitting on top of her head.

Xumifushou Temple

须弥福寿之庙, xūmífúshòuzhī miào • Daily 8am–5.30pm • April–Oct ¥80; Nov–March ¥60 (joint ticket with Putuo Zongcheng Temple) • Bus #118 from Lizhengmen Dajie

The **Xumifushou Temple**, just southwest of Puning, was built in 1780 in Mongolian style for the sixth Panchen Lama when he came to Beijing to pay his respects to the emperor (see box, p.123). The temple centrepiece is the **Hall of Loftiness and Solemnity**, its finest features the eight sinuous gold dragons sitting on the roof, each weighing over a thousand kilograms.

Putuo Zongcheng Temple

普陀宗乘之庙, pǔtuó zōngchéngzhī miào • Daily 8am–5.30pm • April–Oct ¥80; Nov–March ¥60 (joint ticket with Xumifushou Temple) • Bus #118 from Lizhengmen Dajie

The magnificent **Putuo Zongcheng Temple** was built in 1771 and is based on Lhasa's Potala Palace. Covering 220,000 square metres, it's the largest temple in Chengde, with sixty groups of halls, pagodas and terraces. The grand terrace forms a Tibetan-style facade screening a Chinese-style interior, although many of the windows on the terrace are fake, and some of the whitewashed buildings around the base are merely filled-in shapes.

Inside, the **West Hall** is notable for holding a rather comical copper statue of the Propitious Heavenly Mother, a fearsome woman wearing a necklace of skulls and

---

CATCHING THE GHOST

On the thirteenth day of the first lunar month (January or February), monks at Puning Temple's Mahayana Hall observe the ritual of **catching the ghost**, during which a ghost made of dough is placed on an iron rack while monks dressed in white dance around it, then divide it into pieces and burn it. The ritual is thought to be in honour of a ninth-century Tibetan Buddhist, Lhalung Oaldor, who assassinated a king who had ordered the destruction of Tibetan Buddhist temples, books and priests. The wily monk entered the palace on a white horse painted black, dressed in a white coat with a black lining. After killing the king, he washed the horse and turned the coat inside out, thus evading capture from the guards who did not recognize him.

---

riding side-saddle on a mule. According to legend, she vowed to defeat the evil demon Raksaka, so she first lulled him into a false sense of security – by marrying him and bearing him two sons – then swallowed the moon and in the darkness crept up on him and turned him into a mule. The two dancing figures at her feet are her sons; their ugly features betray their paternity. The **Hall of All Laws Falling into One**, at the back, is worth a visit for the quality of the decorative religious furniture on show. Other halls hold displays of Chinese pottery and ceramics and Tibetan religious artefacts, an exhibition slanted to portray the gorier side of Tibetan religion and including a drum made from two children's skulls. The roof of the temple has a good view over the surrounding countryside.

Pule Temple

普乐寺, pǔlè sì • Daily 8.30am–4.30pm • ¥50 (joint ticket with Anyuan Temple) • Bus #10 from Lizhengmen Dajie

Due northeast of Bishu Mountain Resort, the **Pule Temple** was built in 1766 by Qianlong as a place for Mongol envoys to worship, and its style is an odd mix of Han and Lamaist elements. The Lamaist back section, a triple-tiered terrace and hall with a flamboyantly conical roof and lively, curved surfaces, steals the show from the more sober, squarer Han architecture at the front. The ceiling of the back hall is a wood-and-gold confection to rival the Temple of Heaven in Beijing. Glowing at its centre is a mandala of Samvara, a Tantric deity, in the form of a cross. The altar beneath holds a Buddha of Happiness, a life-size copper image of sexual congress; more cosmic sex is depicted in two beautiful mandalas hanging outside. Outside the temple, the view from the car park is spectacular, and just north is the path that leads to Sledgehammer Rock and the cable car.

Anyuan Temple

安远庙, ānyuǎn miào • Daily 8.30am–4.30pm • ¥50 (joint ticket with Pule Temple) • Bus #10 from Lizhengmen Dajie

Anyuan Temple lies within walking distance to the north of the Pule Temple, and enjoys a delightful setting on the tree-lined east bank of the Wulie River. It was built in 1764 for a community of 12,000 Mongolian prisoners of war who were relocated to Chengde by Qianlong after his victorious campaign against them at Ili, right up on China's northwestern frontier.

Sledgehammer Rock

棒锤山, bàngchuí shān • ¥50 • 2km walk from the Pule Temple, or cable car (¥50 return) • Bus #10 from Lizhengmen Dajie

Thinner at the base than at the top, the towering column of **Sledgehammer Rock** is more than 20m high, believed in legends to be a huge dragon's needle plugging a hole in the peak, which was letting the sea through. The rock's obviously phallic nature is tactfully not mentioned in tourist literature, but is acknowledged in local folklore – should the rock fall, it is said, it will have a disastrous effect on the virility of local men.

On the south side of the rock, at the base of a cliff, is **Frog Crag** (蛤蟆石, háma shí), a stone that vaguely resembles a sitting frog – the 2km walk here is pleasant, if the frog itself disappoints.

ARRIVAL AND DEPARTURE
CHENGDE

It's usually quickest to reach Chengde by bus from Beijing (3–5hr); trains can take twice as long.

By train From Beijing train station (7 daily; 4hr 30min–10hr 30min) you'll chug through rolling countryside, with a couple of Great Wall vistas on the way. Chengde train station is in the southeast of town; tickets are easy to buy here, though there's a helpfully located ticket office just east of the *Mountain Villa* hotel.

By bus Beijing's Dongzhimen and Sihui bus stations both offer departures to Chengde daily 6am–6pm. Chengde itself has at least two long-distance bus stations: 4km to the north is Sifang station (四方长途汽车客运站, sìfāng chángtúqìchē kèyùn zhàn); while the East Bus Station (汽车东站, qìchē dōng zhàn) lies 7km to the south of town on bus #118 route. There's also a depot of sorts immediately in front of the train station.

GETTING AROUND

By bus Local buses are infrequent and always crammed. Buses #5 & #11, which go from the train station to Bishu Mountain Resort; bus #6 from here to the Puning Temple; and bus #118 to the northern temples are the most useful.

By taxi Taxis are easy to find, but drivers don't use their meters – a ride into town from transit points shouldn't cost more than ¥20.

By minibus Hotels will be able to help with chartering a minibus for around ¥350 a day (bargain hard).

ACCOMMODATION

★**First Met Hostel** 初见客栈, chūjiàn kèzhàn. Block 4, Yuhua Business Centre, 106 Yuhua Lu ☎0314 7014117. Hidden among modern apartment blocks, rooms here are plain but kept nice and clean with security lockers in the dorms, there's an outdoor terrace for sunny days, and staff are helpful. Bike rental too. Dorms ¥60, twins ¥150

Huilong 会龙大厦酒店, huìlóng dàshà jiǔdiàn. 2 Chezhan Lu ☎0314 2085369. One of the more inexpensive proper hotels that take foreigners, with rooms ranging from the cheap and simple to relatively plush varieties. Not much atmosphere, but perfectly comfortable and convenient for the train station too. ¥300

★**Qiwanglou** 绮望楼宾馆, qǐwànglóu bīnguǎn. 1 Bifengmen Dong Lu ☎0314 2024385. Well-run hotel with imitation Qing-style buildings (though rooms are of modern design), just moments from the Bishu Mountain Resort main entrance. Its flowery grounds make for a pleasant walk even if you're not staying here. Service is excellent, and the staff among the few people in Chengde who speak English. ¥1400

Shang Ke Tang 普宁寺上客堂大酒店, pǔníng sì shàngkètáng dàjiǔdiàn. Puning Temple ☎0314 2058888. This interesting hotel's staff wear period clothing and braided wigs befitting the adjoining Puning Temple, and glide along the dim bowels of the complex to lead you to appealingly rustic rooms. You're a little away from the action here, though this is not necessarily a negative, and there are a few cheap restaurants in the area. ¥550

EATING AND DRINKING

Chengde doesn't offer much in the way of culinary adventure. There are plenty of decent **restaurants** catering to tourists on Lizhengmen Dajie around the main entrance to the Bishu Mountain Resort; on summer evenings, rickety tables are put on the pavement outside, and many diners stay on drinking well into the evening. The best place for a **drink** is busy **Shaanxiying Jie**, a streamside street stretching west of Nanyingzi Dajie.

Daqinghua 大清花, dàqīnghuā. 21 Lizhengmen Dajie ☎0314 2082222. Pine-walled dumpling restaurant that's the best option in the area around the Bishu Mountain Resort entrance. Their dumplings (¥12–20) are great, though there's a full menu of tasty northeastern dishes – including delicious stewed pork hocks, grilled ribs and toffee potatoes at around ¥45 a dish. Daily 11.30am–8.50pm.

Fangyuan 芳园居, fāngyuánjū. Inside Bishu Mountain Resort ☎0314 2161132. This snazzy restaurant serves imperial cuisine, including such exotica as "Pingquan Frozen Rabbit"; prices are pretty high, however, and you won't get much change from ¥150 per person, even without drinks. Daily 11am–5pm.

Qianlong Jiaoziguan 乾隆饺子馆, qiánlóng jiǎoziguǎn. Just off Centre Square, a park at the heart of the shopping district ☎0314 2076377. The best *jiaozi* in town are served here, and far more besides – the menu is full of Chinese staples, with a few more interesting items such as sauerkraut with lung, braised bullfrog in soy, and battered venison. The more adventurous mains clock in at ¥60–100, though penny-pinchers will appreciate the spicy Sichuan noodles (¥12). Daily 11am–9pm.

7

Accommodation

Beijing has a great range of accommodation, from smart five-star international chains and luxury boutique guesthouses, down to no-frills budget hotels and humble youth hostels. You don't always have to pay premium prices for convenient locations, with many within walking distance of major attractions such as the Forbidden City, Tian'anmen Square and the Temple of Heaven – and even if you end up further out, you should be within easy range of a subway station. While not every place to stay has buckets of local character, plenty are set inside converted *siheyuan* courtyard houses, often hidden away in Beijing's backstreet *hutongs*; not only are these tremendously atmospheric, but you don't have to spend a fortune either. Wherever you stay, however, book in advance – especially between June and August – when it becomes especially hard to find budget accommodation.

ESSENTIALS

HOTELS

Upmarket The capital's upmarket hotels (from ¥900 per night for a double room in high season) are legion, and more are appearing all the time. They offer amenities such as gyms, saunas, and business centres; annoyingly, while cheap hotels have free internet, you might have to pay for it at pricey ones. These establishments are comparable to their counterparts elsewhere in the world, though the finer nuances of service might well be lacking. If nothing else, they make useful landmarks, and some have pretty good restaurants that are, by Western standards at least, inexpensive.

Mid-range Mid-range hotels (¥400–900) are well equipped and comfortable, offering spacious double rooms, but can often feel anonymous and unstylish – though there are quite a few exceptions, particularly if you go for a courtyard house option (see box, p.132). Breakfast apart, it's recommended to eat out rather than in the hotel restaurant: hotel food is pretty mediocre at this level.

Budget Budget hotels (up to ¥400) boast little in the way of facilities; you can expect your room to be clean, but it might be poky. There is, however, a lot of choice in this price range, thanks to Chinese chains such as *Hanting Inn* (ⓦ www .huazhu.com) and *Jinjiang Inn* (ⓦ www.jinjianginns.com). Be aware, however, that not all branches of these chains are allowed to accept foreign guests.

HOSTELS

Beijing's hostels (¥70–100 for a dorm bed, en-suite doubles from ¥350) are clean and professionally run. You can expect them to feature a lounge/bar with a TV and a few DVDs, self-service laundry (¥15 or so) and bike rental (around ¥20/day). They have to be given credit for offering free wi-fi and internet access, something the larger hotels charge for. Don't be put off if you don't fit the backpacker demographic; there are a few slightly pricier options in which you won't hear Bob Marley or see tables filled with empty Qingdao bottles. All hostels also have double and some single rooms, sometimes with shared bathrooms – though with prices around ¥350, you

might strike a better deal at a budget hotel. Note that any place billing itself a "youth hostel" will give you a ¥10 per night discount if you have a youth hostel (IYHA) card, which they can sell you for ¥60.

COSTS AND BOOKING

Room rates Unless otherwise stated, the prices we quote represent the cost of the cheapest double room in high season (April–Sept). Almost all hotels, certainly all the more upmarket establishments, have high- and low-season rates; though at all but the cheapest hotels it's possible to bargain the walk-in price down by at least thirty percent. Bear in mind too that most places have a range of rooms, and staff will usually offer you the more expensive ones – it's always worth asking if they have anything cheaper. Most hotels have a few single rooms, priced slightly cheaper than doubles.

Reservations and booking websites The best deals are almost always in advance online, either through the accommodation's own website, or via booking sites. The two main Chinese sites (with English pages) are ⓦ elong .com and ⓦ ctrip.com – the advantage of these two is that often a deposit isn't needed to make a booking – while non-Chinese sites such as ⓦ trivago.com also have plenty of choice. For hostels, use ⓦ hostelworld.com or ⓦ hostelbookers.com, both of which require a small deposit. It's also straightforward enough to reserve a room by phone – at higher-end hotels and all hostels someone on reception will speak English, though at mid-range places you might be less lucky. You can also reserve rooms from counters at the airport, and they will usually offer a small discount – though you'll get a much better deal if you book the same room yourself.

Checking in Reception staff will photocopy your passport for the police and ask for a deposit (押金, yājīn) of a few hundred yuan; keep your receipt to ensure that you get this back when checking out. Remember to grab a few hotel business cards when you check in – vital for letting taxi drivers know where you're staying.

8

WHICH AREA?

The glitzy, expensive hotels are generally in the **centre and east** of the city; a cosmopolitan area with lively restaurants and nightlife, this is the place to stay if you are looking for international-standard style and comfort. Such places are clustered around shop-heavy **Wangfujing**, bar- and restaurant-laden **Sanlitun**, and businesslike **Jianguomen Dajie**.

Overlapping with the east, the **north** of the city, south of the Second Ring Road, has some charmingly ramshackle (and newly fashionable) areas. Head this way if you want to stay in traditional Beijing; it's also the best area for budget and mid-range places.

The **west** and **south** of the city are, on the whole, less interesting – though there are plenty of accommodation options here, including some good hostels. Lastly, a few **country retreats** are reviewed in the "Around Beijing" chapter (see p.104), while it's also possible to stay in Tianjin – almost close enough to commute from (see p.118) – or more distant Chengde (see p.123).

FACILITIES

Breakfast Breakfast is usually included in the rate in mid- and upper-range hotels, where a choice of Western and Chinese food is available. It is generally not included at hostels; exceptions have been noted in our reviews.

Tour offices All hotels and hostels have tour offices offering trips to the obvious sights: the Great Wall, acrobatics and Beijing opera shows. These are usually good value – show tickets generally cost no more than you'd pay at the door but give you free transport there, while the Great Wall and other out-of-town tours are by far the easiest way to reach said sights. Both hotels and hostels will also book train and plane tickets for you, for a small commission (¥30–50, usually slightly cheaper at hostels); for train tickets, you'll pay less if you go to a dedicated train ticket office (see p.24).

HOTELS

THE FORBIDDEN CITY AND TIAN'ANMEN SQUARE

Days Inn 香江戴斯酒店, xiāngjiāng dàisī jiǔdiàn. 1 Nanwanzi Xiang, Nanheyan Da Jie ☎ 010 65127788; subway line #1 to Wangfujing, Exit C1; map p.42. Motel-like doubles with standard facilities (though cheapest rooms are slightly tatty), set back off the main road in a quiet location. It's nothing special, but the staff are helpful and you're just a few minutes' walk from the Forbidden City, Wangfujing and Tiananmen Square. Little English spoken. ¥590

Hanting Express 汉庭快捷酒店, hàntíng kuàijié jiǔdiàn. 102 Nanchizi Da Jie, opposite the east exit of Workers' Park ☎ 010 52828000; subway line #1 to Tian'anmen East, Exit B; map p.42. The simple rooms are bright, clean and perfectly adequate – get a twin, rather than a cheaper double, if you need a bit of elbow room – but there's no soundproofing, and the walls are paper-thin. All told though, a bargain given the location. Doubles ¥390, twins ¥550

★**Kapok** 木棉花酒店, mùmiánhuā jiǔdiàn. 16 Donghuamen Dajie ☎ 010 65259988, ⓦ kapokhotel beijing.com; subway line #1 to Wangfujing, Exit C2; map p.42. Swish boutique hotel between the Forbidden City and Wangfujing, with clean lines, glass walls and a bamboo theme giving it a distinctive, modish look. There aren't too many luxury extras, and it's not especially near a subway station, but overall it's chic, very comfortable, and well located. ¥700

NORTH OF THE CENTRE

Bamboo Garden 竹园宾馆, zhúyuán bīnguǎn. 24 Xiaoshiqiao Hutong ☎ 010 58520088, ⓦ bbgh.com .cn; subway line #2 or #8 to Guloudajie, Exit E; map pp.58–59. Old but not too musty thanks to a recent refurbishment, this hotel was converted from the residence of a Qing official, and today the courtyards and bamboo-filled gardens are by far its best features. The more expensive suites boast period furniture, but the standard rooms are pretty good value, if small, with garden views. It's tucked into an alley in an agreeable part of the city, near Houhai, but still quiet. ¥780

★**Courtyard 7** 秦唐府客栈七号院, qíntángfǔ kèzhàn qīhàoyuàn. 7 Qiangulouyuan Hutong ☎ 010 64060777, ⓦ courtyard7.com; subway line #8 to Shichahai, Exit C; map pp.58–59. Rooms in this courtyard hotel off Nanluogu Xiang might be on the small side for the price – and the few "economic" options (¥560) are also windowless – but it more than makes up for it with a peaceful ambience and good location. It's single storey so all the rooms face the courtyard, and are elegantly furnished throughout, with four-poster beds and colourful tiled bathrooms. Ask about discounts from the rack rate. ¥900

COURTYARD HOTELS

Beijing has many small **courtyard hotels** to suit all budgets. Reminiscent of B&Bs, these intimate back-alley guesthouses are atmospheric and distinctively Chinese, with the central courtyard a venue for guests to mingle. They're often surprisingly well located too, with the greatest concentration north of the centre. On the downside, the alleyways they are found on are often inaccessible to taxis, and can be a bit earthy. In addition, because of the age of the buildings, places at the lower end of the scale can be a little rough around the edges: rooms are sometimes a bit dark, and in winter you'll have to leave the heater on high. Basically, go courtyard if you want ambience and local colour, but be aware that facilities and comfort may not be comparable to a modern hotel at the same price. Here are our favourites:

Chinese Box Courtyard Hostel See p.137
Côte Cour See opposite
Courtyard 7 See above
Double Happiness Courtyard Hotel See opposite

Fly By Knight Courtyard Hostel See p.136
Kelly's Courtyard See p.135
Leo Hostel See p.136
Red Wall Garden See p.134
The Orchid See opposite

Guxiang 20 古巷20号商务会, gǔxiàng èrshí hào shāngwùhuì 20 Nanluogu Xiang ☎010 64005566, ⓦbjguxiang.com; subway line #6 to Nanluoguxiang, Exit E; map pp.58–59. Slick-looking hotel right in the popular nightlife area of Nanluogu Xiang. Once in through the traditional red-painted doorway, there are plenty of "antique" features, from dark wooden furniture and four-poster beds to a virtual museum of porcelain. Unfortunately, staff are fairly offhand, not much English is spoken, and a lack of maintenance is beginning to show. Doesn't maintain much presence on the street, so look for the *Starbucks* sign (there's a branch in the foyer). ¥580

★**The Orchid** 65 Baochao Hutong ☎010 84044818, ⓦtheorchidbeijing.com; subway line #8 to Shichahai, Exit C; map pp.58–59. Located on popular Baochao *hutong*, this is one of the best boutique hotels in the whole city. Its modern, minimalist rooms, all dark wooden floors and crisp white walls, are arranged around a delightful courtyard; their rooftop area offers superlative sunset views over the district's grey-tiled roofs, and staff will encourage you to drink one of their delicious house cocktails up there. ¥1200

Shatan 沙滩宾馆, shātān bīnguǎn. 28 Shatan Hou Jie ☎010 84026688, ⓦshatanhotel.com; subway line #6 or #8 to Nanluoguxiang, Exit A; map pp.58–59. Utterly ordinary mid-range Chinese hotel, but it's well-located at the edge of an interesting *hutong* district close to Jingshan Park, rooms are large, comfortable and clean, and online rates can work out a better deal than hostel doubles – though their cheapest rooms lack windows. ¥450

EAST OF THE CENTRE

WANGFUJING

Beijing 北京饭店, běijīng fàndiàn. 33 Dongchang'an Jie ☎010 65137766, ⓦwww.chinabeijinghotel.com .cn; subway line #1 to Wangfujing, Exit C2; map pp.68–69. One of the most recognizable buildings in Beijing, this mansion block just east of Tian'anmen Square was built in 1900. There's a ludicrously over-decorated entranceway, a huge pool, smart but bland rooms, and superlative vistas over the Forbidden City from the top floors of the west wing (though an office block stops you spying down into militarized Zhongnanhai to the west). ¥1200

Côte Cour 演乐宾馆, yǎnyuè bīnguǎn. 70 Yanyue Hutong ☎010 65237981, ⓦhotelcotecourbj.com; subway line #5 or #6 to Dongsi, Exit C; map pp.68–69. This fourteen-room courtyard-style boutique hotel is bang in the middle of the city but located in a quiet *hutong*. Skilfully decorated with oriental chic, it's a place to consider if style and character are more important to you than lavish facilities. There's no restaurant, but a free breakfast is served in the lounge. Call in advance and they'll arrange a taxi to pick you up, though drivers sometimes won't go down the alley – meaning a 5min walk. ¥1268

Crowne Plaza 国际艺苑皇冠饭店, guójì yìyuàn huángguān fàndiàn. 48 Wangfujing Dajie ☎010 65133388, ⓦcrowneplaza.com; subway line #5 to Dengshikou, Exit A; map pp.68–69. Well-established international five-star chain hotel with arty pretensions (there's an on-site gallery) and a handy location for the shops and sights. The open-plan lobby is pretty impressive, and there's nothing to fault here, from the clean and comfortable rooms to the attentive service and large breakfast. The best of a number of upmarket hotels in the area. ¥1280

Double Happiness Courtyard Hotel 阅微庄宾馆, yuèwēizhuāng bīnguǎn. 37 Dongsi Sitiao ☎010 64007762, ⓦhotel37.com; subway line #5 or #6 to Dongsi, Exit B; map pp.68–69. A traditional-looking option boasting larger rooms than most, with wooden floors and the usual Chinese carved and lacquered decor. The courtyards are very attractive, with red lanterns and plenty of foliage that provides the perfect environment for their weekly performances of music. It's central, but 200m along a narrow alley that most taxis won't tackle – still, the subway station is only a couple of minutes' walk away. ¥990

Grand Hotel Beijing 北京贵宾楼饭店, běijīng guìbīnlóu fàndiàn. 35 Dongchang'an Jie ☎010 65137788, ⓦgrandhotelbeijing.com; subway line #1 to Wangfujing; map pp.68–69. A central, if ageing, five-star palace with splendid views over the Forbidden City. Rooms feature period rosewood furniture, and there's plenty of elegant calligraphy as well as paintings around; facilities include a pool and gym. Service standards are high, making this a better bet than the *Beijing* next door. ¥1100

★**Hilton Wangfujing** 王府井希尔顿酒店, wángfǔjīng xī'ěrdùn jiǔdiàn. 8 Wangfujing Dong Dajie ☎010 58128888, ⓦhilton.com; subway line #5 to Dengshikou, Exit A; map pp.68–69. Luxurious and upscale, the *Hilton* is a safe international choice and there are some major discounts available, though it tends to get booked out. It's near the shopping district of Wangfujing, and some decent restaurants, and you can see the Forbidden City from the upper floors. There's judicious use of incense, rooms have iPod docks, and there's an impressive gym and pool. ¥1300

Home Inn Plus 如家精选酒店, rújiā jīngxuǎn jiǔdiàn. 212 Dongsi Bei Dajie ☎010 65595900, ⓦhomeinns.com; subway line #5 to Zhangzizhonglu, Exit C; map pp.68–69. You can't mistake the over-designed, arty exterior of this boutique budget hotel, all floating white rectangles. Inside there's slick minimalist decor and comfortable rooms with a reasonable amount of space. You're conveniently close to the Confucian and Yonghe Lama temples here, plus a slew of interesting *hutong* bars; the only downside is the location on a busy junction, though rooms are soundproofed. ¥499

8

8

★**Peninsula Palace** 王府饭店, wángfǔ fàndiàn. 8 Jingyu Hutong ☎010 85162888, ⓦpeninsula .com; subway line #5 to Dengshikou, Exit A; map pp.68–69. Discreet local representative of this famous upmarket Hong Kong chain, within walking distance of the Forbidden City. Clever use of space means the Deluxe rooms – barely more expensive than their base rate – have the feeling of a suite. ¥2400

Prime 华侨大厦, huáqiáo dàshà. 2 Wangfujing Dajie ☎010 65136666, ⓦprimehotel-beijing .com; subway line #5 or #6 to Dongsi, Exit G; map pp.68–69. A monumental block of a tourist hotel, catering mostly to Chinese tour groups. Staff are friendly and professional, while rooms are comfortable rather than luxurious, though all but the most basic are nicely decorated with "oriental" artwork. Extras include a pool, sauna and gym, plus an ATM in the lobby. ¥750

★**Red Wall Garden** 红墙花园酒店, hóngqiáng huāyuán jiǔdiàn. 41 Shijia Hutong ☎010 51692222, ⓦredwallgardenhotel.com; subway line #5 to Dengshikou, Exit C; map pp.68–69. Located down a quiet *hutong*, this former Qing-era mansion turned courtyard hotel stands out for its extraordinarily helpful, English-speaking staff and their chic modern rooms with lush floor rugs and handsome, antique-style furniture. There's also a pleasant courtyard bistro and restaurant serving Chinese and Western food, and a patio for sitting out with a drink after dark. Ask about their courses, such as noodle-making and tea appreciation. ¥870

SANLITUN

Ibis Beijing Dongdaqiao 宜必思酒店, yíbìsī jiǔdiàn. 30 Nansanlitun Lu ☎010 65088100, ⓦaccorhotels.com; subway line #6 to Dongdaqiao, Exit B; map pp.68–69. International budget urban chain offering reliable, inexpensive facilities in this often pricey part of town. Rooms are surprisingly large and attractive for the price, and the bars and restaurants of Sanlitun are only 10min up the road. ¥380

★**Opposite House** 瑜舍, yúshè. Sanlitun Lu ☎010 64176688, ⓦwww.theoppositehouse.com; subway line #10 to Tuanjiehu (Exit A); map p.72. This trendy hotel is filled with modern Chinese art; if you think that you've walked into a gallery you'd be half right, since they've connections with UCCA in the 798 Art District (see p.102). Rooms offer minimalist chic with no stinting on comfort; bathrooms have oak-wood tubs and waterfall showers. It's just around the corner from Sanlitun, so there's no shortage of restaurants and nightlife in the area. There's no sign on the outside – look for the green building next to the 3.3 shopping mall. ¥2300

Red Hotel 红驿栈, hóngyìzhàn. 10B Taiping Zhuang, Dongzhimenwai Daji, Chunxiu Lu ☎010 64171066, ⓦwww.red-hotel.com; subway line #2 to Dongsishitiao, Exit B; map pp.68–69. Modern, clean, friendly budget hotel whose overall finish and ambience is a cut above what you'd expect for the very reasonable rate, and it's surrounded by inexpensive restaurants. Not much English spoken. ¥350

Yoyo 优优客酒店, yōuyōu kèjiǔdiàn. Due east of 3.3 Building ☎010 64173388, ⓦwww.yoyohotel.cn; subway line #10 to Tuanjiehu, Exit A; map p.72. A little boutique-style hotel whose sleek, honey-coloured rooms are surprisingly attractive – they may be minuscule, but considering the location you won't do much better for the price. Note that in some rooms the showering facilities are visible from the beds – check before you pay if this isn't your thing. It's located just a hop, skip and jump from Sanlitun on a quiet alley. ¥399

JIANGUOMEN DAJIE AND AROUND

Jianguo 建国饭店, jiànguó fàndiàn. 5 Jianguomenwai Dajie ☎010 65002233, ⓦhoteljianguo .com; subway line #1 to Yong'anli, Exit B; map pp.68–69. Popular, thanks to its convenient (if hardly atmospheric) location just down the road from the Silk Market (see p.165), this old stalwart has rooms of varying quality – ask to stay on the newly renovated executive floor or on a lower floor with a view of the garden. The restaurant, *Justine's* (see p.147), has pretty good French food, and there are plenty of other drinking and dining options outside. Many walk-in rates only include breakfast for one. ¥1000

★**Park Hyatt** 柏悦酒店, bóyuè jiǔdiàn.

BEIJING'S BEST

Best for people-watching Peking Youth Hostel (see p.136)
Best for free kung fu lessons Fly By Knight Courtyard Hostel (see p.136)
Best for partying Leo Hostel (see p.136)
Best for sunset cocktails The Orchid (see p.133)
Best for night-time walks to the Forbidden City Kapok (see p.132)
Best for celeb-spotting St Regis (see p.135)
Best for views Park Hyatt (see above)
Best for art Opposite House (see above)
Best for night-time visits to the Summer Palace Aman@Summer Palace (see opposite)

2 Jianguomenwai Dajie ☎010 85671234, ⓦbeijing
.park.hyatt.com; subway line #1 or #10 to Guomao, Exit
D; map pp.68–69. One of the most architecturally
masterful hotels in the city, set on the 37th to 60th floors of
an almost toy-like block that's illuminated rather
beautifully at night. Rooms here offer all the pared-down
luxury you'd expect of the chain, and there are stupendous
views from all sides. There's a great bar and restaurant up
top, an excellent gym and *Xiu* bar down below. **¥1700**
St Regis 国际俱乐部饭店, guójìjùlèbù fàndiàn.
21 Jianguomenwai Dajie ☎010 64606668,
ⓦstarwoodhotels.com; subway lines #1 or #2 to
Jianguomen, Exit B; map pp.68–69. One of the
plushest hotels in the city, this is the first choice of
visiting dignitaries and celebs, from George Bush to
Quentin Tarantino. It features real palm trees in the lobby,
marble bathrooms, a colossal swimming pool (for a hotel,
at any rate) and there's butler service available for all
guests. **¥1700**

SOUTH OF THE CENTRE
Far East 远东饭店, yuǎndōng fàndiàn. 90 Tieshu Xi
Jie ☎010 51958811, ⓦwww.fareasthotelbeijing.com;
subway line #2 to Qianmen, Exit C, or line #7 to
Hufangqiao, Exit B; map pp.80–81. Despite the pretty
website, this hotel is an unattractive 1980s block of a place,
but inside it's in a good state of repair even if the rooms are
ordinary and slightly scuffed around the edges. The biggest
plus is the location in an interesting residential *hutong*,
within a ten-minute walk of touristy Dazhalan's restaurants
and shops. Though often billed as a hostel, there are no
dorms. **¥360**
Hanting Qianmen 汉庭前门酒店, hàntíng
qiánmén jiǔdiàn. 1 Changxiang Wutiao ☎010
67056668; subway line #2 to Qianmen, Exit B; map
pp.80–81. Basic but decent-value budget hotel; rooms
come with a shower and just enough space to move around
your luggage. It's in a quiet corner of town, though just a
fifteen-minute walk from Qianmen or the Temple of
Heaven Park, with a genuinely old, unrestored block of
alleys to the north – though they're due for a facelift. **¥360**
★**Happy Dragon at the Temple of Heaven (RJ
Brown Hotel)** 瑞洁宾舍酒店, ruìjié bīnshě jiǔdiàn.
17 Xin Nong Jie ☎010 83133338, ⓦhappydragonhostel
.com; subway line #7 to Zhushikou, Exit C; map
pp.80–81. Prominent building (look for the "Brown" sign

on top) in a slightly nondescript area but close to the
Natural History Museum and Temple of Heaven, and within
walking distance of Tian'anmen Square. Inside it's a decent
inner-city budget hotel – there are no dorms – with
compact modern en-suite rooms; some also come with a
balcony. There's a café and bar on site too. Good value and
extremely popular – book ahead. **¥369**

WEST OF THE CENTRE
★**Kelly's Courtyard** 凯丽家, kǎilì jiā. 25 Xiaoyuan
Hutong ☎010 66118515, ⓦkelly'scourtyard.com;
subway line #4 to Xisi, Exit D; map pp.88–89.
Sympathetically restored courtyard home with friendly
management, right at the end of a quiet *hutong* cul-de-
sac. It's bit far away from things, though that's precisely
why most guests are here. The guesthouse itself is
comfortable, with charmingly decorated rooms arranged
around a warm, glassed-in terrace, though you get the
sense that if you dropped a pin in your room, all of the
other guests would know about it. **¥446**
Templeside Deluxe House 广济邻青年旅舍,
guǎngjìlín qīngnián lǚshè. 2 Baita Xiang, off
Zhaodengyu Jie ☎010 66172571, ⓦtempleside.com;
subway line #2 to Fuchengmen, Exit B; map
pp.88–89. This renovated courtyard house has really gone
for a Chinese feel; everything, from the designs on the
carpets to the latticework windows, is red, tassled or
plastered with characters. Even the cisterns are decorated
with Chinese motifs. But if you don't mind a bit of chintz,
this is a pretty successful marriage of *hutong* house and
comfy pad. The central courtyard has been turned into a
sociable lounge by the addition of a glass roof, and it's cute
and quiet with friendly staff; the only problem is that it's just
a little out of the way, near Baita Temple (see p.91). **¥500**

THE FAR NORTH
Aman@Summer Palace 安缦颐和, ānmàn yíhé.
1 Gongmenqian Jie ☎010 59879057, ⓦaman.com;
subway line #4 to Xiyuan, Exit C2; map p.98. About as
close as you'll be able to stay to the Summer Palace, both in
terms of location (it's just outside the east gate) and feel –
parts of the complex are centuries old, with contemporary
rooms decked in period timber. This is a place to get away
from it all; the restaurants, pool and spa facilities are top-
notch, and there's even a secret gate into the palace, which
can be opened at night for a crowd-free stroll. **¥6300**

HOSTELS

FORBIDDEN CITY AND TIAN'ANMEN SQUARE
Feel Inn Youth Hostel 非凡青年旅舍, fēifán
qīngnián lǚshè. 2 Ciqiku Hutong ☎65287418,
ⓦbeijingfeelinn.com; subway line #1 to Tian'anmen
East, Exit B; map p.42. Austere – almost spartan – hostel

with institutional eggshell-blue walls and slightly cramped
dorms, but it's also clean, with friendly staff, there's a bar,
and it's just around the corner from Pudu Temple, well-
located for all the central attractions. A few more
bathrooms would improve things, but you can't argue with
the rate. Dorms **¥60**, doubles **¥268**

NORTH OF THE CENTRE

Downtown Backpackers 东堂青年旅舍, dōngtáng qīngnián lǚshè. 85 Nanluogu Xiang ☎ 010 84002429, ⊛ backpackingchina.com; subway line #6 or #8 to Nanluoguxiang, Exit E; map pp.58–59. Long-time backpacker favourite, with an enviable location among the artsy boutiques of Beijing's trendiest *hutong*; you won't be short of eating and nightlife options. Graffiti all over the walls extol the virtues of the staff, though perhaps they've let it go to their heads. There are a few single and double rooms – priced according to whether they have windows and bathrooms – which get booked up rapidly. Small breakfast included. Dorms ¥70, doubles ¥380

Peking Youth Hostel 北平国际青年旅舍, běipíng guójì qīngnián lǚshè. 113-2 Nanluogu Xiang ☎ 010 84039098, ⊛ peking.hostel.com; subway line #6 or #8 to Nanluoguxiang, Exit E; map pp.58–59. Purpose-built hostel with immaculate rooms (including a women-only dorm for ¥10 extra) and a winning location on Nanluogu Xiang, plus a far quieter annexe a fifteen-minute walk away; there's some great people-watching from the rooftop café, the downstairs component of which is extremely popular with passers-by. The steep prices are difficult to justify, though. Dorms ¥130, doubles ¥500

★ Red Lantern House 红灯笼客栈, hóngdēnglóng kèzhàn. 5 Zhengjue Hutong ☎ 010 83285771, ⊛ redlanternhouse.com; subway line #4 to Xinjiekou, Exit C; map pp.58–59. A converted courtyard house in an engaging market area, close to Houhai. The main building offers reception, restaurant/bar and dorms; these open straight on to the social area and, depending on the clientele, can be noisy. A separate building about 250m west has simple, airy and spotless en-suite doubles with floral wallpaper; it's much quieter overall and there's a small courtyard to sit around in. Dorms ¥85, doubles ¥300

Sitting on the Walls Courtyard House 城墙客栈, chéngqiáng kèzhàn. 57 Nianzi Hutong ☎ 010 64027805, ⊛ www.beijingcitywalls.com; subway line #6 to Nanluoguxiang, Exit A; map pp.58–59. Tucked away in a quiet *hutong*, this is a converted courtyard house that offers an intimate atmosphere, a bit of character, friendly staff, pets, and dodgy plumbing. It's very central, just behind the Forbidden City, though a little tough to find first time; most taxi drivers won't know where it is. Wend your way through the alleyways, following the signs. Dorms ¥100, doubles ¥420

Sleepy Inn 丽舍什刹海国际青年旅店, lìshè shíshàhǎi guójì qīngnián lǚdiàn. 103 Deshengmennei Dajie ☎ 010 64069954; subway line #2 to Jishuitan, Exit B; map pp.58–59. This homely hostel has a great (if tricky-to-find) location, beside a canal just off Xihai Lake, and is probably the most laidback of Beijing's hostels. A terrace, pleasant book-lined café and helpful

staff make up for slightly overpriced doubles; the dorms are good value, though. Dorms ¥100, doubles ¥380

EAST OF THE CENTRE

Beijing Saga Youth Hostel 红都实佳宾馆, hóngdū shíjiā bīnguǎn. 9 Shijia Hutong ☎ 010 65130369, ⊛ sagayouthhostelbeijing.cn; subway line #5 to Dengshikou, Exit C; map pp.68–69. The lobby is a bit bare and dusty, and overall this place won't win any awards for character; but the staff are great, they've got all the usual hostel trimmings, and the rooms are spacious, clean and comfortable. They also specialize in Tibet tours (4 days return package to Lhasa ¥2200) and overnight camping trips to unrestored sections of the Great Wall, including a barbecue and lunch at a local home (¥900). Dorms ¥90, doubles ¥310

★ Fly By Knight Courtyard Hostel 夜奔北京四合院客栈, yèbēn běijīng sìhéyuàn kèzhàn. 6 Dengcao Hutong ☎ 130 41095935; subway line #5 or #6 to Dongsi, Exit C; map pp.68–69. Superb courtyard hostel, tucked into an atmospheric *hutong* area east of the Forbidden City. It's a small, boutiquey place, and so gets booked up early; those lucky enough to bag a room or bed will benefit from a relaxed atmosphere, one livened up with occasional martial arts lessons. Dorms ¥180, doubles ¥550

Sanlitun Youth Hostel 三里屯青年旅舍, sānlǐtún qīngnián lǚshè. Off Chunxiu Lu ☎ 010 51909288, ⊛ sanlitun.hostel.com; subway line #2 to Dongsishitiao, Exit B; map pp.68–69. Most notable for being the closest hostel to Sanlitun, this is a friendly place that boasts a good communal area and a faux-traditional courtyard setting. Rooms are the usual functional deal, though neater and better-maintained than most; and if you do want to stray, it's not far to local restaurants and bars. The only problem is its relative distance from the nearest subway station. Dorms ¥55, doubles ¥250

SOUTH OF THE CENTRE

365 Inn 365 安怡之家宾馆, 365 ānyí zhījiā bīnguǎn. 55 Dazhalan Xijie ☎ 010 63085956, ⊛ china365inn.wixsite.com/365inn; subway line #2 to Qianmen, Exit C; map pp.80–81. Highly popular place on the bustling Dazhalan strip. Its warren of rooms are cheery and relatively spacious, though guests tend to spend more time in the street-facing restaurant, which morphs into a busy bar come evening. Dorms ¥80, doubles ¥270

★ Leo Hostel 广聚园青年旅舍, guǎngjùyuán qīngnián lǚshè. 52 Dazhalan Xijie ☎ 010 63031595, ⊛ leohostel.com; subway line #2 to Qianmen, Exit C; map pp.80–81. The best hostel on Dazhalan, and particularly popular with younger backpackers on account of its cheap bar and fun vibe. Leafy and attractive

8

communal spaces make up for rooms that are slightly tatty round the edges, and some of the dorms are a bit cramped, but there's an army of attentive staff keeping the place running smoothly. It's easy to find, and close to Tian'anmen Square and the Forbidden City. Dorms ¥75, doubles ¥380

WEST OF THE CENTRE

★ **Chinese Box Courtyard Hostel** 团圆四合院客栈, tuányuán sìhéyuàn kèzhàn. 52 Xisi Beiertiao ☎ 010 66186768, ⓦ chinesebox.hostel.com; subway line #4 to Xisi, Exit A; map pp.88–89. This charming little family-run courtyard hotel, hidden behind a sturdy red *hutong* door, only has a couple of rooms, so you'll certainly need to book ahead. The dorms are on the pricey side, but the rather incongruously luxurious double rooms are some of the best in their price range; they feature huge beds, and imperial-style wallpaper and cushions. There are daily events such as musical performances, tea tastings and "dumpling parties". Small breakfast included. Dorms ¥150, doubles ¥550

Pagoda Light 白塔之光, báitǎ zhī guāng. 180 Fuchengmen Da Lu, just west of the Baita entrance ☎ 010 66552188; subway line #4 to Xisi, Exit A, or line #2 to Fuchengmen, Exit B; map pp.88–89. A sparklingly new, purpose-built hostel which, steep prices aside, is hard to fault: clean, spacious, modern and with stylish pine and slate decor, plus an internal light well. Dorms are slightly odd, with rows of mattresses divided by pine boards instead of bunks. Don't miss the sunset view of the Baita Temple from the third-floor café. Dorms ¥138, doubles ¥448

8

Eating

The Chinese are a nation of foodies: even pleasantries revolve around the subject. One way of asking "how are you?" – *nichīfàn le ma?* – translates literally as "have you eaten rice yet?", and they talk food like the British talk about the weather, as a social icebreaker. Meals are considered social events, and the Chinese like their restaurants to be *rènao* – hot and noisy. Given this obsession with food, it follows, perhaps, that China boasts one of the world's most complex cuisines, with each region presenting a host of intricate varieties. The culinary wealth of Beijing is unique; it encompasses every style of Chinese food available, along with just about any Asian fare and most world cuisines. It's no surprise then that, for some visitors, eating becomes the highlight of their trip.

9

Every corner of Beijing is filled with restaurants, though their nature changes as you shift throughout the city. A few compact areas have become quite trendy, and boast a cosmopolitan range of places to eat: there's Sanlitun (and especially the upper levels of the Tai Koo Li complex); the **Yonghe Gong/Beixinqiao** areas to the northeast of the centre; and the **CBD** in the east. **Wangfujing**, near the Forbidden City, caters to the masses with its series of chain restaurants, while south of the centre you'll find good duck south of **Qianmen** and Muslim food around **Niu Jie Mosque**. If you're at a loss you can do far worse than head for the nearest **shopping mall**: all have (air-conditioned) food courts with local and international fast-food chains, smart-casual restaurants and snack bars.

For short **cookery courses** in English, contact The Hutong (ⓦthehutong.com) or the Beijing Cooking School (ⓦbeijingcookingschool.com; see p.27).

ESSENTIALS

BEIJING SPECIALITIES

There's a definite **Manchurian influence** in the capital's cuisine, not least in a common use of pickles and millet in home-style cooking, but also in the very non-Chinese partiality for roasted meats – such as Beijing's most famous restaurant dish, **Peking duck**. Although duck isn't actually eaten that often by locals, you should certainly give it a go while you're here; the same can be said for elaborate **imperial cuisine** (see box, p.141). At the other end of the culinary spectrum, Beijing also has its own version of that Chinese staple, the **hotpot**, while local **street food** is not to be missed either, especially at **breakfast** time (see box, p.140).

Peking duck 北京烤鸭, běijīng kǎoyā. Originating either with the Qing-dynasty Manchurian invaders, or perhaps brought to China by Muslim immigrants from Central Asia way back in the Mongol era, succulent roast duck is Beijing's big culinary hitter, and deservedly so. Locals love to debate the merits of convection roasters over peach-wood ovens and the like, and every venerable restaurant has a different preparation technique, though the basics involve first pumping air between the skin and the meat, to separate them; painting the duck with a maltose syrup and hanging it up until the skin is parchment-dry; then roasting it in a specially designed oven. Once the duck has been brought to your table and carved, the routine is always the same: slather some dark, tangy bean sauce onto elastic, paper-thin pancakes, pop in a few spring onions, add shreds of duck, duck skin (crisp and rich) and cucumber, roll it up and eat. Nothing is wasted; the duck's entrails are usually made into a separate rich soup, then served up alongside the meat. The cost varies depending on where you go and whether you'd like side dishes served with the duck; some places advertise low prices but then charge extra for the sauce, pancakes and spring onions. Expect to pay upwards of ¥170 for a whole duck, or at least double this at any of the city's more famous duck restaurants. Favourite places include *Liqun* (see p.148), *Quanjude* (see p.148), *Siji Minfu* (see p.142) and *Jingzun* (see p.146).

Mongolian hotpot 蒙古火鍋, ménggǔ huǒguō. Not to be confused with the now-ubiquitous spicy Sichuanese hotpot from southwestern China, Mongolian hotpot is Beijing's classic winter warmer, but makes for a fantastic communal meal at any time of year. The brass pot in the centre of the table has an outer trough around a chimney with a charcoal-burner underneath. Stock is boiled in the trough, and diners dip in slices of raw meat, vegetables, bean noodles, mushrooms and bean curd. Lamb is the traditional highlight, and it's sliced so finely that it takes only a few seconds to cook between your chopsticks. Shake to get rid of excess water, then dunk into the sesame-based dipping sauce, and it's ready to eat. Like Peking duck, Mongolian hotpot likely has Muslim origins and many Muslim restaurants offer it, though by far the most famous place is *Dong Lai Shun* (see p.148).

Dumplings Given how cold northeast China gets in winter, it's not surprising that the signature regional snack is piping-hot dumplings, served straight out of bamboo steamers. There are two main types: ravioli-like *jiaozi* (饺子, jiǎozi), typically filled with minced pork and cabbage and served with a dipping sauce of soy sauce, vinegar and pickled garlic; and *baozi* (包子, bāozi), looking like a small bread roll and either plain (馒头, mántou, literally "bald heads") or stuffed with a variety of meat and vegetable fillings – a favourite is beef, carrot and cumin. Miniature *baozi* – called *xiaolongbao* (小笼包, xiǎolóngbāo) – and *jiaozi* are served as a sit-down snack in their steamers (holding ten or so), while the larger *baozi* (good as hand warmers on a cold day) are sold per piece to take away.

FAST FOOD AND STREET FOOD

Street food is everywhere in Beijing (see box, p.140), and trying it is an essential part of the local culinary scene. However grubby the immediate surroundings, almost everything is made to order in front of you, and you can be fairly confident that what's on offer is hygienic. The status of Wangfujing's tourist **night markets**, once infamous for their stalls selling impaled chicken hearts, sparrows,

9

BEIJING SNACKS AND STREET FOOD

Most Beijingers kick off the day at the nearest streetside stall or hole-in-the-wall selling steamers full of **jiaozi** or **baozi** (see p.139); **deep-fried dough** sticks (油条, yóutiáo) served with warm, sweetened soy milk (豆浆, dòujiāng); or mung-bean milk (豆汁, dòuzhī), a real local favourite despite its greyish tinge and faintly repulsive, sour smell. In a country where dairy products are a rarity, Beijing **yoghurt** (老北京酸奶, lǎo běijīng suānnǎi) is also worth a try; sold in cute clay pots, it has a delicious, honey-like taste.

For a memorable mix of street performance and local flavour, you can't beat **jianbing** (煎饼, jiānbǐng), a savoury crêpe which originated in nearby Tianjin but has now become a favourite Beijing staple. Sold from mobile carts or streetside windows, a scoop of batter is cooked until firm on a circular hotplate, then an egg is cracked over the top to make a tasty, omelette-like layer; it's all seasoned with chilli bean paste and sliced spring onions, folded around a rectangular, crispy biscuit, chopped into quarters and handed over – a wonderfully warming winter breakfast, all prepared in under a minute by a deft cook.

If you need a light snack as you wander, try heavily spiced barbecued meat **kebabs** (串, chuàn, though pronounced "chuar" in Beijing's pirate-like accent), often served up by Uyghurs from China's northwest. As these are a Muslim import, lamb skewers (羊肉串, yángròu chuàn) are the de facto choice, though there are usually various cuts of chicken to choose from too. Many Muslim restaurants sell takeaway kebabs from front-of-house windows; you can find them all over town, but for the most authentic places, head to the streets just north of Niu Jie Mosque (see p.84). Not far behind in the popularity stakes is *malatang* (麻辣烫, málà tàng), various skewered comestibles boiled in a spicy broth, and often served with a peanut paste. A sweet alternative are skewers of **toffee haws** (糖葫芦, tánghúlu; also made with grapes, strawberries etc), which were originally sold by street hawkers.

Some restaurants around town specialize in **local snacks**, many of which have entertaining names: there's "rolling donkey" (驴打滚, lú dǎgǔn), steamed sweet soya bean rolls dusted in toasted flour; "sweet ears" (糖耳朵, táng ěrduo) sugary, jelly-soft twists of cooked dough; "door-stud rolls" (门钉肉饼, méndīng ròubǐng), named after the golden studs on imperial household doors, stuffed with various fillings and fried to golden perfection; and "seasoned millet mush" (面茶, miàn chá), hot millet-flour porridge with sesame sauce floating on top. Then there are rice cakes with sweet fillings (艾窝窝, ài wōwō); blocks of syrup-coated flour noodles (沙琪玛, shāqímǎ); "stir-fried" liver (炒肝, chǎo gān), actually a tonic soup flavoured with garlic and ginger; and fried noodles with fermented soya bean paste (炸酱面, zhájiàng miàn).

---

crickets, silkworm pupae, scorpions and sheep testicles, is uncertain; one has definitely been closed by the authorities, citing hygiene regulations (though gentrification of the district is more likely the real reason), and the other is perhaps surviving on borrowed time.

SNACK CHAINS

Ajisen Ramen 味千拉面, wèiqiān lāmiàn. ⓦ ajisen .com.cn. Good-value and filling – if not massively inspiring – fast food from this Japanese chain offering ramen, rice, and fried pork cutlet-style dishes.

Hai Di Lao 海底捞火锅, hǎidǐlāo huǒguō. ⓦ www .haidilao.com. Reasonably priced Sichuan hotpot chain, with a choice of broths and a make-your-own-dipping-sauce counter. There's a 24hr one on the 8th floor of the APM mall, Wangfujing.

Huguosi 护国寺小吃店, hùguósì xiǎochī diàn. Muslim canteen serving a range of Beijing snacks (including "rolling donkey"), restaurant dishes and freshly made, takeaway pastries and breads (try their delicious

shaobing sesame buns). Daily 5.30am–9pm.

Longfusi 隆福寺小吃店, lóngfúsì xiǎochī diàn. Full run of traditional Beijing street food and snacks in relatively smart surroundings; nerve yourself to slurp a bowl of "millet mush" or *douzhr*. Daily 7am–9pm.

Qinfeng Steamed Dumpling 庆丰包子铺, qìngfēng bāozipù. *Baozi* specialist, founded in the 1940s but now doubly famous after Xi Jinping was recently seen sampling their wares. Their buns are a fraction of the cost of better-known Tianjin rival, *Goubuli* (see p.122), and just as tasty. Daily 6.30am–9pm.

Yonghe King 永和大王, yǒnghé dàwáng. Breakfast chain known for its tofu milk with *youtiao* (fried dough sticks), and cheap noodle dishes. Daily 6am–10.30pm.

NIGHT MARKET

Xiaochi Jie 小吃街, xiǎochī jiē. Xiagongfu Jie; subway line #1 to Wangfujing, Exit C2; map pp.68–69. This pedestrianized alley is lined with stalls selling xiǎo chī – literally, "little eats" – from all over China. Though vendors are pushy, it's atmospheric and has tables to sit down at with an ice-cold glass of beer. Daily 10am–midnight.

OTHER CHINESE CUISINES

Many regional Chinese cuisines are represented in Beijing; besides ordinary restaurants, most **provincial government offices** have inexpensive and extremely authentic canteens attached, catering to their staff but open to the public too. A list of the principal dishes from each region is included in our menu reader (see p.199), but here are the most popular regional styles in the capital:

Hunanese Hunan province, in central China, is known for its rural cuisine, featuring fresh fish and river food, unsophisticated (but very tasty) stews, simply cooked vegetable dishes, and an abundance of fresh and picked chillies. Chairman Mao and many of the early Communist hierarchy were from Hunan, which perhaps explains the cuisine's popularity.

Sichuanese Boisterous Sichuanese food, with its extravagant use of fiery chillies, aromatic Sichuan peppercorns and pungent flavours, is a particular favourite among Beijingers and tourists alike. Try *mapo doufu* (麻婆豆腐, mápó dòufu; bean curd with pork), *gongbao jiding* (宫保鸡丁, gōngbǎo jīdīng; chicken and peanuts) and searingly hot *zhushui yu* (水煮鱼, shuǐzhǔyú; boiled fish slices with chilli) for a classic spicy meal.

Xinjiang Food from the Turkic peoples of Xinjiang, in the far northwest, is perennially popular. It has a Central Asian flavour, notable for its lamb kebabs flavoured with cumin, baked breads and handmade "pulled" noodles (拉面, lāmiàn) – watching a skilled cook taking just a few seconds to bang and stretch the raw dough into a skein of fine noodles is one of the wonders of the cuisine. You'll often find Xinjiang food at street stalls (see box opposite).

Yunnanese Stuck way over in China's far southwest, a region bumping up against Burma, Vietnam, Laos and Thailand, Yunnan province is famed for the ethnic diversity of its peoples, and its cuisine reflects this. Among the tropical flavours that you might encounter are pineapple, seasoned pork and lots of mushrooms; dishes are often spicy, and some places serve them on banana leaves.

INTERNATIONAL FOOD

While restaurants serving International food are scattered all through central Beijing, there's a purpose-built strip of them up in the northeast on "**Lucky Street**" (好运街, hǎoyùn jiē; subway line #14 to Zaoyinglu, Exit A; map pp.96–97), featuring Indian, Japanese and Chinese restaurants, plus the *Nashville* bar (see p.155).

Elsewhere in Asia Japanese, Thai, Malay and Middle Eastern cooking are all fairly well represented; you'll also find a limited number of Indian and even Russian places.

Western There's ample opportunity to eat Western fast

IMPERIAL CUISINE

Pity the poor emperor. At mealtimes he wasn't allowed to take more than one mouthful of any one dish for fear that if he showed a preference a poisoner might take advantage. As a lowly citizen however, you are under no such compunction, and the city has a few places where you can indulge in the **imperial cuisine** that originated in the Qing dynasty kitchens. It's an expensive treat, however – expect at least ¥250 per head in a group – though you won't be served anything like the 108 courses that traditionally featured at banquets. As well as meticulously prepared dishes created with extravagant ingredients such as **birds' nests** and **sharks' fins**, imperial cuisine is noted for fish that's so fresh it's still flapping (it's all about keeping the nerves intact) and fine **pastries** such as pea-flour cakes and kidney-bean-flour rolls. Although you'll find dishes made with exotic meats such as **boar** and **camel**, these days you won't come across bear or wolf on the menu. Thankfully, one other ingredient is also no longer included: traditionally, imperial food always came with a strip of silver inside, as it was thought to turn black in the presence of poison.

Bai Family Courtyard 白家大院, báijiā dàyuàn. 15 Suzhou Jie, up towards the Summer Palace ☏010 62658851; subway line #10 to Suzhoujie, Exit A; map pp.96–97. This courtyard restaurant sits inside a beautifully restored mansion garden, hung with red lanterns, serving impeccable traditional dishes. Staff dress in period costume, and the replica *famille rose* porcelain and imperial yellow linen tablecloths are nice touches. Daily 11.30am–2pm & 5–8pm.

Fangshan 仿膳饭庄, fǎngshàn fànzhuāng. 1 Wenjin Jie, inside the east gate of Beihai Park ☏010 64042573; subway line #6 to Beihai North, Exit D; map pp.58–59. Founded in 1925, this is Beijing's longest-running restaurant serving imperial cuisine. The 14-course banquet is good, but can't possibly compare with the insanely opulent decor, dripping with dragon-wrapped pillars, ornamental stone carvings and gilded woodwork. Daily 11am–1.30pm & 5–8pm.

9

BEIJING'S BEST

Best hotpot Dong Lai Shun (see p.148)
Best Yunnanese Lost Heaven (see below)
Best Xinjiang Crescent Moon (see p.144)
Best vegan Veggie Table (see p.144)

Best dumplings Din Tai Fung (see p.147)
Best Manchu Najia Xiaoguan (see p.148)
Best Peking duck Jingzun (see p.146)
Best ambience Mei Mansion (see opposite)

food in the city, with *KFC*, *McDonald's* and *Subway* all well established. All the major International hotels have restaurants serving Western fare, including familiar breakfasts; alternatively, head to one of the many bars or cafés which also offer Western brunch and pub meals.

VEGETARIANS

Thanks to Buddhism, China has a long-established and sophisticated vegetarian cuisine, using tofu in various guises, gluten, mushrooms and even puffed bran to replace or replicate meat. Sadly, there are surprisingly few dedicated options in Beijing, though the wide array of meat-free dishes on Chinese menus means that veggies should have no particular problem in finding plenty to eat. Do be aware, however, that vegetable dishes may be made on the same surfaces, or with the same implements, as those used for meat. Probably the best fully vegetarian establishments are *Fuhui Ciyuan* (see p.144) if you're after Chinese food, and *Veggie Table* (see p.144) if you're not.

PRACTICALITIES

Opening hours The Chinese tend to eat early, sitting down to lunch at noon and dinner at six; many establishments are closing down by 9pm, though a few stay open late or even around the clock. Some places also close for a couple of hours after the lunchtime rush. Opening hours are given for all restaurants listed in this chapter.

Costs Prices are low in comparison with the West. For a roadside noodle or dumpling stop you're looking at under ¥15 for a one-dish meal, and even in quite decent restaurants it's possible to eat well for ¥50 a head – though you can, of course, spend a lot more if you dine lavishly in palatial surroundings. The sample prices of meals in our restaurant reviews are calculated on the basis of each person ordering a couple of dishes plus rice, or a main course and dessert.

Booking You'll only really need to book at the trendiest or most upmarket restaurants; most mid-range and cheaper places won't take bookings at all.

Listings To keep on top of Beijing's ever-changing restaurant scene, check out the expat listings magazines: *Time Out* (ⓦ timeoutbeijing.com), *The Beijinger* (ⓦ issuu .com/thebeijinger), *That's Beijing* (ⓦ thatsmags.com /beijing), and *City Weekend* (ⓦ cityweekend.com.cn /beijing).

Tipping Tipping isn't expected; if there is a service charge (usually at posher places), it will be on the bill.

Chopsticks Many restaurants in areas popular with tourists have knives (刀子, dāozi) and forks (叉子, chāzi), though most visitors are able to crack chopstick use within a few days. Tofu dishes should be eaten with a spoon (勺子, sháozi).

Home delivery Forgo the whole tedious business of leaving your room to eat by contacting the brilliantly named Sherpa (ⓦ sherpa.com.cn) who, for a small service charge, deliver than many of the city's popular restaurants. Your food will likely be a little lukewarm after delivery, but after a night out in Sanlitun it'll taste like manna from the gods.

Supermarkets Supermarkets are covered under "Shopping" (see p.168).

RESTAURANTS

THE FORBIDDEN CITY AND TIAN'ANMEN SQUARE

★**Lost Heaven** 花马天堂, huāmǎ tiāntáng. 23 Ch'ienmen complex, 23 Qianmen Dongdajie ☎ 010 85162698, ⓦ lostheaven.com.cn; subway line #2 to Qianmen, Exit B; map p.42. At the northeast corner of the former US Legation compound, this elegant restaurant features almost romantically subdued lighting, southeast Asian carved wooden furniture, stylish crockery and a range of Yunnanese and Burmese curries, spicy salads flavoured with fresh herbs and tropical fruits, plus taro spring rolls and tamarind juice drinks. ¥150 a head. Daily noon–2pm & 5pm–1am.

Renhe 仁和酒家, rénhé jiǔjiā. 19 Donghuamen Dajie; subway line #1 to Tian'anmen East subway, Exit B; map p.42. A short walk from the Forbidden City's east gate, this is a cut above the area's other (mostly horrendous) restaurants. Here you're far less likely to be ripped off or served yesterday's rice; in fact, the food is rather good, especially their tasty tofu dishes (from ¥32). Its outdoor seats are also a prime place for evening beers. Daily 6am–1am.

★**Siji Minfu** 四季民福, sìjì mínfú. 11 Nanchizi Jie ☎ 65267369; subway line #1 to Tian'anmen East subway, Exit B; map p.42. Smart, modern Beijing restaurant specializing in succulent roast duck, with the open brick ovens and sweating chefs in starched white uniforms as part of the floor show. Try to grab a table at the back overlooking the Forbidden City moat; touristy but easily the best restaurant in the area. No bookings, so get here early or expect to wait. Around ¥150 a head. Daily 11am–9pm.

NORTH OF THE CENTRE

18 Tea Garden 十八茶院, shíbā cháyuàn. 18 Banchang Hutong ☎010 64060918; subway line #6 to Nanluoguxiang; map pp.58–59. Within easy walking distance of Nanluogu Xiang, this is an understated but beautiful courtyard venue, with mint-coloured bead curtains hanging from every ledge. The set-meals-only menu (¥60–120) offers a seemingly unwieldy fusion of Italian and Japanese cuisine, though it's all executed very well indeed. They also serve a large range of tea and Japanese alcohol. Bookings essential. Daily 11am–7pm.

Café Sambal 桑芭, sāng bā. 43 Doufuchi Hutong ☎010 64004875, ⓦcafesambal.com; subway line #8 to Shichahai, Exit A2; map pp.58–59. Authentic Malay food in a laidback setting, tucked away down a *hutong* and quite easy to miss. There are a variety of places to sit, from the bar-like room by the entrance to the floor-cushions abutting the courtyard, and a decent set lunch of *bak ku teh* spare-rib soup, sweet milky tea and dessert (¥68); otherwise mains are around ¥45. Daily 10am–11pm.

Dali Courtyard 大理院子, dàlǐ yuànzi. 67 Xiaojingchang Hutong ☎010 84041430; subway line #8 to Shichahai, Exit C; map pp.58–59. It's a little tricky to find this charming courtyard restaurant, but worth the effort for its excellent Yunnanese home cooking. There's no menu – you simply turn up, pay the fixed price (around ¥180 per head for eight or so dishes), then the chef gives you whatever he feels like making. Portions are generous and generally rice-based, and all sets will have a fish dish. Drinks are extra. Reservations recommended. Daily noon–2.30pm & 6–10.30pm.

Hutong Pizza 胡同披萨, hútòng pīsà. 9 Yindingqiao Hutong ☎010 83228916; subway line #8 to Shichahai, Exit A2; map pp.58–59. A tiny restaurant serving up delicious pizzas from ¥80; they're probably a bit too big for one person, but not quite large enough for two. It's hidden away down an alley; follow the signs from the bridge over the lakes. Daily 11am–11pm.

Kaorouji 烤肉季, kǎoròujì. 14 Qianhai Dongyuan ☎010 64045921; subway line #8 to Shichahai, Exit A2; map pp.58–59. This down-to-earth Muslim restaurant, a three-storied affair run by the same family for 150 years, takes advantage of its lakeside location with big windows and, in summer, balcony tables. While the food isn't exceptional, everything is reliably tasty: the beef and barbecued lamb dishes are recommended. You'll spend around ¥100 a head. Daily 11am–11pm.

Lao Xi'an 老西安饭庄, lǎo xī'ān fànzhuāng. 20 Xinjiekou Nan Da Jie ☎010 66181748; subway line #4 to Xinjiekou, Exit C; map pp.58–59. Busy, eat-and-run Muslim canteen with no English sign or menu, but most people order either kebabs – ¥10 for four, from the window out the front – or the famous, if unsophisticated, Xi'an dish *yangrou paomo* (羊肉泡馍, yángròu pàomó; ¥32), a bowl of spicy lamb broth and ripped-up cubes of bread. Daily 11am–11pm.

★**Mei Mansion** 梅府家宴, méifǔ jiāyàn. 24 Daxiangfeng Hutong, just east of Prince Gong's Palace ☎010 66126845; subway line #6 to Beihai North, Exit B; map pp.58–59. Former royal mansion with attractive garden, serving the traditional, clear-flavoured dishes favoured by the twentieth-century Beijing opera great, Mei Lanfang (see p.62). The stylish Art Deco dining room is filled with photos and operatic mementoes of Mei Lanfang's career. Set menu only and bookings essential; expensive. Daily 11.30am–2pm & 5–10pm.

Nuage 庆云楼, qìngyún lóu. 22 Qianhai Dongzhao ☎010 64019581; subway line #8 to Shichahai, Exit A2; map pp.58–59. Decent Vietnamese food served in a smart upstairs bar-restaurant. Try the steamed garlic prawns and battered squid, and finish with super-strong Vietnamese coffee if you don't intend to sleep in the near future. You'll spend upwards of ¥120 per head. Don't miss the extraordinary tropical fantasy toilets. Daily 11am–2pm & 5.30–10.30pm.

★**Private Kitchen 44** 细管胡同44号, xìguǎnhútóng sìshísìhào. 70 Deshengmennei Dajie ☎010 64001280; subway line #2 to Jishuitan, Exit B; map pp.58–59. Dishes from rural southwestern China, best washed down with rice wine: spare ribs steamed in glutinous rice (¥38); pork knuckle stewed with bamboo shoots (¥188); Miao sour fish soup (¥98); or the house speciality "spicy dry pot", a mix of veg, meat, wild herbs and Sichuan pepper (¥78). The food is excellent and it's always bustling, despite high prices; book ahead. Daily 11am–2pm & 4.30–10pm.

Shuxiangju 蜀乡居家常菜, shǔxiāngjū jiāchángcài. 2 Weikang Hutong, though entrance is on Xinjiekou Dong Jie; look for the "My Home Welcome" sign ☎010 53693353; subway line #2 to Jishuitan, Exit C; map pp.58–59. Friendly, fast-food-style restaurant with Sichuanese name, staff and menu: fish-flavoured pork shreds, dry-fried beans, twice-cooked pork, *mapo doufu*, and even the rarely seen smoked duck. Great value at around ¥50 a head. Daily 24hr.

Xiao Beijing Jiaozi 小北京饺子, xiǎo běijīng jiǎozi. 52 Di'anmen Wai Dajie ☎010 84014598; subway line #8 to Shichahai, Exit C; map pp.58–59. Within spitting distance of touristy Qianhai and the Drum Tower, yet bright, cheerful, reasonably priced food if you want a light meal at around ¥20 a dish: a plate of prawn and cucumber *jiaozi*, or cold side dishes like lotus root in syrup, bashed cucumber or "hemp tofu" (麻豆腐, má dòufu) – actually a fermented

9

soya and mung-bean mash flavoured with chilli and Sichuan pepper. Daily 10.30am–10pm.

EAST OF THE CENTRE
WANGFUJING AND AROUND

★**Dadong** 大董烤鸭店, dàdǒng kǎoyādiàn. Floor 5, Jinbaohui Shopping Centre, 88 Jinbao Jie ☎010 85221234, ⓦdadongdadong.com; subway line #5 to Dengshikou, Exit C; map pp.68–69. A bright, elegant, modish place that's garnered a good reputation for its attentive staff and crispy-skinned, succulent Peking duck (from ¥258). This is by no means their only offering though: the menu runs to 160 pages. Daily 11am–10pm.

Fuhui Ciyuan 福慧慈缘, fúhuì cíyuán. Xila Hutong, 53 Donganmen Dajie ☎010 51385789; subway line #5 to Dengshikou, Exit A; map pp.68–69. Smart, nice-looking place with overhead "vine" trellis and traditional touches in the wooden screen ballustrades and heavy furniture. Purely vegetarian Chinese food, which at first glance you'd be forgiven for thinking contained meat; it's all beautifully presented but not expensive at around ¥70 a head. Daily 11am–9pm.

Lei Garden 利苑酒家, lìyuàn jiǔjiā. 3F Jinbao Tower, 89 Jinbao Jie ☎010 85221212, ⓦleigarden.hk; subway line #5 to Dengshikou, Exit C; map pp.68–69. This well-established, upmarket Cantonese restaurant specializes in seafood, though they go overboard mixing the likes of clams with lobster soup. Other signature dishes include baked chicken in salt, crispy-skinned pork, various clay-pot dishes and an unlikely parade of desserts (such as chilled mango with grapefruit and sago). Best of all, however, is their *dim sum* selection, served throughout the morning. At least ¥200 per head. Daily 11.30am–3pm & 5.30–10.30pm.

★**Made in China** Grand Hyatt (东方君悦大酒店, dōngfāng jūnyuè dàjiǔdiàn), 1 Dongchang'an Jie ☎010 65109024; subway line #1 to Wangfujing, Exit A; map pp.68–69. An element of drama is added to this dim, traditionally styled restaurant by the spectacle of chefs toiling over the giant woks and ovens in the open kitchen. It's one of the swankiest places in town, and the Chinese-with-a-twist food is reliably excellent; their signature menu goes for ¥498 per person (minimum two), but à la carte items average ¥120. Daily 11.30am–2.30pm & 5.30–10.30pm.

YONGHE GONG AND AROUND

Cheung Kee 章记餐厅, zhāngjì cāntīng. 98 Guozijian Jie, west of the Confucian temple and virtually on the corner with Andingmennei Dajie ☎010 64036619; subway line #2 to Andingmen, Exit B; map pp.68–69. Small, dark but comfortable Singaporean Chinese place with a brief menu featuring one-dish meals

– laksa, beef brisket curry and juicy Hainan chicken rice, for example – which it does very well. ¥50 a head. Daily 11am–10pm.

Crescent Moon 弯弯月亮, wānwān yuèliàng. 16 Dongsi Liutiao ☎010 64005281; subway line #5 or #6 to Zhangsizhonglu, Exit C; see map, pp.68–69. Uigur establishment done up in green and yellow paint with Islamic-style domes on the roof. Inside it's unusually clean and orderly: order a roast leg of lamb smothered with cumin (¥130), plus a couple of vegetable dishes, pilau and naan, and you have a substantial meal for two. Surprisingly for a Muslim restaurant, they also stock Xinjiang Black Beer. The dining hall is relatively small but there are private rooms at the rear. Daily 11am–10pm.

Dagui 大贵, dàguì. 69 Daxing Hutong; look for red lanterns just east of the police station ☎010 64071800; subway line #5 to Zhangzizhonglu, Exit D; map pp.68–69. Rustic affair with basic furnishings, serving dishes from Guizhou province – one of China's poorest – which in reality should mean little more than rice with hot-and-sour fish stew (¥48). However, their menu also stretches to a good range of wind-cured meats, stir-fries and vegetable dishes (including pungent *zi'ergen* salad), and the house speciality is a huge platter of grilled spicy ribs (¥75), enough for two. Daily 10am–2pm & 5–10pm.

Huajia Yiyuan 华家怡园, huājiā, yíyuán. 235 Dongzhimennei Dajie ☎010 64037802; subway line #5 to Beixinqiao, Exit B; map pp.68–69. This glassed-over courtyard restaurant, with songbirds and pleasant trellis-shrouded seating, is touristy but also an excellent place to sample Sichuanese food, northern-style dumplings or Beijing duck – a bargain at ¥168. There's also a Chinese Opera-themed floor show. Daily 10.30am–4am.

★**Jin Ding Xuan** 金鼎轩, jīn dǐng xuān. 77 Hepingli Xijie ☎010 64978978; subway line #2 or #5 to Yonghegong Lama Temple, Exit A; map pp.68–69. Antique-style palace on four floors crammed with customers, wooden furniture, chefs and waiters scurrying in all directions, and filled with the competing scents of dishes from around China: Sichuanese *lazi ji*, Peking duck, Hunanese snacks, Cantonese *dim sum*, West Lake Fish from Hangzhou, and more. The menu changes through the day too, with different sittings 6–11am, 11am–2pm, 2–5pm, 5–10pm and 10pm–6am. Despite being open around the clock, expect to have to take a number and wait in the street outside. ¥75 will see you full. Daily 24hr.

Veggie Table 吃素的, chīsù de. 19 Wudaoying Hutong ☎010 64462073; subway line #2 or #5 to Yonghegong Lama Temple, Exit D; map pp.68–69. Top-notch organic vegan menu, featuring couscous, curries and mezes (including superb hummus and falafel). Pride of place goes to their famed mushroom burger

9

GHOST STREET

Nicknamed "Ghost Street" (簋街, guǐ jiē), a 1km-long stretch of **Dongzhimennei Dajie** is lined with hundreds of restaurants, all festooned with red lanterns and neon – a colourful and boisterous scene, particularly on weekends. Note that staff in these restaurants will probably speak little or no English, though plenty have a picture menu to make ordering easy enough. It's an atmospheric experience, though when the crowds arrive in the evening the whole street can resemble a car park.

(¥62), tasty enough even for non-vegetarians. Mon–Fri 11.30am–3.30pm & 5.30–10.30pm, Sat & Sun 11.30am–11.30pm.

★**Vineyard Café** 葡萄院儿, pútáoyuàn'er. 31 Wudaoying Hutong ☎010 64027961, ⓦvineyardcafe .cn; subway line #2 or #5 to Yonghegong, Exit D; map pp.68–69. Good Western wine and food, including pizza, makes this bright, cheery place popular with the local expats. Serves tasty brunches too (from ¥75), making it a target before or after a trip to Yonghe Gong. Tues–Sun 11.30am–midnight.

Zhang's BBQ Lamb 张记烤羊腿, zhāngjì kǎoyángtuǐ. 78 Jiaodaokou Nan Dajie ☎010 84046623; subway line #6 or #8 to Nanluoguxiang, Exit F; map pp.68–69. In the evening it's difficult get past this absurdly popular, noisy barbecue restaurant, what with tables spilling out on to the pavement and a kerbside charcoal grill wafting out the fantastic smell of chargrilled lamb. Somewhere to come in a large group, order a whole grilled leg and plenty of beer, and enjoy people-watching. Under ¥100 a head. Daily 10am–2pm & 5–11pm.

SANLITUN

Bellagio 味千拉面, wèiqiānlāmiàn. Level 3, Tai Koo Li complex ☎010 64177040; subway line #10 to Tuanjiehu, Exit A; map p.72. Despite the Italian-sounding name, this is a busy Taiwanese restaurant offering Chinese favourites in typically generous portions, featuring heavy sauces, plenty of chilli and some specialities such as *migao* (steamed glutinous rice flavoured with shrimp and mushroom) and *caipu dan* (a turnip omelette). Daily 11.30am–9pm.

Blue Frog 藍蛙, lánwā. Level 3, Tai Koo Li complex ☎010 64174030, ⓦbluefrog.com.cn; subway line #10 to Tuanjiehu, Exit A; map p.72. Local representative for this national chain of comfortable American-style restaurants, offering TV screens everywhere you look and hearty meals: big breakfasts (¥88), pasta (¥118) and various grill options including ribeye steak (¥198). Sun–Thurs 10am–midnight, Fri & Sat 10am–1am.

Crystal Jade 翡翠酒家, fěicuì jiǔjiā. Level 3, Tai Koo Li complex ☎010 64166858, ⓦcrystaljade.com; subway line #10 to Tuanjiehu, Exit A; map p.72. Bright and modern Shanghai-style chain known for its excellent *xiaolongbao* dumplings (¥25 for four) and generously sized

spicy *lamian* noodle soups (¥45). Cold side dishes are good too, especially tofu with preserved eggs, pickled white radish in syrup, and wood-ear fungus with vinegar dressing. Around ¥75 a head. Daily 11am–3pm & 5–9pm.

Foodie Town 美食城, měishí chéng. At the foot of Soho Tower, south across the road from the Tai Koo Li complex; subway line #10 to Tuanjiehu, Exit D; map p.72. Tasty fast food from across China eaten off trays at plastic tables in a noisy, rapid-turnover environment – you're here to fuel up, not dine. Infinitely cheaper than most local restaurants, so in demand with local shop staff. Daily 7am–7pm.

Hatsune 隐泉日本料理, yǐnquán rìběnliàolǐ. Level 3, Tai Koo Li complex ☎010 64153939; subway line #10 to Tuanjiehu, Exit A; map p.72. Hip, young, American-styled Japanese restaurant with a reputation for good sushi and sashimi – not to mention grilled head of salmon. Expect around ¥200 per head. Daily 11.30am–2pm & 5.30–10pm.

Hotpot Express 鼎鼎香, dǐngdǐngxiāng. Level 3, Tai Koo Li complex ☎010 64172546; subway line #10 to Tuanjiehu, Exit A; map p.72. The gig at this casual-smart Sichuanese hotpot chain is that everyone gets their own pot, which is handy if one of your party can't take spice or meat. Choose from a wide variety of broths – chicken is recommended – then pick the raw ingredients to cook up. It shouldn't set you back more than ¥100 per head in a group. Daily 11am–midnight.

★**Jingzun** 京尊烤鸭店, jīngzūn kǎoyā diàn. 6 Taiping Nan Li, Chunxiu Lu ☎010 64174075; subway line #2 to Dongsishitiao, Exit B; map pp.68–69. Despite being packed with expats and close to a *Holiday Inn*, this comfortable, informal place isn't the tourist rip-off you might expect: a whole roast duck, excellently cooked, is just ¥168, and you'll pay about ¥100 a head in a group for duck with plenty of side dishes and beer. There's also a front terrace for sitting out in good weather. Daily 11am–10pm.

Karaiya Spice House 辣屋, làwū. 3F Tai Koo Li South ☎010 64153535; subway line #10 to Tuanjiehu, Exit A; map p.72. Hunanese fine dining at this expat favourite, where specialities include various "dry-fried" dishes, smoked ham, hot and sour pork ribs and steamed Mandarin fish. Choose carefully if you can't take too much heat; many dishes are packed with chillies. ¥150 per person. Daily 11.30am–2pm & 5.30–10pm.

Middle 8th 中8楼, zhōngbālóu. Level 3, Tai Koo Li complex ☎010 64158858; subway line #10 to Tuanjiehu, Exit A; map p.72. Smart-casual restaurant with good cross-section of Yunnanese cooking, from *qiguo* steampot, subtly flavoured with herbs, through to grilled pork slices dusted in chilli, stir-fried wild mushrooms and pine nuts, goats' cheese and wild herb salad, roasted bee larvae (nutty), and sweet pineapple rice. Wash it all down with rice wine. ¥100 a head. Daily 11am–11pm.

★**Migas** 6F Nali Patio, Tai Koo Li complex ☎010 52086061, ⊛migasbj.com; subway line #10 to Tuanjiehu, Exit A; map p.72. An artfully decorated place serving the tastiest Spanish food in Beijing, *Migas* consistently rates highly for its seafood (especially the chargrilled octopus) and creative cooking (aged lamb chops with black garlic sponge cake), but pretty much everything here is delicious. Don't forget the rooftop terrace bar for tapas, a drink and a dance (see p.153). Lunchtime set meals are excellent value at ¥95, otherwise ¥200 a head. Booking advised. Daily noon–3.30pm & 6–10pm.

One Thousand and One Nights 一千零一夜, yīqiān língyīyè. 21 Gongti Beilu ☎010 65324050; subway line #10 to Tuanjiehu, Exit A; map pp.68–69. Beijing's oldest Middle Eastern restaurant is still popular both with Western bigwigs, who come here to fill up on kebabs, and with homesick diplomats, who puff on hookahs on the pavement terrace outside. Try the hummus as a starter and the baked chicken, kebabs or lamb platter for a main course, and leave enough room for baklava. Music and frankly cheesy belly dancing nightly. About ¥150 per head. Daily 11am–11pm.

Serve the People 为人民服务, wèi rénmín fúwù. 1 Sanlitun Xiwujie ☎010 84544580; subway line #10 to Agricultural Exhibition Center, Exit D2; map p.72. This trendy Thai restaurant serves staples such as green curry, pork satay with peanut sauce and *tom yum*, all of which are worth trying. Authentically hot, though you can ask them to tone down the spices. About ¥150 per person. Daily 10.30am–10.30pm.

Sureño 榆舍地中海餐厅, yúshè dìzhōnghǎi cāntīng. B1 Opposite House, 11 Sanlitun Lu ☎010 64105240, ⊛surenorestaurant.com; subway line #10 to Tuanjiehu, Exit A; map p.72. This expat favourite, featuring an open kitchen and a wood-fired oven, is the city's best venue for Mediterranean-style fine dining. You can get a pizza here for as little as ¥120, while the seafood platter – including oysters, crab and a whole lobster – will set you back about ¥400 per person; expect to pay around ¥250 for a main course. Daily noon–10.30pm.

THE CBD

★**Chuanban** 川办餐厅, chuānbàn cāntīng. Inside the Sichuan Provincial Government Building, 5 Gongyuan Toutiao, north off Jianguomen Da Jie ☎010 65122277; subway lines #1 or #2 to Jianguomen, Exit A; map pp.68–69. Catering to Sichuanese office workers, this is one restaurant where the staff don't ask if you can eat chilli: if you can't, you're in the wrong place. Big range of snacks and dishes served among faux-antique teahouse decor: *lazi ji*, cold spicy noodles, steamed spare-ribs in rice flour, tea-smoked duck; the slow-simmered soups are a speciality. Large portions; around ¥75 a head. Mon–Fri 11am–2pm & 5–9.30pm, Sat & Sun 11am–9.30pm.

Din Tai Fung 鼎泰丰, dǐngtàifēng LG2, Parkview Green Mall, 9 Dongdaqiao Lu ☎010 85626583, ⊛www.dintaifung.com.tw; subway line #6 to Dongdaqiao; map pp.68–69. Slick, upscale Taiwanese chain famed for its steamed *xiaolongbao* "soup" dumplings, a juicy meat filling packed into a paper-thin dough wrapping – bite a corner off the dumpling and carefully drain the juice into a spoon first, or risk splattering your shirt front. They also do great noodle soups. Around ¥100 a head. Daily 11.30am–10pm.

Justine's Jianguo Hotel (建国饭店, jiànguó fàndiàn), 5 Jianguomenwai Dajie ☎010 65002233; subway line #1 to Yong'anli, Exit B; map pp.68–69. Beijing's oldest French restaurant is suitably fancy, resplendent in super-plush carpets, giant mirrors, golden chandeliers and stained glass. The menu switches around with pleasing regularity; try the lobster soup or grilled lamb. Service is attentive. Around ¥350 per person. Daily 6.30am–10.30am, noon–2pm & 6–10pm.

Lime 青柠, qīng níng. Tower 15-103, Central Park, 6 Chaowai Da Jie ☎010 65970887; subway line #10 to Jintaixizhao, Exit A; map pp.68–69. A friendly Thai venue serving fairly authentic food for ¥40–65 per dish; the *tom yum* and green curries are particularly recommended. Their outdoor seats are the best place from which to gaze over Central Park, a cosmopolitan residential area hidden from the surrounding main roads. Daily 11am–10pm.

Makye Ame 玛吉阿米, mǎjí āmǐ. 2F A11 Xiushui Nanjie ☎010 65069616; subway line #1 to Yong'anli, Exit A1; map pp.68–69. Hearty Tibetan food in a cosy atmosphere, rather more upscale than anywhere in Tibet, featuring plenty of yak meat. Try the *momos* (dumplings), grilled mushrooms or roasted lamb ribs and wash everything down with Tibetan beer – or, if you've the nerve, traditional butter tea. Tibetan singing and dancing on Wed and Fri nights. Daily 10am–2am.

Malacca Legend 马六甲傳奇, mǎliùjiǎ chuánqí. The Place, North Building, 9 Guanghua Lu ☎010 65871393; subway line #6 to Dongdaqiao, Exit D; map pp.68–69. Small place serving Nyonya Malay dishes, pleasantly informal despite the starched tablecloths and straight-backed chairs. Choose from dry curry *rendang*, *pie tie* (crispy pastry "hats" filled with shredded vegetables), whole crab or seafood, and finish with *es kachang*

9

(a mountain of shaved ice and sweet syrup) to help you cool off on a hot day. Lunch sets of curry, rice, prawn crackers, egg sambal and pandan pancakes are good value (¥50). Daily 11am–10pm.

Nadaman 滩万, tānwàn. 4F Shangri La Hotel, 1 Jianguomen Dajie ☏010 65052299; subway lines #1 or #10 to Guomao, Exit D; map pp.68–69. Discreet and stylishly minimalist Japanese restaurant, whose lunchtime set meals (around ¥250) are less financially crippling than either the sashimi or Wagyu beef for dinner (¥700 each). Most of the ingredients are flown in from Japan. Take someone you want to impress. Daily 11.30am–2pm & 5.30–10pm.

★**Najia Xiaoguan** 那家小馆, nǎjiā xiǎoguǎn. 10 Yong'anli Xi Jie, though there's no English sign; look for red lanterns and a "traditional" wooden gateway with the name in gold on the board above the door ☏010 65686553; subway line #1 to Yong'anli, Exit C; map pp.68–69. This superb Manchu place has a similar menu to the higher-profile "imperial cuisine" restaurants (see box, p.141), but scores higher for the friendly service, fair prices and an attractive, tearoom-like interior. Go for the excellent *guotie* (pot-sticker dumplings), slow-cooked *huangtanzi* stew, yam with osmanthus syrup or one of the venison dishes. Mains around ¥70; bookings essential. Daily 11am–11pm.

SOUTH OF THE CENTRE

Deyuan 德缘烤鸭店, déyuán kǎoyā diàn. 57 Dazhalan Xijie ☏010 63085371; subway line #2 to Qianmen, Exit C; map pp.80–81. Elaborate antique-style frontage alive with golden phoenixes, where they advertise a whole Peking duck for just ¥138 – though as they add ¥20 for carving, ¥14 for pancakes etc, you won't see much change from ¥200. Good quality though, and still the cheapest in the district. Daily 10am–2pm & 5–9pm.

★**Dong Lai Shun** 东来顺, dōngláishùn. 7 Dazhalan Dong Jie, inside and upstairs at the tourist market – look for the entranceway lucky Rabbit god statuette ☏010 63165836; subway line #2 to Qianmen, Exit C; map pp.80–81. Founded in 1903 and now with branches all over China, this features Beijing's own – non-spicy – Muslim hotpot. Order clear stock and platters of thinly sliced lamb, vegetables, mushrooms, glass noodles and dipping sauce, and cook your selection in a copper-funnelled "Mongolian" hotpot. You definitely need a group; expect ¥100 a head and don't be cajoled by staff into ordering far too much food. Daily 11am–9pm.

Goubuli 狗不理, gǒubùlǐ. 31 Dazhalan Dong Jie ☏010 63533338; subway line #2 to Qianmen, Exit C; map pp.80–81. Local branch of this famous Tianjin chain (see p.122), serving their signature steamed buns with various fillings (try the pork, shrimp and sea cucumber combo) for ¥68 and up per batch. They're tasty, but it's a lot

to pay for one of China's most basic staples, available on any street corner for a fraction of the price. Daily 7.30am–9pm.

Liqun 利群烤鸭店, lìqún kǎoyādiàn. 11 Beixiangfeng Hutong ☏010 67025681; subway line #2 to Qianmen, Exit B or line #7 to Qiaowan, Exit A; map pp.80–81. Famous but downright grungy, grease-splattered duck specialist, possibly doomed as gentrification of the adjoining *hutong* district edges closer. Quality is decent, but a little overpriced; it's ¥265 for a whole duck with accompaniments, or ¥365 with a host of side dishes as well. Expect to queue even after you've made a reservation (essential, in any case). Daily 11am–10pm.

Niu Jie Hongji 牛街洪记小吃店, niú jiē hóngjì xiǎochīdiàn. 10 Niu Jie ☏010 63550735; subway line #7 to Guanganmennei, Exit C; map pp.80–81. Well-regarded – if no-frills and noisy – multistorey canteen in the heart of Beijing's Muslim quarter. Service is slap-down and most dishes are pretty much standard Chinese, just using lamb or beef instead of pork, but it's crammed at lunchtime and pretty inexpensive: a couple of dishes plus rice shouldn't set you back more than ¥50, while a platter of "local flavour" snacks is ¥20. There's a front-of-house window selling Muslim breads, buns and pastries to take away. Daily 9am–8pm.

Quanjude 全聚德, quánjùdé. 30 Qianmen Dajie ☏010 67011379; subway line #2 to Qianmen, Exit C; map pp.80–81. Beijing's most famous duck restaurant by far, and pretty smart too, in a typically Chinese bright-lights way; reservations are not essential, but advised if you don't want to spend ages in the queue. The duck (¥365) is pricey but also everything you'd expect: rich, juicy and with meltingly crisp copper-coloured skin. Other duck delicacies are available, including seared duck hearts in liquor, and fried duck mince in bird's nest. Daily 11am–1.30pm & 4.30–8pm.

WEST OF THE CENTRE

China Central TV Tower 中央电视楼, zhōngyāng diànshì lóu. 11 Xishanhuangzhong Lu ☏010 68475809; subway line #1 or #10 to Gongzhufen, Exit B; map pp.88–89. Beijing's only rotating restaurant floats 221m above the city, offering generous views (though see p.90). The substantial set-price buffet and hotplate barbecue features Chinese, Japanese and Western food at very decent prices, given the setting (lunch ¥198, dinner ¥298); you can apparently eat for free if you can prove it's your birthday (though you still pay for the tower entry plus drinks). Daily 11am–9pm.

THE FAR NORTH

Ganges 恒河印度餐厅, hénghé yìndù cāntīng. 2 Jiangtai Lu ☏010 51358353, ⓦganges-restaurant .com; subway line #14 to Jiangtai, Exit A; map pp.96–97. Beijing isn't overwhelmed with Indian restaurants, so despite being stuck way up northeast – handy for the 798 Art District, if nowhere else – this place comes as a relief for those on a curry quest who can't live without naan, samosas, chicken korma, vindaloo, chana masala and Tiger beer. ¥100 a head. Daily 11am–11pm.

Lush 2F 1 Huaqing Jiayuan ⊙010 82863566, ⓦlushbeijing.com; subway line #13 to Wudaokou, Exit B; map pp.96–97. Super-popular student hangout serving all sorts of good Western food; most plump for the burgers, sandwiches or fried breakfasts, all of which cost around ¥40. Come evening, it's one of the area's busiest bars (see p.155) – it never, in fact, closes. Don't expect snappy service. Daily 24hr.

Shido Noodles 食度拉面馆, shídù lāmiànguǎn. Taoci Er Jie, 798 Art District; subway line #14 to Jiangtai, Exit B; map pp.96–97. The 798 district's restaurants are overpriced, but the area's single cheapie is where many gallery staff come to eat. It's nothing special,

but you'll get a huge, filling bowl of good noodles for under ¥40. Daily 11am–6pm.

Tantan Dalu 坦坦大炉, tǎntǎn dàlú. 4F 35 Chengfu Lu ⊙010 62560471; subway line #13 to Wudaokou, Exit A; map pp.96–97. The best of the Wudaokou area's many Korean restaurants; there are, indeed, several in this building alone. Try *bibimbap* (mixed rice, veggies and spice) or *naengmyeon* (cold buckwheat noodles) for around ¥35; a little more will buy you a portion of barbecued meat. Daily 10am–11pm.

Tori Tei 鸟亭日本菜, niǎotíng rìběn cài. "Lucky Street" (好运街, hǎoyùn jiē), Chaoyang Gongyuan Lu ⊙010 58670266; subway line #14 to Zaoyinglu, Exit A; map pp.96–97. Informal Japanese barbecue restaurant whose food might not win any prizes but is tasty enough, and goes down well between sips of chilled Kirin beer or sake. Grilled chicken skewers (*yakitori*) are the house speciality, and they also do great grilled mackerel, beef, bacon and asparagus rolls. Around ¥100 a head. Daily 5.30pm–1am.

CAFÉS

Coffee culture has thoroughly infiltrated Beijing, though as the preserve of foreigners and well-to-do locals, prices are relatively high at around ¥25 a cup. Note that some bars are also great spots to linger over a cappuccino; and that many of the places below do decent Western-style light meals and cakes. All have **free wi-fi**.

★**Alley Café** 寻常巷陌, xúncháng xiàng mò. 61 Shatan Houjie ⊙010 84047228; subway line #10 to Tuanjiehu, Exit A; map pp.58–59. Close to Jingshan Park and Forbidden City exits, this street is crowded with mediocre places to eat, of which this informal backpacker-style café is the exception. The coffee is decent (¥25), as are the Western-style set breakfasts and *jiaozi* (¥32); though their rice-and-curry meals are only average. Attractive courtyard patio and very friendly English-speaking staff, plus bike hire too. Daily 8am–8pm.

Bookworm 老书虫, lǎo shūchóng. 4 Sanlitun Nanjie ⊙010 65869507, ⓦbeijingbookworm.com; subway line #10 to Tuanjiehu, Exit D; map p.72. Hugely popular place for an espresso-and-laptop session with Beijing's expat crowd, largely on account of its excellent bookshop and library (see p.163), plus regular literary events and lectures. Check the website for details. Daily 9am–2am.

Café Flatwhite 4 Jiuxianqiao Lu, 798 Art District ⊙010 59789067; subway line #14 to Jiangtai, Exit B; map pp.96–97. Original of now citywide chain, and still the best café in the 798 district, serving good strong coffee (surprisingly cheap for the area at ¥22–28) and a nice range of meals. Try the pasta dishes (from ¥48), some of which use fresh, handmade spaghetti. Daily 9am–9pm.

Café Zarah 飒哈, sàhā. 42 Gulou Dongdajie ⊙010 84039807, ⓦcafezarah.com; subway line #5 to Beixinqiao or line #6 to Nanluoguxiang, Exit E; map

pp.58–59. This is Beijing's prime spot for expats updating their blog/writing a book/thinking of making a film about life in China, so not much talking goes on behind the sea of Apple logos. It's a nice setting though; a cosy, attractively open-plan courtyard house, stripped down to expose timber roof beams and polished concrete floors, serving good continental breakfasts (from ¥45) and plenty of snacks (including home-made ice cream). Wed–Mon 10am–midnight.

Confucius Café 秀冠, xiùguān. 25 Guozijian Lu ⊙010 64052047; subway line #2 or #5 to Yonghegong, Exit D; map pp.68–69. This antique-style grey-brick café faces out onto the semi-pedestrianized avenue, making it a good place to people-watch. The coffee is OK, if not exceptional, but it's a nice place to rest up after a visit to the nearby Confucius Temple. Daily 9am–8pm.

★**HA (High Altitude Coffee)** 高海拔咖啡, gāohǎibá kāfēi. 84 Dongsi Bei Da Jie; subway line #5 to Beixinqiao, Exit C, or Zhangzizhong, Exit B; map pp.68–69. Stylish grey brick and concrete space on two levels, with heavy wooden tables downstairs and comfy sofas above. They roast their own coffee; you can choose generic (¥25) or pay more for Ethiopian, central American or Kenyan beans (from ¥45). Their cheesecake is great too. Daily 10am–8pm.

He Kitchen & Co. 48 Wudaoying Hutong; subway line #2 or #5 to Yonghegong, Exit D; map pp.68–69. Many things recommend this stylish-looking café: the

9

hocks of Spanish ham hanging from the ceiling, the craft beer, the decent coffee... but not, sadly, most of their attempts at Western-style salads and sandwiches. Daily 9am–11pm.

Jiangmai Tang 讲麦堂, jiǎngmài táng. Tower 20-102, 6 Chaowai Dajie ☏010 65970724; subway line #6 to Dongdaqiao, Exit D; map pp.68–69. Antidote to Beijing's many generic, claustrophobic or overly hip alternatives – just a bright, smart, relaxed café at the foot of a residential apartment block, which bakes its own bread and French pastries, and serves good coffee. Daily 7am–7pm.

Najian 那间咖啡, nàjiān kāfēi. 60 Xisi Nan Dajie ☏010 66166607; subway line #4 to Xisi, Exit D; map pp.88–89. Cute place full of young Chinese couples, with a Western-style light-meal menu (sandwiches, salads, "huge slice" pizza etc) and an enormous range of desserts, including durian cheesecake. The freshly ground coffee is really good; there's also a bar serving "Anti-date" and other dubiously named cocktails. Daily 10am–8pm.

Oasis Jingshan Qian Jie; no convenient subway, but close to Jingshan Park and the Forbidden City exit; map pp.58–59. Small place with cheery barista and room for perhaps a dozen customers at a squeeze, with a view over the road to the very photogenic northeastern corner of the Forbidden City. They roast their own beans, and serve espressos to wake you out of a coma. No wi-fi. Tues–Sun 8am–7pm.

★**Soloist** 39 Yangmeizhu Xie Jie, Dazhalan; subway line #10 to Qianmen, Exit C; map pp.80–81. There aren't many cafés down this way, which makes this excellent two-storey place, with its "antique industrial" exposed red-brick interior, doubly welcome – even if it is a haven for coffee snobs. They roast their own beans, and the very chic range includes high-end Kenyan and Hawaiian brews (¥45–100). Daily 10.30am–10pm.

Wen Yu 文宇奶酪店, wényǔ nǎilàodiàn. 49 Nanluogu Xiang; subway line #6 or #8 to Nanluoguxiang, Exit E; map pp.58–59. Take a walk down Nanluogu Xiang, and before long you'll spy people bearing blue-and-white plastic pots. They've all been to *Wen Yu*, a yoghurt café so popular that they've long thrown away the tables – all the better to accommodate a queue that regularly spills way out into the road. ¥10–15 per pot; cold coffee ¥5. Daily noon–6pm.

Xiaoxin's 小新的店, xiǎoxīn de diàn. 103 Nanluogu Xiang ☏010 64036956; subway line #6 or #8 to Nanluoguxiang, Exit E; map pp.58–59. This cosy courtyard hideaway is one of the better Nanluogu Xiang cafés, though the staff could be a little more alert. Limited menu; try their smoothies and locally renowned cheesecakes. Daily 10am–midnight.

VICS

Drinking and nightlife

In 1995, Sanlitun Lu in the east of Beijing had just one bar, and it was losing money. A new manager bought it, believing the place had potential but that the *feng shui* was wrong – the toilet was opposite the door and all the wealth was going down it. He changed the name, moved the loo and – so the story goes – the city's bar scene took off from there. These days Beijing boasts a great range of drinking holes, from British-style pubs to boutique beer breweries, rum bars and even a couple of places distilling their own spirits; while most are aimed at foreign customers, they're becoming popular too with younger, more affluent Chinese. If you're looking for a dance with your drinks, there are slick, International-style clubs (many with imported DJs) and even a few grungy venues where the city's youth vent their angst, though the live music scene is in a slight downturn at present.

BARS

Though you can find places to drink all over the city, the bulk of Beijing's bars are concentrated in two areas. **Sanlitun** has the highest-profile scene, especially along the old strip of Sanlitun Lu, north of Gongrentiyuchang Bei Lu, which has become a gauntlet of pick-up joints whose loud touts try to lure – or physically drag – you inside. The other area spreads eastwards from the **Bell Tower** past the **Yonghe Gong** district, where a growing number of small, boutique venues are hidden among the maze of *hutongs*. "Hidden" is the word; some don't even have signs outside, so you'll have to check house numbers as you go. Most serve a range of imported ales and spirits, but the big thing at the moment is locally brewed **craft beer** – including excellent IPA at around ¥40 a pint. Drinks aside, bars often serve some of the best Western-style fast food in the city – burgers, fish and chips, pizza and the like. We've given **opening hours** throughout, though these can be flexible – a bar tends to close only when its last barfly has lurched off. There's usually a cover charge to get in (around ¥30) when a band is playing. Though Chinese beer can be cheaper than bottled water if bought in a shop, expect a 350ml bottle of local Yanjing beer to cost ¥20–40 at a bar.

NORTH OF THE CENTRE

8-Bit 13 Beiluogu Xiang ☎ 010 80448229; subway line #2 to Andingmen, Exit A; map pp.58–59. Big departure from the rest of the area's stripped-back *hutong* venues: this one's black-tiled and blue-lit, packed with vintage TVs and video-gaming consoles (Super Mario anyone?). The bar deals in craft beer and strange cocktail shots. Tues–Sun 6pm–2.30am.

Dirty Duck 黑天鹅, hēi tiān'é. 19 Beiluogu Xiang ☎ 010 46217796; subway line #2 to Andingmen, Exit A; map pp.58–59. Edwardian-style leather couches and dark woodwork framing the bar, a Union Jack strung over the pool table, and regular curry and quiz nights: the most British pub in town, if that's what you're after – the only deviation being the rooftop terrace, fairly rare back in Blighty, but worth a visit for the view. Their strong English Pale Ale (¥40) is the one to try. Daily 6pm–2am.

East Shore Live Jazz Café 东岸咖啡, dōng'àn kāfēi. 2F 2 Qianhai Nanyan ☎ 010 84032131; subway line #8 to Shichahai, Exit A2; map pp.58–59. Surrounded by brash, noisy cafés and restaurants, this dark, mellow jazz bar is set on the second floor with a view of the lake. They don't generally charge entry for live shows either. Daily 3pm–2am.

★**Mao Mao Chong** 毛毛虫, máomao chóng. 12 Banchang Hutong ☎ 1584 2719052; subway line #6 or #8 to Nanluoguxiang, Exit F; map pp.58–59. Renowned for its locally themed cocktails at ¥40–60: Bloody Mao, Chong Collins, pandan daiquiri and their signature Mala Mule – lime, ginger beer and chilli-infused vodka. It's a tiny

space but the bar staff are cool, there's a jazz soundtrack, and the pizza is good. Mon–Thurs 6pm–midnight, Fri & Sat 4pm–late.

★**Modernista** 44 Baochao Hutong, cnr of Baochao and Wangzuo ☎ 1369 1425744; subway line #2 or #8 to Guloudajie, Exit G; map pp.58–59. Art Deco 1930s-feel interior with red velvet curtain for the stage, floor tiles in domino checks and geometric lines everywhere. French-heavy clientele, tapas (and full meals in the evening) plus Prohibition-era cocktail menu (¥40–75), reconstructing several "lost" recipes. Live music with jazz/funk bias most weekends. Mon–Fri 4pm–2am, Sat & Sun 11am–2am.

Pass By Bar 过客酒吧, guòkè jiǔbā. 108 Nanluogu Xiang; subway line #6 to Nanluoguxiang, Exit E; map pp.58–59. A renovated courtyard house turned comfortable bar/restaurant, popular with backpackers and students. There are lots of books and pictures of China's far-flung places to peruse, and well-travelled staff to chat to – if you can get their attention. Daily 9am–4am.

Siif 如果, rúguǒ 67 Beiluogu Xiang ☎ 010 64069496; subway line #2 to Andingmen, Exit A; map pp.58–59. A highly friendly place to escape the crowds on nearby Nanluogu Xiang, with quirkily designed furniture and a tiny dance space. Head on downstairs for table football, or clamber up to the roof terrace for a drink. Daily 1pm–2am.

EAST OF THE CENTRE

YONGHE GONG AND AROUND

Café de la Poste 云游驿, yún yóu yì. 58 Yonghegong Da Jie ☎ 010 64027047, ⓦ cdlpbeijing.com; subway

---

BEIJING'S BEST

Best for rum Tiki Bungalow (see opposite)
Best for imported beer selection El Nido (see opposite)
Best microbrewery Great Leap (see box, p.154)
Best distillery Distillery (see opposite)
Best place to watch sports Cuju (see opposite)

Best bar-fly hangout Café de la Poste (see above)
Best cocktails Mao Mao Chong (see above)
Best gay club Destination (see p.156)
Best stylish interior Modernista (see above)
Best live music venue Hot Kat Club (see p.155)

line #5 to Beixinqiao, Exit B; map pp.68–69. French-owned and run, so no surprise to find some good informal dining and the bar stocked with absinthe and bottles of cab-sav. Perhaps unfairly renowned for being the only likely place open for a beer (cheap at ¥15) at 4.30am, by which time a fair number of the city's dubious foreign chancers are propping up the bar. Daily: bar noon–very late; food noon–3pm & 6–11pm.

Capital Spirits 北京白酒吧, běijīng báijiǔba. 3 Daju Hutong ☎010 64093319, ⓦcapitalspiritsbj.com; subway line #5 to Beixingqiao, Exit C; map pp.68–69. While most foreigners can't stand the rawness of baijiu, there's probably no other bar dedicated to China's national tipple in the country, so come here if you fancy a challenge – or simply need to learn how to tell a refined Moutai from gutrot erguotou. Tues–Sun 8pm–12.30am.

★**Cuju** 蹴鞠洛哥餐吧, cùjū luògē cānba. 28 Xiguan Hutong ☎010 64079782, ⓦcujubeijing .com; subway line #5 to Zhangzizhonglu, Exit A; map pp.68–69. Eclectic rum selection, including some home-made infusions held in medicine bottles behind the bar (try Pirates' Delight, flavoured with cinnamon and goji). Dampen the effects with filling Moroccan food, such as the Totale (¥68), a plate of sausage slathered in a spicy sauce. Despite lack of space, they've installed two TVs for catching soccer games live. Opens at all hours if there's an international game on, otherwise daily 6am–midnight.

★**Distillery** 23 Xinsi Hutong ☎010 64093319, ⓦcapitalspiritsbj.com; subway line #5 to Zhangzizhonglu, Exit B; map pp.68–69. Beijing's first boutique distillery occupies the front part of an old siheyuan, decked downstairs in spartan-chic concrete and timber; upstairs there's a mellow lounge overlooking grey-tiled rooftops. It produces its own vodka and gin in the copper still at the rear – try a G&T with the juniper-heavy house special, "Uncle Karl" (¥50) – plus there are forty-odd commercial varieties to choose from, alongside a substantial collection of American whiskies. Mon–Sat 7pm–midnight.

El Nido 方家小酒馆, 59 fāng jiā xiǎojiǔguǎn 59. 59 Fangjia Hutong ☎010 84029495; subway line #5 to Beixinqiao, Exit A; map pp.68–69. Tiny bar that somehow manages to squeeze in over a hundred different varieties of imported beer, plus plenty of wines and stronger stuff. A few outside tables too. Daily 6am–late.

Ramo 64 Fangjia Hutong ☎010 84035004; subway line #5 to Beixinqiao, Exit A; map pp.68–69. Quiet spot to chill over a range of imported boutique bottled beers, after exhausting yourself touring the nearby temples. Also serves light bar meals – pizza by the slice (¥20), chicken croquettes (¥28) and burger and chips (¥40). When the weather's right there are tables at the front for watching hutong life. Daily 9.30am–11pm.

For up-to-the-minute reviews, check the expat magazines The Beijinger (ⓦthebeijinger.com), That's Beijing (ⓦthatsmags.com/beijing), City Weekend (ⓦcityweekend.com.cn/beijing) and Time Out (ⓦtimeoutbeijing.com).

★**Tiki Bungalow** 34 Jiaodaokou San Tiao; subway line #5 to Beixinqiao, Exit A; map pp.68–69. Quirky place for a Beijing backstreet: there's a Great White shark called Wilson hanging from the ceiling, a palm-frond-fringed bar, Tiki mugs, an affable manager in a Hawaiian shirt and the biggest wall of rum you could ever hope to lay eyes on. If you like your spirits straight, try one of the more unusual brands – Burmese, Japanese, even Scottish – otherwise all your favourites are here, plus a long list of cocktails (including a classic Mai Tai). Mon–Sat 7pm–2am.

SANLITUN

First Floor 壹楼, yī lóu. Tongli Building, behind Tai Koo Li, Sanlitun ☎010 64130587, ⓦfirstfloorbj.com; subway line #10 to Tuanjiehu, Exit A; map p.72. Generally horrible service, but decent imported draught beer and pub food; outdoor tables make it a favourite with expats watching the endless parade of bohemian Beijingers. Gets busier and sleazier as the night progresses. Daily 11am–midnight.

Jazz Ya 爵士屋, juéshì wū. Nali Patio ☎010 64151227, ⓦjazzya.com.cn; subway line #10 to Tuanjiehu, Exit A; map p.72. Just off the main road, this mellow Japanese place – a courtyard full of rough-hewn wooden tables – has a better drinks menu than most of its neighbours. Regular live jazz too. Daily noon–2am.

The Local 4 Gongti Bei Lu, tucked away in a compound behind Bookworm ☎010 65919525, ⓦbeijing-local .com; subway line #10 to Tuanjiehu, Exit D; map p.72. Spacious, comfortable American-style bar with upstairs balcony, live sports on a big screen, bar food of the pizza, ribeye and buffalo wings sort, and a good selection of Belgian draught beers and bourbon. Happy Hour daily 4–8pm. Daily noon–midnight.

Mesh At the Opposite House (瑜舍, yúshè), 11 Sanlitun Lu ☎010 64105220, ⓦtheoppositehouse.com; subway line #10 to Tuanjiehu, Exit A; map p.72. Cosy, classy lounge bar in the basement of a chic hotel, attracting a trendy, international crowd. Dress up, order a cocktail (from ¥80), and try to look sophisticated. Daily 5pm–2am.

★**Migas** 6F Nali Patio (那里花园, nàlǐ huāyuán); subway line #10 to Tuanjiehu, Exit A; map p.72. The upstairs bar at this Spanish restaurant has long been a favourite with Beijing's young-and-well-heeled set; views from here are simply superb, and there's barely room to wiggle your butt during the weekend DJ sets. Weekdays are

10

BEIJING'S MICROBREWERIES

Microbrewed beer has really taken hold in Beijing, with strong, hop-scented varieties of IPA very much to the fore at the moment. Aside from the following four (foreign-owned) heavyweights, look out for Chinese-run operations *Panda*, just south of Beixinqiao station on Dongsi Bei Dajie; and *Pei Ping*, opposite the *Tiki Bungalow* on Jiaodaokou San Tiao.

Arrow Factory 箭厂啤酒, jiànchǎng píjiǔ. 9 Jianchang Hutong ☏010 64076308, ⓦwww .arrowfactorybrewing.com; subway line #2 or #5 to Yonghegong Lama Temple, Exit D; map pp.58–59. Slightly downbeat exterior, with their *Stuff'd* restaurant at the front (go for the home-made sausages) and bar – decked in requisite bare-concrete-and-timber decor – tucked away to the side. Current pick of their beers is the English Archer and the aptly named Seeing Double. They also have a larger branch at 1 Xin Dong Lu on Liangma He Nan Lu, which is open all day (closed Mon). Mon–Thurs 5pm–1am, Fri 5pm–2am, Sat 11.30am–2am, Sun 11.30am–1am.

★**Great Leap** 大跃啤酒, dàyuè píjiǔ. 6 Doujiao Hutong, ⓦgreatleapbrewing.com; subway line #5 to Shichahai, Exit C; map pp.58–59. Hidden behind a wall at the corner of a square, there's a pleasantly shaded courtyard garden and a bar with exposed beams, heavy wooden furniture and brick floor. East City Porter and Little General IPA are good, but the thing to try is Edmund Backhouse pilsner, named after the infamous Sinologist and literary forger (see *Hermit of Peking*, p.192). Tues–Thurs 5–10.30pm, Fri 5–11pm, Sat 2–11pm, Sun 2–10pm.

Jing A Taproom 京A, jīng A. 1949 Complex, 4 Gongti Bei Lu, Sanlitun ☏010 65018883, ⓦjingabrewing.com; subway line #10 to Tuanjiehu, Exit D; map p.72. Brick-walled compound hidden at the back of an entertainment complex, with outdoor tables, spacious bar and smart junior executives as clientele. Try their Flying Fist ale. Mon–Wed 5pm–midnight, Thurs 4pm–midnight, Fri 4pm–2am, Sat 11am–2am, Sun 11am–midnight.

Slow Boat Taproom 悠航鲜啤, yōu háng xiān pí. 56 Dongsi Ba Tiao ☏010 65385537, ⓦslowboatbrewery.com; subway line #5 to Zhangzizhonglu, Exit C; map pp.68–69. Cramped concrete box, tiled white on the inside (the rumour is that it was indeed once a toilet block) jam-packed with communal wooden tables and benches. You usually end up standing but the excellent beer – try Monkey's Fist IPA – more than compensates. Filling bar meals too. Mon–Thurs 5pm–midnight, Fri 5pm–1am, Sat 2pm–1am, Sun 11.30am–10pm.

---

a different story, with lounge music pulsing over a nattering crowd, all seated on funky furniture. Daily 6pm–late.

Tree 树酒吧, shù jiǔbā. Behind 3.3 Mall, Sanlitun ☏010 64151954; subway line #10 to Tuanjiehu, Exit A; map p.72. Relaxed and unassuming little bar, with a selection of Belgian white beers and decent pizza; if you'd like to mix things up a bit, note that they have a great sister bar within stumbling distance. Daily midday–late.

THE CBD

Atmosphere 云酷就把, yúnkù jiùbà. 80F World Trade Center ☏010 85716459; subway line #1 or #10 to Guomao, Exit E2; map pp.68–69. Dress up (no shorts or slippers), catch the lift inside the *Shangri-la* hotel's east entrance, and step out eighty floors up at Beijing's loftiest bar. Come prepared for some shocking prices and (on clear days) stunning views. Book ahead for a window seat. Mon–Fri 2pm–2am, Sat & Sun noon–2am.

Ichikura 一藏酒吧, yīcáng jiǔbā. Chaoyang Theatre, 36 Dongsanhuan Beilu ☏010 65071107; subway line #2 or #6 to Chaoyangmen, Exit A; map pp.68–69. This two-storey Japanese whisky bar is as tasteful and understated as the acrobatic shows next door are glitzy and vulgar. A great range of single malts – including superb Japanese varieties – and fine attention to detail (check out the round ice cubes) make this dark, cosy venue a hidden gem. Daily 8pm–2am.

★**Xiu** 秀, xiù. 6F Park Hyatt, 2 Jianguomenwai Dajie ☏010 85671107; subway line #1 or #10 to Guomao, Exit D; map pp.68–69. With some of the most wonderful views of any Beijing bar from its outdoor terrace, *Xiu* has been among the most popular in the city for several years, serving up good cocktails amid a stylish, yet raucous, atmosphere. There's a dancefloor inside, though be warned that it's a notorious hunting ground for local prostitutes. Daily 6pm–late.

SOUTH OF THE CENTRE

365 Inn 365 安怡之家宾馆, 365 ānyí zhījiā bīnguǎn. 55 Dazhalan Xijie ☏010 63085956; subway line #2 Qianmen, Exit C; map pp.80–81. The bar fronting this hostel (see p.136) is just about the best place to settle in for a bottled beer in the backpacker-heavy Dazhalan area; *Leo Hostel* across the road has a good bar too, but this one has the added benefit of prime people-watching opportunities. Daily 7am–late.

THE FAR NORTH

★Lush 1 Huaqing Jiayuan ⓦlushbeijing.com; subway line #13 to Wudaokou, Exit A; map pp.96–97. A café/restaurant by day, beer bottles start to pop as soon as the sun dares to approach the horizon. Prices are cheap, in keeping with the area's student population – though it can get a bit quiet here outside term time. Daily 24hr.

Nashville Bar 乡谣酒吧, xiāngyáo jiǔbā. Chaoyang Gongyuan Lu ☎010 58670298; subway line #14 to Zaoying, Exit A; map pp.96–97. Long-running watering hole relocated to "Lucky Street" from its original Sanlitun location, taking the expat clientele along with it. There's the usual cavernous wood interior and strip of pavement tables, reasonably priced pilsner (¥30) and expensive Guinness (¥80). Well-sited for sharpening the appetite, before eating at nearby restaurants. There's a Philippino rock band in nightly. Daily 11am–3am.

CLUBS

Chinese clubs are pretty slick these days, with hip-hop and house music proving enduringly popular. There's a concentration of unashamedly trashy, commercial places northeast of the centre around the west side of Workers' Stadium on Gongren Tiyuchang Xilu (usually shortened to **Gongti Xilu**), and on Saturday night the car park here is full of white Mercedes dropping off the *dakuans* (big moneys) and their *xiaomis* (little honeys). All places listed here have a **cover charge**, which generally increases at weekends. If you just want to dance, and aren't too fussy about the latest music, check our bar reviews (see p.152) for venues with their own dancefloor.

NORTH OF THE CENTRE

Dada 大大酒吧, dàdà jiǔbā. 206 Gulou Dong Dajie ☎0183 11080818; subway line #8 to Shichahai, Exit C; map pp.58–59. Beijing extension of this understated, arty and unpredictable Shanghai club, with definite leanings towards anything avant-garde, alternative and electronic; the sound system is excellent. It also hosts movie nights among other things. Daily 9pm–4.30am.

Vics 威克斯, wēikèsī. Workers' Stadium North Gate ☎010 52930333, ⓦvics.com.cn; subway line #2 to Dongsishitiao, Exit C; map pp.58–59. One of many unapologetically trashy clubs in the area, this long-running hip-hop place features a sweaty dancefloor filled with enthusiastic booty grinders. The low cover charge and cheapish drinks (bottled beer is ¥25) make it popular with students and embassy brats. ¥50 on weekends, free Mon–Thurs. Daily 9.30pm–2am.

EAST OF THE CENTRE

Coco Banana 赛特饭店, sàitè fàndiàn. 8 Gongti Xilu ☎010 85999999; subway line #2 or #6 to Chaoyangmen, Exit A; map pp.68–69. Gaudy and brash, this glitzy club with a tiny dancefloor provides loud techno to an enthusiastic, young, moneyed-up Chinese crowd. Cover charge ¥30 weekdays, ¥50 weekends, and more when a big-name DJ is playing. Daily 9pm–2am.

THE FAR NORTH

Propaganda East Gate, Huaqing Jiayuan; subway line #13 to Wudaokou, Exit B; map pp.96–97. "Oh god, *that* place..." is the stock reaction when mentioning this bar to someone who's been in Beijing for a while. This infamous Wudaokou student club is a shameless meat market, whose ¥50 all-you-can-drink nights (every Wed) are crazily popular. The spirits are dodgy for sure, though; stick to the beer. Daily 8pm–late.

LIVE MUSIC VENUES

Mainstream **Chinese pop** (mostly slushy ballads sung by Hong Kong or Taiwanese heart-throbs) is hard to avoid, though Beijing has also long harboured an edgier **underground** scene – even if it's reeling a little after the abrupt recent closure of *2 Kolegas* and *Mao Livehouse*, two of its mainstay venues – and a few **jazz** bars. There will generally be a cover of around ¥30–80 at the following venues. Chinese and Western classical music are covered in the "Entertainment and the arts" chapter (see p.157).

INDIE

Dusk Dawn Club (DDC) 14 Shanlao Hutong; subway line #6 or #8 to Nanluoguxiang, Exit B; map pp.68–69. Small-scale venue hosting live jazz, folk and indie bands; it's aimed at young, arty, upwardly mobile Chinese and many come as much for the bar and funky ambience as for the music. Tues–Sun 1pm–2am.

★Hot Cat Club 热力猫, rèlì māo. 46 Fangjia Hutong ☎010 64007868; subway line #5 to Beixinqiao, Exit A; map pp.68–69. Perfect venue – it always feels just a bit too small – and mainstay of Beijing's live music scene, hosting foreign and domestic bands hammering out blues, rock, reggae and indie. Mon–Thurs Tiger beer is just ¥10, Wed is Comedy Club night, Thurs has open-mike music, with Beijing bands Fri–Sun. Daily 10am–late.

Modernsky Lab Floor B1, Building D, Galaxy Soho; subway line #2 or #6 to Chaoyangmen, Exit G; map pp.68–69. This Chinese indie record label and music festival organizer now has its own live venue, though it's

10

THE MIDI FESTIVAL

The **Midi Rock Music festival** (ⓦ www.midifestival.com) started as a student bash in Haidan Park, and has since grown to a China-wide extravaganza, with Beijing's event now attended by thousands and held out in the countryside. It has always been controversial, banned in 2008 and with foreign acts occasionally refused permission to play. Still, plenty of local talent is on display, and the audience is enthusiastic. You can even camp, for the full-on "Chinese Glastonbury" experience. Check the website for dates, venue and ticket prices.

surprisingly low-key and barely advertised – check free weekly listings magazines to see what's on.

★**School Bar** 53 Wudaoying Hutong; subway line #2 or #5 to Yonghegong Lama Temple, Exit D; map pp.68–69. Long-running place with an underground bar vibe, a sometimes angry young crowd and a strong punk and grunge bias; a bit hit and miss, but definitely somewhere to catch up-and-coming local bands. Beer is cheap at ¥25 a bottle. Daily 8pm–late.

Yugong Yishan 寓公移山, yúgōngyíshān. 3–2 Zhangzizhong Lu ⓣ010 64042711, ⓦ yugongyishan .com; subway line #5 to Zhangzizhonglu, Exit A; map pp.68–69. With a big dancefloor, an up-for-it crowd and an eclectic mix of live acts, this has to be the best all-round venue in town. The sounds on offer here are mostly rock and electro, though there's a pleasing genre mix across each month. Daily 5pm–midnight.

JAZZ

Blue Note 23 Ch'ienmen complex, Qianmen Dong Dajie ⓣ010 65270288, ⓦ bluenotebeijing.com;

subway line #2 to Qianmen, Exit A; map p.42. Beijing venue for the famous New York jazz club, housed in the former US Legation compound (see p.66) and offering a stellar line-up of International and domestic talent. Tues-Sun according to programme; check website for times.

East Shore Live Jazz Café 东岸咖啡, dōng'àn kāfēi. 2F 2 Qianhai Nanyanlu ⓣ010 84032131; subway line #8 to Shichahai, Exit A2; map pp.58–59. A fine bar outside performance time (see p.152), this has live jazz from the house band – fronted by legendary Chinese musician Liu Yuan – from around 10pm Thurs to Sun. No cover charge. Daily 3pm–2am.

MAINSTREAM

Workers' Stadium 工人体育场, gōngrén tǐyùchǎng. Off Gongti Beilu ⓣ010 65016655, ⓦ gongti.com.cn; subway line #6 to Dongdaqiao, Exit A; map pp.68–69. This is where giant gigs are staged, mostly featuring Chinese pop stars, though the likes of Björk have also played here (though, given her views on Tibet, that'll never happen again).

GAY BEIJING

China has relatively relaxed attitudes towards homosexuality – it's no longer a crime – and in cosmopolitan Beijing, pink power has a big influence on fashion and the media. However, bars for gay or lesbian *tongzhi* (literally, comrades) are still few and far between, though note some "regular" places – such as the classy lounge bar *Mesh* (see p.153) – host dedicated gay nights.

Alfa 阿尔法, ā'ěrfǎ. 6 Xingfu Yicun, opposite North Gate of Workers' Stadium ⓣ010 64130086; subway line #2 to Dongsishitiao, Exit B; map pp.68–69. Not gay but certainly gay-friendly, especially on their irregular gay and lesbian nights; keep an eye on the city listings magazines for details. It's free to get into the bar area (which makes surprisingly good food); for the dancefloor you'll have to

cough up an extra ¥30. Daily 8pm–late.

★**Destination** 目的地, mùdìdì. 7 Gongti Xi Lu; ⓦ bjdestination.com; line #2 to Dongsishitiao, Exit C; map pp.68–69. Beijing's biggest and most popular gay club by far, with two floors full of half-naked men (mainly local), as well as women who'd rather avoid non-gay men for the night. Entry ¥60. Daily 8pm–late.

ACROBATIC SHOW, CHAOYANG THEATRE

Entertainment and the arts

Most visitors to Beijing make a trip to see Beijing opera – whether in a
dedicated opera venue or in a traditional teahouse – and the superb Chinese
acrobatics displays. Fewer investigate the contemporary side of the city's
entertainment scene: the indie music (see p.155), classical music, theatre and
dance events. There are also a number of cinemas screening foreign and
domestic blockbusters (you might have look elsewhere to check out
provocative movies emerging from new, underground film-makers). Some of
the venues are a little inconveniently located; many, in particular, lie in a
wide stretch south of Tian'anmen Square but it's worth remembering that
many "tours" to the most popular shows often cost the same as the regular
ticket price, yet throw transport in for free.

ESSENTIALS

Listings For mainstream cultural events – ballet troupes, large-scale concerts and so forth – check the listings in the *China Daily* (available at most hotels). For more in-depth reviews and wider venue coverage, try the expat magazines: *The Beijinger* (ⓦthebeijinger.com), *That's Beijing* (ⓦthatsmags.com/beijing), *City Weekend* (ⓦcityweekend .com.cn/beijing) and *Time Out* (ⓦtimeoutbeijing.com).

Tickets Tickets for all big shows are available at box offices, or from China Ticket Online (☎400 6103721, ⓦen .damai.cn). It's amazing how many of them cost exactly ¥180. However, for opera, martial arts and acrobatic performances, it's usually better to book directly through your accommodation, since transport to the venue (but not back) is often included for free.

TRADITIONAL OPERA

A trip to see Beijing's famous opera (see box below) is one of the most popular diversions for international travellers. If the regular shows seem too long, you could visit a teahouse to get your fix, where you'll be served snacks and, of course, tea – such performances are short and aimed at visitors.

OPERA VENUES

★**Chang'an Grand Theatre** 长安大戏院, cháng'ān dàxìyuàn. 7 Jianguomennei Dajie ☎010 65101308; subway line #1 or #2 to Jianguomen, Exit A; map pp.68–69. A modern, central theatre seating 800 and putting on a wide range of performances throughout the day – it's probably the most popular place in town for Beijing opera. From ¥180.

Huguang Guildhall 湖广会馆, húguǎng huìguǎn. 3 Hufangqiao Lu ☎010 63045396; subway line #7 to Hufangqiao, Exit C; map pp.80–81. The appeal of this place is its traditional wooden stage and teahouse – see p.79. Seats ¥180–380. Performances nightly at 6.30pm.

Liyuan Theatre 梨园剧场, líyuán jùchǎng. 1F Qianmen Jianguo hotel (前门建国饭店, qiánmén jiànguó fàndiàn), 175 Yong'an Lu ☎010 63016688, ⓦqianmenhotel.com; subway line #7 to Hufangqiao, Exit B; map pp.80–81. Accessible place to see opera; as you go in you pass the actors putting on their make-up – a great photo op. The opera itself is a visitor-friendly bastardization, lasting an hour and jazzed up with some martial arts and slapstick. Tickets can be bought from the office in the front courtyard (daily 9–11am, noon–4.45pm & 5.30–8pm; ¥90–280). Performances nightly at 7.30pm.

Zhengyici Theatre 正义祠剧场, zhèngyìcí jùchǎng. 220 Qianmen Xiheyanjie ☎010 63189454; subway line #2 to Hepingmen, Exit C2; map pp.80–81. A genuinely old wooden opera stage, even grander than that at the Huguang Guildhall and worth a visit just to check out the architecture. Tickets from ¥280. Performances nightly at 8pm.

TEAHOUSE THEATRES

Lao She Teahouse 老舍茶馆, lǎoshě cháguǎn. 3F Dawancha Building, 3 Qianmen Xidajie ☎010 63036830; subway line #2 to Qianmen, Exit C; map pp.80–81. Teahouse theatre that puts on shadow puppet, folk music and opera performances on separate floors. Free 10min shadow puppet shows through the day; otherwise performance timetables are posted in the lobby. Seats from ¥180. Daily 10am–2pm & 5–8.30pm.

Tianqiao Teahouse Theatre 天桥乐茶园 tiānqiáolè cháyuán 113 Tianqiao Nandajie ☎010 51655060; subway line #7 to Zhushikou, Exit A; map pp.80–81. Restored 1930s venue whose organizers try hard to create an authentic atmosphere, right down to the period costumes worn by the staff. "Crosstalk" performances begin at 7pm and last 3hr, and mostly comprise segments of traditional opera with a little acrobatics in between. It's popular with tour groups, so book in advance. ¥180 including tea and snacks; ¥330 including a duck dinner as well.

BEIJING OPERA

Beijing opera (京戏, jīng xì) is the most celebrated of China's 350 or so regional operatic styles – a unique combination of song, dance, acrobatics and mime. Highly stylized, to the outsider the performances can often seem obscure and wearying, punctuated as they are by a succession of crashing gongs and piercing, discordant songs. But it's worth seeing once, especially if you can acquaint yourself with the story beforehand. Most of the plots come from historical or mythological romances – the most famous, which any Chinese will explain to you, are *Journey to the West*, *The Three Kingdoms*, *Madame White Snake* and *The Water Margin* – and full of moral lessons. Offering an interesting, if controversial, variation on the traditions are those operas that deal with contemporary themes – such as the struggle of women to marry as they choose. The **colours** used on stage, from the costumes to the make-up on the players' faces, are highly symbolic: red signifies loyalty; yellow, fierceness; blue, cruelty; and white, evil.

DRAMA AND DANCE

Most evenings you can catch Chinese song and dance simply by turning on the TV, though there's plenty of opportunity to see it live. There are also a number of places in which to see **theatre**, both traditional and imported; in addition to the venues listed below, check the Poly Theatre (see p.160).

Beijing Exhibition Theatre 北京展览馆剧场, běijīng zhǎnlǎnguǎn jùchǎng. 135 Xizhimenwai Dajie ☎010 68354455; subway line #4 to Beijing Zoo, Exit C2; map pp.88–89. This giant hall, containing nearly 3000 seats, stages classical ballet, folk dance and large-scale song-and-dance revues. Prices vary, but expect to pay at least ¥400 for any big-name event.

Capital Theatre 首都剧场, shǒudū jùchǎng. 22 Wangfujing Dajie ☎010 65121598, ⓦbjry.com; subway line #5 or #6 to Dongsi, Exit G; map pp.68–69. Look out for the People's Art Theatre company here – their photo archive, documenting their history, is displayed in the lobby. Tickets generally start at ¥120. Most performances are in Chinese.

Penghao Theatre 蓬蒿剧场, pénghāo jùchǎng. 35 Dongmianhua Hutong ☎010 64006452, ⓦpenghao theatre.com; subway line #6 to Nanluoguxiang, Exit E; map pp.68–69. In a *hutong* just behind the Central Academy of Drama, this intimate, privately run theatre set in a beautifully converted courtyard house also has a rather nice rooftop bar. Check website for performance prices.

Puppet Theatre 中央木偶剧院, zhōngyāng mù'ǒu jùyuàn. Cnr of Anhua Xili & Third Ring Rd ☎010 64254798, ⓦpuppetchina.com; subway line #8 to Anhuaqiao, Exit D1 – but bizarrely there is no road crossing at this exit, leaving you in the middle of a busy road; map pp.96–96. Once as important for commoners as opera was for the elite, Chinese puppetry usually involves hand puppets and marionettes. Shows here, both live and recorded, are aimed at kids, involve Beijing opera, short stories and Western fairy tales; ticket.s cost from ¥100. Five shows daily 10am–3pm.

11

ACROBATICS AND MARTIAL ARTS

Certainly the most accessible and exciting of the traditional Chinese entertainments, **acrobatics** covers anything from gymnastics through to magic tricks and juggling. The tradition of professional acrobatics has existed in China for two thousand years and continues today at the country's main training school, Wu Qiao in Hebei Province, where students are enrolled at the age of five. The style may be vaudeville, but performances are spectacular, with truly awe-inspiring feats of dexterity – sixteen people stacked atop a bicycle and the like. Just as impressive are martial arts displays, which usually involve a few mock fights and feats of strength, such as breaking concrete slabs with one blow.

Beijing Workers' Club 北京工人俱乐部, běijīng gōngrén jùlèbù. 7 Hufang Lu ☎010 63528910, ⓦthelegendofjinsha.com; subway line #7 to Hufangqiao, Exit B; map pp.80–81. Popular for its "Legend of Jinsha" show, which adds a few interesting quirks to the old acrobatic routines – silk-rope dancing, water cannon, and some zany motorbike stunts. Tickets from ¥110. Daily 3.50pm & 5.30pm.

★**Chaoyang Theatre** 朝阳剧场, cháoyáng jùchǎng. 36 Dongsanhuan Beilu ☎010 65072421, ⓦchaoyangtheatre.com; subway line #6 or #10 to Hujialou, Exit C1; map pp.68–69. If you want to see acrobatics, come to one of the shows here. At the end, the Chinese tourists rush off as if it's a fire drill, leaving the foreign tour groups to do the applauding. There are plenty of souvenir stalls in the lobby – make your purchases after the show rather than during the interval, as prices reduce at the end. Tickets from ¥180. Daily 7.15–8.30pm.

Red Theatre 红剧场, hóng jùchǎng. 44 Xingfu Dajie ☎010 67142473, ⓦredtheatre.cn; subway line #5 to Tiantandongmen, Exit B; map pp.80–81. A lively kung fu routine, featuring smoke, fancy lighting and some incredible action. Tickets from ¥180. Daily 5.15pm & 7.30pm.

CLASSICAL MUSIC VENUES

Traditional Han Chinese music is usually played on the *erhu* (a kind of fiddle) and *qin* (a seven-stringed zither). Contemporary compositions tend to be in a pseudo-romantic, Western-influenced style – easy on the ear, they can be heard live in upmarket hotels and restaurants. To hear traditional pieces, however, visit the concert halls. **Western classical music** is popular – the best place to catch it is the Beijing Concert Hall – as is jazz, which you can hear at a few venues, such as *Blue Note* (see p.156).

Beijing Concert Hall 北京音乐厅, běijīng yīnyuètīng. 1 Beixinhua Jie ☎010 66057006; subway line #1 or #4 to Xidan, Exit D; map pp.88–89. This hall seats 1000 people and hosts regular concerts of Western classical and Chinese traditional music by Beijing's resident orchestra and visiting orchestras from the rest of China and overseas. Tickets from ¥80.

Century Theatre 世纪剧院, shìjì jùyuàn. Sino-Japanese Youth Centre, 40 Liangmaqiao Lu ☎010 64663311; subway line #10 to Liangmaqiao, Exit C; map pp.68–69. This is an intimate venue for soloists

THE BIRTH, DEATH AND RESURRECTION OF CHINESE DRAMA

Spoken **drama** was only introduced into Chinese theatres in the twentieth century. The **People's Art Theatre** in Beijing became the best-known company and staged Chinese-language translations of European plays – Ibsen and Chekhov were among the favourite playwrights. But with the onset of the Cultural Revolution in 1968, Jiang Qing, Mao's third wife, declared that "drama is dead". The company, along with most of China's cinemas and theatres, was almost completely out of action for nearly a decade afterwards, with a corpus of just eight plays (deemed socially improving) continuing to be performed. Many of the principal actors, directors and writers were banished, generally to rural hard labour. In 1979, the People's Art Theatre re-formed and quickly re-established its reputation.

11

and small ensembles. Mostly Chinese modern and traditional classical compositions. ¥120–150. Evening performances.

Forbidden City Concert Hall 北京中山公园音乐堂, běijīng zhōngshān gōngyuán yīnyuètáng. Zhongshan Park, Xichang'an Jie ☎010 65598285, ⓦfcchbj.com; subway line #1 to Tian'anmen West, Exit C; map p.42. A stylish hall, with regular performances of Western and Chinese classical music, and occasionally jazz too. Tickets from ¥80.

★ **National Centre for the Performing Arts** 国家大剧院, guójiā dàjùyuàn. 2 Xichang'an Jie ☎010 66550000; subway line #1 to Tian'anmen West, Exit C; map p.42. This is one venue you can't miss: it's that giant egg west of Tian'anmen Square. The opera hall seats over 2000, with fantastic acoustics and lighting; tickets start from ¥180 (box office opens daily from 9.30am, or ring to reserve). Also hosts Beijing opera shows. Performances nightly at 7.30pm.

Poly Theatre 保利大厦国际剧场, bǎolìdàshà guójì jùchǎng. Poly Plaza, 14 Dongzhimen Nandajie ☎010 65001188; subway line #2 to Dongsishitiao, Exit B; map pp.68–69. A gleaming hall that presents diverse performances of jazz, ballet, classical music, opera and modern dance for the edification of Beijing's cultural elite. Tickets from ¥180. Daily 7.30pm.

CINEMAS

Despite the prevalence of cheap, pirated DVDs and the internet, Beijing still has an abundance of cinemas, many of them on the upper floors of shopping malls. Foreign movies will either be dubbed into Chinese or shown in the original language with subtitles; ⓦwww.247cinema.cn is an invaluable English-language booking site, as it tells you which performances are in English. Tickets cost around ¥80. If your Chinese is up to scratch, pay a visit to the atmospheric **Daguanlou cinema** (see p.73) – which shows films only in Chinese – in Dazhalan.

MAINSTREAM CINEMAS

Broadway 百老汇电影, bǎilǎohuì diànyǐng. B1 Oriental Plaza Mall, 1 Dongchang'an Jie ☎010 85185804, ⓦwww.b-cinema.cn; subway line #1 to Wangfujing, Exit A; map pp.68–69. Large option located in the highly presentable Oriental Plaza Mall.

East Gate Cinema 东环影城, dōnghuán yǐngchéng. B1 Building B, East Gate Plaza, 9 Dongzhong Jie ☎010 64185930; subway line #2 or #13 to Dongzhimen, Exit C; map pp.68–69. Small and a little ragged, which makes this a good choice if you don't fancy the whole multiplex experience.

★**Megabox** 美嘉欢乐影城, měijiāhuānlè yǐngchéng. Tai Koo Li ☎010 64176118, ⓦwww.imegabox.com; subway line #10 to Tuanjiehu, Exit A. Beijing's most reliable option for international, non-dubbed films.

Wanda Cineplex 万达电影, wàndá diànyǐng. 3F Building 8, Wanda Plaza, 93 Jianguo Lu ☎010 59603399, ⓦwandafilm.com; subway line #1 to Dawanglu, Exit D; map pp.68–69. Big, comfortable cinema that usually has at least one international film going.

ART-HOUSE CINEMAS

★**Broadway Cinematheque** 当代MOMA, dāngdài MOMA. F3 Building 4, MOMA North, 1 Xiangheyuan Lu ☎010 84388258; subway line #2 or #13 to Dongzhimen, Exit G; map pp.68–69. Runs regular themed events, often international in nature.

Space for Imagination 盒子咖啡馆, hézi kāfēiguǎn. 5 Xiwangzhuang Xiaoqu, Haidian ☎010 62791280; subway line #13 to Wudaokou, Exit A. A charming cineastes' bar opposite the east gate of Qinghua University, showing avant-garde films every Saturday at 7pm.

Shopping

Appropriately for the capital of a major commercial power, Beijing has some first-class shopping. Much of it is concentrated in three districts: Wangfujing has mostly mid-market shops and malls selling famous Chinese brands; Xidan hosts giant department stores; and Qianmen has been reinvented as an open-air mall. Elsewhere, Liulichang, a street of imitation Ming buildings, is a good spot to furnish yourself with tourist-friendly souvenirs; shops here are much of a muchness, though there are some better places on nearby Dazhalan Lu. Jianguomenwai Dajie is the place to head for clothes, and Guomao is where you'll find the really high-end stuff. Shopping is more exciting, and cheaper, in the city's many markets, even though they offer no guarantee of quality; you can – and should – bargain.

ESSENTIALS

Opening hours Shops generally open Monday to Saturday from 9am to 6pm or 7pm, closing earlier on Sunday; the large shopping centres are open every day until around 9pm. Outdoor markets don't have official opening times, but tend to trade from about 7am to 6pm. We have listed opening times throughout.

Addresses Phone numbers are given for shops contactable in this way; if you're stuck for directions, head there in a taxi and ask the driver to call.

ANTIQUES, CURIOS AND SOUVENIRS

There's no shortage of curio stores and markets in the capital, offering opium pipes, jade statues, porcelain, jewellery, mahjong sets, Fu Manchu glasses, and all manner of bric-a-brac, often masquerading as carefully grimed "antiques". While most of these pieces are indeed reproductions (or, if you like, fakes), you might strike lucky: small pieces, such as hairpins, wood carvings, embroideries and prints are often the genuine article, if expensive by international standards. Good places to explore include the eastern branch of **Liulichang Jie** (subway line #2 or #4 to Xuanwumen, Exit H; map p.78), which is thick with curio stores; and any of the markets below. For inexpensive **art supplies** – Chinese paper, writing brushes, ink, and frames – try stores opposite the National Art Museum on Wusi Da Jie (see p.67).

SHOPS

Beijing Arts and Crafts 工美大厦, gōngměi dàshà. 200 Wangfujing Dajie ☎ 010 65140170; subway line #1 to Wangfujing, Exit C2; map pp.68–69. Good quality but hideously gaudy tourist tat: Buddha beads, silk embroideries of pandas, scroll paintings of pheasants, white jade jewellery, cloisonné, fans, porcelain statues, traditional wooden furniture and carvings. Expect to bargain at least thirty percent off marked prices. They issue certificates of authenticity for jade and antiques. Daily 10am–9pm.

Delia 地利亚, dìlìyà. 52 Wudaoying Hutong ☎ 010 64010375; subway line #2 or #5 to Yonghegong, Exit D; map pp.68–69. 1960s retro, Chinese-style – which means chirpy communist booklets and trinkets depicting a bright future for all – plus some vintage European clothing, accessories and jewellery. Good fun. Daily 2.30–10pm.

Rongbaozhai 荣宝斋, róngbǎozhāi. Liulichang Xi Jie ⓦ rongbaozhai.cn; subway line #2 or #4 to Xuanwumen, Exit H; map pp.80–81. Beijing's most famous supplier of anything to do with traditional calligraphy and painting: brushes, paper, inkstones, water droppers, scroll weights, brush rests and inksticks. The rest of the street is full of similar shops with lower prices, as is most of nearby Nanxinhua Jie. Daily 9am–5.30pm.

★**Soul Art Shop** 创艺无限, chuàng yì wúxiàn. 97 Nanluogu Xiang ⓦ ruantao.com; subway line #6 or #8 to Nanluoguxiang, Exit E; map pp.58–59. Fun and colourful acrylic models of animals, plants and deities – including Beijing's own Rabbit god – based on traditional dough sculptures. Cheerful and creative souvenirs. Daily 10am–8pm.

★**Three Stone** 三石斋风筝坊, sāndànzhāi fēngzhēngfǎng. 25 Di'anmen Xidajie ⓦ cnkites.com; subway line #6 to Nanluoguxiang, Exit E; map pp.58–59. A specialist kite shop with a rich history – the ancestors of the current owner once made kites for the Qing royals. Though there are plenty of fancy designs here, they also sell a fair few cheapies. Daily 9am–8pm.

Xuhua Zhai 旭华寨, xùhuá zhài. 120 Liulichang Xi Jie ☎ 1355 2698708; subway line #2 or #4 to Xuanwumen, Exit H; map pp.80–81. Small, dark store with affable owner and a wealth of trinkets stuffed into glass-fronted cases. You won't find any rare Ming vases here, but it's worth a browse for low-key, genuinely old curios. Bargain hard. Daily 10am–6pm.

MARKETS

Baoguo Temple 报国寺, bàoguó sì. Subway line #7 to Guanganmennei, Exit B, turn left and you're there; map pp.80–81. Deconsecrated temple whose halls are now full of curio dealers – especially of coins and old books, but also wood carvings, prints and all manner of bric-a-brac. Individual dealers keep their own hours, but Saturday mornings are best overall. Daily from 9am.

ON THE SOUVENIR HUNT

Good, widely available, inexpensive **souvenirs** include kites, art materials, papercuts (images cut into thin card), knotwork, tea sets, jade bracelets, mahjong sets and ornamental chopsticks (try any department store). Seals are another popular choice, with your name put into a soapstone "chop" in either Chinese characters or Roman letters; prices start at around ¥50, and if you want to see ancient traditions meeting modern technology, go round the back and watch them laser-cut it. For something a little unusual, you could get some Cultural Revolution kitsch – porcelain Mao figurines, the Little Red Book, Red Guard alarm clocks – from an antique store.

BEIJING'S BEST

Best for tea Ten Fu (see p.168)

Best for riot-cop key-fobs Police Museum (see p.66)

Best for goat-penis aphrodisiac Tongrentang pharmacy (see box, p.34)

Best for drily witty T-shirts Plastered T-Shirts (see p.165)

Best for antiques Beijing Antique City (see below)

Best for local music C Rock (see p.164)

Best for artsy local fashion Jixiangzhai (see p.165)

Best for lengths of silk Daxin Textiles (see p.165)

Best for traditional kites Three Stone (see opposite)

Best for kitsch statuettes Soul Art Shop (see opposite)

★**Beijing Antique City** 北京古玩城, běijīng gǔwánchéng. Huawei Nanlu; subway line #10 to Panjiayuan, Exit C2 and it's 250m south; map pp.6–7. A huge cube of a building with tat on the ground floor and upper three levels a warren of real and replica antiques, everything from Song dynasty ceramics to wooden cake moulds, silver jewellery and court regalia. Fascinating, but asking prices are very steep – some dealers even import stock from overseas for sale to wealthy Beijingers. Best visited on a Sunday. Daily 9.30am–6.30pm.

Liangma International Jewel and Antiques Market 亮马国际珠宝古玩城, liàngmǎ guójì zhūbǎo gǔwán chéng. 27 Liangmaqiao Lu; subway line 10 to Sanyuanqiao, Exit B; map pp.68–69. Two floors of jade and jewellery, with curios and carpets on the third floor. If

you know what you're after, there are some interesting pieces here, from Tibetan and Mongolian woollen "tiger" rugs to antique militaria. Daily 10am–6pm.

Panjiayuan Market 潘家园市场 pānjiāyuán shìchǎng. Panjiayuan Lu; subway line #10 to Panjiayuan, Exit B; map pp.6–7. Beijing's biggest and best-known antique market, selling everything from secondhand books to paintings, huge stone carvings, gaudy porcelain and ethnic embroideries. You might strike lucky at the small stalls inside the entrance, but this is largely the domain of trinket wholesalers with vast stocks of whatever "old" things are in vogue at the moment – polished stones, Song-style ceramics, bronze teapots etc. Busiest at the weekends. Mon–Fri 8am–6pm, Sat & Sun 6am–6pm.

12

BOOKS

There are plenty of English-language books on Chinese culture for sale in Beijing, including many hard to find in the West, ranging from giant coffee-table tomes celebrating new freeways in China to comic-book versions of Chinese classics. Even if you're not buying, Beijing's **bookshops** are pleasant environments in which to browse; some have cafés and art galleries attached.

★**Bookworm** 老书虫书吧, lǎoshūchóng shūbā. 4 Sanlitun Nanjie ☏010 65869507, ⊛beijingbookworm .com; subway line #10 to Tuanjiehu, Exit D; map p.72. Lots of English-language books, both used and new, to buy here at this popular café, which also hosts regular literary events and lectures. Strong on paperbacks about China. Daily 9am–2am.

Cathay Bookshop 中国书店, zhōngguó shūdiàn. Liulichang Xi Jie ⊛zgsd.net; map pp.80–81. There are several branches of this art-focused store across the city but this is the biggest and best: mostly new books downstairs in the front, with secondhand to the rear, and a huge stock of antique volumes and prints – not just Chinese either – upstairs. As usual in China, anything vaguely collectable is expensive. Daily 9am–5.30pm.

Foreign Language Bookstore 外文书店, wàiwén shūdiàn. 218 Wangfujing Dajie ⊛bpiec.com.cn; subway line #1 to Wangfujing, Exit C2; map pp.68–69. This dowdy store has the biggest selection of foreign-language books in mainland China: art books,

textbooks on Chinese medicine, translations of Chinese classics, and imported fiction. Daily 8am–5pm.

Sting Like a Bee 摘刺古本店, zhāicì gǔběndiàn. 72 Nanjianzi Xiang; subway line #5 to Zhangzizhonglu, Exit D; map pp.68–69. Contender for the oddest shop in all Beijing, a vintage art space and bookshop lined with antique leather-bound volumes, almost all in German (plus a few Chinese museum catalogues). Worth a browse if you're passing. Daily 10am–10pm.

Wangfujing Bookstore 王府井书店, wángfǔjǐng shūdiàn. 218 Wangfujing Dajie ☏010 65132842; subway line #1 to Wangfujing, Exit C2; map pp.68–69. As well as checking out the useful Chinese maps and road atlases near the entrance, head to the third floor for classics in translation – including Romance of the *Three Kingdoms*, *Outlaws of the Marsh*, *Dream of Red Mansions*, *Midnight*, the *True Story of Ah Q* and even some Tibetan authors – plus a big cache of imported paperbacks at relatively low prices. Daily 10am–9pm.

CARPETS

Created mainly in Xinjiang, Tibet and Tianjin, the beautiful handmade **carpets** on sale in Beijing aren't cheap, but are nevertheless pretty good value. Tibetan carpets are yellow and orange and usually have figurative mythological or religious motifs; rugs from Xinjiang in the northwest are red and pink with abstract patterns, while weaves from Tianjin are multicoloured. Check the colour for consistency at both ends – sometimes, large carpets are hung up near a hot lamp, which causes fading. As well as at the following, you can get carpets at the Friendship Store (see p.166; bargain hard here), Yuanlong Silk Corporation (see p.166) and Liangma International Jewel and Antiques Market (see p.163).

Qianmen Carpet Company 前门地毯厂, qiánmén dìtǎnchǎng. Tiantan Mansion, 59 Xingfu Jie, just north of the Tiantan hotel ☎010 67151687; line #5 to Tiantandongmen, Exit A1; map pp.6–7. A converted air-raid shelter selling carpets mostly from Xinjiang and Tibet; the silk carpets from Henan in central China are very popular. A typical 2m by 3m carpet can cost around ¥50,000, though the cheapest rugs start at around ¥2000. Mon–Fri 8.30am–5pm.

CDS AND DVDS

Pirated CDs and DVDs are sold by chancers who approach foreigners around the Silk Market (see opposite), on Dazhalan and in bars in Houhai and Sanlitun. You can get DVDs for as little as ¥10, CDs for ¥5. Note that with DVDs of newly released films, you're likely to get a version shot illicitly in a cinema, with heads bobbing around at the bottom of the screen. Otherwise, music shops selling **legitimate CDs** can be found throughout the city; a couple of the best are reviewed below.

Beijing Huashiweiye In the pedestrian street behind Tai Koo Li; subway line #10 to Tuanjiehu, Exit A; map p.72. Forget the name of this place, since even the proprietors aren't sure; it's marked from the outside as "CD DVD SHOP", and that's what they sell; thanks to a wide selection of films, they've a regular base of expat customers. Daily 8am–5pm.

C Rock 99 Gulou Dongdajie; subway line #2 to Nanluoguxiang, Exit E; map pp.58–59. One of the best places in the city to go hunting for CDs by local bands; the friendly owner will be pleased to make recommendations, and give you a listen to a few choice tracks. Hours vary; generally 11am–5pm.

CLOTHES AND FABRICS

Clothes are a bargain in Beijing. Head to the nearest shopping mall for well-made smart-casual wear at reasonable prices from domestic, quaintly named brands such as *Yishion*, *Raidy Boer* and *I'm David*. If you're after something personal – a figure-hugging *qipao* dress, for example, much in vogue during the 1930s – there are tailors who can run up a piece in a week or so; and even fabric shops where you can buy silk or cloth by the metre. Cheap and cheerful clothes are easily found too, as is modern designer wear. If you're particularly tall or have especially large feet you'll have difficulty finding clothes and shoes to fit you, though there's a reasonable chance of striking lucky at the Silk Market.

TAILORS

Hongdu Tailor 红都, hóngdū. 28 Dongjiaomin Xiang ☎010 63519282; subway line #2 to Qianmen, Exit A; map pp.68–69. This tailor, just opposite the former Yokahama Bank, once made suits for Chairman Mao himself; he may not have been much of a fashion icon but the offerings here are of very high quality. A full suit will set you back about ¥10,000, and take a month to make. Mon–Sat 9am–5pm.

Lisa Tailor 5F, 3.3 Mall, 33 Sanlitun Beilu ☎010 51365879, ⊚beijingtailor.com; subway line #10 to Tuanjiehu, Exit A; map p.72. A reliably good bet for bargain tailoring, with English-speaking staff; suits start at around ¥1000, and ladies' *qipao* at around the same price. Next-day service is available for a little more. Mon–Sat 9am–6pm.

Mr King Tailor Shop 金先生裁缝店, jīn xiānsheng cáiféng diàn. 90 Dazhalan Xi Jie ☎010 63180990; subway line #2 to Qianmen, Exit C; map pp.80–81. If you want handmade clothes but prices at the larger stores east down towards Qianmen make your eyes water, check out this small, one-man operation, with its surprisingly good range of Chinese and Western styles and fabrics. Daily 9am–10pm.

FAKING IT

China has a massive industry in **fakes** – nothing escapes the counterfeiters. You'll no doubt hear assurances to the contrary, but you can assume that many antiques and collectable stamps, coins and posters are replicas, that paintings are prints and that Rolex watches will stop working as soon as you turn the corner. Piracy does rob artists of their livelihood, but the pirated CDs and DVDs are indeed very cheap, while even more of a bargain are the widely available fake designer-label clothes and accessories.

SHOPS

A You 阿尤, āyóu 108 Xinjiekou Beidajie ☎010 65242400; subway line #4 to Xinjiekou, Exit C; map pp.58–59. Trendy, ethnic-style designer clothes from an established local design brand. Prices start at around ¥200 for striking summer dresses. Mon–Sat 9am–5pm.

Beijing Silk Store 北京谦祥益丝绸商店, běijīng qiānxiángyì sīchóu shāngdiàn. 50 Dazhalan Xijie ☎010 63016658; subway line #2 to Qianmen, Exit C; map pp.80–81. Going since the 1840s, this Dazhalan store is an excellent place to buy quality Chinese silk, with a wider selection and keener prices than any of the tourist stores. The ground floor sells silk fabrics by the metre, while clothes can be bought upstairs. Daily 8am–5pm.

Dong Liang Studio 栋梁, dòngliáng. 102, 2-Building, Central Park, Jinghua Lu ☎010 84047648, Ⓦdongliangchina.com; subway line #10 to Jintaixizhao, Exit A; map pp.68–69. Chic, elegant and affordable clothes by local designers; look out for beautiful dresses by JJ, Ye Qian and Shen Ye. Mon–Sat 9am–5pm.

Five Colours Earth 五色土, wǔsètǔ. F5, Building 6, Jianguomen Diplomatic Compound ☎010 58692923, Ⓦfivecoloursearth.net; subway line #1 or #2 to Jianguomen, Exit B; map pp.68–69. Interesting and unusual collections by a talented local designer, often incorporating fragments of old embroidery. Not too expensive either: you can pick up a coat for ¥600. Mon–Fri 10am–4pm by appointment.

★**Jixiangzhai** 吉祥斋, jíxiáng zhāi. 3.3 Building, shop 1017, Tai Koo Li, Sanlitun ☎010 51365330, Ⓦwww.jixiangzhai.cn; subway line #10 to Tuanjiehu, Exit A; map p.72. High-end, very stylish Chinese silk dresses, rich in colour and embroidery, with definite "ethnic" and traditional leanings. Daily 11am–11pm.

Neiliansheng Shoes 内联升布鞋, nèiliánshēng bùxié. 34 Dazhalan Dong Jie ☎010 63013041, Ⓦnls1853.com; subway line #2 to Qianmen, Exit C; map pp.80–81. One of Dazhalan's great old shops, with a giant shoe in the window and all manner of handmade traditional flat, slip-on shoes and slippers inside. Prices from ¥300 or so – they make great gifts. Daily 9am–8pm.

★**Plastered T-Shirts** 创可贴T恤, chuàngkětiē tīxù. 61 Nanluogu Xiang Ⓦplasteredtshirts.com; subway line #6 to Nanluoguxiang, Exit E; map pp.58–59. Hipster T-shirts and sweatshirts whose witty designs reference everyday Beijing life – subway tickets, thermoses and so on. It's a standard ¥180 per shirt. Daily 9am–7pm.

Ruifuxiang Store 瑞蚨祥丝绸店, ruìfúxiáng sīchóudiàn. 5 Dazhalan, off Qianmen Dajie ☎010 63035313, Ⓦrefosian.com; subway line #2 to Qianmen, Exit C; map pp.80–81. Shot silk from ¥128 per metre, up to rich dragon-emblazoned brocades at a staggering ¥8800. Also a good selection of shirts and dresses, with a tailor specializing in made-to-measure qipaos. Aim to

barter a little off the quoted price. Daily 9.30am–8.30pm.

Shanghai Tang 上海滩, shànghǎi tān. B1 Grand Hyatt, 1 Dongchang'an Jie ☎010 85187228, Ⓦshanghaitang.com; subway line #1 to Wangfujing, Exit A; map pp.68–69. This renowned Hong Kong designer label offers brightly coloured luxury chinoiserie. Nice bags and cufflinks, as well as cushions, purses, robes and neo-Mao jackets, though it's all very pricey. It's straight down the steps from the Hyatt lobby. Daily 10am–10pm.

Sheng Xifu Hat Store 盛锡福帽店, shèngxīfú màodiàn. 196 Wangfujing Dajie ☎010 65130620; subway line #1 to Wangfujing, Exit B; map pp.68–69. China's most famous hat brand, with a display in the store of headwear worn by luminaries. A cap of cotton is ¥128, rabbit fur ¥680. Daily 8am–6pm.

Ullens Center for Contemporary Art 尤伦斯当代艺术中心, yóulúnsī dāngdài yìshùzhōngxīn. 798 Art District ☎010 64386675, Ⓦucca.org.cn; subway line #14 to Jintai, Exit B; map pp.96–97. The shop connected to this excellent gallery (see p.103) sells limited-edition fashion by local designers for around ¥1000 and handwoven bags for ¥300. Tues–Sun 10am–7pm.

MARKETS

Aliens Street Market 老番街, lǎofān jiē. Yabao Lu, north of Ritan Park; subway line #2 or #6 to Chaoyangmen, Exit A; map pp.68–69. Bustling warren of stalls on two floors, offering cheap clothing, practical household items, cosmetics and tea – all being bought in bulk by Russian customers. It's especially good for clothes and accessories; don't believe any marked sizes and take a close look at the stitching before you hand over your cash. Daily 9.30am–7pm.

★**Daxin Textiles** 大新纺织品东四市店, dàxīn fǎngzhīpǐn dōngsìshì diàn. 227 Chaoyangmen Nei Dajie; subway line #5 or #6 to Dongsi, Exit B; map pp.68–69. A dozen or more booths under one roof selling silk and cloth by the metre; tailors here can make suits, qipaos etc to your order. About twenty percent cheaper than other dealers in town. Daily 9am–7.30pm.

Silk Market 秀水市场, xiùshuǐ shìchǎng. Off Jianguomenwai Dajie, Ⓦxiushui.com.cn; subway line #1 to Yong'anli, Exit A; map pp.68–69. This huge six-storey tourist mall has electronics, jewellery and souvenirs, but its main purpose is to profit through flouting international copyright laws, with hundreds of stalls selling fake designer labels. You'll need to haggle hard. There are also a few tailors – pick out your material, then bargain, and you can get a suit made in 24hr for ¥800 or so. It's incredibly busy, attracting over 50,000 visitors a day on weekends, and vendors are tiresomely pushy. Daily 9.30am–9pm.

Yansha Outlets Mall 燕莎奥特莱斯购物中心, yànshā àotèláisī gòuwù zhōngxīn. 9 Dongsihuannan Lu ☎010 67395678, Ⓦyanshaoutlets.com; subway line

12

#10 to Jinsong, then a taxi (¥15); map pp.6–7. At the southern end of the eastern section of the Fourth Ring Road, this is a huge outlet for genuine designer clothes and bags, all old lines, at discounts of 30–50 percent. Very popular with expats. Daily 10am–10pm.

Yuanlong Silk Corporation 元隆顾绣绸缎商场,

yuánlóng gùxiù chóuduàn shāngchǎng. 55 Tiantan Lu 📞010 67052451; subway line #5 or #7 to Ciqikou, Exit D; map pp.80–81. There's a good selection of silk clothes, blankets and bedding at this large, mall-like building, located just opposite the Tiantan Park wall. Mon–Sat 9am–6.30pm.

COMPUTER EQUIPMENT

You can pick up memory sticks, an MP3 player, webcams, laptops, phones, tablets and more for less than at home if you go for stock Chinese brands such as Acer and Lenovo, but don't expect after-sales support. **Pirated software**, though a steal (in more ways than one), should be given a wide berth. The main area for electronic goodies is **Zhongguancun** in northwest Beijing (subway line #4 to Zhongguancun), nicknamed "Silicon Alley" for its plethora of computer shops and high-tech businesses.

Buy Now Mall 百脑汇, bǎinǎohuì. 10 Chaoyangmen Wai Dajie, across from the Dongyue Temple; subway line #2 or #6 to Chaoyangmen, Exit A; map pp.68–69. Convenient and orderly four-storey mall of stores, and a good place to load up on cheap laptops, phones or tablets. You can barter, but this isn't the Silk Market – you might get, at most, a quarter off. Daily 9am–8pm.

Hailong Electronics City 海龙大厦, hǎilóng dàshà. 1 Zhongguancun Dajie; subway line #4 or #10 to Haidian Huangzhuang; map pp.96–97. The biggest in

the area, with six storeys, is a veritable bazaar, piled high with all manner of gadgetry. There is a little leeway for bargaining. Mon–Sat 9am–6pm.

Sundan 顺电, shùndiàn. LG, Tai Koo Li, Sanlitun 🌐sundan.com; take the escalator down from the courtyard; subway line #10 to Tuanjiehu, Exit A; map p.72. Branch of citywide electronic accessories chain stocking decent-quality generic gear; there's no bargaining but prices are reasonable and some staff speak English. Daily 10am–9pm.

DEPARTMENT STORES AND MALLS

For general goods, and an idea of current Chinese taste, check out the city's **department stores** and **malls**. Maybe it's the air of exclusivity and sophistication, or just a reaction to Beijing's bad weather, but the appetite for vast and sterile shopping warrens seems insatiable. Aside from clothing stores, they house supermarkets, coffee shops, restaurants, chemists and food courts, and sometimes cinemas and bowling alleys.

★**APM** 北京, APM běijīng APM. 138 Wangfujing Jie 🌐beijingapm.cn; subway line #1 to Wangfujing, Exit B; map pp.68–69. Large, bright mall that's probably the cheeriest in the city. All your favourite Western high-street names are here, and the top two levels have some good places to eat. Daily 9am–10pm.

Friendship Store 北京友谊商店, běijīng yǒuyì shāngdiàn. Jianguomenwai Dajie 📞010 65003311; subway line #1 or #2 to Jianguomen, Exit B, or line #1 to Yong'anlin, Exit A1; map pp.68–69. Once the only place foreigners could easily shop for souvenirs in Beijing, today there's hardly anyone moving around the four floors of pricey paintings, porcelain, silk, jade and tea. Daily 9.30am–8.30pm.

Galaxy Soho 银河SOHO, yínhé SOHO. Nanshuiguan Hutong 🌐galaxysoho.sohochina.com/en; subway line #2 or #6 to Chaoyangmen, Exit G; map pp.68–69. Newest venue for the Galaxy empire is an architectural delight: a range of interconnected, cocoon-like structures with a distinctive horizontal "slatting" effect. Its shops are worth a poke around, though it's mostly office space. Daily 10am–8pm.

Oriental Plaza 东方广场, dōngfāng guǎngchǎng.

1 Dongchang'an Jie 🌐www.orientalplaza.com; subway line #1 to Wangfujing, Exit A; map pp.68–69. Extremely long mall featuring a number of excellent international boutiques – see p.67. Daily 9.30am–10pm.

Parkview Green Fangcaodi 芳草地, fāngcǎodì. Fangcaodi Hutong 🌐parkviewgreen.com/eng; subway line #6 to Dongdaqiao, Exit D; map pp.68–69. Four interconnected glass buildings with vast open-plan interior, whose climate is apparently controlled using green technology – if so, something of a first for the city. The usual upmarket chains have a presence. Daily 10am–8pm.

Sanlitun Soho 三里屯SOHO, sānlǐtún SOHO. Gongren Tiychang Beilu 🌐sanlitunsoho.sohochina.com; subway line #10 to Tuanjiehu, Exit D; map p.72. You probably won't be coming here for the shops – though there are a couple of places to eat – but this mix of office space and shops is certainly striking, its black-and-white striped towers rising up like giant barcodes. Daily 10am–8pm.

Tai Koo Li 太古里, tàigǔlǐ. Off Sanlitun Lu 🌐www.taikoolisanlitun.com; subway line #10 to Tuanjiehu, Exit A; map p.72. Some of Beijing's malls are beautiful constructions, and others are merely excellent places to shop. These twin malls, however, are a successful blend of

12

both, with their mix of elegant dining and high-end consumerism. The north mall is a little bit snobby, but its southern counterpart is a favourite strolling and dating spot with young Beijingers. Mall open 24hr; shop times vary.

JEWELLERY AND ACCESSORIES

Jewellery is a good buy in Beijing, though some of the prices will make your eyes water. Handmade pieces by minorities such as the Miao and Tibetans are perennially popular with foreigners, and are currently trendy with the Chinese.

Chow Tai Fook 周大福, zhōu dàfú. 20 Qianmen Dajie ☎010 67028771, ⓦchowtaifook.com; subway line #2 to Qianmen, Exit C or B; map pp.80–81. Beijing headquarters of this reliable Hong Kong chain; somewhere to buy stylish pearl, diamond, sapphire, emerald and ruby jewellery at – relatively speaking – competitive prices. Daily 10am–8pm.

Memory of China 青花的记忆, qīnghuā de jìyì. 30 Nanluoguxiang ☎13621132120; subway line #6 or #8 to Nanluoguxiang, Exit E; map pp.58–59. Shards of colourful antique ceramics set in creatively crafted silver mounts. The idea is enchanting and pieces are certified as genuine, but prices are astronomical; you could just about buy a whole Song dynasty bowl for the cost of a pendant here. Daily 10am–8pm.

Hongqiao Department Store 红桥百货中心, hóngqiáo bǎihuò zhōngxīn. 52 Tiantan Donglu; subway line #5 to Tiantandongmen, Exit B; map pp.80–81. Also known as the Pearl Market, this giant mall comprises five floors, of which the top two are dedicated to pearls and the others a mix of souvenirs, Middle Eastern carpets, scarves, T-shirts and electronics. Popular with tourists but not a great experience; it's always overcrowded, asking prices are absurd, and dealers are very pushy. Daily 9am–8pm.

SUPERMARKETS

Beijing is well stocked with supermarkets, especially useful if you want to get a picnic, or have **self-catering** facilities. All sell plenty of Western food alongside the Chinese, though few have a decent range of dairy products. Most new malls also have supermarkets in their basements.

Carrefour 家乐福, jiālèfú. Guangqumen Neidajie ⓦcarrefour.com.cn; subway line # to Guangqumennei, Exit A; map pp.6–7. The most conveniently located Beijing outpost of the French hypermarket empire; like the others, it's a decent hunting ground for bicycles, wines, cheese, nappies and much more. Daily 8am–10pm.

City Shop B1 The Place, 9 Guanghua Lu ⓦcityshop .com.cn; subway line #10 to Jintaixizhao, Exit A or D; map pp.68–69. A particularly well-stocked supermarket, and conveniently located right in the centre of Beijing's prime business district. Daily 9am–9pm.

★**Jenny Lou** 6 Sanlitun Beilu ⓦwww.jennylou.com.cn; subway line #10 to Agricultural Exhibition Center, Exit D2; map p.72. A chain of small, almost deli-like supermarkets with branches all over the east of the city. All sorts of goodies line their crowded shelves, making this the place to head if you want exotic treats like olives, cheese (often incredibly cheap), or international cereals. Daily 8am–11pm.

Marketplace LGF Tai Koo Li, Sanlitun, take the escalator down from the courtyard ☎010 64158226; subway line #10 to Tuanjiehu, Exit A; map p.72. Huge cornucopia of imported Western products, alongside fresh fruit and veggies; expect premium prices but should you need Branston Pickle or Marmite, odds are that you'll find it here. Daily 10am–10pm.

TEA

There are tea shops all over the city, and many offer free samples; some also double as places in which to buy **tea sets**, though these will be cheaper in dedicated pottery or souvenir shops.

Maliandao Tea Street 马连道茶叶街, mǎliándào cháyèjiē. Behind Beijing West train station; subway line #7 to Wanzi, Exit A; map pp.6–7. If you're in the mood for something truly special, this street hosts hundreds of tea shops along a 1.5km-long stretch. They all offer free tastings, but remember that you're expected to bargain for the actual product. You're spoilt for choice, of course, but check out four-storey Tea City, about halfway down.

Ten Fu 天福茶, tiānfú chá. 53 Qianmen Dajie ⓦtenfu .com/en; subway line #2 to Qianmen, Exit C; map pp.80–81. Huge chain with stores across the city; one of their best is here on pedestrianized Qianmen Dajie (there's another nearby on Dazhalan Dong Jie). Some staff speak English, and there's little pressure to buy – it's so busy that they don't need to hassle for custom. All sorts of tea is available, from the extremely cheap to the extraordinarily expensive. Daily 8am–9pm.

Zhang Yiyuan 张一元茶, zhāngyīyuán chá. 86 Qianmen Dajie ⓦzhangyiyuan.net; subway line #2 to Qianmen, Exit C; map pp.80–81. Fantastic tearoom with a great location on Qianmen Dajie; as well as a wide range of teas and tea sets, in summer months they serve delectable green-tea ice cream from a shopfront window. Other branches across the city. Daily 8am–9pm.

BEIJING DUCKS

Sports and fitness

During the 2008 Olympics, a passion for athletic activity became a patriotic duty. Now the dust has settled, the legacy of the Games includes a range of good sports facilities across the capital, from the outdoor workout machines placed in every neighbourhood to the showpiece stadiums themselves. However, the most visible kinds of exercise need no fancy equipment; head to any park in the morning and you'll see citizens going through all sorts of martial arts routines, as well as performing popular exercises deemed beneficial for the *qì* (气, life force), such as walking backwards, chest slapping, and tree hugging. In addition, plenty of people cycle, play table tennis (often with a line of bricks as a net) and street badminton (with no net at all), while in the evening many public spaces – parks in particular – become the venue for mass ballroom dancing.

13

GYMS

Gyms are becoming as popular as they are in the West. Private gyms charge from ¥3000 per year, though some offer monthly rates and you might well be able to negotiate a shorter-term deal. Most large hotels also have at least some equipment, or even fully-equipped gyms plus a pool; non-guests get charged upwards of ¥200 a session.

B Active F2, Building 6, Sanlitun SOHO, 8 Gongti Bei Lu Ⓦ bactive24h.com; subway line #10 to Tuanjiehu, Exit D. Small but extremely popular gym with filtered air system for smoggy days, good equipment and plenty of classes in kick boxing and the like. It's open 24hr.

E-52 Enter Total Fitness 17 Hepingli Zhong Jie Ⓣ 010 84216385; subway line #5 to Hepinglibeijie, Exit C. Big gym with plenty of no-frills, conventional treadmills, bikes and cross trainers – they've even got a boxing ring.

★Park Hyatt 柏悦酒店, bǎiyuè jiǔdiàn. 2 Jianguomenwai Dajie Ⓣ 010 85671101, Ⓦ beijing .park.hyatt.com; subway line #1 or #10 to Guomao, Exit D; map pp.68–69. The most attractive gym in the city, based on the 59th floor of the fancy *Park Hyatt* hotel. The views over the CBD are fantastic, especially from the nearby lap-pool. The only problem is the price, which for non-guests starts at a princely ¥500 per day.

HIKING

Beijing Hikers Ⓣ 010 64322786, Ⓦ beijinghikers .com. Expat-run group organizing frequent, imaginative hikes in the city's environs to dilapidated sections of the Great Wall, caves and the like. Reservations are required. Meets every Saturday at the *Starbucks* in the *Lido Holiday Inn*.

ICE SKATING

In winter, try Qianhai, the Summer Palace or the Shicha Lakes for **ice skating**. Otherwise, there are a couple of indoor venues around town. However, you may not fancy visiting any of these places as a novice, as Chinese skaters are very good and expect a certain degree of confidence.

Le Cool B2 China World Trade Centre Ⓦ www.cwtc .com; subway line #1 or #10 to Guomao, Exit A; map pp.68–69. The city's most accessible indoor rink: small, but still a lot of fun, and family-friendly. From ¥50 for 90min. Mon–Sat 10am–10pm, Sun 10am–8pm.

MARTIAL ARTS

Beijing has long been a decent place to study Chinese **martial arts** such as *tai ji*, Shaolin kung fu, *xingyi* and *bagua* (see box, p.82). You'll see people training, especially at weekends, in many of the city's parks – Temple of Heaven is a good place to look – but while Chinese-speakers might find a teacher this way, in general it's hard to do so without a proper introduction.

Beijing Milun Kung Fu School 36 Ganyu Hutong, off Wangfujing Ⓦ kungfuinchina.com; subway line #5 to Dengshikou. Renowned school, if somewhat generic, set in a wonderful *hutong* location (though they decamp to Ritan Park during the summer months). Rates start at ¥200 a session; tuition in English available.

China Yiquan Academy 中意武馆, zhōngyì wǔguǎn. 17 Zhengjiaojia Dao, Xinjiekou, in the same compound as the Red Lantern hostel's second building Ⓣ 010 66055289, Ⓦ www.yiquan-zywg .com; subway line #4 to Xinjiekou, Exit B. The strange but powerful art of *yiquan*, as taught by the indefatigable Yao Chengrong. While *yiquan* works well in its own right, it's also a great foundation for studying *tai ji*, *xingyi* and *bagua*. You'll need to speak Chinese and be prepared to take a few knocks.

ATHLETIC EVENTS AROUND BEIJING

Some intriguing events take place around Beijing. Most interesting is the **Genghis Khan Extreme Grasslands Marathon** (Ⓦ genghiskhanmtbadventure.com), which sees runners pound a standard-length marathon course through some of China's most enchantingly beautiful scenery. This usually takes place in early July, and is immediately followed by the **Genghis Khan Mountain Bike Adventure**, a three-day, 206km race organized by the same team. Do them back to back and live to tell the tale, and you'll have had the ideal preparation for September's **Beijing International Triathlon** (Ⓦ beijinginternationaltriathlon.com), an event resuscitated in 2013.

MASSAGE AND SPA

13

Beijing is full of dodgy **massage** joints, but reliable venues do exist – plenty of them, too. Prices are rising, but are still less than you'd pay in most Western countries. **Spa** services are even easier to track down – most upper-end hotels offer such treatments.

Aibosen 爱博森盲人按摩院, àibósēn mángrén ànmóyuàn. 11A Liufang Beilijia ☎010 64652044; subway line #13 to Liufang, Exit B; map pp.96–97. The blind staff at this clinic are trained in Chinese medical massages. Most popular with foreigners are the 1hr deep-tissue massages (¥138). If you like them and are sticking around for a while, you can pick up discount cards for ten (¥850) or twenty (¥1480) massages. Daily 10am–1.30am.

Bodhi 菩提, pútí. 17 Gongti Beilu, opposite Workers' Stadium ☎010 64130226, ⊛www.bodhi.com.cn; subway line #2 to Dongsishitiao, Exit B; map pp.68–69. Ayurvedic and Thai massages are among the many options available at this Southeast Asia-styled clinic. Ayurvedic massage ¥288 for 1hr. Daily 11am–12.30pm.

Chi Shangri-La Hotel 29 Zizhuyuan Lu ☎010 68412211; subway line #9 or #4 to National Library, Exit A; map pp.88–89. Therapies at this luxurious New Age spa claim to use the five Chinese elements – metal, fire, wood, water and earth – to balance your *yin* and *yang*. It might look like a Tibetan temple, but there can't be many real Tibetans who could afford to darken its doors; a Chi Balance massage costs ¥1430, a Himalayan Healing Stone Massage ¥1700 (and there's a 15 percent service charge). Daily 10am–midnight.

Dragonfly 悠庭, yōutíng. ⊛dragonfly.net.cn. This well-reputed Shanghai chain has opened two centres in the capital – check the website for locations. Their classic Chinese massage (60min; ¥188) is always popular, as are the foot massages. Daily 10am–11pm.

St Regis Spa Centre St Regis Hotel, 21 Jianguomenwai Dajie ☎010 64606688, ⊛starwoodhotels.com/stregis; subway line #1 or #2 to Jianguomen, Exit B; map pp.68–69. Traditional Chinese massage, aromatherapy and facials are among the treatments on offer at this very upscale hotel. Prices start at ¥450 for a head and shoulders massage. Daily 10am–10pm.

Taipan 6 Ritan Lu ⊛taipan.com.cn. A popular chain, with branches all over the city – no frills, but clean and cheap. ¥228 for a 75min foot massage or a 60min body massage.

ROCK CLIMBING

O'le 5 Shimencun Lu ☎186 18461002, ⊛ole-sports .org; subway line #7 to Baiziwan, Exit A. This outfit has a great climbing wall geared to all experience levels, and also runs weekend trips to outdoor venues in the hills around Beijing. There's a useful store too. Day sessions cost ¥65.

SKIING

Nanshan 南山滑雪场, nánshān huáxuěchǎng. 60km northeast of the city ☎010 89091909, ⊛nanshanski.com; bus #980 from Dongzhimen bus station to Miyun Xidaqiao (¥14), then taxi (about ¥20); direct shuttle bus (¥45 return) daily 8.30am from Wudaokou subway (line #13). The best of Beijing's ski resorts, with thirteen 1500m-long runs. For snowboarders there are two kickers, a mini pipe and more than a dozen boxes and rails, and there's also sledging and cable gliding. Entrance ¥20; 2hr skiing session from ¥150, whole day from ¥310; gear rental will come to just under ¥100.

SNOOKER AND POOL

Pool and **snooker** are very popular in China, and increasingly so, thanks to the exploits of Ding Junhui, who won his first China Open in 2005 – aged just 17 – and in 2016 became the first Chinese player to qualify for the World Championship finals. A great many wish to follow in his footsteps, and some locals are expert cue-wielders; you can take them on at any number of halls around town (some say there are over 2000), so just ask at your accommodation for the nearest. It'll be around ¥20 per hour for a table and, even at swankier venues, beer is usually available.

SWIMMING

Avoid **swimming pools** at the weekends, when they're full of teenagers doing just about everything but swimming. Bear in mind that some **hotels** open their lavish pools and gym facilities to non-guests; we've listed the most impressive of them below.

HOTEL POOLS

CITIC Hotel 9 Xiaotianzhi Nan Lu ☎010 64565588, ⊛www.citichotelbeijing.com. For family pool fun, this hotel up by the airport has hot springs and the capital's only indoor-outdoor pool. ¥130/day.

Doubletree by Hilton 168 Guang'anmenwai Dajie ☎010 63381888, ⊛doubletree3.hilton.com; subway line #7 to Daguanying; map pp.6–7. ¥150/day.

Ritz-Carlton 1 Jinchengfang Dong Jie ☎010 66016666, ⊛ritzcarlton.com; subway line #1 or #2 to

13

SPECTATOR SPORTS

The Chinese now have more leisure time than ever before, and many spectator sports have seen large gains in attendance figures. Introduced by Americans in the early twentieth century, **basketball** is king here, though fans of Beijing Guo'an **football** team may beg to differ. In addition, the Chinese excel at "small ball" games such as **squash**, **badminton**, **snooker** and **table tennis**; tournaments – like snooker's China Open – take place all the time, but it's perhaps more interesting to see the champions of the future being coached at outdoor tables in places such as Ritan Park. In theory, it's possible to buy tickets for all major sporting events online at ⓦ en.damai.cn, though these often sell out in minutes, usually ending up in the hands of scalpers; you'll have to haggle them down to a good price (try ¥50) outside the stadium.

BASKETBALL

The **Beijing Ducks** (北京鸭篮球俱乐部, běijīng yā lánqiú jùlèbù) are the capital's main basketball team; they compete in the CBA (Chinese Basketball Academy) and won their first national title in 2011–12. They play at the MasterCard Center (subway line #1 to Wukesong, Exit B1), which also hosted basketball games in the 2008 Olympics.

FOOTBALL

European football leagues have a surprisingly strong following, and English, Spanish and German games are shown on CCTV5 and BTV. Premier Xi Jinping is a big footie fan, and – partly to curry favour with him – China's billionaires are throwing money into the **Chinese Super League**. The league's resources have improved accordingly, and decent wages have attracted a fair few foreign players and coaches, though it continues to be rocked by match-fixing scandals.

In season (mid-March to mid-Oct), **Beijing Guo'an** football team (北京国安足球俱乐部, běijīng guó'ān zúqiú jùlèbù) is one of its big hitters; they play most of their games in the 66,000-capacity Workers' Stadium (subway line #2 to Dongsishitiao, Exit C). Games with local rivals Tianjin Teda and title challengers Shanghai Shenhua are the liveliest, but even at these, the atmosphere is relaxed, and there's no trouble; no one sees the need to segregate fans, for example. Glamorous foreign teams often include Beijing on their pre-season warm-up tours, usually playing at the National Stadium (aka Bird's Nest; see p.102).

Fuxingmen, Exit A; map pp.88–89. ¥220/day.
Westin Chaoyang 1 Xinyuan Nan Lu ☎010 59228888, ⓦ starwoodhotels.com; subway line #10 to Liangmaqiao, Exit A; map pp.68–69. ¥250 for a weekend pass.

PUBLIC POOLS

Ditan Swimming Pool 地坛游泳馆, dìtán yóuyǒng guǎn. 8 Hepingli Zhong Jie ☎010 64264483; subway line #2 to Andingmen, Exit B; map pp.68–69. If you just want a cheap swim, try this place, open year-round (entry ¥30). In the summer, there are outdoor pools open for the same price at nearby Qingnian Lake. Daily 7am–10pm.

National Aquatics Centre 国家游泳中心, guójiā yóuyǒng zhōngxīn. Olympic Green ☎010 84370112, ⓦ www.water-cube.com/en; subway line #8 to Olympic Green, Exit B1; map pp.96–97. Since the games, the famous Water Cube (see p.102) has reopened as a water theme park, featuring spas, slides and a wave pool. ¥60. Daily 10am–9.30pm.

Sino-Japanese Youth Centre 中日青年交流中心, zhōngrì qīngnián jiāoliú zhōngxīn. 40 Lianmaqiao Lu, by the Century Theatre ☎010 64683311; subway line #10 to Liangmaqiao, Exit C; map pp.68–69. Serious swimmers should check out this Olympic-size pool. Entry ¥88. Daily 9am–9pm.

TEAM SPORTS

FOOTBALL

Beijing Barbarians ⓦ beijingbarbarians.com. Beijing's "United Nations of Football", with two 11-a-side and two 5-a-side teams playing weekly.

Club Football ⓦ clubfootball.com.cn. Year-round 5-a-side competitions for men, women and kids alike.

International Friendship Football Club ⓦ new .iffc1994.com. Relatively serious, this club controls two leagues' worth of teams. The standard is pretty high.

HANDBALL

Handball in China ⓦ handballinchina.org. Group that meets every Thurs evening for some handball fun. Free for first-timers and a good mix of skills.

RUGBY

Beijing Devils ⓦ beijingdevils.com. Extremely cosmopolitan rugby club, whose men's, women's and touch teams meet for training at least once per week.

SCULPTURE AT 798 ART DISTRICT

Contexts

History

Zip through Beijing in a taxi, and you'd be hard-pressed to guess that this relentlessly forward-marching city – all eight-lane expressways, multistorey office blocks and cutting-edge designer architecture – has much of a history at all. Yet, aside from brief periods of civil strife, Beijing has been at the centre of the Chinese empire for over seven hundred years, ever since the Mongol Yuan dynasty under Kublai Khan set up camp here in the thirteenth century. During the subsequent Ming and Qing dynasties (1368–1911), Beijing developed into a truly grand metropolis, as any number of surviving sights from these times still proves; a national capital that was also arguably the centre of the civilized world – a title that it clearly wants back.

Beginnings

Peking man (*Homo erectus pekinensis*) walked the Beijing area from 750,000–250,000 BC, as evidenced by a number of fossils unearthed in caves between 1921 and 1937 near the village of Zhoukoudian, a site around 60km southwest of what is today the city centre. *Homo sapiens* inhabited the same area at a later date (c.30,000 BC); tools and bone fragments from this time have also been discovered in Wangfujing, right in the middle of the modern city. The first actual settlements in and around Beijing go back almost as far, to the end of the **Paleolithic era**; evidence of dozens of **Neolithic** settlements, including burial sites, has also been discovered across the city and its environs.

While the city's pre-imperial history is shrouded in myth and legend, the first recorded event occurred in the eleventh century BC, when the **Zhou dynasty** conquered the Shang, and went on to use Beijing as a regional capital. Evidence suggests that this base city-state, named Ji after one particular Zhou leader, was near Guang'anmen, not too far at all from the centre of modern Beijing. Around 690 BC, during what is now known as the **Spring and Autumn Period**, Ji was absorbed by the competing Yan state (eleventh century to 222 BC), based just to the south, and it was during the last decades of Yan's existence that the city received its first protective walls. Far greater fortifications, though still earthen in nature, were built during the **Qin dynasty** (221–207 BC); Beijing was at this time a mere regional base, with the imperial capital way out west in Xi'an. It remained relatively unimportant for half a millennium until the Former Yan, one of the **Sixteen Kingdoms** which jostled for power during – and after – the latter part of the **Jin dynasty** (265–420 AD), moved their capital here in 352; this only lasted for five years, but the Northern Wei restored Beijing as capital four decades later. This on-off arrangement became a pattern – increasing in importance after being connected to Shanghai by the **Grand Canal** during the Sui dynasty (581–618), Beijing served as an occasional regional capital during the Tang (618–907), Five dynasties (907–960) and Liao (907–1125) periods.

11th century BC	690 BC	Late 2nd century BC	250 AD
Zhou dynasty conquers Shang; Beijing becomes a regional capital for the first time	Beijing absorbed by Yan state	First protective walls built	First extensive irrigation systems installed, increasing agricultural productivity

HISTORICAL CHRONOLOGY

21st–16th centuries BC Xia dynasty
16th–11th centuries BC Shang dynasty
11th century to 771 BC Zhou dynasty
770–476 BC Spring and Autumn Period – China fragments into city states and small kingdoms
457–221 BC Warring States – China's fragmentation continues
221–207 BC Qin dynasty
206 BC–220 AD Han dynasty
222–280 Three Kingdoms Period: China is divided into three competing territories, the Wei, Shu Han and Wu
265–420 Jin dynasty
420–581 Southern dynasties and Northern dynasties – rapid succession of short-lived dynasties

581–618 Sui dynasty – China united for the first time since Han dynasty
618–907 Tang dynasty
907–1125 Liao dynasty
1125–1234 Jin (Jurchen) dynasty
1271–1368 Yuan dynasty
1368–1644 Ming dynasty
1644–1911 Qing dynasty
1912–45 Republic founded, its fall followed by civil war between Nationalists and Communists, and Japanese occupation
1945–49 Further period of civil conflict between Guomindang and the Communist People's Liberation Army
1949 Communists take power over mainland China; establishment of People's Republic

The **Liao dynasty** saw the Khitan, a nomadic barbarian tribe from the northern grasslands, erect another major series of city walls, and make full use of the Grand Canal as a means of trade. The city walls could not prevent the Khitan being overthrown by the Southern Song, who razed Beijing but failed to fully defeat the Liao. This was eventually accomplished with the aid of the Jurchen, another nomadic group, who made Beijing capital of the Jurchen or (second) **Jin dynasty** (1125–1234) in 1153. The city's walls were then expanded as the population swelled to half a million, and it became one of the first places in the world in which paper currency was used.

The Yuan dynasty

Beijing's true pre-eminence dates back to the latter half of the thirteenth century, and the formation of Mongol China under **Genghis Khan** (1162–1227), and subsequently **Kublai Khan** (1215–94). It was Genghis who conquered Beijing in 1215, his army breaking through the walls and demolishing the city. The Mongols initially took **Shangdu** in Mongolia (the "Xanadu" of Coleridge's poem) as their capital; **Marco Polo** visited Kublai here and was impressed with the city's sophistication. "So great a number of houses and of people, no man could tell the number…", he wrote. "I believe there is no place in the world to which so many merchants come, and dearer things, and of greater value and more strange, come into this town from all sides than to any city in the world…" The wealth he depicted stemmed from Shangdu's position at the start of the **Silk Road**, the trading route that stretched all the way to Central Asia; Marco Polo described "over a thousand carts loaded with silk" arriving in the city almost every day.

By 1264 the Mongols had consolidated their hold over China, and, as emperor, Kublai decided to move his power base out of Mongolia and down south into the Chinese heartlands. He pragmatically chose Beijing as his new capital – well within

Early 7th century	1122	1125	1214
Grand Canal fully connected, linking Beijing to Shanghai	City captured by Jurchen tribe, given to Song	Jurchens retake Beijing	City under siege from Mongol army, led by Genghis Khan; surrender follows the next year, and the city is sacked

Chinese territory, yet close enough to the Mongolian heartlands – incidentally bringing the wealth of the Silk Road along with him and ensuring that the city would develop in grand style.

The Ming dynasty

With the accession of the **Ming dynasty**, who defeated the Mongols in 1368, the capital shifted temporarily to Nanjing. However, the second Ming emperor, **Yongle**, returned to Beijing, building around him prototypes of the city's two great monuments, the Forbidden City and the Temple of Heaven. It was during Yongle's reign, too, that the city's basic layout took shape, rigidly symmetrical, extending in squares and rectangles from the palace and inner-city grid to the suburbs, much as it is today. It's estimated that over 250,000 prisoners of war were used as slaves during these epic waves of construction, numbers which – along with arrivals (sometimes forced) from the previous capital of Nanjing – swelled the city's population to over one million. The city almost certainly became the first place on earth to reach that figure.

The Great Wall

Though the Yuan dynasty had been brought to a close, the threat from the north remained. Beijing found itself under regular attack from Mongol horsemen, who occasionally reached the very gates of the city; they also hampered communications with the rest of the empire, with the situation coming to a head in the early fifteenth century. The solution was simple but incredibly ambitious: it was at this time that construction of the famed **Great Wall** got going in earnest. Unlike previous walls, this was no mere barrier of rammed earth, but a sinuous snake of brick and stone – several of them, in fact. Mighty as the wall may have been, it was only as strong as its weakest link – the fact that guards will always be conducive to bribery meant that it became a grandiose but ultimately futile attempt to stem the incursions of northern Manchu tribes into China.

The Qing dynasty

Beijing's subsequent history is dominated by the rise and eventual collapse of the **Manchu** who, as the **Qing dynasty**, ruled China from the city from 1644 to the beginning of the twentieth century. Three outstanding Qing emperors brought an infusion of new blood and vigour to government early on. **Kangxi**, who began his 61-year reign in 1654 at the age of 6, was a great patron of the arts, as borne out by the numerous scrolls and paintings blotted with his seals, indicating that he had viewed them – you'll see plenty in the Forbidden City. His fourth son, the Emperor **Yongzheng** (1678–1735), ruled over what is considered one of the most efficient administrations ever enjoyed by China; as well as cracking down on the corruption that had plagued the rules of previous emperors, he formed the Grand Council, a high-level body whose policies went on to shape much of Qing society. He was succeeded by **Qianlong** (1711–99), whose reign saw China's frontiers greatly extended and the economy stimulated by peace and prosperity. In 1750, the capital was perhaps at its zenith, the centre of one of the strongest, wealthiest and most powerful countries in

1266	1271	1272	1302	1403	1420
Marco Polo visits Shangdu	Kublai Khan declares new Yuan dynasty with Beijing as capital	Drum Tower erected	Confucius Temple constructed	The city is named Beijing for the first time	Forbidden City completed; Beijing likely the largest city in the world at this time

HISTORY TODAY: THE MING AND QING

Ancient Observatory An underrated sight, this old observatory boasts a clutch of breathtakingly beautiful Ming-dynasty astrological instruments. See p.74

Chengde A wonderful small city in Hebei Province, featuring Bishu Shanzhuang, an old imperial retreat, and a series of stunning temples. See p.123

Drum Tower Looming over the Shicha Lakes, just north of the Forbidden City, this tower can be climbed for great views. The neighbouring Bell Tower is also Ming, but has since been rebuilt. See p.63

The Forbidden City One of China's biggest tourist draws, this old imperial stomping ground goes back to the Mongol era, but its present structure is essentially

Ming. Also of note here are a series of splendid exhibition halls – one of them houses one of the world's finest collections of Ming vases. See p.41

The Great Wall Another world-famous sight, the wall also pre-dates the Ming, but it's the work from this period that's most visible. See p.105

The Ming Tombs The resting place of several Ming-dynasty emperors. See p.110

The Temple of Heaven Justly regarded as the epitome of Ming design, and a real Beijing must-see. See p.79

Zhihua Temple Built for a favoured palace eunuch, this contains the oldest wooden structures in Beijing. See p.74

the world. It was at this time that the extraordinary **Summer Palace** was constructed. With two hundred pavilions, temples and palaces, and immense artificial lakes and hills, it was the world's most remarkable royal garden, and, along with the Forbidden City, a magnificent symbol of Chinese wealth and power.

European expansionism and the Opium Wars

In the late eighteenth century expansionist European nations were sniffing around Asia, looking for financial opportunities. China's rulers, immensely rich and powerful and convinced of their own superiority, had no wish for direct dealings with foreigners. When a British envoy, **Lord Macartney**, arrived at Chengde in 1793 to propose a political and commercial alliance between King George III and the emperor, his mission was unsuccessful. This was partly because he refused to kowtow to the emperor, but also because the emperor totally rejected any idea of allying with one whom he felt was a subordinate. Macartney was impressed by the vast wealth and power of the Chinese court, but later wrote perceptively that the empire was "like an old crazy first-rate man-of-war which its officers have contrived to keep afloat to terrify by its appearance and bulk".

Foiled in their attempts at official negotiations with the Qing court, the British decided to take matters into their own hands and create a clandestine market in China for Western goods. Instead of silver, they began to pay for tea and silk with **opium**, cheaply imported from India. As the number of addicts escalated during the early nineteenth century, China's trade surplus became a deficit as silver drained out of the country to pay for the drug. The emperor suspended the traffic in 1840 by ordering the **destruction** of more than twenty thousand chests of opium, an act that led to the outbreak of the **Opium Wars**. Flaring on and off for the next twenty years, these culminated in China's defeat by Western powers, the forced opening up of the country to foreign trade, and the **destruction of the Summer Palace** by Anglo-French forces in 1860.

1643	1644	1669	1750s
Plagues hit, claiming over 200,000 lives	Beijing taken in peasant rebellion, then taken back by Manchu; Qing dynasty begins	Tongrentang pharmacy (see p.34) opens its doors for the first time	Summer Palace constructed

HISTORICAL NAMES OF BEIJING

Ji (11th century BC–607 AD), the first recorded name of Beijing, employed from the Zhou to the Northern Dynasties periods; "Yan" was also used at times, and referred to a separate settlement to the south.

Zhuojun (607–616) Used for a short time during the Sui dynasty.

Youzhou (616–938) During the Tang and Five dynasties periods; "Fanyang" and "Yanjing" were also used at times.

Nanjing (938–1125) During the Liao dynasty; the name "Yanjing" was also employed.

Yanjing (1125–1271) In addition to its earlier use, this became the city's official name in the Jin dynasty, as well as the early Yuan; it remains a nickname for the city, best evidenced as the brand name of its best-selling beer.

Dadu (1271–1368) The name given to Beijing when it was chosen to serve as the Yuan dynasty capital.

Beiping (1368–1403) The name chosen following the Ming conquest; it was also used at points after the proclamation of the Republic.

Beijing (1403–present) "North Capital" was first chosen as a name under the Ming, used as a sole name under the Qing, occasionally eschewed by the Republic in favour of Beiping (see above), then brought back in 1949 by the People's Republic.

Peking Never an official name in Mandarin, though used as a transliteration by the Western world until the dawn of *pinyin* in 1958. Though "Beijing" has been the official romanized spelling since then, the name still lives on in the form of Peking duck and Peking man, and in various European languages.

The Empress Dowager Cixi

While the imperial court lived apart, within the gilded cage of the **Forbidden City**, conditions in the capital's suburbs for the civilian population were starkly different. Kang Youwei, a Cantonese visiting in 1895, described this dual world: "No matter where you look, the place is covered with beggars. The homeless and the old, the crippled and the sick, with no one to care for them, fall dead on the roads. This happens every day. And the coaches of the great officials rumble past them continuously."

The indifference spread from the top down. China was now run by the autocratic, out-of-touch **Empress Dowager Cixi** (see box, p.99), who could hardly have been less concerned with the fate of her people. She squandered money meant for the modernization of the navy on building a new Summer Palace of her own, a project which became the last grand gesture of imperial architecture and patronage. By this time, in the face of successive waves of defeats by foreign powers, the Chinese empire was near collapse.

The Boxer Rebellion and Xinhai revolution

Towards the end of the nineteenth century, a rebel peasant movement now known as the **Boxers** attempted to stymie the Western advance; though initially suppressed by the Qing court, Cixi soon allowed them greater leeway. In 1900, they laid siege to Beijing's legations quarter for almost two months, before being beaten by an eight-nation alliance of over 20,000 troops. These forces proceeded to loot the city (a substantial amount of treasure remains abroad to this day), occupy much of northern China and impose crippling indemnities on the ailing Qing government.

1860	1864	1900	1911	1915
French and British armies victorious in Second Opium War; both loot Summer Palace	*Quanjude* restaurant introduces new kind of oven, heralding birth of what is now known as Peking duck	Legation quarter besieged during Boxer Rebellion	Qing dynasty overthrown; Republic of China founded in 1912	Empire of China declared

A full-scale **revolution** took place in 1911 after trouble bubbled up in the south of China; **Yuan Shikai** (1859–1916) led an army sent to suppress the rebellion, but ended up negotiating with them instead. Newly returned from exile, the idealistic revolutionary **Sun Yatsen** (1866–1925) declared the **Republic of China** at the very dawn of 1912, offering Yuan Shikai its stewardship on the condition that he compel the Qing court to abdicate. They duly did so a month later – the end of two millennia of imperial rule, though **Puyi** (1906–67), the last emperor, was kept on as a powerless figurehead.

The republic

The short-lived republic was in trouble from the outset, with its first months marked by infighting, factionalism and the not insignificant matter of where to base the national capital. One of Sun's preconditions for transferring power to Yuan was that **Nanjing** should become capital; the Senate, ignoring this, voted for Beijing instead. Sun insisted on a second vote, with Beijing not one of the options, and this saw Nanjing emerge victorious; not to be stopped, Yuan engineered reasons to stay put in Beijing, with forces loyal to him setting off a wave of rioting and destruction down south in Nanjing.

In 1913, Sun Yatsen's second attempt at a revolution failed and he was forced into exile once again, while the senate was cleared of any Nationalist members who may have supported his return. Yuan went a step further the next year, dissolving parliament and a constitution whose ink was still wet; in 1915 he went further still, declaring himself emperor of the new **Empire of China**. Rebellion inevitably bubbled up once more in the south, and Yuan resumed the mantle of president in March 1916; he died a few months later. China fell under the control of warlords, with eight presidents in the twelve years following Yuan's death, together with a twelve-day resuscitation of Manchu rule. Amazingly, the city managed to grow and modernize itself during this period of chaos, with streets widened, city gates smartened up, and a new tram system inaugurated.

The Guomindang

In 1928, Beijing came under the military dictatorship of the Nationalist **Guomindang** party, led by **Chiang Kaishek** (1887–1975), losing its mantle as capital to Nanjing, and nine years later was taken by Japanese forces after a firefight at the Marco Polo Bridge (see p.116). World War II began immediately afterwards, and at its close Beijing was controlled by an alliance of Guomindang troops and American marines.

World war was followed by **civil war** – the Nationalists and Chinese Communists had been allies during the fight against Japan, but following a hastily arranged, oft-broken truce they entered a full state of war as soon as 1947. The **Communist People's Liberation Army (PLA)** took Beijing in early 1949, and advanced south; despite appeals from Nanjing for a truce, they crossed the Yangtze soon afterwards, and took southern China from the Nationalists too.

The communist era

On October 1, 1949, **Mao Zedong** (see box, p.52), Chairman of the Communist Party, proclaimed the inauguration of the **People's Republic of China** from Tian'anmen gate, in the process making Beijing the nation's capital once more. The city that Mao

1921	1928	1937	1945
Bones of Peking man unearthed; tram lines introduced	Beijing falls under Nationalist control; replaced as capital of nation, then as capital of Hebei Province	Empire of Japan takes over Beijing, and makes the city capital once more	Nationalists retake control following Japanese defeat in World War II

inherited for the Chinese people was in most ways primitive. Imperial laws had banned the construction of houses higher than the official buildings and palaces, so virtually nothing was more than one storey high. The roads, although straight and uniform, were narrow and congested, and there was scarcely any industry.

The rebuilding of the capital, and the erasing of symbols of the previous regimes, was an early priority for the communists. They wanted to retain the city's sense of ordered planning, with **Tian'anmen Square**, laid out in the 1950s, as its new heart. Initially their inspiration was Soviet, with an emphasis on heavy industry and a series of poor-quality high-rise housing programmes. Most of the traditional courtyard houses, which were seen to encourage individualism, were destroyed. In their place anonymous concrete buildings were thrown up, often with inadequate sanitation and little running water. Much of the new social planning was misguided; after the destruction of all the capital's dogs – for reasons of hygiene – in 1950, it was the turn of **sparrows** in 1956. This was a measure designed to preserve grain, but it only resulted in an increase in the insect population. To combat this, all the grass was pulled up, which in turn led to dust storms in the windy winter months.

The Great Leap Forward and the Cultural Revolution

Dogs, sparrows and grass were one thing, but the regime had loftier aims. Mao announced the so-called **Great Leap Forward** in 1958, with the intention of dramatically reorganizing the nation along communist lines. In theory, farms were to be collectivized in order to improve agricultural output, with the resultant extra food taken to cities to feed the workers in communal mess halls, leading to greater industrial output. What it actually resulted in was, of course, poverty and mass malnutrition; even when the mess halls were phased out, people had nothing left to cook with, since they'd all been required to have their pots and pans melted down for communal use. In addition, in the zeal to be free of the past and create a modern "people's capital", much of Beijing was destroyed or co-opted. In the 1940s, there were eight thousand temples and monuments in the city; by the mid-1960s, there were only around 150. Even the city walls and gates, relics mostly of the Ming era, were pulled down, their place taken by ring roads and avenues.

More destruction was to follow during the **Great Proletarian Cultural Revolution** – to give it its full title – that began in 1966. Under Mao's guidance, Beijing's students organized themselves into a political militia, the **Red Guards**, who were sent out to destroy the Four Olds: old ideas, old culture, old customs and old habits. The students attacked anything redolent of capitalism, the West or the Soviet Union. Few of the capital's remaining ancient buildings escaped destruction.

The end of Mao

Mao's hold on power finally slipped in the 1970s, when his health began to decline. A new attitude of pragmatic reform prevailed, deriving from the moderate wing of the Communist Party, headed by Premier **Zhou Enlai** (1898–1976) and his protégé, **Deng Xiaoping** (1904–1997).

In July 1976, a catastrophic earthquake in the northeast of the country killed half a million people. The Chinese hold that natural disasters always foreshadow great events, and no one was too surprised when Mao himself died on September 9. Deprived of

1949	1958	1966	1971
Communist army marches into Beijing; Mao Zedong declares People's Republic of China from Tian'anmen	Great Leap Forward begins	Cultural Revolution begins	Nixon visits

their figurehead, and with memories of the Cultural Revolution clear in everyone's mind, Mao's supporters in the Party quickly lost ground to the right, and Deng was left running the country.

Capitalism with Chinese characteristics

The subsequent move away from Mao's policies was rapid: in 1978, anti-Maoist dissidents were allowed to display wall posters in Beijing, some of which actually criticized Mao by name. Though such public airing of political grievances was later forbidden, by 1980 Deng and the moderates were secure enough to officially sanction a cautious questioning of Mao's actions. In the capital, his once-ubiquitous portraits and statues began to come down. However, criticism of Mao was one thing, but criticism of the Party was viewed quite differently. When demonstrators assembled in **Tian'anmen Square** in 1989, protesting at corruption and demanding more freedom, the regime dealt with them brutally, sending tanks and soldiers to fire on them (see box, p.51).

Deng's "open door" policies of economic liberalization and welcoming foreign influences brought about new social (though not political) freedoms, massive westernization, and the creation of a consumer culture. Western fast food, clothes and music and Japanese motorbikes became – and remain – all the rage.

Deng stepped down in the early 1990s and was succeeded by **Hu Jintao** (1942–) and **Wen Jiabao** (1942–), pragmatic technocrats under whose stewardship the Chinese economy grew at a sustained rate of around ten percent a year. Urban Chinese became much better off: in the 1970s, the "three big buys" – consumer goods that families could realistically aspire to – were a bicycle, a watch and a radio; in the 1980s, they were a washing machine, a TV and a refrigerator. Now, like their counterparts in South Korea and Japan, the middle classes own cars and computers.

Beijing today

Beginning with the build-up to Beijing hosting the Olympic games in 2008, the city has benefited from massive **investment in infrastructure** – not least the subway system, which has expanded from just three lines in 2007 to its current nineteen, with more planned. As the city's restless reinvention continues, a certain ramshackle charm – not to mention any sense of overall cohesion – has been lost as the former network of antique *hutongs* have either been demolished wholesale or gentrified. Overall, Beijing has improved; it will never perhaps be memorable for attractiveness, but it's undeniably dynamic, inventive and exciting.

The economy and corruption

Xi Jinping (1953–) became the People's Republic's seventh president in 2013, with Li Keqiang (1955–) as his premier. Xi has proved himself far more authoritarian and conservative than any of China's recent leaders, and is clearly concerned that political liberalism and creeping westernization has created social instability through loss of faith in both the authorities and traditional Chinese culture. This comes on top of increasing public discontent at **rising inflation** and living costs after two decades of double-digit economic growth, coupled with the issue of **guanxi** – a well-used term describing personal connections, whether derived from family, business, friendships or

1976	1987	1989	1995	1997
Death of Chairman Mao	*The Last Emperor* released	Tian'anmen protests halted by massacre	Artists first start to trickle into 798 factory district	Midi Music Festival first held

out-and-out power. As success is largely dependent on *guanxi*, the potential for corruption is enormous; even before being installed as president, Xi Jinping was vowing to crack down on it from the "tigers" at the top to the "flies" at the bottom (though some found this amusing, since Xi himself is the son of one of the Communist Party's founding fathers).

To deal with these issues, Xi has started to rein in the economy, which is now running at seven to eight percent annual growth, by shifting the focus from overseas trade to domestic consumption; and his promised **crackdown on corruption** has seen many high-profile figures imprisoned or executed. There has also been a drive against further westernization (such as banning any new "bizarre or xenocentric" architecture in Beijing), in favour of promoting "traditional Chinese values" – which seems to mean putting love of the Party before all else. At same time, a tightening up of **media control** means that most bad-news stories simply aren't reported on: internet access to foreign websites is increasingly restricted, and in 2015 Xi Jinping himself dropped in to visit all the major national papers, just to reinforce the message that they should behave themselves.

Class and the hukou system

Beijing's mammoth **income disparities** play a part in daily life. Peasants, attracted by the big city's prospects, now flood in en masse as **migrant workers**. The lucky ones end up working on building sites, though even they are often exploited and treated with suspicion by most city-dwellers, a sign of China's current class divisions. Steps are being taken to combat this, including a minimum wage of 40 percent of urban salaries.

A reform of Beijing's restrictive **hukou** policies has also been on the agenda for some time. These residence permits were introduced as a means of keeping the population in check and in place during the Great Leap Forward, and while restrictions on work and movement were gradually lifted from the 1980s on, migrant workers remain unable to benefit fully from healthcare or other important urban services. Of course, those who own a Beijing *hukou* don't want these reforms to take place, since the city's funds will have to be spread across more people.

The environment

One issue on the lips of all locals – sometimes in a depressingly literal sense – is **pollution**. Despite the fact that factories were moved far from the city before the Olympics rolled into town, things only seem to be getting worse, even according to the generally untrusted official statistics. In 2009, the US embassy in Beijing began tweeting their own hourly pollution reports; the rest of the world looked on with quizzical amusement on a particularly particle-filled day in 2010, when the hitherto sober reading sailed past "bad" and "hazardous" to a whole new level – "crazy bad". And it really was: the level had passed beyond 500, a full twenty times higher than WHO guidelines, and up until then supposedly the top of the scale. In December 2015, the Beijing authorities issued their first ever "red" air quality warning, and promptly decided to change the way air quality was reported. In 2016, a poll among Beijingers suggested that the majority of residents would even favour cutting back on economic expansion if it brought pollution under control, and at the G20 Summit that year China indeed signed up to the **Paris Global Climate Agreement**.

2003	2007	2008	2016
SARS hits Beijing	Line 5, the first of Beijing's "new" subway lines and only the fourth in the city, opens	Beijing hosts Summer Olympics	After air quality in the capital worsens, China signs up to the Paris Global Climate Agreement

Temple life

Beijing's Taoist and Buddhist temples are valuable repositories of heritage: as well as being often the only recognizably Chinese buildings around, they are rich with artefacts and long-preserved traditions. Outside, you'll see a glorious array of tat for sale – from flashing Buddhas to credit-card-sized images of gods to be kept in your wallet for luck. Inside, smoke billows from burners – as well as incense, you'll see worshippers burning fake money, ingots or even paper cars to enrich ancestors in heaven.

Design

In Beijing, as in China as a whole, temples are not as old as they may look; most were trashed during the Cultural Revolution and have been rebuilt from scratch. But the layout and design elements are genuinely ancient, and based on principles set down thousands of years ago. Like private houses, all Chinese temples face **south** (barbarians and evil spirits come from the north), and are surrounded by walls. Gates are sealed by heavy doors and guarded by **statues** – Buddhists use the four Heavenly Kings, while Taoists have a dragon and a lion. Further protection is afforded by a **spirit wall** in the first courtyard – easy enough for the living to walk around but a block to evil, which can supposedly only travel in straight lines.

Following this, there'll be a succession of **halls** and **courtyards**, arranged symmetrically – it's all about maintaining harmony. The courtyards will be enclosed by walls – creating so-called "sky wells" – and will usually feature ornate incense burners full of ash, venerable trees, and perhaps a pond. The buildings are placed according to a strict hierachy, with those facing front and at the rear being the most important. The halls are supported by lacquered **pillars** – Buddhists colour them bright red, Taoists use black. Some of the most elegant details are in the roof, where interlocking beams create a characteristic curved roofline and elegantly made and beautifully painted brackets (*dougongs*) allow the jauntily curving eaves to extend well beyond the main pillars. Look out for the procession of figures, including a dragon and a man riding a phoenix among various mythological beasties, that run along the edges of the roof. They're put there for luck and protection.

Symbols

The main hall of a **Buddhist temple** is dominated by three large **statues** – the Buddhas of the past, the present and the future – while the walls are lined by rather outlandish **arhats**, or saints. Around the back of the Buddhist trinity will probably be a statue of

---

TEMPLE FAIRS

Every Beijing temple holds a fair at **Chinese New Year**, integrating worship, entertainment and commerce. At these boisterous carnivals, the air is thick with incense, and locals queue to kneel at altars and play games that bring good fortune – lobbing coins at the temple bell, for example. Priests are on hand to perform rituals and write prayers.

Beijing's biggest fairs are at the Tibetan **Yonghe Gong** (see p.67) and the Taoist **Baiyun Guan** (see p.87): pick one or the other, as it's considered inauspicious to visit both during the same festival. To help you decide, note that Taoist festivals concentrate on renewal, Tibetan Lamaist ones on enlightenment.

A MONK'S LIFE

Buddhist monks wear orange robes and keep their heads shaved, while **Taoist monks** wear blue and keep their long hair tied up. Both sets of monks are celibate and vegetarian, and avoid garlic or onion, which are said to enflame the passions. Under the strict rule of an abbot, the monks and nuns live a regimented and quiet life, taken up with study, prayer and observance and celebration of significant dates. There are also plenty of practical tasks concerning the day-to-day running of the institution. Meals are communal and there will be at least three hours of prayer and meditation every day.

Guanyin, the multi-armed Goddess of Mercy. Believed to help with childbirth, she's very popular, and you'll see the same figure in Taoist temples.

Taoist temples are much more diverse in iconography. The Taoist holy trinity is made up of the three **immortals**, who each ride different animals (a crane, tiger and deer) and represent the three levels of the Taoist afterlife. You'll see dragons and phoenixes depicted in all Chinese temples, but **animal carvings** are more popular with the animist Taoists, too: look out for bats and cranes – symbols, respectively, of good luck and longevity. Other figures in Taoist temples include the red-faced God of War, Guan Yu, and the general Zhuge Liang – characters in the ancient story of the *Romance of the Three Kingdoms* (see p.192), and based on real-life figures. Around the edges of the halls you'll see often fantastical depictions of other immortals and saints, usually shown with a magical talisman and evidence of some kind of special power. All are presided over by the stern-looking Jade Emperor.

Confucian temples are rather formal, with little imagery, though you will see plenty of tombstone-like steles supported by stone tortoises – perhaps a nod towards the Indian story that a tortoise carries the world on its back. Recently, new statues of the great sage have been erected following approval of his official likeness.

Film

Although Chinese cinema goes back a long way, much of its early produce came from Shanghai, rather than Beijing. The capital finally started to pump out films in quantity during the Great Leap Forward, but output across the nation was choked off with the Cultural Revolution – no film was produced anywhere in the country between 1966 and 1970. Recovery, understandably, took time, but since the early 1980s China in general, and Beijing in particular, have been making larger and larger ripples in world cinema.

The fifth generation

In 1984 the Chinese film industry was suddenly brought to international attention for the first time by the arrival of the so-called "**fifth generation**" of Chinese film-makers. That year, director **Chen Kaige** and his cameraman Zhang Yimou, both graduates from the first post-Cultural Revolution class (1982) of the Beijing Film School, made the superb art-house film *Yellow Earth*, which told a somewhat sobering tale of peasant life in early communist times. The film was not particularly well received in China, either by audiences, who expected something more modern, or by the authorities, who expected something more optimistic. Nevertheless, it set the pattern for a series of increasingly overseas-funded films, such as *The Last Emperor* and *Farewell My Concubine*, comprising stunning images of a "traditional" China, irritating the censors at home and delighting audiences abroad.

Zhang Yimou

Chen Kaige's protégé **Zhang Yimou** was soon stealing a march on his former boss with his first film *Red Sorghum*, based on the Mo Yan novel (see p.192). This film was not only beautiful, and reassuringly patriotic, but it also introduced the world to heart-throb actress **Gong Li**. The fact that Gong Li and Zhang Yimou were soon to be lovers added to the general media interest in their work, both in China and abroad. They worked together on a string of hits, including *Judou*, *The Story of Qiu Ju*, *Raise the Red Lantern*, *Shanghai Triad* and *To Live*. None of these could be described as art-house in the way that *Yellow Earth* had been, and the potent mix of Gong Li's sexuality with exotic, mysterious locations in 1930s China was clearly targeted at Western rather than Chinese audiences. Chinese like to point out that the figure-hugging *qipao* regularly worn by Gong Li are entirely unlike the period costume they purport to represent. Zhang Yimou has since been warmly embraced by the authorities (as evidenced by his selection as director of the Olympic ceremonies in 2008), though his films have got worse.

The sixth generation and recent developments

In the 1990s, a new "**sixth generation**" of directors set out to make edgier work. Their films, usually low-budget affairs difficult to catch in China, depict what their makers consider to be the true story of modern urban life: cold apartments, ugly streets, impoverished people. Good examples include *Beijing Bastards* and *In the Heat of the Sun* (see box, p.186). Some commercial films from this period, such as *Beijing Bicycle* and *Spring Subway* (see box, p.186) were influenced by this social realist aesthetic.

The most recent trends in Chinese cinema have seen continuations of the sixth-generation patterns. The **mainstream** directors have become more influenced by Western works, and are making big bucks in China's increasing array of multiplex

BEIJING ON FILM

Beijing Bastards (1993). A story of apathetic, fast-living youths, this was one of China's first independently produced films; it stars rock singer and rebel Cui Jian (see p.189), who is depicted drinking, swearing and playing the guitar.

Beijing Bicycle (2001). Given social realist treatment, this is the story of a lad trying to get his stolen bike back – a lot more interesting than it may sound.

Cell Phone (2003). Perhaps the most successful work of Feng Xiaogang, one of China's most revered directors, this satirical comedy revolves around two men having affairs. If you like it, try Be There or Be Square, Sorry Baby, A World Without Thieves and Big Shot's Funeral – all light, clever comedies set in Beijing, made during the 1990s.

★**Farewell My Concubine** (1994). Chen Kaige's superb take on modern Chinese history. Although the main protagonist – a homosexual Chinese opera singer – is hardly typical of modern China, the tears induced by the film are wept for the country as a whole.

In the Heat of the Sun (1995). Directed by Jiang Wen, In the Heat of the Sun perfectly captures the post-revolutionary ennui of 1970s Beijing in its tale of a street gang looking for kicks. Written by Wang Shuo, the bad boy of contemporary Chinese literature,

it displays his characteristic irreverence and earthy humour.

The Last Emperor (1987). This sumptuously shot tale of Puyi, the last of China's long, long line of emperors, remains the most famous Western-made film about China – no surprise, really, since it scooped a full seven Oscars.

New Socialist Climax (2009). Jian Yi documentary which explores the way in which revolutionary sites have been turned into tourist attractions.

★**Out of Phoenix Bridge** (1997). Li Hong's superb documentary, looking at the lives of four young women who move from the countryside to Beijing in search of a new life.

Spring Subway (2002). Austere film which employs the capital's gleaming subway stations as a backdrop to the protagonist's soul-searching.

Red Light Revolution (2010). Comedy about a hapless Beijing taxi driver who unexpectedly finds himself with a stock of Viagra and decides to open a sex shop – only to run afoul of government regulations. Great local rock soundtrack too.

The World (2004). Jia Zhangke film set in a world-culture theme park in Beijing, where the workers squabble and fail to communicate against a backdrop of tiny replicas of the world's famous monuments.

cinemas – in this they've been assisted by a government that still limits the number of Hollywood films shown each year, and pulls them from the screens in order to give home-grown films better sales. Conversely, those at the **art-house** end of the scale have found themselves making low-budget, introspective fare, developed almost exclusively for international consumption and the global film festival circuit.

The mainstream output is by no means all bad. By way of example, local spaghetti western (does that make it a spaghetti eastern, or a noodle western?) *Let the Bullets Fly* (2010) broke local box-office records, yet also went on to scoop a few international awards. However, the most telling films are those coming from new directors such as **Ying Liang**, whose *The Other Half* (2006) won awards for its depiction of gambling and dysfunctional families in a polluted industrial town, and **Liu Jiayin**, whose *Oxhide* (2004) showed Beijing family life in a documentary style.

Documentaries

Beijing does, indeed, have a promising **documentary movement** of its own, one which often skirts, then goes beyond, the line of what's acceptable to the state. Some pertinent (and important) tales of the city have been told in works such as *Out of Phoenix Bridge* (see box above) and *Bumming* (1990), which consists of a series of interviews with disaffected local artists. *Beijing Taxi* (2011), which takes a trip around the city with local cabbies, isn't, perhaps, as self-consciously meaningful, but is illuminating in its own way – expats tend to deplore Beijing's taxi drivers, but here they're painted in a more sympathetic light. *New Socialist Climax* (see box above) is another good example.

Art

Chinese painting has an ancient history. The earliest brush found in China, made out of animal hairs glued to a hollow bamboo tube, dates from about 400 BC. The Chinese used silk for painting on as early as the third century BC, with paper being used as early as 106 AD. Nowadays, Beijing's modern art scene is up there with the most vibrant in the world, revolving around the superb 798 Art District just to the northeast of the city centre (see p.102). The scene is particularly lively during the Beijing Biennale (◍bjbiennale.com.cn), held in late September in even-numbered years.

Traditional art

The earliest Chinese art dates back to the Neolithic period – **pottery** vessels painted with geometric designs. From the same period come decorated clay heads, and pendants and ornaments of polished stone or jade – a simplified sitting bird in polished jade is a very early example of the Chinese tradition of animal sculpture. The subsequent era, from around 1500 BC, is dominated by **Shang and Zhou bronze vessels** used for preparing and serving food and wine; their design often featured geometric and animal motifs, as well as grinning masks of humans and fabulous beasts. Later, under the **Zhou**, the style of the bronzes became more varied and rich: some animal vessels are fantastically shaped and extravagantly decorated, others seem to be depicting not so much a fierce tiger, for example, as utter ferocity itself.

Although the Shang produced a few small sculpted human figures and animals in marble, **sculptures** and works in stone begin to be found in great quantities in **Han-dynasty** tombs. Indian-style art marked the advent of **Buddhism**; not until the **Tang** do you get the full flowering of a native Chinese style, where the figures are rounder, with movement, and the positions, expressions and clothes are more natural and realistic. The **Song** continued to carve religious figures, but less statuary was produced until the **Ming**, with their taste for massive tomb sculptures, as still seen in Beijing.

Painting

Traditional Chinese paintings are light and airy, with empty spaces playing an important element in the design, and rich in symbolism; they're decorated with a few lines of poetry and several names in the form of seals – the marks of past owners. The great flowering of landscape painting came with the **Song dynasty**; an academy was set up under imperial patronage, and different schools of painting emerged which analysed the natural world with great concentration and intensity. Their style has set a mark on Chinese landscape painting ever since. The **Ming dynasty** saw a willingness by painters to be influenced by tradition: as well as the famous landscapes, look for examples of bamboo and plum blossom, and bird and flower paintings being brought to a high decorative pitch.

The arrival of the Manchu **Qing dynasty** did not disrupt the continuity of Chinese painting, but the art became wide open to many influences. It included the Italian **Castiglione** (Lang Shi-ning in Chinese) who specialized in horses, dogs and flowers under imperial patronage, and individualists such as the Eight Eccentrics of Yangzhou, who objected to derivative art and sought a more distinctive approach to subject and style.

Even today, Chinese art schools emphasize traditional techniques, but many students have been quick to plug themselves into international trends; at its best, this leads to art that is technically proficient and conceptually strong. Recent decades of seismic change in China has, in keeping with the rules of development, seen a recent shift towards more traditional forms of painting, or at least the weaving of the traditional into the contemporary. It has led to works from artists such as **Zhang Daqian** commanding huge prices at auction.

Contemporary art

Contemporary art is flourishing in Beijing, and well worth checking out. The best galleries are owned by expats, and Chinese art is seen as an attractive investment by foreign buyers. Galleries in the city centre are rather more commercial than those in the suburban artsy areas, tending to focus on selling paintings rather than making a splash with a themed show. Still, there are some that display interesting and challenging work.

The scene began in earnest in the 1990s with a group who, with little chance of selling their work – or even exhibiting – banded together to form an arts village in the suburbs of Beijing, near the old Summer Palace. These artists developed a school of painting that expressed their individualism and their sceptical, often ironic and jaundiced view of contemporary China; this was, of course, the generation that had seen its dreams of change shot down at Tian'anmen Square. Nurtured by curator **Li Xianting**, known as "the Godfather of Chinese art", as well as sympathetic foreign collectors, they built the foundations of the art scene as it is today.

The most famous of these so-called **cynical realists** is **Fang Lijun**, whose images of disembodied heads against desolate landscapes are some of the most characteristic images of modern Chinese art. Other art stars who began their career here include **Yue Minjun**, who paints sinister laughing figures, and the satirists **Wang Jinsong** and **Song Yonghong**.

Artists such as **Wang Guangyi** developed a second, distinctly Chinese school of art called **political pop**, where the powerful iconography of the Cultural Revolution was co-opted to celebrate consumerism – workers wave iPods instead of Little Red Books. This kind of thing, perennially popular with foreign visitors, is regarded these days as pretty hackneyed in China. Rather more interesting was the deliberately brash "**gaudy art**" movement of the 1990s, whose aesthetic celebrated the tacky and vulgar; look out for **Xu Yihui**'s ceramic confections and the **Luo Brothers**' kitsch extravaganzas.

Today's trends

It's much harder to pick out trends in today's ferment of activity, but many artists are unsurprisingly preoccupied with documenting the destruction of the Chinese urban landscape and the gut-wrenching changes that have accompanied **modernization**. As spaces for viewing art have increased, artists have diversified into **new media** such as performance and video; two to look out for are **Cao Fei**, who films and photographs fantasy tableaux, and **Yang Fudong**, who makes wistful images of modern life. With all the noise, you need to shout to make yourself heard – and the loudest modern artists are the impresario **Zhang Huang**, who produces witty sculptures on an enormous scale, and art celebrity **Ai Weiwei**, who helped design the concept behind the Bird's Nest Olympic stadium (see p.102).

The contemporary art scene is, however, facing a few major challenges. Artists and photographers have fewer problems with **censorship** than writers or musicians, though the governmental shackles are still in place. Counterfeiting has also become a real issue – unlike Chinese copies of overseas-brand handbags, smartphones or golf clubs, this is having a discernibly negative local impact. There has been a massive surge in **forgeries**, compounded by the fact that only 70 percent of works bought at auction are actually getting paid for. In addition, some of what does actually sell goes for an inflated price – either as status symbols to the nouveau riche, or (allegedly) as tools of high-level bribery. Government regulation may take some time to catch up with these dark inner workings of the local art scene.

Music

The casual visitor to China could be forgiven for thinking that the only traditional style of music to compete with bland pop is that of the kitsch folk troupes to be heard in hotels and concert halls. Beijing opera, however, is now famous across the globe, while a very different, edgier sound can be heard in certain smoky city bars – the new Chinese rock, with its energetic expressions of urban angst.

Beijing opera

Chinese musical drama dates back at least two thousand years, and became overwhelmingly popular with both the elite and common people from the Yuan dynasty onwards. Of the several hundred types of regional opera, **Beijing opera**, a rather late hybrid form dating from the eighteenth century, is the most widely known – now heard throughout China, it's the closest thing to a "national" theatre. Many librettos now performed date back to the seventeenth century and describe the intrigues of emperors and gods, as well as love stories and comedy. The rigorous training the form demands – and the heavy hand of ideology that saw it as the most important of "the people's arts" – is graphically displayed in Chen Kaige's film *Farewell My Concubine* (see box, p.186).

While Chinese opera makes a great visual spectacle, musically it is, frankly, an acquired taste, resembling to the uninitiated the din of cats fighting in a blazing firework factory. The singing style is tense, guttural and high-pitched, while the music is dominated by the bowed string accompaniment of the *jinghu*, a sort of sawn-off *erhu*. It also features plucked lutes, flutes and – for transitional points – a piercing *shawm*. The action is driven by percussion, with drum and clappers leading an ensemble of gongs and cymbals in an assortment of set patterns. Professional opera troupes exist in the major towns but rural opera performances, which are given for temple fairs and even weddings, tend to be livelier. Even in modern Beijing, you may come across groups of old folk meeting in parks to go through their favourite Beijing opera excerpts.

Indie and electronic music

Controversial local legend **Cui Jian**, a sort of Chinese Bob Dylan, was China's first real rock star, giving up a job as a trumpeter in a Beijing orchestra to perform gravel-voiced guitar rock with lyrics as risqué as he could get away with – look out for his albums *Power to The Powerless* and *Egg Under the Red Flag*. Cui Jian is now seen as the granddaddy of Beijing's thriving **indie music** scene. Nobody makes any money out of it – venues and bands struggle to survive against all-pervasive pop pap, and when an act does take off, piracy eats up any profits the recordings might have made – but fierce dedication keeps the scene alive. Most **bands** of note, many of which perform in English or have a mixed set, are on the Scream, Badhead or Modern Sky labels. Bands to look out for include Rolling Stones-wannnabes Joyside, indie noise merchants Carsick Cars, Mongolian rockers Voodoo Kungfu, indie pros Lonely China Day, and electro popsters Pet Conspiracy. Veteran punks Brain Failure folded in 2013, passing the mantle of nuttiest punks on to younger bands like Demerit.

The best new **electronic music** is on Shanshui Records; look out for iLoop and Sulumi. Not so well represented is **hip-hop** (odd, as it has made plenty of inroads in fashion) though old favourites CMCB carry it off pretty well.

Books

You won't find much variety in English-language reading materials when buying books in Beijing; your best bet may be the many cheap editions of the Chinese classics, published in English translation by two Beijing-based firms, Foreign Languages Press (FLP) and Panda Books (some of whose titles are published outside China, too). In the reviews below, books that are especially recommended are marked ★; o/p signifies that a book is out of print. Note that the Chinese put surnames before first names, and we've listed authors here in alphabetical order accordingly (though westernized Chinese names follow the English format).

HISTORY

Peter Fleming *The Siege at Peking.* A lively account of the events that led up to June 20, 1900, when the foreign legations in Beijing were attacked by the Boxers and Chinese imperial troops.

Paul French *Midnight in Peking.* A real-life murder mystery, revolving around the search for the killer of Pamela Warner, an English girl whose body was found in Beijing, minus heart and blood, in 1937.

Reginald Johnston *Twilight in the Forbidden City.* The memoirs of a British official and scholar who from 1919 until 1924 served as tutor to China's luckless last emperor, Puyi. It's a haunting work, full of unique personal insights into the characters and events that ushered in the closing years of imperial China.

Li Kunwu and Philippe Ôtié *A Chinese Life.* Manga-format autobiography, written from street level, about the changes China has undergone since the postwar period, through the disastrous social experimentation of the 1950s and 1960s, and into the post-Maoist, "socialist capitalism"

of today. Unusual in that its unheroic author is unapologetically pro-Party and doesn't attempt to pander to Western sensibilities, this is an honest and sometimes ugly tale of an ordinary person living in difficult times.

Morris Rossabi (ed.) *The Travels of Marco Polo.* Said to have inspired Columbus, *The Travels* is a fantastic read, full of amazing insights picked up during Marco Polo's 26 years of wandering in Asia between Venice and the Peking court of Kublai Khan. It's not, however, a coherent history, having been ghost-written by a romantic novelist from Marco Polo's notes.

Jan Wong *Red China Blues.* Jan Wong, a Canadian of Chinese descent, went to China as an idealistic Maoist in 1972 at the height of the Cultural Revolution, and was one of only two Westerners permitted to enrol at Beijing University. She describes the six years she spent in China and her growing disillusionment, which led eventually to her repatriation. A touching, sometimes bizarre, inside account of the bad old days.

CULTURE AND SOCIETY

★Jasper Becker *The Chinese; City of Heavenly Tranquility: Beijing in the History of China.* *The Chinese* is a classic, weighty, erudite but very comprehensible introduction to Chinese society and culture; lighter and breezier, *City of Heavenly Tranquility* is a great collection of stories about Beijing's history, including a hard-hitting condemnation of how most physical remains of that history have recently been destroyed.

Ian Buruma *Bad Elements: Chinese Rebels from Los Angeles to Beijing.* Interviews with Chinese dissidents, both at home and in exile, make for a compelling, if inevitably rather jaundiced, view of the country.

Martin Jacques *When China Rules the World.* Comprehensive overview, both troubling and enlightening, of the ascendancy of the Chinese state and the impact that it is having on the rest of the world.

James Kynge *China Shakes the World.* Another critical but

acute overview of Chinese society and government and the challenges ahead.

★Michael Meyer *The Last Days of Old Beijing.* Combines a history of Beijing's *hutongs* with a memoir of what it was like to live in them, immersed in the local community.

Yiyun Li *A Thousand Years of Good Prayers; Gold Boy, Emerald Girl.* Two short stories looking at how China's rapid changes have affected the lives of ordinary folk, from a Beijinger now living in the States.

Yu Hua *China in Ten Words.* A former country dentist – now one of the country's most acclaimed authors – explores modern Chinese society by investigating the overt and subtle meanings behind ten colloquial phrases. An interesting mosaic of a book, bound together by Yu Hua's deeply human insights.

GUIDES AND REFERENCE BOOKS

Giles Beguin and Dominique Morel *The Forbidden City: Heart of Imperial China*. A good introduction to the complex, and to the history of the emperors who lived there, though the best thing about this pocket book (as with most books about the Forbidden City) is the illustrations.

Jonathan Campbell *Red Rock*. Written by a Canadian music promoter and journalist with long links to the Beijing music scene, this book traces the history of modern Chinese rock, and how the last twenty years' melange of Western-influenced protest balads, punk, indie and grunge has gradually mutated into a distinctly Chinese sound.

Lin Xiang Zhu and Lin Cuifeng *Chinese Gastronomy* (o/p). A classic work, relatively short on recipes but strong on cooking methods and the underlying philosophy. It wavers in and out of print, sometimes under different titles – look for "Lin" as the author name. Essential reading for anyone serious about learning the finer details of Chinese cooking.

Derek Sandhaus *Baijiu*. Useful handbook for anyone trying to get beyond their first mouthful of China's favourite raw spirit, with the history and individual characteristics of dozens of brands laid out in thumbnail sketches. Everything you need to know, from *baijiu* drinking culture to separating "rice aroma" brands from the finest Wuliangye. Don't miss the useful cocktail recipes at the back.

Mary Tregear *Chinese Art*. Authoritative summary of the main strands in Chinese art from Neolithic times, through the Bronze Age and up to the twentieth century. Clearly written and well illustrated.

Richard Vine *New China Art*. Good handbook if you're looking for something to untangle the confusing and over-hyped contemporary art scene in China, with solid background information on the social changes shaping it all – well worth reading before you head out to the 798 Art District.

RELIGION AND PHILOSOPHY

Asiapac Comics Series. Available at Beijing's Foreign Language Bookstore, this entertaining series of books presents ancient Chinese philosophy in cartoon format, making the subject accessible without losing too much complexity. They're all well written and well drawn; particularly good is the *Sayings of Confucius*.

Confucius *The Analects*. There are various good translations of this classic text, a collection of Confucius's teachings focusing on morality and the state. *I Ching*, also known as *The Book of Changes*, is another classic volume

from Confucius that teaches a form of divination. It includes coverage of some of the fundamental concepts of Chinese thought, such as the duality of *yin* and *yang*.

Lao Zi *Tao Te Ching*. The *Daodejing* in *pinyin*, this is a collection of mystical thoughts and philosophical speculation that form the basis of Taoist philosophy.

Arthur Waley (trans.) *Three Ways of Thought in Ancient China*. Translated extracts from the writings of three of the early philosophers – Zhuang Zi, Mencius and Han Feizi. A useful introduction.

BIOGRAPHY AND AUTOBIOGRAPHY

Pallavi Aiyar *Smoke and Mirrors: An Experience of China*. There are plenty of memoirs about the expat experience in Beijing; this one stands out as it was written from an Indian perspective. Amusing, anecdotal and full of acute observations.

E. Backhouse and J.O. Bland *China Under the Empress Dowager* (o/p). Classic work on imperial life in late nineteenth-century China. It's based around the diary of a court eunuch, which is now generally accepted to have been forged. (Backhouse was the prime suspect; see the review of *Hermit of Peking* by Hugh Trevor-Roper below.)

Rachel Dewoskin *Foreign Babes in Beijing*. Breezy account of an American girl's adventures among the city's artsy set in the 1990s. The most interesting parts concern the author's experiences working as an actress on a Chinese soap opera.

Jia Yinghua *The Last Eunuch of China: the Life of Sun Yaoting*. The title of this book basically says it all: it's a fantastic peek at the colourful life of Sun Yaoting, who died in 1996 after rising from humble farmyard origins to the imperial court.

★**Jung Chang** *Wild Swans*; *Mao: The Untold Story* and *Empress Dowager Cixi: The Concubine Who Launched Modern China*. Enormously popular in the West, *Wild Swans* is a family saga covering three generations that chronicles the horrors of life in turbulent twentieth-century China. A massive and well-researched character assassination, *Mao* serves as an excellent introduction to modern Chinese history, as well as being a good read. Lastly, *Cixi* is one of several recent books to paint the dowager in a more forgiving light, arguing that she was more savvy, and less evil, than the world gives her credit for.

David Leffman *The Mercenary Mandarin*. Set against a late-Qing-dynasty backdrop, this lively biography documents the unlikely life of British adventurer William Mesny, who jumped ship at Shanghai in 1860 and spent the rest of his 59 years in China as a gun-runner, smuggler, customs official, arms instructor, botanist, explorer, journalist and decorated general in the Chinese military.

Pu Yi *From Emperor to Citizen*. The autobiography of the last Qing emperor, Pu Yi, who lost his throne as a boy and was later briefly installed as a puppet emperor during the

Japanese occupation. He ended his life employed as a gardener.

Hugh Trevor-Roper *Hermit of Peking: The Hidden Life of Sir Edmund Backhouse*. Sparked by its subject's thoroughly obscene memoirs, *Hermit of Peking* uses external sources in an attempt to uncover the facts behind the extraordinary and convoluted life of Edmund Backhouse – Chinese scholar, eccentric recluse and phenomenal liar – who lived in Beijing from the late nineteenth century until his death in 1944.

Frances Wood *Hand-grenade Practice in Peking*. Slightly surreal account of how Wood (later a curator at the British Library and writer on Chinese history) spent a year studying Chinese in Beijing during the Cultural Revolution, much of it picking cabbages with local farmers or taking part in compulsory sports – such as throwing hand grenades. A great insight into how the lunacy of the times affected ordinary people.

CHINESE LITERATURE

Cao Xueqin *Dream of Red Mansions*. Sometimes published under the English title *Dream of the Red Chamber*, this intricate eighteenth-century comedy of manners follows the fortunes of the Jia clan through the emotionally charged adolescent lives of Jia Baoyu and his two female cousins, Lin Daiyu and Xue Baochai. *The Story of the Stone*, a version published in the West by Penguin, fills five paperbacks; the FLP edition, available in Beijing, is much simplified and abridged.

Chun Sue *Beijing Doll*. This rambling confessional details the teenage writer's adventures in the indie music scene. With plenty of sex and drugs, it caused quite a stir when it came out and was, predictably, banned.

Lao She *Rickshaw Boy*. One of China's great modern writers, Lao She was driven to suicide during the Cultural Revolution. This story is a haunting account of a young rickshaw puller in pre-1949 Beijing.

★**Lu Xun** *The Real Story of Ah Q and Other Tales of China*. Widely read in China today, Lu Xun is regarded as the father of modern Chinese writing. *Ah Q* is one of his best tales: short, allegorical and cynical, about a simpleton who is swept up in the 1911 revolution.

Luo Guanzhong *Romance of the Three Kingdoms*. One of the world's greatest historical novels. Though written 1200 years after the events it depicts, this vibrant tale vividly evokes the battles, political schemings and myths surrounding China's turbulent Three Kingdoms period.

★**Ma Jian** *Red Dust*; *The Noodle Maker*; *Beijing Coma*. Satirist Ma Jian is one of China's most insightful living writers, though most of his work is banned in China. *Red Dust* is a travelogue about an epic, beatnik-style jaunt around China in the 1980s, documenting a set of chaotic lives, not least the narrator's own. *The Noodle Maker* is a dark novel concerning the friendship between a writer of propaganda and a professional blood donor; and *Beijing Coma*, his weightiest tome, concerns the events of 1989.

★**Mo Yan** *The Red Sorghum Clan*; *The Garlic Ballads*. China's only winner of the Nobel Prize for Literature, Mo Yan (whose name, meaning "don't speak", speaks volumes about how popular he is with the regime) is most famed for *The Garlic Ballads*, a hard-hitting novel of rural life; and *The Red Sorghum Clan*, parts of which were turned into *Red Sorghum*, a Zhang Yimou film (see p.185). Both books were banned in China; though neither were set in Beijing, their thinly veiled social commentary is still appropriate reading.

Wang Shuo *Playing For Thrills*; *Please Don't Call Me Human*. The bad boy of contemporary Chinese literature, Wang Shuo writes in colourful Beijing dialect about the city's seamy underbelly. These are his only novels translated into English: the first is a mystery story whose boorish narrator spends most of his time drinking, gambling and chasing girls; the second, banned in China, a bitter satire portraying modern China as a place where pride is nothing and greed is everything, and a dignified martial artist is emasculated in order to win an Olympic gold medal.

★**Wu Cheng'en** *Journey to the West*. Absurd, lively rendering of the Buddhist monk Xuanzang's pilgrimage to India to collect sacred scriptures, aided by – according to popular myth – Sandy, Pigsy, and the irrepressible Sun Wu Kong, the monkey king. Arthur Waley's version, published in the West under the title *Monkey*, retains the tale's spirit while shortening the hundred-chapter opus to paperback length.

Mandarin Chinese

As the most widely spoken language on earth, Chinese is hard to overlook. Mandarin Chinese, derived from the language of Han officialdom in the Beijing area, has been systematically promoted over the past hundred years to be the official, unifying language of the Chinese people, much as modern French, for example, is based on the original Parisian dialect. It is known in mainland China as *putonghua*, "common language". All Beijingers will speak and understand it, but note that working-class Beijingers have a distinctively purring, piratical accent, which softens hard consonants and often adds an "r" sound to the end of many words – hence the district of Dazhalan comes out as "Darshirlar". It's most noticeable with older folk, particularly men who've been at the beer or *baijiu*.

Chinese **grammar** is delightfully simple. There is no need to conjugate verbs, decline nouns or make adjectives agree – Chinese characters are immutable, so words simply cannot have different "endings". Instead, context and fairly rigid rules about word order are relied on to make those distinctions of time, number and gender that Indo-European languages are so concerned with. Instead of cumbersome tenses, the Chinese make use of words such as "yesterday" or "tomorrow" to indicate when things happen; instead of plural endings they simply state how many things there are. For English speakers, Chinese word order is very familiar, and you'll find that by simply stringing words together you may well be producing perfectly grammatical Chinese. Basic sentences follow the subject–verb–object format; adjectives, as well as all qualifying and describing phrases, precede nouns.

From the point of view of foreigners, the main thing that distinguishes Mandarin from familiar languages is that it's a **tonal** language. In order to pronounce a word correctly, it is necessary to know not only the sounds of its consonants and vowels but also its correct tone – though with the help of context, intelligent listeners should be able to work out what you are trying to say even if you don't get the tones quite right.

Pinyin

Back in the 1950s, the communist government hoped to eventually replace Chinese characters with an alphabet of Roman letters; thought the threat of mass riots brought an end to this plan, the *pinyin* system, a precise and exact means of representing all the sounds of Mandarin Chinese, had already been devised. It comprises all the Roman letters of the English alphabet, with the four tones represented by diacritical marks, or accents, which appear above each syllable. The old aim of replacing Chinese characters with *pinyin* was abandoned long ago, but in the meantime *pinyin* has one very important function, that of helping foreigners pronounce Chinese words. However, there is the added complication that in *pinyin*

THERE'S AN APP FOR THAT

Travellers are increasingly using their mobile phones to counter linguistic difficulties faced during their time in China. We review essential dictionary apps – even one that converts a Chinese menu to English via your smartphone camera – in Basics (see box, p.36).

the letters don't all have the sounds you would expect, and you'll need to spend an hour or two learning the correct sounds.

You'll often see *pinyin* in Beijing, on street signs and shop displays, but only well-educated locals know the system very well. The establishments in this book have been given both in characters and in *pinyin*; the pronunciation guide below is your first step to making yourself comprehensible. For more information, see the *Rough Guide Mandarin Chinese Phrasebook*.

PRONUNCIATION

There are four possible **tones** in Mandarin Chinese, and every syllable of every word is characterized by one of them, except for a few syllables, which are considered toneless. In English, to change the tone is to change the mood or the emphasis; in Chinese, to change the tone is to change the word itself. The tones are:

First or "high" ā ē ī ō ū A high, flat pitch often used in English when mimicking robotic or very boring, flat voices.

Second or "rising" á é í ó ú Used in English when asking a question showing surprise, for example "eh?" Try raising your eyebrows when attempting to make a sound with this tone – it never fails.

Third or "falling-rising" ǎ ě ǐ ǒ ǔ Used in English when echoing someone's words with a measure of incredulity. For example, "John's dead." "De-ad?!"

Fourth or "falling" à è ì ò ù Often used in English when counting in a brusque manner – "One! Two! Three! Four!" Try stamping your foot lightly when attempting to make a sound with this tone.

Toneless A few syllables do not have a tone accent. These are pronounced without emphasis, much like that lovely word "meh".

Note that when two words with the third tone occur consecutively, the first word is pronounced as though it carries the second tone. Thus nĕ (meaning "you") and hǎo ("well, good"), when combined, are pronounced ní ǎǎo, meaning "how are you?"

CONSONANTS

Most consonants, as written in *pinyin*, are pronounced in a similar way to their English equivalents, with the following exceptions:

c as in ha**ts**

g is hard as in **g**od (except when preceded by "n", when it sounds like sa**ng**)

q as in **ch**eese

x has no direct equivalent in English, but you can make the sound by sliding from an "s" to an "sh" sound and stopping midway between the two

z as in su**ds**

zh as in fu**dge**

VOWELS AND DIPHTHONGS

As in most languages, the vowel sounds are rather harder to quantify than the consonants. The examples below give a rough description of the sound of each vowel as written in *pinyin*.

a usually somewhere between f**a**r and m**a**n

ai as in **eye**

ao as in c**ow**

e usually as in f**ur**

ei as in g**ay**

en as in hyph**en**

eng as in s**ung**

er as in b**ar** with a pronounced "r"

i usually as in b**ee**, except in zi, ci, si, ri, zhi, chi and shi, when i is a short, clipped sound, like the American military "sir".

ia as in **ya**k

ian as in **yen**

ie as in **yeah**

o as in s**aw**

ou as in sh**ow**

ü as in the German ü (make an "ee" sound and glide slowly into an "oo"; at the mid-point between the two sounds you should hit the ü-sound); in *pinyin*, it's sometimes written as a V

u usually as in f**oo**l, though whenever u follows j, q, x or y, it is always pronounced **ü**

ua as in s**ua**ve

uai as in **why**

ue as though contracting "you" and "air" together, **you'air**

ui as in **way**

uo as in w**ore**

USEFUL WORDS AND PHRASES

When writing or saying the name of a Chinese person, the surname is given first; thus Mao Zedong's family name is Mao. Also note that Chinese famously has no precise words for "yes" and "no"; the terms for "is" (是, shì) or "correct" (对, duì) are usually used as a positive response, while for negatives the term 不 (bù) goes behind the verb in question.

BASICS

I	我	wǒ
You (singular)	你	nǐ
He	他	tā
She	她	tā
We	我们	wǒmen
You (plural)	你们	nǐmen
They	他们	tāmen
I want...	我要	wǒ yào...
No, I don't want...	我不要	wǒ bú yào...
Is it possible...?	可不可以	kě bù kěyǐ...?
It is (not) possible	(不)可以...	(bù) kěyǐ
Is there any…/Have you got any…?	你有没有	nǐ yǒu méiyǒu...?
There is/I have	有...	yǒu...
There isn't/I haven't	没有...	méiyǒu
Please help me	请帮我忙..	qǐng bāng wǒ máng
Mr...	...先生	xiānshēng
Mrs...	...太太	tàitai
Miss...	...小姐	xiǎojiě

COMMUNICATING

I don't speak Chinese	我不会说中文	wǒ búhuì shuō zhōngwén
Can you speak English?	你会说英语吗	nǐ huì shuō yīngyǔ ma?
Can you get someone who speaks English?	请给我找一个会说英文的人	qǐng gěiwǒ zhǎo yīgè huìshuō yīngwén de rén?
Please speak slowly	请说得慢一点	qǐng shuōde màn yīdiǎn
Please say that again	请再说一遍	qǐng zài shuō yī biàn
I understand	我听得懂	wǒ tīngdedǒng
I don't understand	我听不懂	wǒ tīngbùdǒng
I can't read Chinese characters	我看不懂汉字	wǒ kànbùdǒng hànzì
What does this mean?	这是什么意思	zhèshì shénme yìsi?
How do you pronounce this character?	这个字怎么念	zhègè zì zěnme niàn?

GREETINGS AND BASIC COURTESIES

Hello/How do you do?/How are you?	你好	nǐhǎo
I'm fine	我很好	wǒ hěnhǎo
Thank you	谢谢	xièxie
Don't mention it/You're welcome	不客气	búkèqi
Sorry to bother you...	麻烦你	máfán nǐ...
Sorry/I apologize	对不起	duìbùqǐ
It's not important/No problem	没关系	méiguānxì
Goodbye	再见	zàijiàn
Excuse me (when getting attention)	不好意思	bùhǎoyìsi

CHIT-CHAT

What country are you from?	你哪个国家来的？	nǐ nǎgè guójiā lái de mǎ?
Britain	英国	yīngguó
England	英国/英格兰	yīngguó/yīnggélán
Scotland	苏格兰	sūgélán
Wales	威尔士	wēi'ěrshì
Ireland	爱尔兰	ài'érlán
America	美国	měiguó
Canada	加拿大	jiānádà
Australia	澳大利亚	àodàlìyà

New Zealand	新西兰	xīnxīlán
South Africa	南非	nánfēi
China	中国	zhōngguó
Outside China	外国	wàiguó
What's your name?	你叫什么名字	nǐ jiào shénme míngzi?
My name is...	我叫....	wǒ jiào...
Are you married?	你结婚了吗？	nǐ jiéhūn le ma?
I am (not) married	我(没有)结婚了	wǒ (méiyǒu) jiéhūn le
Have you got children?	你有没有孩子？	nǐ yǒu méiyǒu háizi?
Do you like...?	你喜不喜欢.....？	nǐ xǐ bù xǐhuān....?
I (don't) like...	我不喜欢....	wǒ (bù) xǐhuān...
What's your job?	你干什么工作？	nǐ gàn shénme gōngzuò?
I'm a foreign student	我是留学生	wǒ shì liúxuéshēng
I'm a teacher	我是老师	wǒ shì lǎoshī
I work in a company	我在一个公司工作	wǒ zài yígè gōngsī gōngzuò
I don't work	我不工作	wǒ bù gōngzuò
I'm retired	我退休了	wǒ tuìxiū le
Clean/dirty	干净/脏	gānjìng/zāng
Hot/cold	热/冷	rè/lěng
Fast/slow	快/慢	kuài/màn
Good/bad	好/坏	hǎo/huài
Big/small	大/小	dà/xiǎo
Pretty	漂亮	piàoliang
Interesting	有意思	yǒuyìsi

NUMBERS

Zero	零	líng
One	一	yī
Two	二/两	èr/liǎng*
Three	三	sān
Four	四	sì
Five	五	wǔ
Six	六	liù
Seven	七	qī
Eight	八	bā
Nine	九	jiǔ
Ten	十	shí
Eleven	十一	shíyī
Twelve	十二	shíèr
Twenty	二十	èrshí
Twenty-one	二十一	èrshíyi
One hundred	一百	yībǎi
Two hundred	二百	èrbǎi
One thousand	一千	yīqiān
Ten thousand	一万	yīwàn
One hundred thousand	十万	shíwàn
One million	一百万	yībǎiwàn
One hundred million	一亿	yīyì
One billion	十亿	shíyì

* 两/liǎng is used when enumerating, for example "two people" is liǎnggè rén.
二/èr is used when counting.

TIME

Now	现在	xiànzài
Today	今天	jīntiān
(In the) morning	早上	zǎoshàng
(In the) afternoon	下午	xiàwǔ
(In the) evening	晚上	wǎnshàng
Tomorrow	明天	míngtiān
The day after tomorrow	后天	hòutiān
Yesterday	昨天	zuótiān
Week/month/year	星期/月/年	xīngqī/yuè/nián
Next/last week/month/year	下/上星期/月/年	xià/shàng xīngqī/yuè/nián
Monday	星期一	xīngqī yī
Tuesday	星期二	xīngqī èr
Wednesday	星期三	xīngqī sān
Thursday	星期四	xīngqī sì
Friday	星期五	xīngqī wǔ
Saturday	星期六	xīngqī liù
Sunday	星期天	xīngqī tiān
What's the time?	几点了？	jǐdiǎn le?
Morning	早上	zǎoshàng
Afternoon	中午	zhōngwǔ
Evening	晚	wǎn
10 o'clock	十点钟	shídiǎn zhōng
10.20	十点二十	shídiǎn èrshí
10.30	十点半	shídiǎn bàn

TRAVELLING AND GETTING AROUND TOWN

North	北	běi
South	南	nán
East	东	dōng
West	西	xī
Airport	机场	jīchǎng
Ferry dock	船码头	chuánmǎtóu
Left-luggage office	寄存处	jìcún chù
Ticket office	售票处	shòupiào chù
Ticket	票	piào
Can I have a ticket to…?	可不可以卖给我到…的票	kěbùkěyǐ màigěi wǒ dào…de piào?
I want to go to…	我想到…去	wǒ xiǎng dàoqù
I want to leave at (8 o'clock)	我想(八点钟)离开	wǒ xiǎng (bādiǎnzhōng) líkāi
When does it leave?	什么时候出发？	shénme shíhòu chūfā?
When does it arrive?	什么时候到？	shénme shíhòu dào?
How long does it take?	路上得多长时间？	lùshàng děi duōcháng shíjiān?
CITS	中国国际旅行社	zhōngguó guójì lǚxíngshè
Train	火车	huǒchē
(Main) train station	(主要)火车站	(zhǔyào) huǒchēzhàn
Bus	公共汽车	gōnggòng qìchēzhàn
Bus station	汽车站	qìchēzhàn
Long-distance bus station	长途汽车站	chángtú qìchēzhàn
Express train/bus	特快车	tèkuài chē
Fast train/bus	快车	ku‡i chē
Ordinary train/bus	普通车	pǔtōng chē

Timetable	时间表	shíjiān biǎo
Map	地图	dìtú
Where is…?	…在哪里？	…zài nǎlǐ?
Go straight on	往前走	wǎng qián zǒu
Turn right	往右走	wǎng yòu zǒu
Turn left	往左拐	wǎng zuǒ guǎi
Taxi	出租车	chūzū chē
Please use the meter	请打开记价器	qǐng dǎkāi jìjiàqì
Underground/subway station	地铁站	dìtiě zhàn
Bicycle	自行车	zìxíng chē
Can I borrow your bicycle?	能不能借你的自行车	néngbùnéng jiè nǐdē zìxíngchē?
Bus	公共汽车	gōnggòng qìchē
Which bus goes to…?	几路车到…去？	jǐlùchē dào … qù?
Number (10) bus	(十)路车	(shí) lù chē
Does this bus go to…?	这车到…去吗？	zhè chē dào … qù ma?
When is the next bus?	下一班车几点开？	xiàyìbānchē jǐdiǎn kāi?
The first bus	头班车	tóubān chē
The last bus	末班车	mòbān chē
Please tell me where to get off	请告诉我在哪里下车？	qǐng gàosù wǒ zài nǎlǐ xiàchē?
Museum	博物馆	bówùguǎn
Temple	寺庙	sìmiào
Church	教堂	jiàotáng

ACCOMMODATION

Accommodation	住宿	zhùsù
Hotel (upmarket)	宾馆	bīnguǎn
Hotel (cheap)	招待所, 旅馆	zhāodàisuǒ, lǚguǎn
Hostel	旅舍	lǚshè
Do you have a room available?	你们有房间吗？	nǐmen yǒu fángjiān ma?
Can I have a look at the room?	能不能看一下方向？	néngbùnéng kàn yíxià fángjiān?
I want the cheapest bed you've got	我要你这里最便宜的床位	wǒ yào nǐ zhèlǐ zuìpiányi de chuángwèi
Single room	单人房	dānrén fáng
Twin room	双人房	shuāngrén fáng
Double room with a big bed	双人房间带大床	shuāngrénfángjiān dài dà chuáng
Three-bed room	三人房	sānrén fáng
Dormitory	多人房	duōrén fáng
Suite	套房	tàofáng
(Large) bed	(大)床	(dà) chuáng
Passport	护照	hùzhào
Deposit	押金	yājīn
Key	钥匙	yàoshi
I want to change my room	我想换房	wǒ xiǎng huànfáng

SHOPPING, MONEY AND THE POLICE

How much is it?	这是多少钱？	zhèshì duōshǎo qián?
That's too expensive	太贵了	tài guì le
I haven't got any cash	我没有现金	wǒ méiyǒu xiànjīn
Have you got anything cheaper?	有没有便宜一点的？	yǒu méiyǒu piányì yìdiǎn de?

Do you accept credit cards?	可不可以用信用卡？	kě bù kěyǐ yòng xìnyòngkǎ?
Department store	百货商店	bǎihuò shāngdiàn
Market	市场	shìchǎng
¥1 (RMB)	一块（人民币）	yí kuài (rénmínbì)
US$1	一块美金	yí kuài měijīn
£1	一个英镑	yí gè yīngbàng
€1	一欧元	yí ōuyuán
Change money	换钱	huàn qián
Bank	银行	yínháng
Travellers' cheques	旅行支票	lǚxíngzhīpiào
ATM	提款机	tíkuǎnjī
PSB	公安局	gōng'ānjú

COMMUNICATIONS

Post office	邮电局	yóudiànjú
Envelope	信封	xìnfēng
Stamp	邮票	yóupiào
Airmail	航空信	hángkōngxìn
Surface mail	平信	píngxìn
Telephone	电话	diànhuà
Mobile/cell phone	手机	shǒujī
SMS message	短信	duǎnxìn
International telephone call	国际电话	guójì diànhuà
Reverse charges/collect call	对方付钱电话	duìfāngfùqián diànhuà
Phone card	电话卡	diànhuàkǎ
I want to make a telephone call to (Britain)	我想给（英国）打电话	wǒ xiǎng gěi (yīngguó) dǎ diànhuà
Internet	网路	wǎngluò
Internet café/bar	网吧	wǎngbā
Email	电子邮件	diànzǐyóujiàn

HEALTH

Hospital	医院	yīyuàn
Pharmacy	药店	yàodiàn
Medicine	药	yào
Doctor	医生	yīshēng
Chinese medicine	中药	zhōngyào
Diarrhoea	腹泻	fùxiè
Vomit	呕吐	ǒutù
Fever	发烧	fāshāo
I'm ill	我生病了	wǒ shēngbìng le
I've got flu	我感冒了	wǒ gǎnmào le
I'm (not) allergic to...	我对...(不)过敏	wǒ duì ... (bù) guòmǐn
Antibiotics	抗生素	kàngshēngsù
Condom	避孕套	bìyùntào
Tampons	卫生棉条	wèishēng miántiáo

A MENU READER

GENERAL

Restaurant	餐厅	cāntīng
House speciality	招牌菜	zhāopái cài
How much is that?	多少钱	duōshǎo qián?
I don't eat (meat)	我不吃(肉)	wǒ bùchī (ròu)
I would like...	我想要...	wǒ xiǎng yào...

Local dishes	地方菜	dìfāng cài
Snacks	小吃	xiǎochī
Menu/set menu/English menu	菜单/套菜/英文菜单	càidān/tàocài/ yīngwéncàidān
Small portion	少量	shǎoliàng
Chopsticks	筷子	kuàizi
Knife and fork	刀叉	dāochā
Spoon	勺子	sháozi
Waiter/waitress	服务员	fúwùyuán
Bill/cheque	买单	mǎidān
Cook these ingredients together	原料混合一块儿做	yuánliào hùnhé yíkuàir zuò
Not spicy/no chilli please	请不要辣椒	qǐng búyào làjiāo
Only a little spice/chilli	一点辣椒	yìdiǎn làjiāo
50 grams	两	liǎng
250 grams	半斤	bànjīn
500 grams	斤	jīn
1 kilo	1公斤	yī gōngjīn

DRINKS

Beer	啤酒	píjiǔ
Coffee	咖啡	kāfēi
Milk	牛奶	niúnǎi
(Mineral) water	(矿泉)水	(kuàngquán) shuǐ
Wine	葡萄酒	pútáojiǔ
Yoghurt	酸奶	suānnǎi
Tea	茶	chá
Black tea	红茶	hóngchá
Green tea	绿茶	lǜchá
Jasmine tea	茉莉花茶	mòlìhuā chá
Juice	果汁	guǒzhī

STAPLE FOODS

Aubergine	茄子	qiézi
Bamboo shoots	笋尖	sǔnjiān
Bean sprouts	豆芽	dòuyá
Beans	豆子	dòuzi
Beef	牛肉	niúròu
Bitter gourd	苦瓜	kǔguā
Black bean sauce	黑豆豉	hēidòuchǐ
Bread	面包	miànbāo
Buns (filled)	包子	bāozi
Buns (plain)	馒头	mántou
Carrot	胡萝卜	húluóbo
Cashew nuts	腰果	yāoguǒ
Cauliflower	菜花	càihuā
Chicken	鸡	jī
Chilli	辣椒	làjiāo
Chocolate	巧克力	qiǎokèlì
Coriander (leaves)	香菜	xiāngcài
Crab	蟹	xiè
Cucumber	黄瓜	huángguā
Dough stick (fried)	油条	yóutiáo
Duck	鸭	yā

Dumplings	饺子	jiǎozi
Eel	鳝鱼	shànyú
Eggs (fried/ordinary)	煎鸡蛋/鸡蛋	jiānjīdàn/jīdàn
Fish	鱼	yú
Garlic	大蒜	dàsuàn
Ginger	姜	jiāng
Lamb	羊肉	yángròu
Lotus root	莲藕	liánǒu
MSG	味精	wèijīng
Mushrooms	磨菇	mógū
Noodles	面条	miàntiáo
Omelette	摊鸡蛋	tānjīdàn
Onions	洋葱	yángcōng
Oyster sauce	蚝油	háoyóu
Pancake	摊饼	tānbǐng
Peanut	花生	huāshēng
Pepper (green)/capsicum	青椒	qīngjiāo
Pork	猪肉	zhūròu
Potato (stir-fried)	(炒)土豆	(chǎo) tǔdòu
Prawns	虾	xiā
Preserved egg	皮蛋	pídàn
Rice noodles	河粉	héfěn
Rice porridge (aka "congee")	粥	zhōu
Rice, boiled	白饭	báifàn
Rice, fried	炒饭	chǎofàn
Salt	盐	yán
Sesame oil	芝麻油	zhīma yóu
Shuijiao (dumplings in soup)	水饺	shuǐjiāo
Sichuan pepper	四川辣椒	sìchuān làjiāo
Snake	蛇肉	shéròu
Soup	汤	tāng
Soy sauce	酱油	jiàngyóu
Squid	鱿鱼	yóuyú
Straw mushrooms	草菇	cǎogū
Sugar	糖	táng
Tofu	豆腐	dòufu
Tomato	蕃茄	fānqié
Vegetables (green)	绿叶蔬菜	lǜyè shūcài
Vinegar	醋	cù
Water chestnuts	马蹄	mǎtí
White radish	白萝卜	báiluóbo
Wood-ear fungus	木耳	mùěr
Yam	红薯	hóngshǔ

COOKING METHODS

Boiled	煮	zhǔ
Casseroled (see also "Claypot")	焙	bèi
Deep-fried	油煎	yóujiān
Fried	炒	chǎo
Poached	白煮	báizhǔ
Red-cooked (stewed in soy sauce)	红烧	hóngshāo
Roast	烤	kǎo
Steamed	蒸	zhēng
Stir-fried	清炒	qīngchǎo

EVERYDAY DISHES

Braised duck with vegetables	蔬菜炖鸭	shūcài dùnyā
Cabbage rolls (stuffed with meat or vegetables)	菜卷	càijuǎn
Chicken and sweetcorn soup	玉米鸡丝汤	yùmǐ jīsī tāng
Chicken with bamboo shoots and baby corn	笋尖嫩玉米炒鸡片	sǔnjiān nènyùmǐ chǎojīpiàn
Chicken with cashew nuts	腰果鸡片	yāoguǒ jīpiàn
Claypot/sandpot (casserole)	砂锅	shāguō
Crispy aromatic duck	香酥鸭	xiāngsū yā
Egg flower soup with tomato	蕃茄蛋汤	fānqié dàntāng
Egg fried rice	蛋炒饭	dànchǎofàn
Fish ball soup with white radish	白萝卜鱼蛋汤	báiluóbo yúdàn tāng
Fish casserole	砂锅鱼	shāguōyú
Fried shredded pork with garlic and chilli	大蒜辣椒炒肉片	dàsuàn làjiāo chǎo ròupiàn
Hotpot	火锅	huǒguō
Kebab	串肉	chuànròu
Noodle soup	汤面	tāngmiàn
Pork and mustard greens	芥菜叶炒猪肉	jiècàiyè chǎo zhūròu
Pork and water chestnut	马蹄猪肉	mǎtízhūròu
Prawn with garlic sauce	蒜汁虾	suànzhīxiā
"Pulled" noodles	拉面	lā miàn
Roast duck	烤鸭	kǎyā
Scrambled egg with pork on rice	滑蛋猪肉饭	huádàn zhūròufàn
Sliced pork with yellow bean sauce	黄豆肉片	huángdòu ròupiàn
Squid with green pepper and black beans	豆豉青椒炒鱿鱼	dòuchǐ qīngjiāo chǎo yóuyú
Steamed eel with black beans	豆豉蒸鳝	dòuchǐ zhēng shàn
Steamed rice packets wrapped in lotus leaves	荷叶蒸饭	héyè zhēngfàn
Stewed pork belly with vegetables	回锅肉	huíguōròu
Stir-fried chicken and bamboo shoots	笋尖炒鸡片	sǔnjiān chǎo jīpiàn
Stuffed bean curd soup	豆腐汤	dòufu tāng
Sweet and sour spare ribs	糖醋排骨	tángcù páigǔ
Sweet bean paste pancakes	赤豆摊饼	chìdòu tānbǐng
White radish soup	白萝卜汤	báiluóbo tāng
Wonton soup	馄饨汤	húntun tāng

VEGETABLES AND EGGS

Aubergine with chilli and garlic sauce	大蒜辣椒炒茄子	dàsuàn làjiāo chǎoqiézi
Aubergine with sesame sauce	芝麻酱拌茄子	zhīmájiàng bànqiézi
Egg fried with tomatoes	蕃茄炒蛋	fānqié chǎodàn
Fried tofu with vegetables	豆腐炒蔬菜	dòufu chǎoshūcài
Fried bean sprouts	炒豆芽	chǎodòuyá
Pressed tofu with cabbage	白菜豆腐	báicài dòufu
Spicy braised aubergine	炖香辣茄子条	dùn xiānglà qiézitiáo
Stir-fried bamboo shoots	炒冬笋	chǎodōngsǔn
Stir-fried mushrooms	炒鲜菇	chǎo xiānggū
Tofu and spinach soup	菠菜豆腐汤	bōcài dòufu tāng
Tofu slivers	豆腐花	dòufuhuā
Tofu with chestnuts	栗子豆腐	lìzi dòufu
Vegetable soup	蔬菜汤	shūcài tāng

REGIONAL DISHES
NORTHERN

Aromatic fried lamb	炒羊肉	chǎoyángròu
Fish with ham and vegetables	火腿蔬菜鱼片	huǒtuǐ shūcài yúpiàn
Fried prawn balls	炒虾球	chǎoxiāqiú
Mongolian hotpot	蒙古火锅	ménggǔ huǒguō
Beijing (Peking) duck	北京烤鸭	běijīng kǎoyā
Red-cooked lamb	红烧羊肉	hóngshāo yángròu
Lion's head (pork rissoles casseroled with greens)	狮子头	shīzitóu

SICHUAN AND WESTERN CHINA

Boiled beef slices (spicy)	水煮牛肉	shuǐzhǔ niúròu
Crackling-rice with pork	爆米肉片	bàomǐ ròupiàn
Crossing-the-bridge (spicy) noodles	过桥米线	guòqiáo mǐxiàn
Carry-pole noodles (with a chilli-vinegar-sesame sauce)	担担面	dàndànmiàn
Deep-fried green beans with garlic	大蒜煸四季豆	dàsuàn biǎnsìjìdòu
Dong'an chicken (poached in spicy sauce)	东安鸡子	dōng'ān jīzi
Doubled-cooked pork	回锅肉	huíguōròu
Dry-fried pork shreds	油炸肉丝	yóuzhà ròusi
Fish-flavoured aubergine	鱼香茄子	yúxiāng qiézi
Gongbao chicken (with chillies and peanuts)	公保鸡丁	gōngbǎo jīdīng
Green pepper with spring onion and black bean sauce	豆豉洋葱炒青椒	dòuchǐ yángcōng chǎo qīngjiāo
Hot and sour soup (flavoured with vinegar and white pepper)	酸辣汤	suānlà tāng
Hot-spiced bean curd	麻婆豆腐	mápódòufu
Rice-flour balls, stuffed with sweet paste	汤圆	tāngyuán
Smoked duck	熏鸭	xūnyā
Strange-flavoured chicken (with sesame-garlic-chilli)	怪味鸡	guàiwèijī
Stuffed aubergine slices	馅茄子	xiànqiézi
Tangerine chicken	桔子鸡	júzijī
"Tiger-skin" peppers (pan-fried with salt)	虎皮炒椒	hǔpí qīngjiāo
Wind-cured ham	扎肉	zhāròu

SOUTHERN CHINESE/CANTONESE

Baked crab with chilli and black beans	辣椒豆豉焙蟹	làjiāo dòuchǐ bèi xiè
Barbecued pork ("char siew")	叉烧	chāshāo
Casseroled bean curd stuffed with pork mince	豆腐碎肉煲	dòfu suìròu bǎo
Claypot rice with sweet sausage	香肠饭	xiāngchángfàn
Crisp-skinned pork on rice	脆皮肉饭	cuìpíròufàn
Fish-head casserole	焙鱼头	bèiyútóu
Fish steamed with ginger and spring onion	清蒸鱼	qīngzhēngyú
Fried chicken with yam	芋头炒鸡片	yùtóu chǎo jīpiàn
Honey-roast pork	叉烧	chāshāo
Lemon chicken	柠檬鸡	níngméngjī

| Litchi (lychee) pork | 荔枝肉片 | lìzhīròupiàn |
| Salt-baked chicken | 盐鸡 | yánshuǐjī |

DIM SUM

Dim sum	点心	diǎnxīn
Barbecued pork bun	叉烧包	chāshāobāo
Crab and prawn dumpling	蟹肉虾饺	xièròu xiājiǎo
Custard tart	蛋挞	dàntà
Doughnut	油炸圈饼	yóuzhà quānbǐng
Pork and prawn dumpling	烧麦	shāomài
Fried taro and mince dumpling	蕃薯糊饺	fānshǔ hújiǎo
Lotus paste bun	莲蓉糕	liánrónggāo
Moon cake (sweet bean paste in flaky pastry)	月饼	yuèbǐng
Paper-wrapped prawns	纸包虾	zhǐbāoxiā
Prawn crackers	虾片	xiā piàn
Prawn dumpling	虾饺	xiā jiǎo
Spring roll	春卷	chūnjuǎn
Steamed spare ribs and chilli	辣椒蒸排骨	làjiāo zhēngpáigǔ
Stuffed rice-flour roll	肠粉	chángfěn
Stuffed green peppers with black bean sauce	豆豉馅青椒	dòuchǐ xiànqīngjiāo
Sweet sesame balls	芝麻球	zhīmá qiú

FRUIT

Fruit	水果	shuǐguǒ
Apple	苹果	píngguǒ
Banana	香蕉	xiāngjiāo
Grape	葡萄	pútáo
Honeydew melon	哈密瓜	hāmìguā
Longan	龙眼	lóngyǎn
Lychee	荔枝	lìzhī
Mandarin orange	橘子	júzi
Mango	芒果	mángguǒ
Orange	橙子	chéngzi
Peach	桃子	táozi
Pear	梨	lí
Persimmon	柿子	shìzi
Plum	李子	lǐzi
Pomegranate	石榴	shíliú
Pomelo	柚子	yòuzi
Watermelon	西瓜	xīguā

GLOSSARY

Arhat Buddhist saint

Bei North

Binguan Hotel; generally a large one, for tourists

Bodhisattva A follower of Buddhism who has attained enlightenment, but has chosen to stay on earth to teach rather than enter nirvana; Buddhist god or goddess

Boxers The name given to an anti-foreign organization that originated in Shandong in 1898 Encouraged by the Qing Empress Dowager Cixi, they roamed China attacking westernized Chinese and foreigners in what became known as the Boxer Rebellion

Canting Restaurant

Cheongsam Cantonese name for a *qipao*

Cultural Revolution Ten-year period beginning in 1966 and characterized by destruction, persecution and fanatical devotion to Mao

Dagoba Another name for a stupa

Dong East

erhu Sometimes known as a Chinese violin, a two-stringed bowed instrument

Fandian Restaurant or hotel

Feng Peak

Feng shui A system of geomancy used to determine the positioning of buildings

Gong Palace

Guanxi Literally "connections": the reciprocal favours inherent in the process of official appointments and transactions

Guanyin The ubiquitous Buddhist Goddess of Compassion, who postponed her entry into paradise in order to help ease human misery Derived from the Indian deity Avalokiteshvara, she is often depicted with up to a thousand arms

Gulou Drum tower; traditionally marking the centre of a town, this was where a drum was beaten at nightfall and in times of need

Guomindang (GMD) The Nationalist Peoples' Party Under Chiang Kaishek, the GMD fought Communist forces for 25 years before being defeated and moving to Taiwan in 1949, where it remains a major political party

Han Chinese The main body of the Chinese people, as distinct from other ethnic groups such as Uigur, Miao, Hui or Tibetan

Hui Muslims; officially a minority, China's Hui are, in fact, ethnically indistinguishable from Han Chinese

Hutong A narrow alleyway

Immortal Taoist saint

Jiao (or mao) Ten fen

Jie Street

Jiuba Bar or pub

Lamaism The esoteric Tibetan and Mongolian branch of Buddhism, influenced by local shamanist and animist beliefs

Laowai A slang term for foreigner

Ling Tomb

Little Red Book A selection of "Quotations from Chairman Mao Zedong", produced in 1966 as a philosophical treatise for Red Guards during the Cultural Revolution

Lu Street

Luohan Buddhist disciple

Maitreya Buddha The Buddha of the future, at present awaiting rebirth

Mandala Mystic diagram which forms an important part of Buddhist iconography, especially in Tibet; they usually depict deities and are stared at as an aid to meditation

Men Gate/door

Miao Temple

Middle Kingdom A literal translation of the Chinese words for China

Nan South

Pagoda Tower with distinctively tapering structure

Palanquin A covered sedan chair, used by the emperor

Peking The old English term for Beijing

Pinyin The official system of transliterating Chinese script into Roman characters

PLA The People's Liberation Army, the official name of the Communist military forces since 1949

PSB Public Security Bureau, the branch of China's police force which deals directly with foreigners

Putonghua Mandarin Chinese; literally "Common Language"

Qiao Bridge

Qipao Long, narrow dress slit up the thigh

Red Guards The unruly factional forces unleashed by Mao during the Cultural Revolution to find and destroy brutally any "reactionaries" among the populace

Renmin The people

Renminbi (RMB) The official term for the Chinese currency, literally, "people's money"

Shawm A shrill-sounding, double-reed woodwind instrument

Si Temple, usually Buddhist

Siheyuan Traditional courtyard house

Spirit wall Wall behind the main gateway to a house, designed to thwart evil spirits, which, it was believed, could move only in straight lines

Spirit Way The straight road leading to a tomb, lined with guardian figures

Stele Freestanding stone tablet carved with text

Stupa Multitiered tower associated with Buddhist temples; usually contains sacred objects

Ta Tower or pagoda

Tai ji A discipline of physical exercise, characterized by slow, deliberate, balletic movements

Tian Heaven or the sky

Uigur Substantial minority of Turkic people, living mainly in Xinjiang

Waiguoren Foreigner

Xi West

Yuan China's unit of currency. Also a courtyard or garden (and the name of the Mongol dynasty)

Zhan Station

Zhong Middle

Zhongnanhai The compound, next to the Forbidden City, that serves as Communist Party headquarters

Zhonglou Bell tower, usually twinned with a drum tower. The bell it contained was rung at dawn and in emergencies

Zhuang Villa or manor

Small print and index

A ROUGH GUIDE TO ROUGH GUIDES

Published in 1982, the first Rough Guide – to Greece – was a student scheme that became a publishing phenomenon. Mark Ellingham, a recent graduate in English from Bristol University, had been travelling in Greece the previous summer and couldn't find the right guidebook. With a small group of friends he wrote his own guide, combining a contemporary, journalistic style with a thoroughly practical approach to travellers' needs.

The immediate success of the book spawned a series that rapidly covered dozens of destinations. And, in addition to impecunious backpackers, Rough Guides soon acquired a much broader readership that relished the guides' wit and inquisitiveness as much as their enthusiastic, critical approach and value-for-money ethos. These days, Rough Guides include recommendations from budget to luxury and cover more than 120 destinations around the globe, from Amsterdam to Zanzibar, all regularly updated by our team of roaming writers.

Browse all our latest guides, read inspirational features and book your trip at **roughguides.com**.

Rough Guide credits

Editor: Lucy Kane
Layout: Anita Singh, Pradeep Thapliyal
Cartography: Swati Handoo
Picture editor: Michelle Bhatia
Proofreader: Susanne Hillen
Managing editor: Andy Turner
Assistant editor: Payal Sharotri

Production: Jimmy Lao
Cover photo research: Marta Bescos
Photographer: Tim Draper
Editorial assistant: Freya Godfrey
Senior DTP coordinator: Dan May
Programme manager: Gareth Lowe
Publishing director: Georgina Dee

Publishing information

This sixth edition published June 2017 by
Rough Guides Ltd,
80 Strand, London WC2R 0RL
11, Community Centre, Panchsheel Park,
New Delhi 110017, India
Distributed by Penguin Random House
Penguin Books Ltd, 80 Strand, London WC2R 0RL
Penguin Group (USA), 345 Hudson Street, NY 10014, USA
Penguin Group (Australia), 250 Camberwell Road,
Camberwell, Victoria 3124, Australia
Penguin Group (NZ), 67 Apollo Drive, Mairangi Bay,
Auckland 1310, New Zealand
Penguin Group (South Africa), Block D, Rosebank Office
Park, 181 Jan Smuts Avenue, Parktown North, Gauteng,
South Africa 2193
Rough Guides is represented in Canada by DK Canada, 320
Front Street West, Suite 1400, Toronto, Ontario M5V 3B6
Printed in Singapore
© Rough Guide 2017
Maps © Rough Guides

224pp includes index
A catalogue record for this book is available from the
British Library
ISBN: 978-0-24127-399-9
The publishers and authors have done their best to
ensure the accuracy and currency of all the information in
The Rough Guide to Beijing, however, they can accept
no responsibility for any loss, injury, or inconvenience
sustained by any traveller as a result of information or
advice contained in the guide.
1 3 5 7 9 8 6 4 2

MIX
Paper from
responsible sources
FSC
www.fsc.org FSC™ C018179

Help us update

We've gone to a lot of effort to ensure that the sixth
edition of **The Rough Guide to Beijing** is accurate and up-
to-date. However, things change – places get "discovered",
opening hours are notoriously fickle, restaurants and
rooms raise prices or lower standards. If you feel we've got
it wrong or left something out, we'd like to know, and if
you can remember the address, the price, the hours, the
phone number, so much the better.

Please send your comments with the subject line
"**Rough Guide Beijing Update**" to mail@uk.roughguides.
com. We'll credit all contributions and send a copy of the
next edition (or any other Rough Guide if you prefer) for
the very best emails.

ABOUT THE AUTHOR

David Leffman first visited in China in 1985 and has since clocked up over five years there in total, mostly working as a travel writer. Among other things, he has written guidebooks to China, Hong Kong, Australia, Indonesia and Iceland. Find out more at: ◉davidleffman.com.

Acknowledgements

Narrell, Peter Goff, Oscar Holland, Pete & Sue, Derek Sandhaus, Shan Shan, Paul Tomic, Yao Chengrong and Lucy Kane for editing

Index

Maps are marked in grey

C

W

X

Y

Z

Map index

Listings key

- ■ Accommodation
- ● Eating
- ▩ Drinking and nightlife
- ● Shopping

City plan

The **city plan** on the pages that follow is divided as shown:

N

0	500
metres

Ditan Park

3

2

SANLITUN

DONGCHENG

DIANMEN

FUCHENGMEN

Yuyuantan Park

Forbidden City

Zhongnanhai (out of bounds)

Ritan Park

XI CHENG

1

Tian'anmen Square

QIANMEN

ZHUSHIKOU

CAISHIKOU

Temple of Heaven Park

XUANWU

Taoranting Park

Map symbols

✈ Airport	♦ Place of interest	▦ Building
Provincial boundary	★ Bus stop	▣ Parking	⬭ Stadium
Chapter division boundary	Ⓢ Subway	☉ Statue	☐ Park
Motorway	⊘ Bus station/depot	⛳ Golf course	🕌 Mosque
Road	ⓘ Information office	Swimming/pool	Chinese temple
Pedestrianized road	⊞ Hospital	▲ Hill	Dagoba
Rail line	⊠ Post office	♥ Museum	
Coastline	⊠ Gate	∴ Ruins	
Wall	E Embassy	⌣ Bridge	
Cable car			

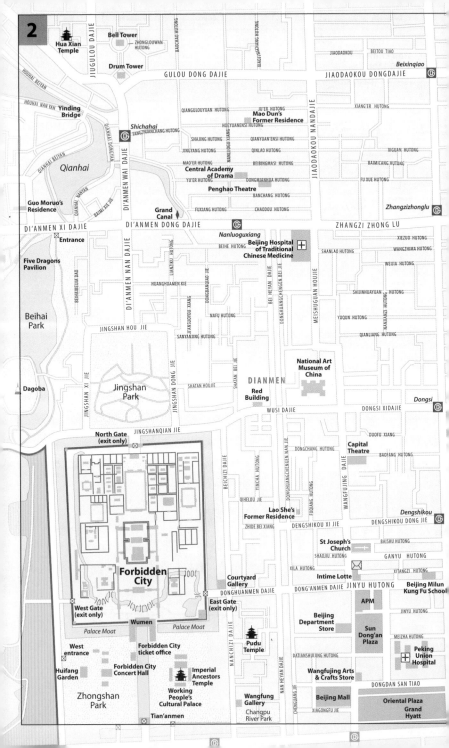